U.S. Operating Experience With Thermally Treated Alloy 600 Steam Generator Tubes

I0438958

U.S. Nuclear Regulatory Commission
Office of Nuclear Reactor Regulation
Washington, DC 20555-0001

AVAILABILITY OF REFERENCE MATERIALS
IN NRC PUBLICATIONS

U.S. Operating Experience With Thermally Treated Alloy 600 Steam Generator Tubes

Manuscript Completed: February 2003
Date Published: April 2003

Prepared by
K. J. Karwoski

Division of Engineering
Office of Nuclear Reactor Regulation
U.S. Nuclear Regulatory Commission
Washington, DC 20555-0001

ABSTRACT

Steam generators placed in service in the 1960s and 1970s had tubes primarily fabricated from mill-annealed Alloy 600. Over time, this material proved to be susceptible to stress corrosion cracking in the highly pure primary and secondary water chemistry environments of pressurized-water reactors. The corrosion ultimately led to the replacement of steam generators at numerous facilities, the first U.S. replacement occurring in 1980. Many of the steam generators placed into service in the 1980s used tubes fabricated from thermally treated Alloy 600. This tube material was thought to be less susceptible to corrosion. Because of the safety significance of steam generator tube integrity, this paper evaluates the operating experience of thermally treated Alloy 600 by looking at the extent to which it is used and results from steam generator tube examinations.

CONTENTS

ABSTRACT . . . . -iii-

CONTENTS . . . . -v-

LIST OF FIGURES . . . . -vii-

LIST OF TABLES . . . . -viii-

EXECUTIVE SUMMARY . . . . -xi-

ACKNOWLEDGMENTS . . . . -xiv-

1 INTRODUCTION . . . . -1-
   1.1 Safety Significance . . . . -1-
   1.2 Tube Integrity Program . . . . -2-
      1.2.1 Purpose of Inspections . . . . -2-
      1.2.2 Eddy Current Testing . . . . -3-
      1.2.3 Tube Repairs . . . . -5-
      1.2.4 Leakage Monitoring . . . . -6-
   1.3 Mill-Annealed Alloy 600 Steam Generator Operating Experience . . . . -6-
   1.4 Thermally Treated Alloy 600 Tubes . . . . -7-

2 STEAM GENERATOR DESIGNS IN PLANTS WITH
THERMALLY TREATED ALLOY 600 TUBES . . . . -11-
   2.1 Introduction . . . . -11-
   2.2 Model D5 Steam Generators . . . . -12-
   2.3 Model F Steam Generators . . . . -14-
   2.4 Replacement Steam Generators . . . . -14-

3 THERMALLY TREATED ALLOY 600 STEAM GENERATOR TUBE
OPERATING EXPERIENCE . . . . -31-
   3.1 Data Gathering Methodology and Introduction . . . . -31-
   3.2 Model D5 Steam Generator Operating Experience . . . . -31-
      3.2.1 Braidwood 2 . . . . -31-
      3.2.2 Byron 2 . . . . -34-
      3.2.3 Catawba 2 . . . . -40-
      3.2.4 Comanche Peak 2 . . . . -45-
   3.3 Model F Steam Generator Operating Experience . . . . -47-
      3.3.1 Callaway . . . . -47-
      3.3.2 Millstone 3 . . . . -49-
      3.3.3 Seabrook . . . . -52-
      3.3.4 Vogtle 1 . . . . -55-
      3.3.5 Vogtle 2 . . . . -58-
      3.3.6 Wolf Creek . . . . -61-
   3.4 Replacement Model Steam Generator Operating Experience . . . . -64-

3.4.1 Indian Point 2 .... -64-
3.4.2 Point Beach 1 .... -64-
3.4.3 Robinson 2 .... -67-
3.4.4 Salem 1 .... -72-
3.4.5 Surry 1 .... -73-
3.4.6 Surry 2 .... -77-
3.4.7 Turkey Point 3 .... -80-
3.4.8 Turkey Point 4 .... -84-

4 SUMMARY .... -153-
    4.1 Model D5 Summary .... -153-
    4.2 Model F Summary .... -154-
    4.3 Replacement Model Summary .... -154-
    4.4 Overall Summary .... -155-
        4.4.1 Forced Outages .... -155-
        4.4.2 Tube Pulls .... -157-
        4.4.3 Selected Inspection Findings .... -158-
        4.4.4 Summary and Observations .... -160-

APPENDIX A: ACRONYMS .... -214-

APPENDIX B: BIBLIOGRAPHY .... -215-

LIST OF FIGURES

Figure 1-1: Mill-Annealed Alloy 600 Steam Generator Tube Degradation . . . . -10-
Figure 2-1: Typical PWR Recirculating Steam Generator Without a Preheater . . . . -18-
Figure 2-2: Typical PWR Recirculating Steam Generator With a Preheater . . . . -19-
Figure 2-3: U-Bend Features . . . . -20-
Figure 2-4: Number of Plants with Thermally Treated Alloy 600 Steam Generator Tubes as a
Function of Year . . . . -21-
Figure 2-5: Westinghouse Model D5 Steam Generator Tube Support Locations . . . . -22-
Figure 2-6: Westinghouse Model D5 Steam Generator Tubesheet Map . . . . -23-
Figure 2-7: Preheater Region of Westinghouse Model D5 Steam Generator . . . . -24-
Figure 2-8: Westinghouse Model F Steam Generator Tube Support Locations . . . . -25-
Figure 2-9: Westinghouse Model F Steam Generator Tubesheet Map . . . . -26-
Figure 2-10: Westinghouse Model 44F Steam Generator Tube Support Locations . . . . . . -27-
Figure 2-11: Westinghouse Model 44F Steam Generator Tubesheet Map . . . . -28-
Figure 2-12: Westinghouse Model 51F Steam Generator Tube Support Locations . . . . . . -29-
Figure 2-13: Westinghouse Model 51F Steam Generator Tubesheet Map . . . . -30-
Figure 4-1: Model D5: Causes of Tube Plugging (12/01) . . . . -196-
Figure 4-2: Model D5: Plugging Per Year . . . . -197-
Figure 4-3: Model D5: Cumulative Plugging Per Refueling Outage . . . . -198-
Figure 4-4: Model D5: Causes of Tube Plugging Per Year . . . . -199-
Figure 4-5: Model F: Causes of Tube Plugging (12/01) . . . . -200-
Figure 4-6: Model F: Plugging Per Year . . . . -201-
Figure 4-7: Model F: Cumulative Plugging Per Refueling Outage . . . . -202-
Figure 4-8: Model F: Causes of Tube Plugging Per Year . . . . -203-
Figure 4-9: Replacement Models: Causes of Tube Plugging (12/01) . . . . -204-
Figure 4-10: Replacement Models: Plugging Per Year . . . . -205-
Figure 4-11: Replacement Models: Cumulative Plugging Per Refueling Outage . . . . -206-
Figure 4-12: Replacement Models: Causes of Tube Plugging Per Year . . . . -207-
Figure 4-13: Number of Thermally Treated Alloy 600 Tubes in Service Per Year . . . . . . -208-
Figure 4-14: All Models: Tubes Plugged Per Grouping/Model (12/01) . . . . -209-
Figure 4-15: All Models: Causes of Tube Plugging (12/01) . . . . -210-
Figure 4-16: All Models: Number of Tubes Plugged Per Year . . . . -211-
Figure 4-17: All Models: Percentage of Tubes Plugged Per Year . . . . -212-
Figure 4-18: All Models: Causes of Tube Plugging Per Year . . . . -213-

LIST OF TABLES

Table 1-1: Plants With Replacement Steam Generators . . . . -9-
Table 2-1: Plants With Thermally Treated Alloy 600 Tubes . . . . -16-
Table 2-2: Age of Steam Generators at Plants With Thermally Treated Alloy 600 Tubes . . -17-
Table 3-1: Braidwood 2: Summary of Bobbin Inspections and Tube Plugging . . . . -87-
Table 3-2: Braidwood 2: Causes of Tube Plugging . . . . -88-
Table 3-3: Braidwood 2: Tubes Plugged for Indications Other Than AVB Wear . . . . -89-
Table 3-4: Byron 2: Summary of Bobbin Inspections and Tube Plugging . . . . -90-
Table 3-5: Byron 2: Causes of Tube Plugging . . . . -91-
Table 3-6: Byron 2: Tubes Plugged for Indications Other Than AVB Wear . . . . -92-
Table 3-7: Catwaba 2: Summary of Bobbin Inspections and Tube Plugging . . . . -95-
Table 3-8: Catawba 2: Causes of Tube Plugging . . . . -96-
Table 3-9: Catawba 2: Tubes Plugged for Indications Other Than AVB Wear . . . . -97-
Table 3-10: Comanche Peak 2: Summary of Bobbin Inspections and Tube Plugging . . . . -102-
Table 3-11: Comanche Peak 2: Causes of Tube Plugging . . . . -103-
Table 3-12: Comanche Peak 2: Tubes Plugged for Indications Other Than AVB Wear . . -104-
Table 3-13: Callaway: Summary of Bobbin Inspections and Tube Plugging (TT Tubes Only)
. . . . -105-
Table 3-14: Callaway: Causes of Tube Plugging (Thermally Treated Tubes Only) . . . . . . -106-
Table 3-15: Callaway: Tubes Plugged for Indications Other Than AVB Wear . . . . -107-
Table 3-16: Millstone 3: Summary of Bobbin Inspections and Tube Plugging . . . . -109-
Table 3-17: Millstone 3: Causes of Tube Plugging . . . . -110-
Table 3-18: Millstone 3: Tubes Plugged for Indications Other Than AVB Wear . . . . -111-
Table 3-19: Seabrook: Summary of Bobbin Inspections and Tube Plugging . . . . -113-
Table 3-20: Seabrook: Causes of Tube Plugging . . . . -114-
Table 3-21: Seabrook: Tubes Plugged for Indications Other Than AVB Wear . . . . -115-
Table 3-22: Vogtle 1: Summary of Bobbin Inspections and Tube Plugging . . . . -116-
Table 3-23: Vogtle 1: Causes of Tube Plugging . . . . -117-
Table 3-24: Vogtle 1: Tubes Plugged for Indications Other Than AVB Wear . . . . -118-
Table 3-25: Vogtle 2: Summary of Bobbin Inspections and Tube Plugging . . . . -119-
Table 3-26: Vogtle 2: Causes of Tube Plugging . . . . -120-
Table 3-27: Vogtle 2: Tubes Plugged for Indications Other Than AVB Wear . . . . -121-
Table 3-28: Wolf Creek: Summary of Bobbin Inspections and Tube Plugging . . . . -122-
Table 3-29: Wolf Creek: Causes of Tube Plugging . . . . -123-
Table 3-30: Wolf Creek: Tubes Plugged for Indications Other Than AVB Wear . . . . -124-
Table 3-31: Indian Point 2: Summary of Bobbin Inspections and Tube Plugging . . . . -125-
Table 3-32: Indian Point 2: Causes of Tube Plugging . . . . -126-
Table 3-33: Indian Point 2: Tubes Plugged for Indications Other Than AVB Wear . . . . . -127-
Table 3-34: Point Beach 1: Summary of Bobbin Inspections and Tube Plugging . . . . -128-
Table 3-35: Point Beach 1: Causes of Tube Plugging . . . . -129-
Table 3-36: Point Beach 1: Tubes Plugged for Indications Other Than AVB Wear . . . . . -130-
Table 3-37: Robinson 2: Summary of Bobbin Inspections and Tube Plugging . . . . -131-
Table 3-38: Robinson 2: Causes of Tube Plugging . . . . -132-
Table 3-39: Robinson 2: Tubes Plugged for Indications Other Than AVB Wear . . . . -133-
Table 3-40: Salem 1: Summary of Bobbin Inspections and Tube Plugging . . . . -134-
Table 3-41: Salem 1: Causes of Tube Plugging . . . . -135-
Table 3-42: Salem 1: Tubes Plugged for Indications Other Than AVB Wear . . . . -136-

Table 3-43: Surry 1: Summary of Bobbin Inspections and Tube Plugging . . . . -137-
Table 3-44: Surry 1: Causes of Tube Plugging . . . . -138-
Table 3-45: Surry 1: Tubes Plugged for Indications Other Than AVB Wear . . . . -139-
Table 3-46: Surry 2: Summary of Bobbin Inspections and Tube Plugging . . . . -141-
Table 3-47: Surry 2: Causes of Tube Plugging . . . . -142-
Table 3-48: Surry 2: Tubes Plugged for Indications Other Than AVB Wear . . . . -143-
Table 3-49: Turkey Point 3: Summary of Bobbin Inspections and Tube Plugging . . . . -144-
Table 3-50: Turkey Point 3: Causes of Tube Plugging . . . . -145-
Table 3-51: Turkey Point 3: Tubes Plugged for Indications Other Than AVB Wear . . . . . -146-
Table 3-52: Turkey Point 4: Summary of Bobbin Inspections and Tube Plugging . . . . -150-
Table 3-53: Turkey Point 4: Causes of Tube Plugging . . . . -151-
Table 3-54: Turkey Point 4: Tubes Plugged for Indications Other Than AVB Wear . . . . . -152-
Table 4-1: Model D5: Total Number and Percentage of Tubes Plugged (12/01) . . . . -165-
Table 4-2: Model D5: Number of Tubes Plugged As a Function of Mechanism (Detailed)
    (12/01) . . . . -166-
Table 4-3: Model D5: Cumulative Plugging Per Year . . . . -167-
Table 4-4: Model D5: Plugging Per Year . . . . -168-
Table 4-5: Model D5: Cumulative Plugging Per RFO . . . . -169-
Table 4-6: Model D5: Number of Tubes Plugged As a Function of Mechanism Per Year
    (Detailed) . . . . -170-
Table 4-7: Model D5: Number of Tubes Plugged As a Function of Mechanism Per Year
    (Summary) . . . . -171-
Table 4-8: Model D5: Fraction of Tubes Plugged As a Function of Mechanism Per Year
    (Summary) . . . . -172-
Table 4-9: Model F: Total Number and Percentage of Tubes Plugged (12/01) . . . . -173-
Table 4-10: Model F: Number of Tubes Plugged As a Function of Mechanism (Detailed)
    (12/01) . . . . -174-
Table 4-11: Model F: Cumulative Plugging Per Year . . . . -175-
Table 4-12: Model F: Plugging Per Year . . . . -176-
Table 4-13: Model F: Cumulative Plugging Per RFO . . . . -177-
Table 4-14: Model F: Number of Tubes Plugged As a Function of Mechanism Per Year
    (Detailed) . . . . -178-
Table 4-15: Model F: Number of Tubes Plugged As a Function of Mechanism Per Year
    (Summary) . . . . -179-
Table 4-16: Model F: Fraction of Tubes Plugged As a Function of Mechanism Per Year
    (Summary) . . . . -180-
Table 4-17: Replacement Models: Total Number and Percentage of Tubes Plugged (12/01)
    . . . . -181-
Table 4-18: Replacement Models: Number of Tubes Plugged As a Function of Mechanism
    (Detailed) (12/01) . . . . -182-
Table 4-19: Replacement Models: Cumulative Plugging Per Year . . . . -183-
Table 4-20: Replacement Models: Plugging Per Year . . . . -184-
Table 4-21: Replacement Models: Cumulative Plugging Per RFO . . . . -185-
Table 4-22: Replacement Models: Number of Tubes Plugged As a Function of Mechanism Per
    Year (Detailed) . . . . -186-
Table 4-23: Replacement Models: Number of Tubes Plugged As a Function of Mechanism Per
    Year (Summary) . . . . -187-

Table 4-24: Replacement Models: Fraction of Tubes Plugged As a Function of Mechanism Per Year (Summary) .... -188-
Table 4-25: All Models: Total Number and Percentage of Tubes Plugged (12/01) ...... -189-
Table 4-26: All Models: Number of Tubes Plugged As a Function of Mechanism (Detailed) (12/01) .... -190-
Table 4-27: All Models: Number of Tubes Plugged As a Function of Mechanism (Summary) (12/01) .... -191-
Table 4-28: All Models: Plugging Per Year .... -192-
Table 4-29: All Models: Number of Tubes Plugged As a Function of Mechanism Per Year (Detailed) .... -193-
Table 4-30: All Models: Number of Tubes Plugged As a Function of Mechanism Per Year (Summary) .... -194-
Table 4-31: All Models: Fraction of Tubes Plugged As a Function of Mechanism Per Year (Summary) .... -195-

EXECUTIVE SUMMARY

The susceptibility of steam generator tubes to degradation is affected by various factors, including the steam generator design, the operating environment (temperature and water chemistry), and operating and residual stresses. Two of the most important factors affecting the susceptibility of a tube to degradation are the tube material and the tube's heat treatment.

Tubes installed in U.S. nuclear steam generators placed in service in the 1960s and 1970s were usually only mill-annealed (passed through a furnace at a high temperature). Over 25 years of operating experience has shown that mill-annealed Alloy 600 is susceptible to degradation in the steam generator operating environment. The degradation includes pitting, wear, thinning, wastage, and stress corrosion cracking.

The extensive tube degradation at pressurized-water reactors (PWRs) with mill-annealed Alloy 600 steam generator tubes resulted in numerous tube leaks, approximately nine tube ruptures, numerous midcycle steam generator tube inspections, and the replacement of steam generators at numerous plants. In addition, extensive tube degradation contributed to the permanent shutdown of other plants. Haddam Neck, Maine Yankee, Trojan, Zion 1, Zion 2, and San Onofre 1 ceased operation with significant amounts of tube degradation.

As mill-annealed Alloy 600 steam generator tubes began exhibiting degradation in the early 1970s, the industry pursued improvements in the design of future steam generators to reduce the likelihood of corrosion. In the late 1970s, some mill-annealed Alloy 600 tubes were subjected to high temperatures for 10 to 15 hours to relieve fabrication stresses and to improve the tubes' microstructure. This thermal treatment process was first used on tubes installed in replacement steam generators put into service in the early 1980s. Thermally treated Alloy 600 is presently used in the steam generators at 17 plants. At another plant, Callaway, the steam generators have thermally treated Alloy 600 tubes in the first 10 rows and mill-annealed Alloy 600 tubes in the remaining rows. Therefore, thermally treated Alloy 600 is used in approximately 25% of the currently operating PWRs (18 of 69).

The operating experience of plants with mill-annealed Alloy 600 steam generator tubes is well documented. The experience with thermally treated Alloy 600 has not been well documented, although thermally treated Alloy 600 is generally recognized to perform better. This report summarizes the steam generator operating experience of U.S. PWRs with thermally treated Alloy 600 steam generator tubes as of December 2001.

A historical review of operating experience identified only six unplanned outages as a result of steam generator issues in plants with thermally treated Alloy 600 tubes: two plants shut down after discovering primary-to-secondary leakage, and four after loose part monitors provided indications that a loose part may be present.

Of the 281,262 thermally treated Alloy 600 tubes placed in service at 18 plants between 1980 and 2001, only 1397 tubes (0.5%) have been plugged. All together, these 18 plants have operated for approximately 260 calendar years (as of December 2001). On the average each of these plants has commercially operated for 14 calendar years (as of December 2001). The dominant degradation mode for thermally treated Alloy 600 tubes is wear. Of the approximately 1400 tubes plugged, approximately 53% of the tubes were plugged as a result of wear. Tube wear occurs when the tube contacts a support structure (e.g., an antivibration bar) or a foreign object (e.g., a loose part).

Far fewer tubes have been plugged in the steam generators with second-generation tube materials (i.e., thermally treated alloy 600) than in earlier steam generators with comparable operating times. Improvements in the design and operation of the second-generation steam generators appear to have increased the corrosion resistance of the tubes, as evidenced by the general lack of any significant amounts of corrosion degradation. The increased corrosion resistance is largely due to the thermal treatment process that has superseded the mill annealing process used in earlier steam generator designs.

The relatively good operating experience of plants with thermally treated Alloy 600 steam generator tubes can be attributed to several factors besides the heat treatment: hydraulic expansion of the tubes into the tubesheet, the quatrefoil design of the tube support plates, and the stainless steel material used to fabricate the plates. The residual stress levels at the expansion transition in tubes hydraulically expanded into the tubesheet are lower than observed in plants whose tubes were expanded mechanically or explosively. Since crack growth rate and time to crack initiation depend in part on the stress level, lower stresses may result in slower crack growth rates and/or longer times before crack initiation.

A number of issues identified in this historical review may warrant additional investigation in the future. These issues are summarized in Section 4.4.4. Some of the issues discussed in Section 4.4.4 include the potential for tubes to continue to degrade following plugging (which raises questions about the need to stabilize these tubes to prevent them from damaging adjacent tubes), the potential for mechanically induced tube denting to occur at tube supports, and the usefulness of the destructive examination of pulled tubes in assessing the causal mechanism for various types of eddy current indications (e.g., volumetric indications).

Although the operating experience with thermally treated Alloy 600 tubes has been favorable to date, licensees still need to monitor the tubes to detect the onset of tube degradation (including cracking) and assure the structural and leakage integrity of the tubes during the intervals between inspections. A better understanding of some of these issues would be useful in determining appropriate intervals for future monitoring of tube degradation.

During the preparation of this report in the first half of 2002, several noteworthy events occurred in plants with thermally treated Alloy 600 steam generator tubes. There were two additional unplanned outages attributed to steam generator issues, and cracklike indications at a plant. One of the unplanned outages began after the licensee observed a 75 gallon per day primary-to-secondary leak due to damage from a loose part, and the other was prompted by an indication of a loose part (not associated with primary-to-secondary leakage). The cracklike indications were detected at Seabrook and were discussed in NRC Information Notice 2002-21, "Axial Outside-Diameter Cracking Affecting Thermally Treated Alloy 600 Steam Generator Tubing," which was issued on June 25, 2002. At Seabrook, portions of two tubes were removed for destructive examination. The root cause evaluation, including the destructive examination of these two pulled tubes, confirmed that the indications were axially oriented outside diameter stress corrosion cracking, and also identified unusually high levels of residual stress in the straight leg sections of both the hot and cold legs. Nonoptimal tube processing during steam generator manufacturing was strongly suspected to be the primary cause of the high residual stresses and the principal factor increasing the susceptibility of the affected tubes to stress corrosion cracking. The precise processing steps responsible for the adverse stress state could not be conclusively determined from a review of the tube processing records.

ACKNOWLEDGMENTS

The author thanks April Smith and Matt Yoder for their assistance in compiling, summarizing, and graphing some of the information contained within this report. The author also thanks Cheryl Khan and Ted Sullivan for their careful review of this report and helpful comments.

1 INTRODUCTION

1.1 Safety Significance

Heat generated in pressurized-water reactors (PWRs) is removed from the reactor core by the primary coolant. Each primary coolant loop in U.S. PWR designs has one reactor coolant pump and one vertically mounted steam generator. There are two to four reactor coolant loops per plant. The hot primary coolant enters and leaves the steam generator through nozzles in the hemispherical head of the steam generator. The transfer of heat from the primary system water to the water on the secondary side of the steam generator is accomplished primarily through the steam generators tubes. This heat transfer boils the water on the secondary side of the steam generator. The primary coolant then returns to the reactor core via the reactor coolant pump, where it is reheated and the cycle is repeated.

Feedwater (secondary coolant) is pumped into the secondary or shell side of the steam generator, where it boils into steam. The steam exits the steam generator through an outlet nozzle and flows to the turbine generator, where it spins the turbine, generating electricity. After exiting the turbine, the steam is condensed into water and pumped back to the steam generator, where the cycle repeats.

Steam generator tubes constitute well over 50% of the surface area of the primary pressure boundary in a PWR. This pressure boundary is an important element in the defense in depth against release of radioactive material from the reactor into the environment. Unlike other parts of the reactor coolant pressure boundary, the barrier to fission product release provided by the steam generator tubes is not reinforced by the reactor containment. That is, fission products released through leaking or ruptured steam generator tubes can escape directly into the environment through the secondary side of the steam generator. Consequently, the integrity of the steam generator tubes must be ensured with high confidence.

Because of the potential consequences of steam generator tube leakage, regulatory limits exist for the amount of primary-to-secondary leakage permitted during normal operation. In addition, PWRs are designed such that operators can rapidly and effectively respond to steam generator tube leakage during power operation. For postulated accidents, primary-to-secondary leakage is assumed to exist and is assessed in evaluating the radiological consequences of postulated accidents such as a feedwater or steam line break. In the event of leakage during normal operation or postulated accidents such as the rupture of the main steam line or feed line, leakage of reactor coolant through the tubes could contaminate the flow in these lines. In addition leakage of primary coolant through openings in the steam generator tubes could deplete the inventory of water available for the long-term cooling of the core in the event of an accident.

For normal operation, the amount of primary-to-secondary leakage is limited by a plant's technical specifications. The limit is plant-specific and ranges from approximately 150 to 720 gallons per day (gpd) through any one steam generator. Leakage through all steam generators is also limited typically to 1 gallon per minute (gpm). For postulated accidents such as the rupture of a main steam line or feed line, the radiological dose consequences associated with approximately 1 gpm primary-to-secondary leakage were evaluated as part of the design basis of the plant. Plant response to a rupture of the main steam line and any leakage of radioactive material through the steam generators is a design basis accident considered in the safety evaluation of PWRs. Typically, plants were designed assuming that primary-to-secondary leakage during postulated accidents would be less than 1 gpm.

Although limits exist for the amount of primary-to-secondary leakage during normal operation (e.g., 150 gpd), there is a possibility that a tube can rupture during normal operation. Leakage from a ruptured tube can result in primary-to-secondary leak rates in the range of 100 to 700 gpm (depending on the severity of the tube rupture and the capacity of the safety injection/charging system pumps). PWRs are designed such that operators can rapidly and effectively respond to the accidental rupture of one steam generator tube during power operation. Although the rupture of a tube during normal power operation is considered in the design of PWRs, a tube rupture concurrent with a postulated accident is not.

1.2 Tube Integrity Program

1.2.1 Purpose of Inspections

Because of the importance of steam generator tube integrity, the NRC requires the performance of periodic inservice inspections of steam generator tubes. The requirements for the inspection of steam generator tubes are intended to ensure that this portion of the reactor coolant system maintains its structural and leakage integrity. Structural integrity refers to maintaining adequate margins against gross failure, rupture, and collapse of the steam generator tubes. Leakage integrity refers to limiting primary-to-secondary leakage during normal operation and postulated accidents to within acceptable limits.

The structural criteria that the tubes are intended to meet are specified in Regulatory Guide 1.121, "Bases for Plugging Degraded PWR Steam Generator Tubes." Adequate leakage integrity during transients and postulated accidents is demonstrated by showing that the resulting leakage from the tubes will not exceed a rate that would violate offsite or control room dose criteria. These criteria are specified, in part, in Part 100 to Title 10 of the *Code of Federal Regulations* (10 CFR Part 100) and in General Design Criteria 19 of Appendix A to 10 CFR Part 50.

To provide assurance of adequate structural and leakage integrity, inspections are performed with the intent of detecting mechanical or corrosive damage to the tubes from manufacturing and/or inservice conditions. In addition, the inservice inspections of the steam generator tubes provide a means of characterizing the nature and cause of any tube degradation so that corrective measures can be taken. Tubes that show an indication of degradation that exceeds the tube repair limits specified in a plant's technical specifications are removed from service by plugging or are repaired by sleeving, as discussed in Section 1.2.3.

The frequency of the inservice inspections of the steam generator tubes is generally every 12 to 24 calendar months, as specified in a plant's technical specifications. The specified maximum interval may need to be reduced to every 20 months in cases where previous inspections have shown extensive degradation, and may be increased to as much as every 40 months in cases where previous inspections have revealed minor degradation. These intervals are reduced or extended on the basis of the categorization of inspection results, as defined in the plant's technical specifications.

Although many plants' technical specifications include a general provision to extend surveillances by 25% of the specified interval, this provision is not considered applicable to steam generator tube inspections; the above criteria indicate the only conditions under which the surveillance interval for steam generator tube inspections may be changed. This position was delineated in NRC Generic Letter 91-04, "Changes in Technical Specification Surveillance Intervals to Accommodate a 24-Month Fuel Cycle," issued on April 2, 1991. As a practical matter, however, utilities with extensive tube degradation (e.g., plants with mill-annealed Alloy 600 steam generator tubes) generally perform steam generator tube inspections at all refueling outages, which typically occur every 12 to 24 months.

The minimum number of steam generators inspected and the number of tubes inspected in these steam generators are specified in the plant's technical specifications. The technical specifications typically permit a subset of steam generators to be examined provided all steam generators are performing in a similar manner. The steam generators inspected during a given outage are alternated so as to ensure the material condition of each steam generator is monitored over time. Depending on the results of the inspections (i.e., the number and severity of the flaws identified), additional steam generators may need to be examined during an outage.

Since the purpose of the steam generator tube inspections is, in part, to ensure adequate structural and leakage integrity of the tube bundle, more frequent inservice inspections may be required, depending on the severity of the indications detected. To ensure that the frequency was adequate for the prior cycle, licensees for PWRs should assess the inspection results following every outage to ensure that the tubes retained adequate structural and leakage integrity. This type of assessment is referred to as "condition monitoring." In addition, licensees should project the condition of the tubes from the current inspection to the next inspection to ensure that the tubes will retain adequate integrity for the next operating interval. This type of assessment is referred to as an "operational assessment." These assessments should be performed because the inspection frequencies and tube repair criteria specified in the technical specifications were established on the basis of specific assumptions concerning various parameters such as the forms of degradation (if any) to which the tubes may be susceptible, limitations of nondestructive examination techniques, and the rate of steam generator tube degradation. If any of these parameters exceed what was assumed during the development of the inspection intervals, the basis for the inspection frequency and tube repair criteria are no longer considered valid.

In summary, the inservice inspection of steam generator tubes is to be conducted at appropriate intervals, such that the structural and leakage integrity of the steam generator tubes is maintained with appropriate margins. These inspections should be adequate to detect degradation at a sufficiently early stage to preclude the progression of the degradation to the point that the regulatory criteria regarding steam generator tube structural and leakage integrity can no longer be met during the interval between inspections.

1.2.2 Eddy Current Testing

Eddy current testing (ECT) is the primary means for inspecting steam generator tubes. This method involves inserting a test coil inside the tube (i.e., the primary side of the tube) and pushing and pulling the coil so that it traverses the tube length. The test coil is then "excited" by alternating current, thereby creating a magnetic field that induces eddy currents in the tube wall. Disturbances of the eddy currents caused by flaws in the tube wall (such as cracks, holes, thinned regions, and other defects) produce corresponding changes in the electrical impedance as seen at the test coil terminals. Instruments are used to translate these changes in test coil impedance into an output that can be monitored by the data analyst. The depth of certain types of flaws can be determined by the observed phase angle response of this output signal. The test equipment is calibrated using tube specimens containing artificially induced flaws of known depth. Geometric discontinuities (such as the expansion transition and dents) and support structures (such as the tubesheet and tube support plates) also produce eddy current signals, making it very difficult to discriminate defect signals at these locations. NUREG/CR-6365 contains a discussion of some of the basic principles of ECT.

Bobbin coil eddy current probes are routinely used to inspect steam generator tubes. The bobbin coil probe permits a rapid screening of the tube for axially oriented and volumetric forms of degradation; however, it has several limitations:

- a general inability to permit characterization of identified degradation (e.g., axial, circumferential, or volumetric; single or multiple axial indications; etc.)

- relative insensitivity to detecting circumferentially oriented tube degradation

- limited capability to detect degradation in regions with geometric discontinuities (e.g., expansion transitions, U-bends, and dents) and deposits

As a result of the bobbin coil's limitations, the emergence of new forms of tube degradation (e.g., stress corrosion cracking), and advancements in computer technology, additional inspection probes were utilized. Currently, inspections of steam generator tubes generally employ both a bobbin coil probe and an additional probe, such as a rotating probe. The bobbin coil probe permits rapid screening of the tube for degradation and can be pulled through a tube at speeds exceeding 40 inches per second, while the rotating probes are used to detect forms of degradation at specific locations since they do not suffer from many of the limitations of the bobbin coil (discussed above).

Rotating probes generally contain one to three specialized test coils. The coils used in the rotating probe head at a specific plant depend on many factors, including optimizing the coils for detecting the forms of degradation to which a tube may potentially be susceptible. The coils used on a rotating probe include (1) a pancake coil which is sensitive to both axially and circumferentially oriented degradation, (2) an axially wound coil (which is sensitive to circumferentially oriented degradation), (3) a circumferentially wound coil (which is sensitive to axially oriented degradation), or (4) a plus-point coil (which reduces the effects of geometry variations in the tube and is sensitive to both axially and circumferentially oriented degradation).

Each of the above-mentioned test coils can be designed and driven at specific frequencies to ensure an optimal inspection of the tubing. In general, lower frequencies are better for detecting degradation initiating from the outside diameter of the tube, while higher frequencies are better for detecting degradation initiating from the inside diameter of the tube. The advantages of the rotating probes are that they are sensitive to circumferentially oriented degradation (which the bobbin coil probe is not), can better characterize the defect, and are less sensitive to geometric discontinuities. The major disadvantage of the rotating probes is their slow inspection speed (typically less than 1 inch per second). Because of this slow inspection speed, rotating probes are only used at specific locations (e.g., U-bends, sleeves, expansion transitions, dents, locations where there is a bobbin coil probe indication, locations where a more sensitive inspection is needed, and locations susceptible to circumferential cracking).

Tubes are generally selected for eddy current testing on a random basis except where experience indicates critical areas requiring inspection and tubes previously found to contain detectable wall penetrations (greater than 20%) or imperfections. A preservice inspection of all steam generators is performed to establish a baseline condition of the tubes. The inservice inspection frequency is adjusted to account for the history of tube degradation encountered within the unit's steam generators.

1.2.3 Tube Repairs

The plant technical specifications set plugging and repair limits for the maximum allowable wall degradation beyond which the tubes must be removed from service by plugging or repaired by sleeving. Tube degradation is typically discovered during scheduled inservice examinations of steam generator tubes, and tube repair (plugging or sleeving) is required for all tubes with indications of tube degradation exceeding the tube repair limits. All plants have a depth-based repair limit that is applicable to all forms of steam generator tube degradation. Alternatives to this depth-based limit have been approved; however, no alternatives have been approved for plants with thermally treated Alloy 600 steam generator tubes. The depth-based repair limit varies from plant to plant, but is typically 40% of the tube wall thickness. That is, tubes with indications of degradation greater than or equal to 40% must be plugged or repaired. For plants with thermally treated Alloy 600 steam generator tubes, there are plants which do do not have the standard 40% depth-based repair limit in their technical specifications. These plants include Robinson 2 and Callaway, which have depth-based repair limits of 47% and 48%, respectively.

The plugging and repair limits are established on the basis of the minimum tube wall thickness necessary to provide adequate structural margins in accordance with Regulatory Guide 1.121 during normal operating and postulated accident conditions. These limits allow for eddy current error and incremental wall degradation that may occur before the next inservice inspection of the tube. These plugging and repair limits are conservatively established according to an assumed mode of degradation in which the walls are uniformly thinned over a significant axial length of tubing. These limits do not consider additional structural margins associated with defects such as small-volume thinning and pitting, and they do not consider the external structural constraints against gross tube failure provided by such support structures as the tubesheet and tube support plates.

Because of its conservative basis, the depth-based limit tends to be overly restrictive for highly localized flaws (such as stress corrosion cracks) and flaws within the tubesheet. As a result, the industry has developed, and the NRC has approved, various alternative forms of repair criteria for specific forms of steam generator tube degradation.

The plugging technique involves installing plugs at the tube inlet and outlet. After plugging, the tube no longer functions as the boundary between the primary and secondary coolant systems. To prolong the life of severely degraded steam generator tubes, some utilities, with prior NRC approval, have repaired defective tubes by sleeving. After sleeving, the repaired tube may remain in service. Of the plants with thermally treated Alloy 600 tubes, only Braidwood 2, Byron 2, and Callaway have NRC approval to sleeve tubes as of December 2001. Of these three plants, only Callaway has installed sleeves in its steam generators. In the case of Callaway, most of the sleeves (but not all) were installed in mill-annealed Alloy 600 tubes.

1.2.4 Leakage Monitoring

Between tube inspections, plants monitor for a loss of tube integrity by monitoring for primary-to-secondary leakage. Various methods are used to monitor for tube leakage, including periodically sampling and analyzing the steam generator secondary water for radioactivity and continuously monitoring various streams (the steam generator blowdown, each main steam line, and the condenser air ejector exhaust) for the presence of or increases in radioactivity. The plant technical specifications limit the amount of primary-to-secondary leakage that can be present during plant operation. These limits vary from plant-to-plant, ranging from approximately 150 to 720 gpd. Additionally, technical specifications limit the specific activity of the secondary coolant (typically to 0.1 microcurie per gram of dose equivalent I-131). The specific activity is used in determining the radiological consequences of steam generator tube leakage.

1.3 <u>Mill-Annealed Alloy 600 Steam Generator Operating Experience</u>

A variety of steam generator designs exist in the U.S. The susceptibility of steam generator tubes to degradation is affected by a number of factors, including the operating environment (temperature and water chemistry), the tube material and its heat treatment, and operating and residual stresses. One of the most important factors affecting the susceptibility of a tube to degradation is the tube material and its heat treatment. Early steam generator designs utilized tubes fabricated from Alloy 600, which was typically mill-annealed by passing the tubes through a furnace at a temperature high enough to recrystallize the material and dissolve the carbon. The carbon content and the mill annealing temperature are important parameters for controlling the mechanical and corrosion properties of Alloy 600. As discussed in NUREG/CR-6365, "Steam Generator Tube Failures," the object of the mill annealing is to dissolve all the carbides, enlarge the grain size, and then cover the grain boundaries with carbides during slow cooling in air. Alloy 600 with insufficient carbides at the grain boundaries is more susceptible to primary water stress corrosion cracking (PWSCC). Undissolved intragranular carbides are undesirable because they provide nucleation sites for the dissolved carbon and prevent precipitation of the carbides on the grain boundaries. Undissolved carbides also prevent the grains from growing. The smaller grains have a much larger grain boundary area per unit of volume, and the carbides do not properly cover the boundaries.

Tubes installed in U.S. nuclear steam generators placed in service in the 1960s and 1970s were usually only mill-annealed. The annealing temperature depended on the manufacturer's practice at the time. Over 25 years of operating experience has shown mill-annealed Alloy 600 is susceptible to various forms of degradation in the steam generator operating environment. The types of degradation affecting mill-annealed Alloy 600 steam generator tubes include pitting, wear, thinning, wastage, and stress corrosion cracking. The orientation of the stress corrosion cracking can be either axial, circumferential, or volumetric. Degradation, of one form or another, has been observed on virtually every portion of the tube. Figure 1-1 illustrates most of the forms of degradation experienced. Although this figure represents a steam generator with U-shaped tubes, once-through steam generators (with straight tubes) have also experienced many of the same types of degradation.

The extensive tube degradation at PWRs with mill-annealed Alloy 600 steam generator tubes resulted in numerous tube leaks, approximately nine domestic tube ruptures, numerous midcycle steam generator tube inspections, and the replacement of steam generators at numerous plants. In addition, extensive tube degradation has contributed to the shutdown of other plants. Haddam Neck, Maine Yankee, Trojan, Zion 1, Zion 2, and San Onofre 1 permanently ceased operation with significant amounts of tube degradation. As of December 2001, 30 plants in the U.S. had replaced their original mill-annealed Alloy 600 steam generators. With one exception (Palisades), the replacement steam generators typically had more advanced tube materials. A listing of the plants that replaced their steam generators is provided in Table 1-1. This table also provides the model and tube material of the replacement steam generator.

Operating experience for plants with mill-annealed Alloy 600 steam generator tubes is well documented.

1.4 Thermally Treated Alloy 600 Tubes

As mill-annealed Alloy 600 steam generator tubes began exhibiting degradation in the early 1970s, improvements in the design of future steam generators were pursued to limit the likelihood of corrosion. Mill-annealed Alloy 600 tubes are generally resistant to chloride stress corrosion cracking, but are susceptible to caustic stress corrosion cracking. The tube material and its heat treatment were of particular importance in these improved designs. The first major advance in limiting the corrosion susceptibility of the steam generator tubes was the use of a thermal treatment process to improve the tube's microstructure and thereby its corrosion resistance.

In the late 1970s, some mill-annealed Alloy 600 tubes were subjected to this thermal treatment process to relieve fabrication stresses and to further improve the tube's microstructure. In this process, the tubes were subjected to high temperatures (approximately 705°C) for 10 to 15 hours. This process promotes carbide precipitation at the grain boundaries and diffusion of chromium to the regions adjacent to the grain boundaries. Alloy 600 with insufficient carbides at the grain boundaries is more susceptible to PWSCC, and chromium depletion at the grain boundaries makes the material more susceptible to outside diameter stress corrosion cracking (ODSCC).

This thermal treatment process was first used on tubes installed in replacement steam generators placed into service in the early 1980s. Thermally treated Alloy 600 is presently used in 17 plants. Another plant, Callaway, has steam generators in which only the first 10 rows have thermally treated Alloy 600 tubes; the remaining rows have mill-annealed Alloy 600 tubes. Other plants (e.g., South Texas 2) may have some thermally treated tubes in their steam generators; however, the number of tubes made from this material is insignificant and are not discussed in this report. Thermally treated Alloy 600 is considered to be highly resistant but not immune to PWSCC compared to mill-annealed Alloy 600 tubes. The experience with thermally treated Alloy 600 has not been well documented although thermally treated Alloy 600 is generally recognized to have better performance. This report provides a summary of the steam generator operating experience at PWRs with thermally treated Alloy 600 steam generator tubes.

It is important to evaluate the operating experience of thermally treated Alloy 600 because although it is no longer the material of choice for new or replacement steam generators, it is used in a number of plants and has been in service for over 20 years. The evaluation may provide insights into the behavior of newer steam generator materials such as thermally treated Alloy 690, which is currently the preferred material for tubes in new and replacement steam generators. Of the 69 operating PWRs in December 2001, approximately 45% have mill annealed Alloy 600 steam generator tubes, approximately 25% have thermally treated Alloy 600 steam generator tubes, and approximately 30% have thermally treated Alloy 690 steam generator tubes.

Table 1-1: Plants With Replacement Steam Generators

Plant Name	No. of Loops	SG Manufacturer/Model		Completion Date	Tube Material[1]
		Original	Replacement		
Surry 2	3	W/51	W/51F	9/80	600 TT
Surry 1	3	W/51	W/51F	7/81	600 TT
Turkey Point 3	3	W/44	W/44F	4/82	600 TT
Turkey Point 4	3	W/44	W/44F	5/83	600 TT
Point Beach 1	2	W/44	W/44F	3/84	600 TT
Robinson 2	3	W/44	W/44F	10/84	600 TT
Cook 2	4	W/51	W/54F	3/89	690 TT
Indian Point 3	4	W/44	W/44F	6/89	690 TT
Palisades	2	CE	CE	3/91	600 MA
Millstone 2	2	CE-67	BWC	1/93	690 TT
North Anna 1	3	W/51	W/54F	4/93	690 TT
Summer	3	W/D3	W/D75	12/94	690 TT
North Anna 2	3	W/51	W/54F	5/95	690 TT
Ginna	2	W/44	BWC	6/96	690 TT
Catawba 1	4	W/D3	BWC	9/96	690 TT
Point Beach 2	2	W/44	W/D47	12/96	690 TT
McGuire 1	4	W/D2	BWC	5/97	690 TT
Salem 1	4	W/51	W/F	7/97	600 TT
McGuire 2	4	W/D3	BWC	12/97	690 TT
St. Lucie 1	2	CE-67	BWC	1/98	690 TT
Byron 1	4	W/D4	BWC	1/98	690 TT
Braidwood 1	4	W/D4	BWC	11/98	690 TT
South Texas Project 1	4	W/E	W/D94	5/00	690 TT
Farley 1	3	W/51	W/54F	5/00	690 TT
Cook 1	4	W/51	BWC	12/00	690 TT
Arkansas Nuclear One 2	2	CE/2815	W/D109	12/00	690 TT
Indian Point 2	4	W/44	W/44F	12/00	600 TT
Farley 2	3	W/51	W/54F	5/01	690 TT
Kewaunee	2	W/51	W/54F	12/01	690 TT
Harris	3	W/D4	W/D75	12/01	690 TT

[1]TT= thermally treated, MA = mill-annealed

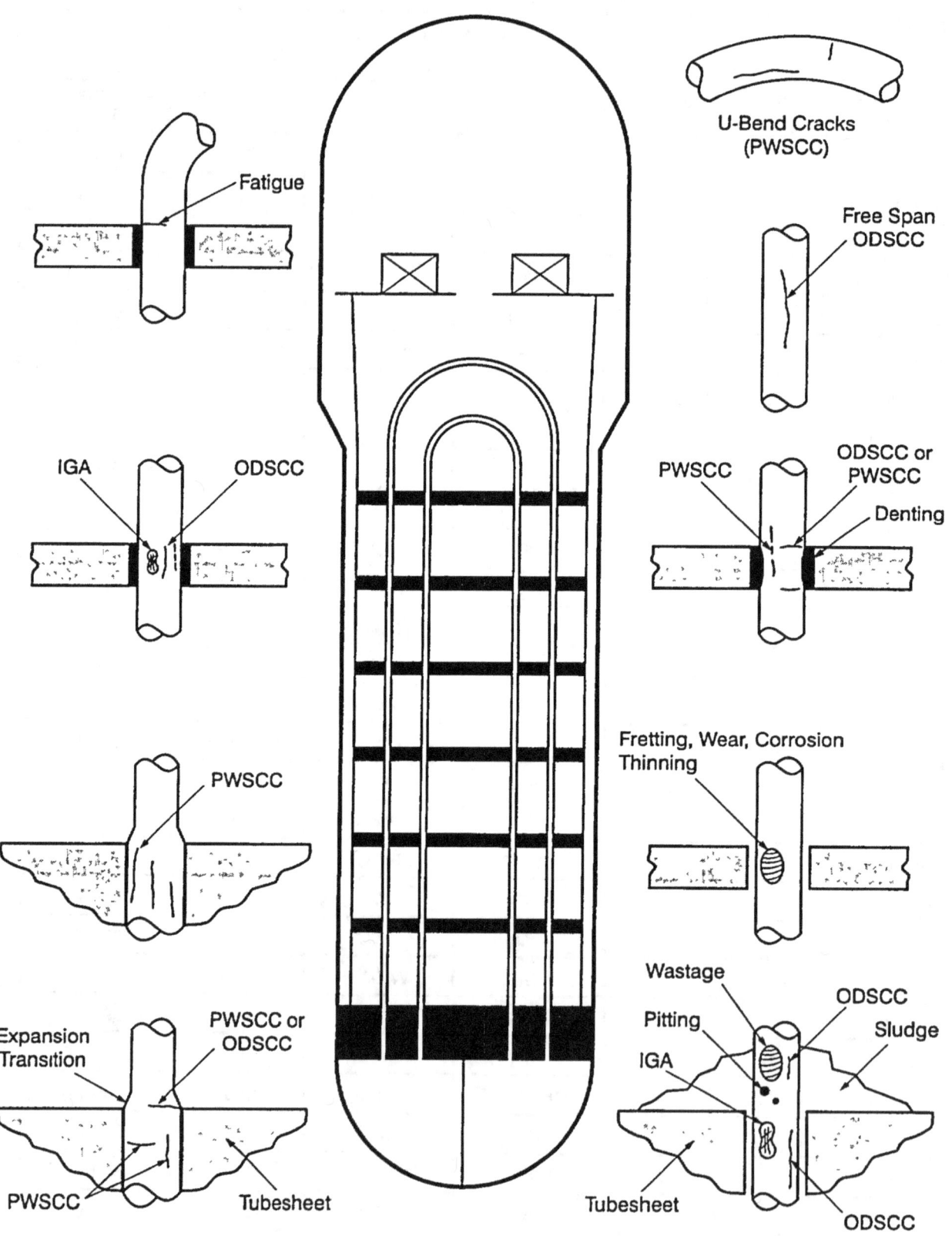

Figure 1-1. Mill Annealed Alloy 600 Steam Generator Tube Degradation

2 STEAM GENERATOR DESIGNS IN PLANTS WITH THERMALLY TREATED ALLOY 600 TUBES

2.1 Introduction

Steam generators in plants with thermally treated Alloy 600 tubes are vertical shell and U-tube heat exchangers with integral moisture-separating equipment (refer to Figure 2-1 or 2-2). Heat is transferred from the hot primary coolant as it flows through the inverted U-tubes to the water on the secondary side of the steam generator. The primary coolant enters and leaves the steam generators through nozzles in the hemispherical bottom head of the steam generator. The transfer of heat from the primary system to the water on the secondary side of the steam generator is accomplished primarily through the steam generator U-tubes. After the primary coolant flows through the U-tubes, it exits the lower plenum of the steam generator through an outlet nozzle. A plate in the lower plenum below the tubesheet, called a "divider plate", separates the inlet and outlet primary coolant and directs the flow through the tubes.

The steam generators are designed with an evaporator section and a steam drum section. The steam drum section is the upper part containing the moisture separators. The evaporator section, sometimes called the "tube bundle", is an inverted U-tube heat exchanger containing the tubes. Typical features of a U-tube are shown in Figure 2-3. The evaporator section may have a preheater region depending on the model. The preheater enhances heat transfer to the incoming feedwater and is a series of baffle plates around a portion of the cold-leg side of the steam generator. Figure 2-1 depicts a typical PWR recirculating steam generator without a preheater, and Figure 2-2 depicts one with a preheater.

The number of tubes in each steam generator depends on the model but varies from 3,000 to nearly 6,000 for the plants with thermally treated Alloy 600 tubes. The tubes are welded to a thick plate, called a "tubesheet", with a hole for each tube end. The tubesheet is approximately 2-feet thick. The tubes are expanded against the tubesheet walls for the full depth of the tubesheet The tubes are supported with plates at a number of fixed axial locations along the tube bundle and with V-shaped bars in the U-bend region of the tube bundle. These V-shaped bars are called "antivibration bars" (AVBs).

Steam generators with thermally treated Alloy 600 tubes were first placed in service in 1980. Figure 2-4 is a graph of the deployment of steam generators with thermally treated Alloy 600 tubes. Currently, 17 plants have steam generators with thermally treated Alloy 600 tubes. Another plant, Callaway, has steam generators in which only the first 10 rows have thermally treated Alloy 600 tubes; the remaining rows have mill-annealed Alloy 600 tubes. All plants with thermally treated Alloy 600 tubes are Westinghouse-designed plants.

Table 2-1 lists all the plants with thermally treated Alloy 600 tubes as of December 2001. The table reveals two populations of plants with thermally treated Alloy 600 tubes: (1) plants which replaced their original steam generators (containing mill-annealed tubes) with ones containing thermally treated Alloy 600 tubes, and (2) plants whose original steam generators were initially fabricated with thermally treated Alloy 600 tubes. All of the latter plants have Westinghouse model D5 and F steam generators.

In addition to the advanced tubing material, steam generators with thermally treated Alloy 600 tubes have other design improvements to increase the tubes' resistance to degradation. One design improvement was to expand the tubes into the tubesheet by hydraulic means rather than by roll expansion or explosive expansion methods. Hydraulic expansion reduces the residual stresses at the expansion transition region, reducing the potential for stress corrosion cracking, and the expansion process (as with all full-depth expansion processes) closes the crevice between the tube and the tubesheet hole (which is a region where dryout can concentrate chemicals if the crevice remains open). Another design improvement in these newer steam generators is the use of stainless steel tube supports rather than carbon steel tube supports. Stainless steel is less susceptible to corrosion than the carbon steel used for the tube support plates in earlier designs. The carbon steel plates corroded and formed magnetite, which filled the crevice between the tubes and the tube support plates, denting the tubes. Another design improvement was the use of quatrefoil-shaped holes rather than round holes. The quatrefoil-shaped holes promote high-velocity flow along the tube, sweeping impurities away from the support plate locations. The quatrefoil-shaped hole design also limits the contact between the tube and the support plate to four narrow lands, minimizing local dryout and chemical concentration.

Table 2-2 indicates the number of calendar years that steam generators in plants currently using thermally treated Alloy 600 tubes have been in service. This table also includes the number of years the original steam generators with mill-annealed Alloy 600 tubes were in service for plants that replaced their steam generators with ones containing thermally treated Alloy 600 tubes. It is interesting to note that many plants which replaced their steam generators in the early 1980s have operated over twice as long with their replacement steam generators. This table clearly illustrates the improvements made in the design and operation of early replacement steam generators. The average age of steam generators with thermally treated Alloy 600 tubes is approximately 14 calendar years.

As alluded to previously, steam generators with thermally treated Alloy 600 tubes can be divided into three categories, model D5, model F, and replacement steam generators. The latter category includes all plants that replaced their original steam generators (which had mill-annealed Alloy 600 tubes) with steam generators containing thermally treated Alloy 600 tubes. The designs of the steam generators in these three categories are discussed further below.

2.2 Model D5 Steam Generators

Westinghouse model D5 steam generators have 4,570 thermally treated Alloy 600 tubes with an outside diameter of 0.750-inch and a 0.043-inch nominal wall thickness. The tubes are hydraulically expanded for the full depth of the tubesheet at each end. The tubes are supported by stainless steel support plates with quatrefoil-shaped holes and V-shaped chrome plated Alloy 600 anti-vibration bars (AVBs). Figure 2-5 depicts the model D5 steam generator tube support configuration. As shown in this figure, several naming conventions are used for the tube support plates. Model D5 steam generator tubes have a square tube pitch as depicted in Figure 2-6 with a tube spacing of 1.063 inches.

The model D5 steam generators have several design features that set them apart from other steam generators with thermally treated Alloy 600 tubes. These features include a preheater and a T-slot. The preheater is a region in the tube bundle which preheats the incoming feedwater (secondary coolant) prior to entering the main region of the tube bundle. The design and operation of the preheater are discussed further below. The T-slot is an untubed portion of the tube bundle. It has a T shape and is used in steam generator blowdown for sludge removal. The T-slot is depicted in Figure 2-6.

The preheater region (near the feedwater inlet) and its relation to the tube bundle are shown in Figure 2-2. The preheater region is located on the cold-leg side of the tube bundle and faces the feedwater inlet. A more detailed view of the preheater region is given in Figure 2-7. As can be inferred from Figure 2-7, the first five rows of tubes in the periphery of the tube bundle are not supported at baffle plates E and H. These tubes are sometimes called "window tubes."

Feedwater flowing into the steam generator first passes through a venturi insert in the main feed nozzle. The insert serves as a backflow restrictor to limit the rate of blowdown from the steam generator in the event of a main feedwater line break. In the preheater section, as illustrated in Figure 2-7, the incoming feedwater enters the inlet waterbox and encounters the impingement plate, which directs the water outward to fill the waterbox volume and downward to the preheater inlet located between baffle plates B and D. In the lower section of the preheater, or first pass, the feedwater enters the tube bundle. The water then flows around the tubes and baffles until it enters the main region of the tube bundle. Because the water changes direction between the baffle plates of the preheater (i.e., right-to-left between B and D and then left-to-right between D and E), this type of preheater design is called a "counterflow preheater."

In the early 1980s, when Westinghouse steam generators with preheaters were first deployed, tube wear attributed to tube vibration in the preheat section of the steam generator was discovered at several foreign plants. The wear was occurring primarily in the outer three rows of tubes in the preheater section (rows 47, 48, and 49). The tube wear was due to large tube-to-baffle-plate clearances and relatively high velocities of the nonuniform, turbulent inlet flow, which allowed the tubes to vibrate within the clearance.

The root cause of the tube wear and design modifications to mitigate its occurrence are discussed in NUREG-0966, "Safety Evaluation Report Related to the D2/D3 Steam Generator Design Modification," and NUREG-1014, "Safety Evaluation Report Related to the D4/D5/E Steam Generator Design Modification." The design modifications for plants with D5 steam generators involved expanding selected tubes (approximately 124 tubes) at baffle plates B and D to make the tubes stiffer and splitting feedwater flow by diverting a fraction of the main feedwater flow through an auxiliary feedwater nozzle to reduce the flow velocities and the potential for tube vibration. For plants with four model D5 steam generators, approximately 10% of the main feedwater flow was diverted. The auxiliary nozzle is located in the upper portion of the steam generator as illustrated in Figure 2-2.

The expansion of tubes at baffle plate locations was intended to limit the tube movement at the baffle plate intersections to a few thousandths of an inch. Westinghouse developed a proprietary process for hydraulically expanding the steam generator tubes at the baffle plates. The hydraulic expansion was intended to minimize the residual stresses from the expansion such that combined with the relatively low temperature in the preheater region there would be no significant increase in the potential for stress corrosion cracking at the expanded locations.

-13-

The expansions were designed to be located entirely within the baffle plate to prevent bulging of the tube outside of the baffle plates.

The model D5 steam generator design incorporated many enhancements compared to earlier models including (1) utilizing stainless steel, a more corrosion-resistant material, as the material for the tube support plates and baffles, (2) changing the shape of the holes in the tube support plates from circular to a quatrefoil shape to improve flow, (3) expanding the tubes within the tubesheet by means of a hydraulic device in lieu of mechanical rollers to reduce stresses, (4) thermally treating the Alloy 600 tubes to enhance their resistance to corrosion, and (5) changing the holes in the flow distribution baffles from slotted to circular shape to improve flow.

Model D5 steam generators are used at Braidwood 2, Byron 2, Catawba 2, and Comanche Peak 2.

2.3 Model F Steam Generators

The model F steam generators were designed in the mid 1970s. Except for the model F steam generators at Callaway, all model F steam generators have 5,626 thermally treated Alloy 600 tubes. At Callaway, only the first 10 rows of tubes in each steam generator have thermally treated tubes (i.e., only 1,214 tubes per steam generator are thermally treated). The tubes have an outside diameter of 0.688-inch and a nominal wall thickness of 0.040 inch. The tubes are hydraulically expanded for the full depth of the tubesheet at each end. The tubes are supported by stainless steel support plates with quatrefoil-shaped holes and V-shaped chrome plated Alloy 600 AVBs. The first 10 rows of tubes were stress-relieved to improve corrosion resistance. Figure 2-8 depicts the model F steam generator tube support configuration. As shown in this figure, several naming conventions are used for the tube support plates. Model F steam generator tubes have a square tube pitch as depicted in Figure 2-9 with a tube spacing of 0.980 inch.

Unlike the model D5 steam generator, the model F steam generator does not have a preheater region. In the model F steam generator, the secondary-system water (feedwater) is fed through a feedwater nozzle to a feedring into the downcomer where it mixes with recirculating water draining from the moisture separators. This downcomer water flows to the bottom of the steam generator, across the top of the tubesheet, and then up through the tube bundle, where steam is generated (refer to Figure 2-1).

Model F steam generators are used at Callaway, Millstone 3, Salem 1, Seabrook, Vogtle 1, Vogtle 2, and Wolf Creek. As discussed above, the model F steam generators at Callaway use thermally treated Alloy 600 only in the first 10 rows of tubes. The model F steam generators at Salem 1 are replacement steam generators which were originally intended to be installed in the canceled Seabrook Unit 2 plant. As a result, the Salem 1 steam generators are discussed as replacement steam generators.

2.4 Replacement Steam Generators

Three different steam generator models are used at plants that replaced their original steam generators with steam generators with thermally treated Alloy 600 tubes, namely the Westinghouse models 44F, 51F, and F. These models do not have a preheater region.

Westinghouse model 44F steam generators have 3,214 thermally treated Alloy 600 tubes with an outside diameter of 0.875 inch and a 0.050-inch nominal wall thickness. The tubes are hydraulically expanded for the full depth of the tubesheet at each end. The tubes are supported by stainless steel support plates with quatrefoil-shaped holes and V-shaped AVBs. Figure 2-10 depicts the model 44F steam generator tube support configuration, using the typical naming convention. Model 44F steam generator tubes have a square tube pitch as depicted in Figure 2-11 with a tube spacing of approximately 1.2 inches.

Model 44F steam generators are used at Indian Point 2, Point Beach 1, Robinson 2, and Turkey Point 3 and 4.

Westinghouse model 51F steam generators have 3,342 thermally treated Alloy 600 tubes with an outside diameter of 0.875 inch and a 0.050-inch nominal wall thickness. The tubes are hydraulically expanded for the full depth of the tubesheet at each end. The tubes are supported by stainless steel support plates with quatrefoil-shaped holes and V-shaped AVBs. The tubes in rows 1 through 8 received a supplemental thermal treatment (stress relieving) after bending, while still in the manufacturing facility. Also, starting with the model F steam generators (including the model 44F and 51F steam generators), a set of geometric controls were implemented for bending the tubes (i.e., manufacturing the U-bends). The controls included strict requirements for ovality, the U-bend-to-leg flatness, and leg spacing. These improved manufacturing requirements helped to provide consistent U-bends, which in turn translated into uniform stresses. The geometric controls helped to eliminate localized stress discontinuities present in earlier steam generators. Figure 2-12 depicts the model 51F steam generator tube support configuration, using the typical naming convention. Model 51F steam generator tubes have a square tube pitch as depicted in Figure 2-13 with a tube spacing of approximately 1.281 inches.

Model 51F steam generators are used at Surry 1 and 2.

Although the steam generators at Salem 1 are replacement steam generators, the steam generators are true model F steam generators. They were initially scheduled to be installed in Seabrook Unit 2, which was never completed. The design of the model F steam generators is discussed in Section 2.3.

Table 2-1: Plants With Thermally Treated Alloy 600 Tubes

Plant	Date[1]	Model	Number of SGs	Replacement[2]
Braidwood 2	1988	D5	4	N
Byron 2	1987	D5	4	N
Callaway[3]	1984	F	4	N
Catawba 2	1986	D5	4	N
Comanche Peak 2	1993	D5	4	N
Indian Point 2	2000	44F	4	Y
Millstone 3	1986	F	4	N
Point Beach 1	1984	44F	2	Y
Robinson 2	1984	44F	3	Y
Salem 1	1997	F	4	Y
Seabrook 1	1990	F	4	N
Surry 1	1981	51F	3	Y
Surry 2	1982	51F	3	Y
Turkey Point 3	1982	44F	3	Y
Turkey Point 4	1983	44F	3	Y
Vogtle 1	1987	F	4	N
Vogtle 2	1989	F	4	N
Wolf Creek 1	1985	F	4	N

[1]Date of commercial operation or date of steam generator replacement, whichever is later
[2]N means the plant has its original steam generators; Y means the steam generators are replacements.
[3]Only the first 10 rows of the Callaway steam generators have thermally treated tubes; the remaining are mill-annealed Alloy 600.

Table 2-2: Age of Steam Generators at Plants With Thermally Treated Alloy 600 Tubes

Plant	Operating Time[1] Original SG	Operating Time[1] Replacement SG
Braidwood 2	13	N/A
Byron 2	14	N/A
Callaway	17	N/A
Catawba 2	15	N/A
Comanche Peak 2	8	N/A
Indian Point 2	26	1
Millstone 3	16	N/A
Point Beach 1	13	18
Robinson 2	14	17
Salem 1	20	4
Seabrook 1	11	N/A
Surry 1	8	20
Surry 2	7	21
Turkey Point 3	9	20
Turkey Point 4	10	19
Vogtle 1	15	N/A
Vogtle 2	13	N/A
Wolf Creek 1	16	N/A

[1]Operating Time = calendar years of operation as of 12/31/01

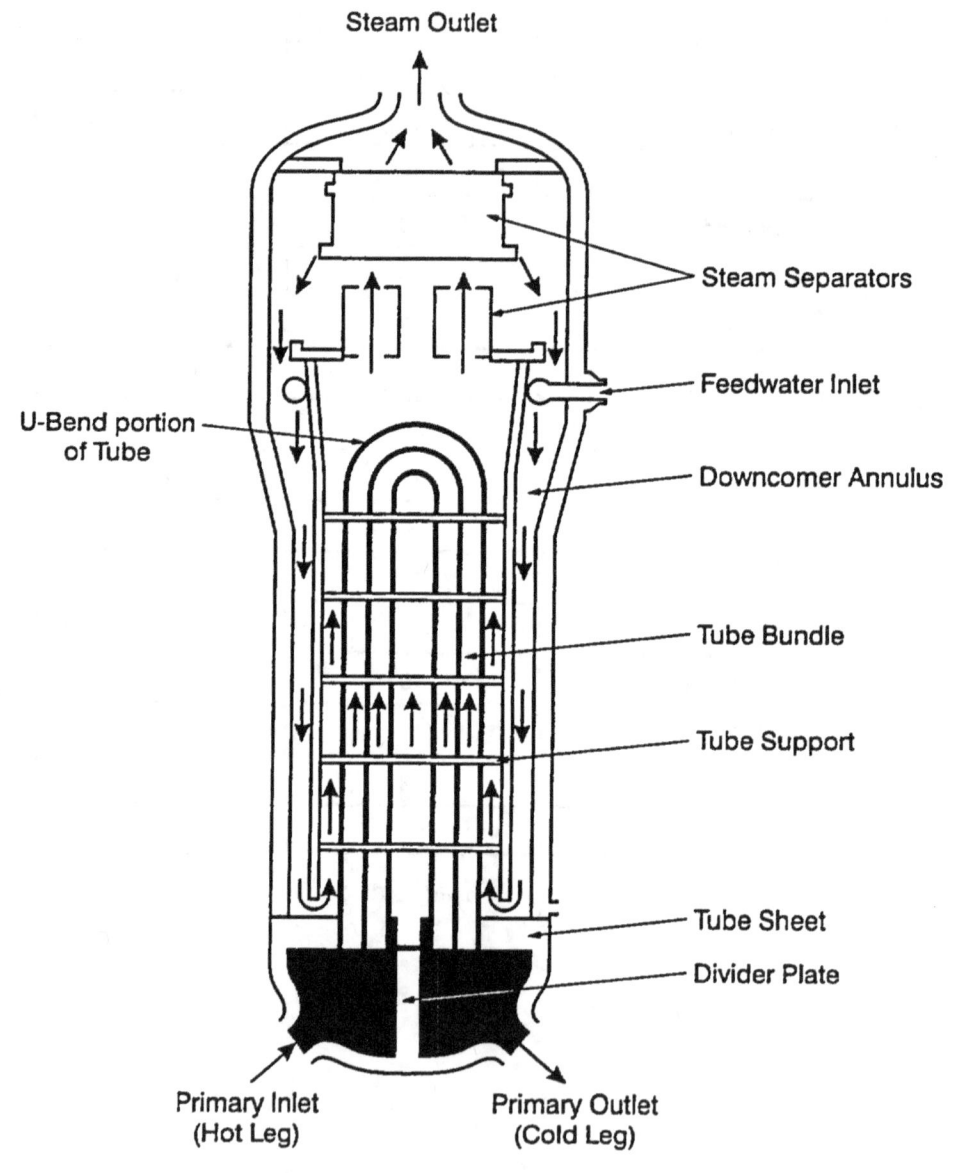

Figure 2-1. Typical PWR Recirculating Steam Generator Without a Preheater

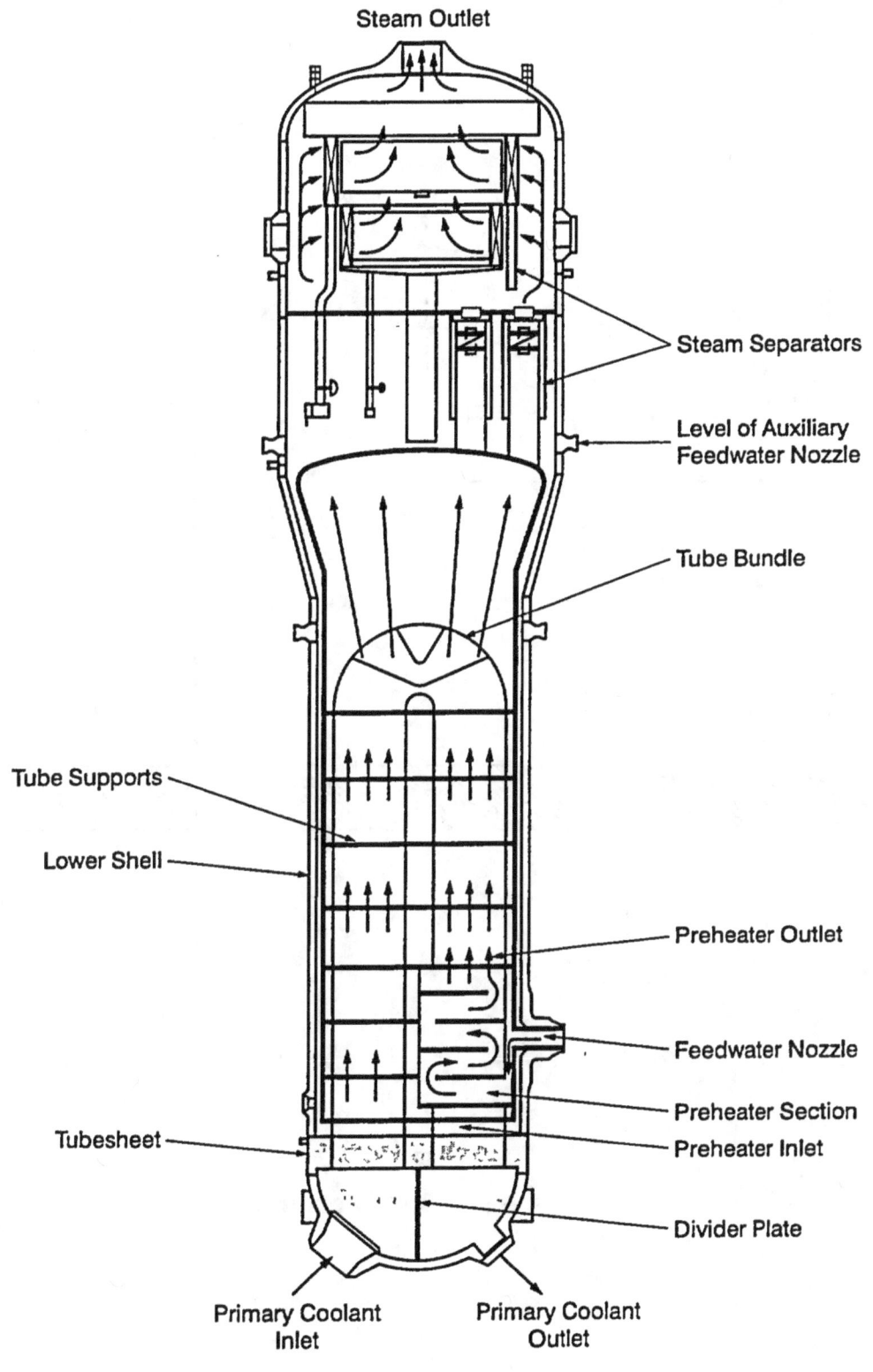

Figure 2-2. Typical PWR Recirculating Steam Generator With a Preheater

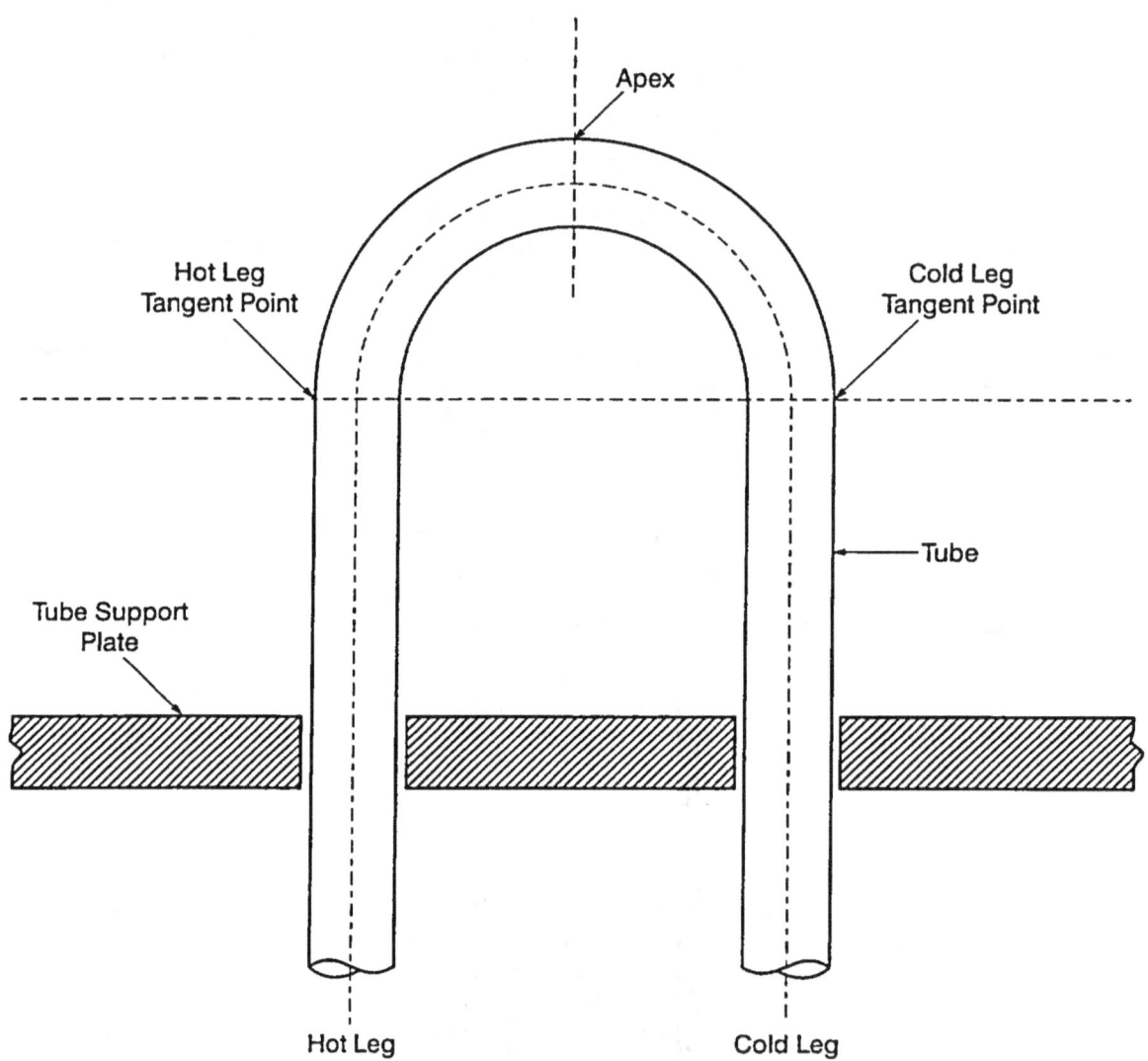

Figure 2-3. U-Bend Features

Figure 2-4: Number of Plants With Thermally Treated Alloy 600 Steam Generator Tubes as a Function of Year

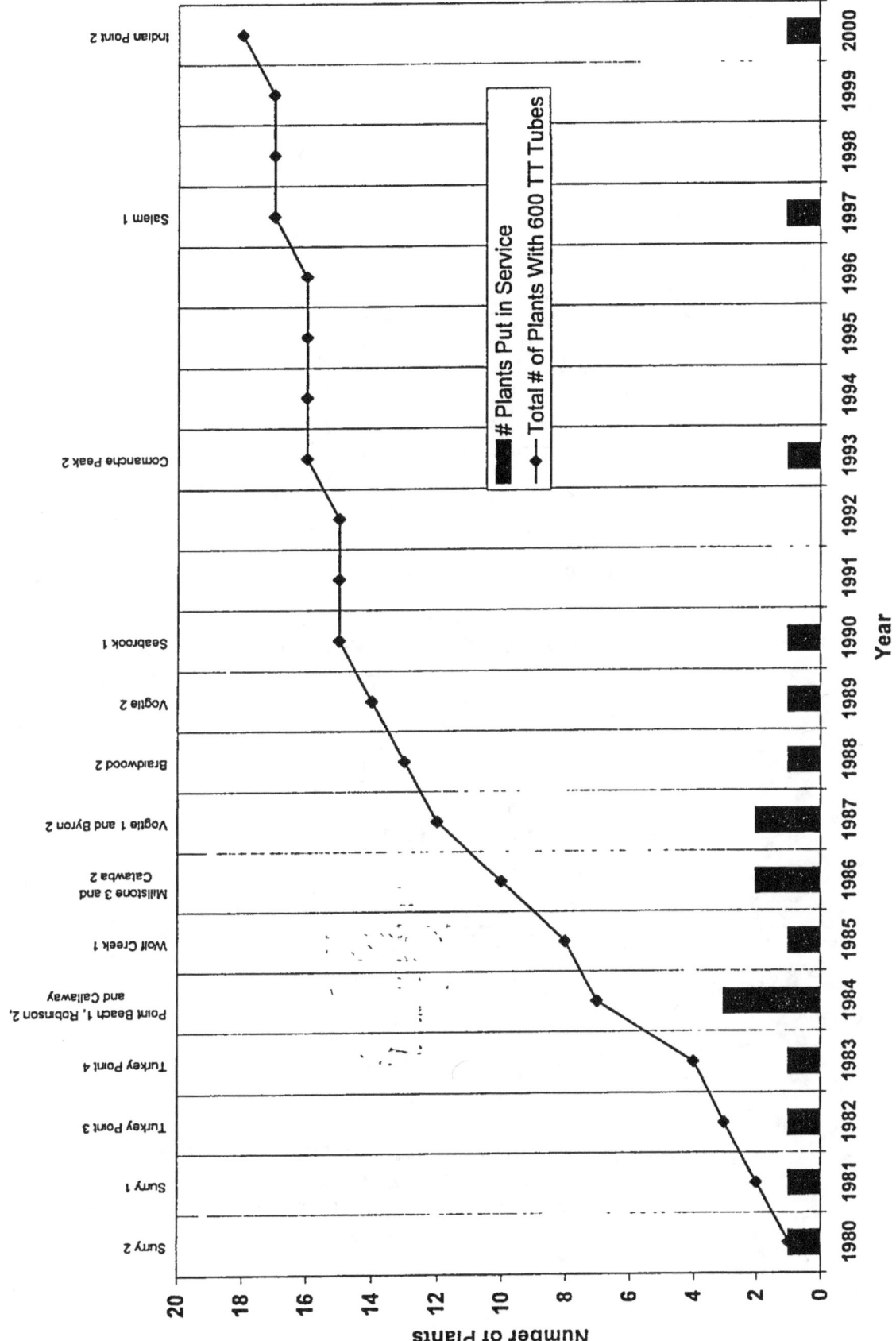

As of December 2001, there were 69 operating PWRs, 18 of which had thermally treated Alloy 600 steam generator tubes

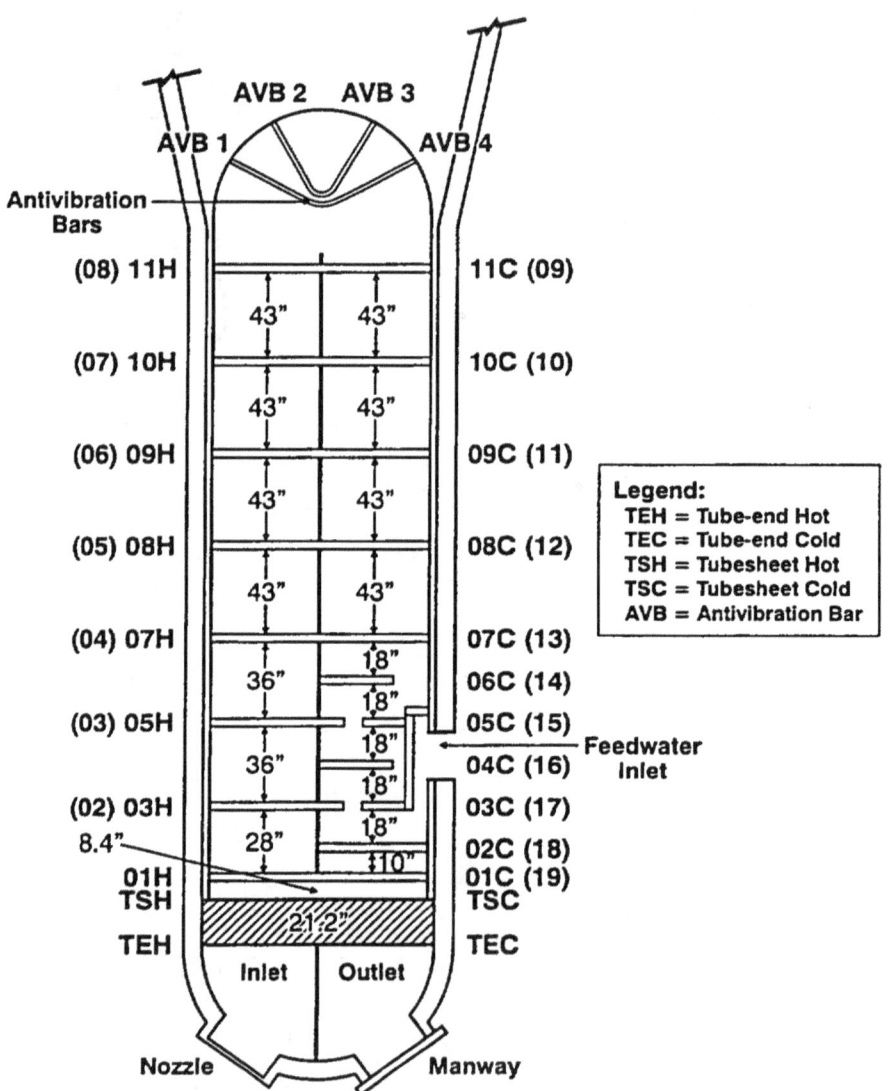

**Figure 2-5. Westinghouse Model D5 Steam Generator
Tube Support Locations**
(Alternate Naming Convention in Parentheses)

Row

50
45
40
35
30
25
20
15
10
5
1

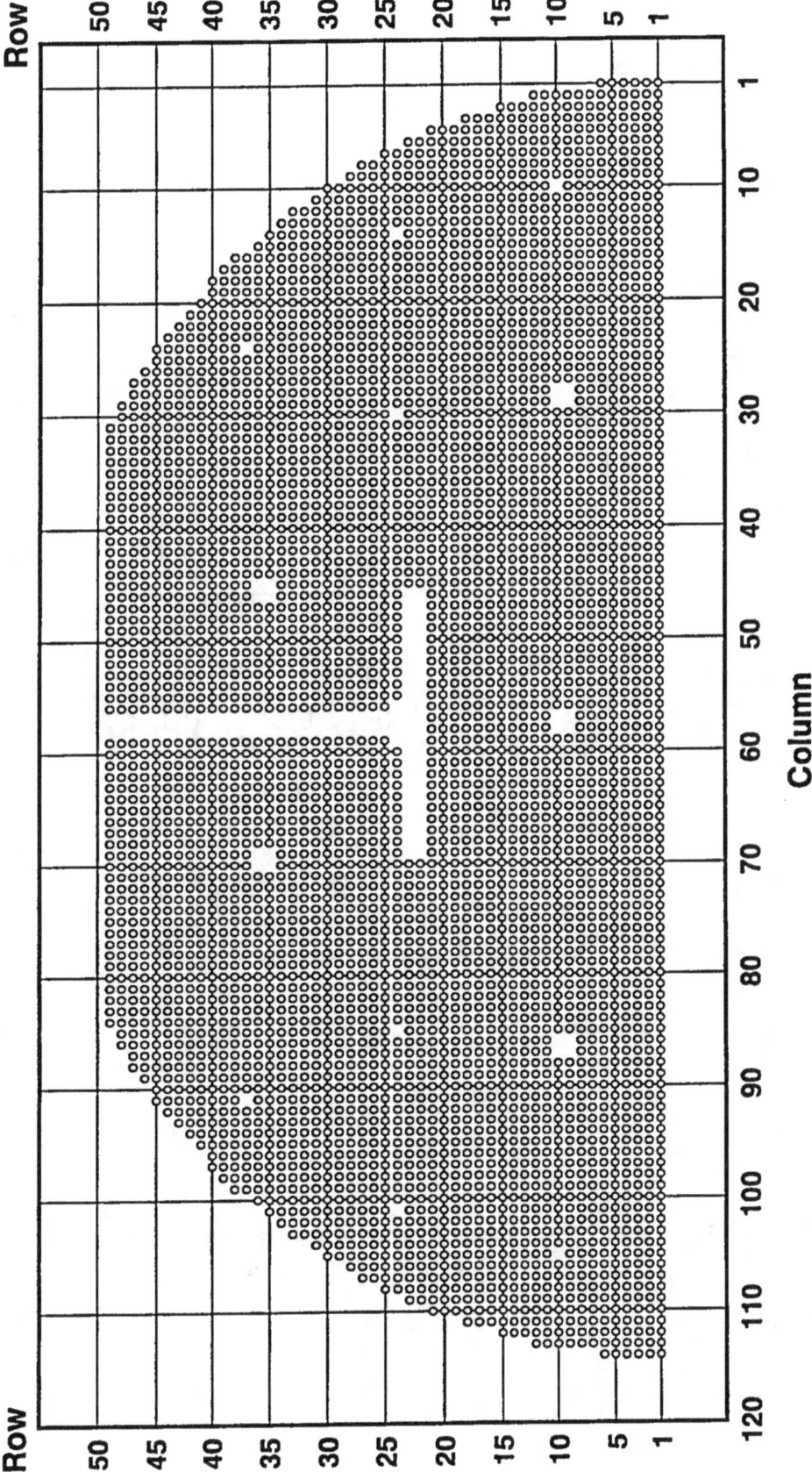

Row

50
45
40
35
30
25
20
15
10
5
1

Column

Figure 2-6. Westinghouse Model D5 Steam Generator Tubesheet Map

-23-

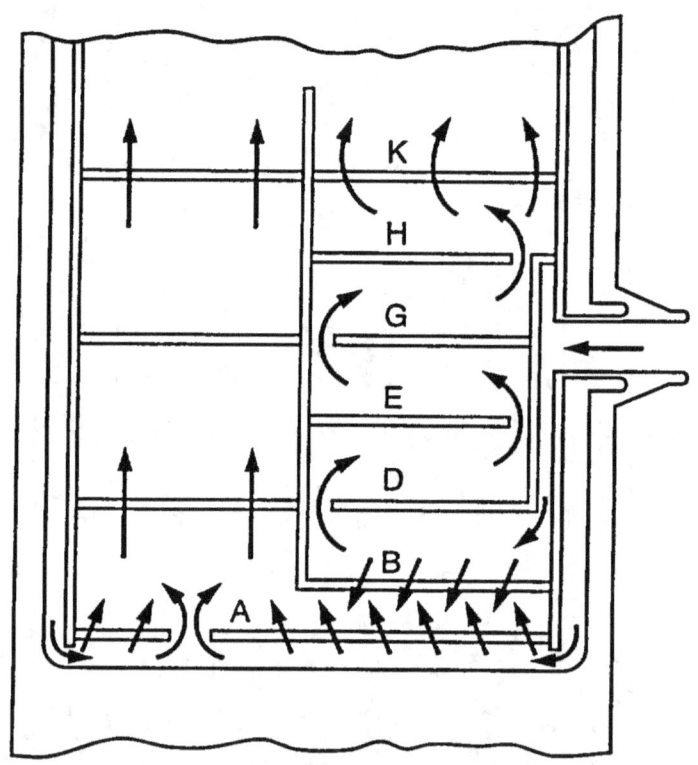

**Figure 2-7. Preheater Region of Westinghouse Model
D-5 Steam Generator**

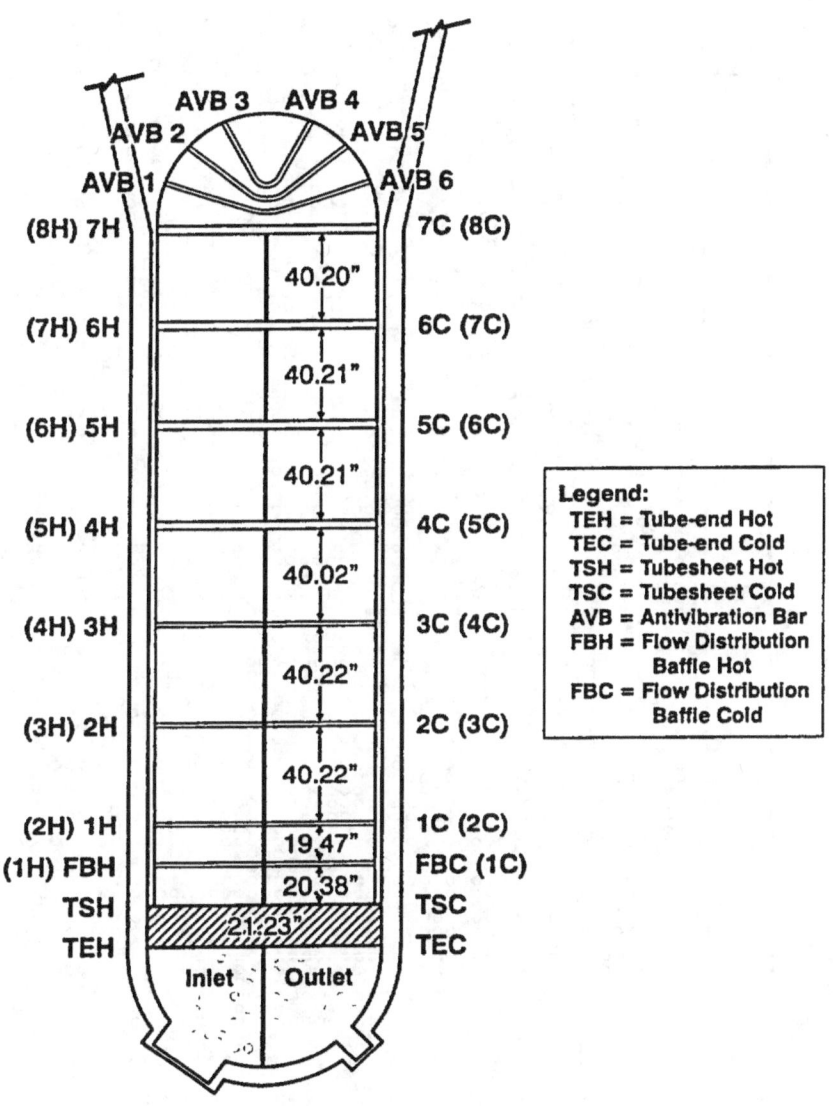

**Figure 2-8. Westinghouse Model F Steam Generator
Tube Support Locations**
(Alternate Naming Convention in Parentheses)

-25-

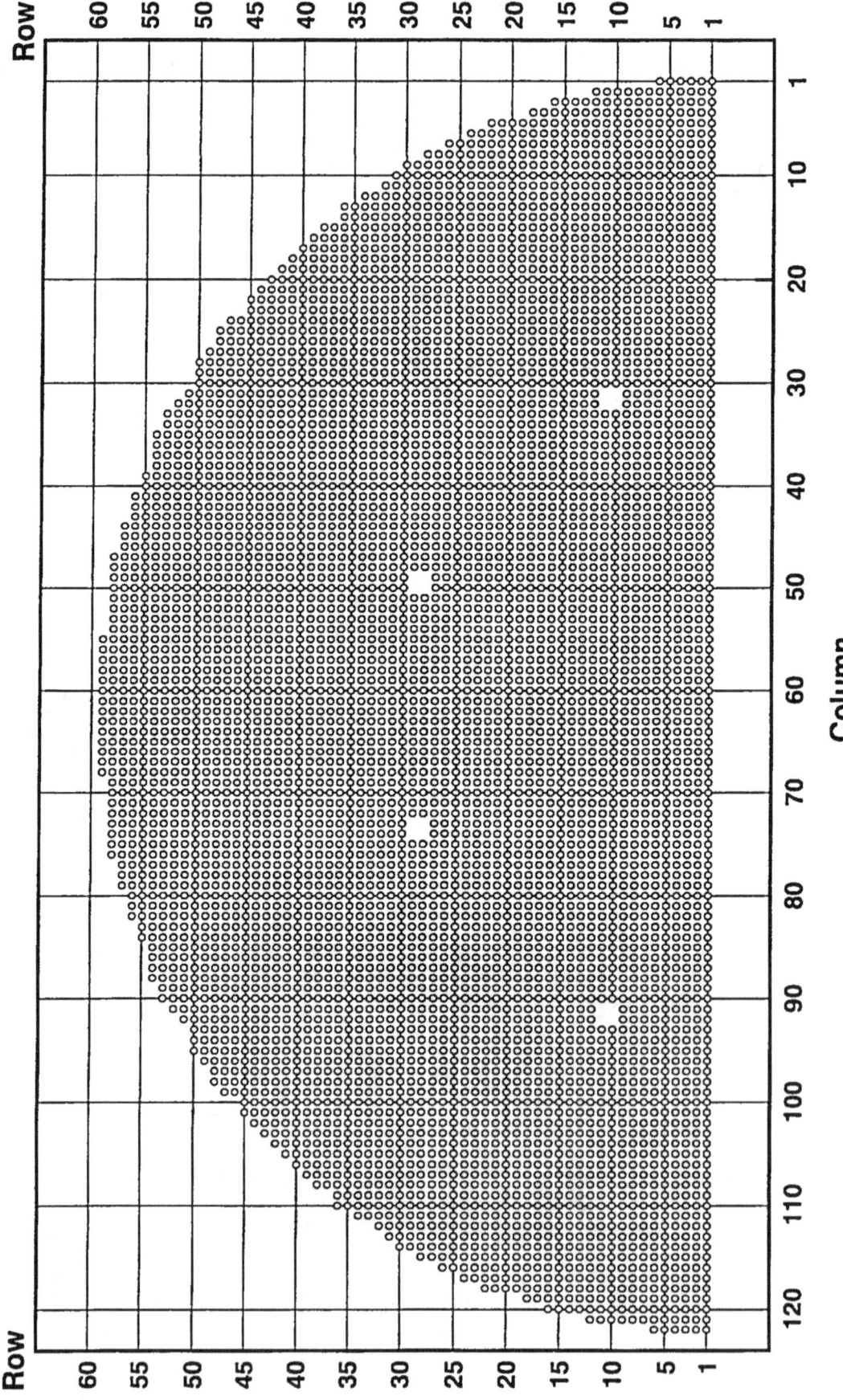

Figure 2-9. Westinghouse Model F Steam Generator Tubesheet Map

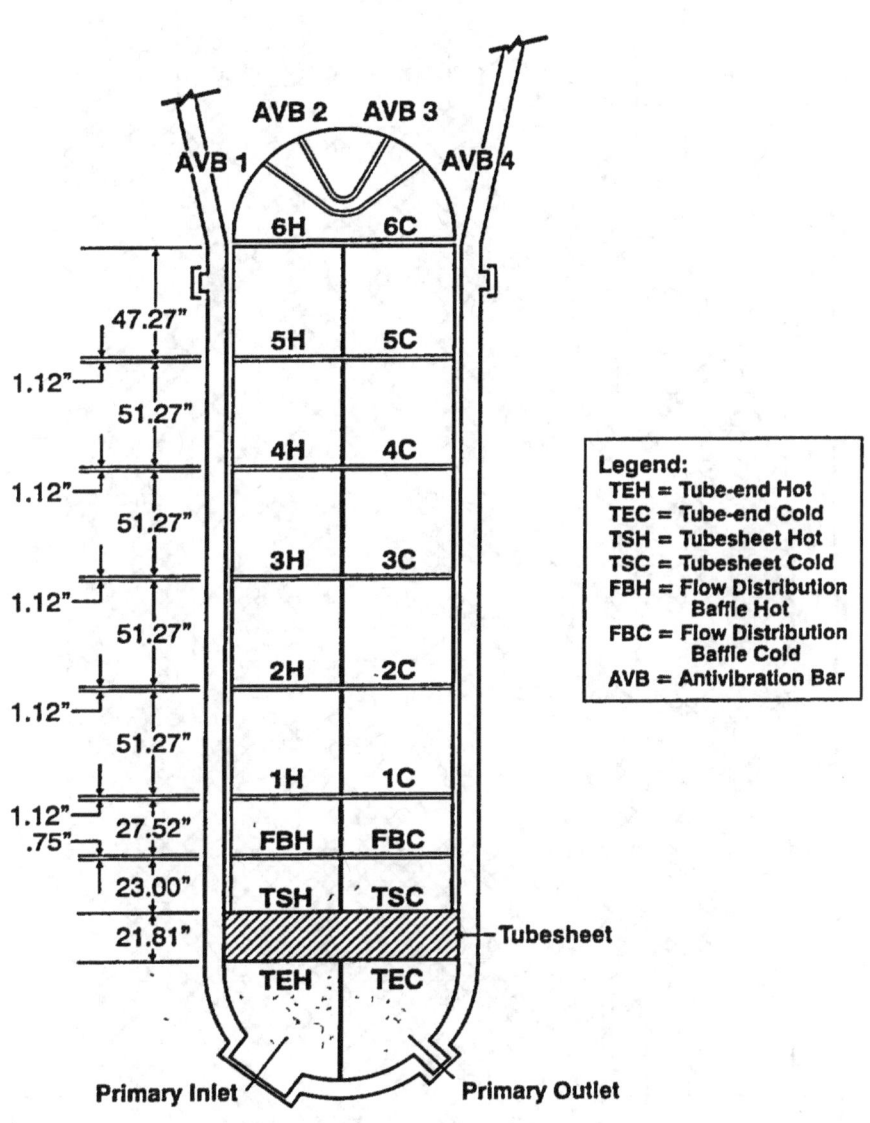

Figure 2-10. Westinghouse Model 44F Steam Generator Tube Support Locations

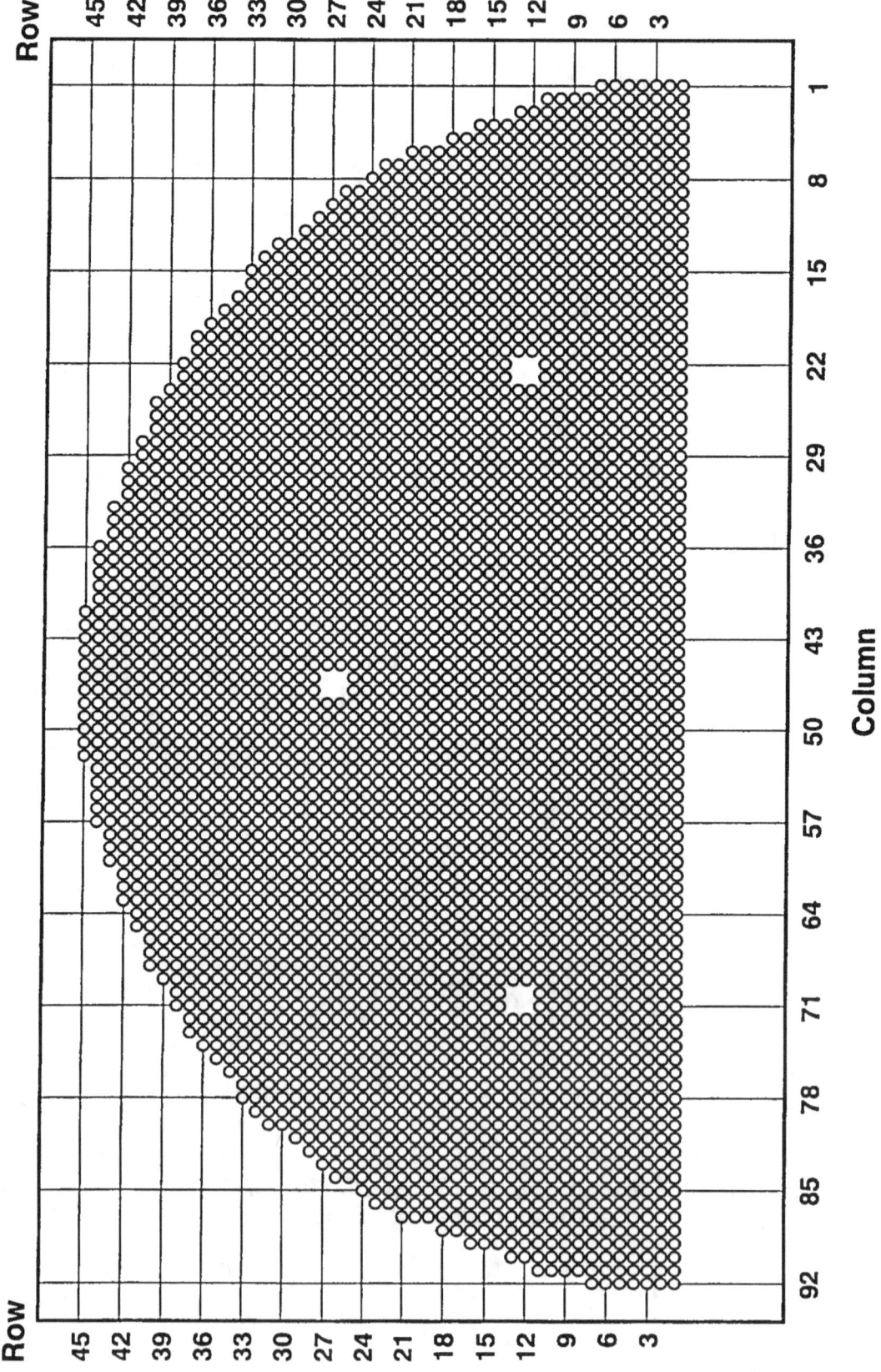

Figure 2-11. Westinghouse Model 44F Steam Generator Tubesheet Map

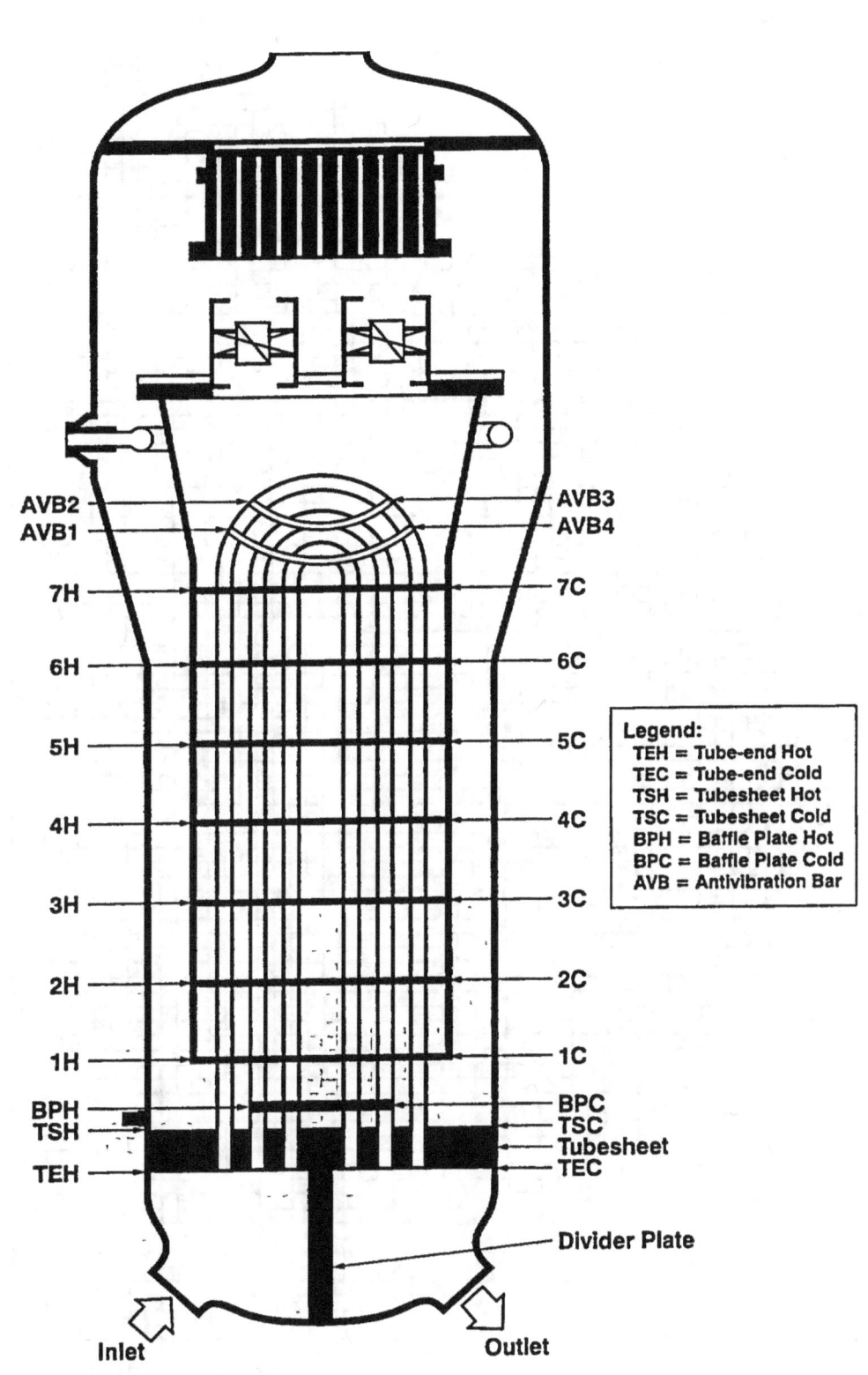

Figure 2-12. Westinghouse Model 51F Steam Generator Tube Support Locations

Row

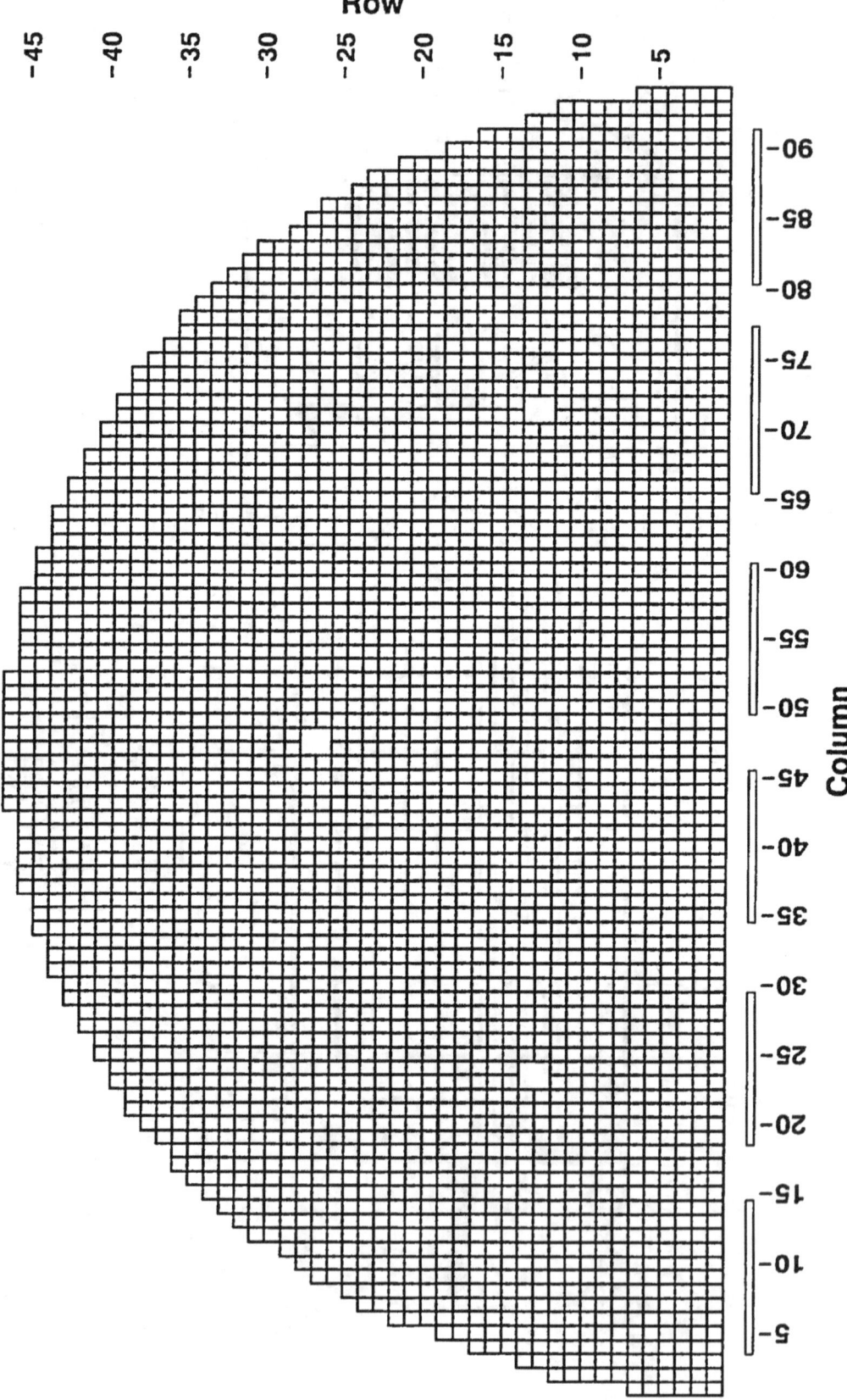

Column

Figure 2-13. Westinghouse Model 51F Steam Generator Tubesheet Map

-30-

3 THERMALLY TREATED ALLOY 600 STEAM GENERATOR TUBE OPERATING EXPERIENCE

3.1 Data Gathering Methodology and Introduction

This section summarizes inspection results for plants with thermally treated Alloy 600 steam generator tubes through December 2001. Significant additional information from the first half of 2002 is summarized in the Executive Summary and in Section 4. The information was primarily gathered from reports provided by licensees to the NRC in accordance with their technical specifications. These licensee reports typically discuss the number and extent of tubes inspected, the number and location of tubes plugged, and the location and percent of wall thickness penetration for each indication of an imperfection. The level of detail provided in these reports varies from plant to plant and frequently from tube inspection outage to outage. As a result, some plants may not have reported all steam generator tube inspection activities during a given inspection outage and/or may not have provided all of their insights in their reports. In addition, the results and interpretation of the results represent the licensee's analysis and evaluation at the time the report was submitted. This may have changed over time. In spite of these limitations, this report provides useful insights into the extent of tube inspections and repairs and the general conclusions of the report are valid.

Some inspection results were also obtained through regional inspection reports, summaries of conference calls with licensees, and meeting summaries. A detailed review of regional inspection reports was not conducted, and that data was not compiled.

In this section, the plants with thermally treated Alloy 600 steam generator tubes are divided into one of three categories: plants with model D5 steam generators, plants with model F steam generators, and plants with replacement model steam generators. For each plant, there is (1) a summary of the inspections, (2) a table summarizing the full-length bobbin coil examinations and number of tubes plugged during each outage, (3) a table summarizing the reasons for plugging each tube, and (4) a table listing the tubes plugged for reasons other than wear at the antivibration (AVBs). In the tables which summarize the reasons for tube plugging, a category referred to as "other" was used to capture tubes that were plugged and for which the specific reason for plugging was not provided or was not clear. Tubes in this category were subdivided based on the location where the degradation was reported (e.g., at the top of the tubesheet). None of these indications were considered to have resulted from stress corrosion cracking.

3.2 Model D5 Steam Generator Operating Experience

Inspection results for Braidwood 2, Byron 2, Catawba 2, and Comanche Peak 2 are provided in this section of the report.

3.2.1 Braidwood 2

Tables 3-1, 3-2, and 3-3 summarize the information discussed below for Braidwood 2. Table 3-1 provides the number of full-length bobbin inspections and the number of tubes plugged and deplugged during each outage for each of the four steam generators. Table 3-2 lists the reasons why the tubes were plugged. Table 3-3 lists tubes plugged for reasons other than wear at the AVBs.

Braidwood 2 has four Westinghouse model D5 steam generators. The licensee numbers its tube supports from 1H to 11H on the hot-leg side of the steam generator and from 1C to 11C on the cold-leg side (refer to Figure 2-5). Based on accident analysis considerations, a maximum of 30% of the tubes can be plugged in any one steam generator and a maximum of 24% of the tubes in the four steam generators can be plugged. Braidwood 2 is authorized in the plant technical specifications to use Westinghouse laser-welded sleeves as a repair method.

During refueling outage (RFO) 1 in 1990, 100% of the tubes in each of the four steam generators were inspected full length with a bobbin coil. As a result of these inspections, two tubes were plugged. Both of these tubes were plugged as a result of indications of AVB wear. The maximum depth reported for the AVB wear indications was 53% throughwall.

During RFO 2 in 1991, approximately 50% of the tubes in each of the four steam generators were inspected full length with a bobbin coil and the remaining tubes in each steam generator were inspected from the hot-leg tube end through the U-bend (i.e., to the uppermost support plate on the cold-leg side). As a result of these inspections, 11 tubes were plugged. All of these tubes were plugged as a result of indications of AVB wear. The maximum depth reported for the AVB wear indications was 51% throughwall.

During RFO 3 in 1993, approximately 50% of the tubes in each of the four steam generators were inspected full length with a bobbin coil and the remaining tubes in each steam generator were inspected from the hot-leg tube end through the U-bend (i.e., to the uppermost support plate on the cold-leg side). As a result of these inspections, 16 tubes were plugged. All of these tubes were plugged as a result of indications of AVB wear. The maximum depth reported for the AVB wear indications was 54% throughwall.

During RFO 4 in 1994, 100% of the tubes in steam generators B and C were inspected full length with a bobbin coil. In addition to the bobbin coil inspections, the rotating pancake coil probe was used to inspect the hot-leg expansion transition region in approximately 10% of the tubes in steam generators B and C. As a result of these inspections, 6 tubes were plugged. All of these tubes were plugged as a result of indications of AVB wear. The maximum depth reported for the AVB wear indications was 47% throughwall.

During RFO 5 in 1996, 100% of the tubes in each of the four steam generators were inspected full length with a bobbin coil. In addition to the bobbin coil inspections, the rotating pancake coil probe was used to inspect the hot-leg expansion transition region in 28% of the tubes, 64% of the dents greater than 5 volts at the hot-leg tube support plates, and the U-bend region of 100% of the row 1 and 2 tubes. These inspections were performed in each of the four steam generators. The rotating pancake coil probe was also used to inspect 20% of the tube expansions at preheater baffles B and D in steam generator A.

As a result of these inspections, 35 tubes were plugged. Of the 35 tubes plugged, 29 tubes were plugged as a result of indications of AVB wear, 2 tubes were plugged as a result of volumetric indications at the first hot-leg tube support plate, 1 tube was plugged for a single axial indication in the U-bend, 2 interior tubes were plugged due to a loose part at hot-leg tube support 8H (the part could not be retrieved), and 1 tube was plugged for a volumetric indication at the top of the tubesheet on the hot-leg side. The maximum depth reported for the AVB wear indications was 67% throughwall.

During RFO 6 in 1997, 100% of the tubes in each of the four steam generators were inspected full length with a bobbin coil. In addition to the bobbin coil inspections, a rotating probe with a plus-point coil was used to inspect the hot-leg expansion transition region in 100% of the tubes, 100% of the dents greater than 5 volts at the hot-leg tube support plates, and the U-bend region of 100% of the row 1 and 2 tubes. These inspections were performed in each of the four steam generators. A rotating probe equipped with a plus-point coil was also used to inspect 20% of the tube expansions at preheater baffles B and D in steam generator B.

As a result of these inspections, 28 tubes were plugged. Of the 28 tubes plugged, 12 tubes were plugged as a result of indications of AVB wear, 15 tubes were plugged as a result of circumferential indications at the hot-leg expansion transition region, and 1 tube was plugged as a result of a volumetric cold-leg free-span indication at cold-leg tube support 2C. This latter indication was reported during the 1994 and 1996 inspections and did not exhibit any significant change since those inspections. Nonetheless, it was plugged. The maximum depth reported for the AVB wear indications was 47% throughwall. Prior to tube plugging, in situ pressure testing was performed on three of the tubes with circumferential indications, including the indication with the largest maximum and average plus-point coil voltage, the longest arc length, and one additional indication characterized as possibly inner diameter initiated. None of these tubes leaked at a pressure of 5000 pounds per square inch (psi). At Byron 2 in 1998 similar circumferential indications were identified. Portions of several tubes were removed from Byron 2 to characterize the nature of these indications. Based on the results from the destructive examinations of the pulled tubes, the indications were determined not to be the result of service-induced cracking or corrosion but rather may have been caused during initial steam generator fabrication or the first few cycles of operation.

During RFO 7 in 1999, 100% of the tubes in each of the four steam generators were inspected full length with a bobbin coil. In addition to the bobbin coil inspections, a rotating probe with a plus-point coil was used to inspect the hot-leg expansion transition region in 25% of the tubes, 25% of the dents and dings greater than 5 volts at the hot-leg tube support plates and in the tube free span, and the U-bend region of 25% of the row 1 and 2 tubes. These inspections were performed in each of the four steam generators. A rotating probe equipped with a plus-point coil was also used to inspect 20% of the tube expansions at preheater baffles B and D in steam generator C. In addition, visual inspections were performed on all of the tube plugs and on the secondary side tubesheet region in all four steam generators.

As a result of these inspections, six tubes were plugged. All of these tubes were plugged as a result of indications of AVB wear. The maximum depth reported for the AVB wear indications was 44% throughwall.

Secondary side visual inspections were performed during this outage. In steam generator C, the upper tube bundle was examined, including the divider lane, the tube periphery lane, and the inner tube bundle. In addition to these upper tube bundle inspections, the top of the tubesheet region was inspected after sludge lancing in all four steam generators. No degradation was found; however, a foreign object, which could not be retrieved, was identified on the top of tubesheet region in steam generator D. The object was wedged between the row 6 column 2 (R6C2) tube and the R7C2 tube. This object was originally identified during RFO 6 in 1997, at which time an evaluation was performed, and the tubes were allowed to remain in service since there was no degradation. The RFO 7 inspections did not show any tube degradation at these locations. An evaluation was performed, and tubes were allowed to remain in service provided they were inspected for degradation each refueling outage.

During RFO 8 in 2000, 100% of the tubes in each of the four steam generators were inspected full length with a bobbin coil. In addition to the bobbin coil inspections, a rotating probe equipped with a plus-point coil was used to inspect the hot-leg expansion transition region in 50% of the tubes, 50% of the dents and dings greater than 5 volts at the hot-leg tube support plates and in the tube free span, and the U-bend region of 50% of the row 1 and 2 tubes (75% in steam generators B and C and 25% in steam generators A and D). These inspections were performed in each of the four steam generators. A rotating probe equipped with a plus-point coil was also used to inspect 20% of the expansions at preheater baffles B and D in steam generators A and D. In addition, visual inspections were performed on all of the tube plugs and on the secondary side tubesheet region in all four steam generators.

As a result of these inspections, 11 tubes were plugged. Of these 11 tubes, 10 were plugged as a result of indications of AVB wear and one row 1 tube was plugged due to a permeability signal with no sign of tube degradation. The maximum depth reported for the AVB wear indications was 45% throughwall. The permeability indication had not changed since RFO 6 in 1997, but a conservative decision was made to plug this indication due to the possibility that the permeability signal could mask future degradation.

The top of tubesheet region was inspected after sludge lancing in all four steam generators. No degradation was found. The foreign object wedged between tubes R6C2 and R7C2 was verified to be present. This foreign object has not resulted in any tube degradation.

Of the tubes plugged at Braidwood 2 as of December 2001, the vast majority (77%) were plugged as a result of AVB wear. The second leading cause of tube plugging was manufacturing related flaws, which accounted for 17% of the tube plugging. Loose parts, inspection issues, and other indications accounted for the remaining 6% of tubes plugged.

3.2.2 Byron 2

Tables 3-4, 3-5, and 3-6 summarize the information discussed below for Byron 2. Table 3-4 provides the number of full-length bobbin inspections and the number of tubes plugged and deplugged during each outage for each of the four steam generators. Table 3-5 lists the reasons why the tubes were plugged. Table 3-6 lists tubes plugged for reasons other than wear at the AVBs.

Byron 2 has four Westinghouse model D5 steam generators. The licensee numbers its tube supports from 1H to 11H on the hot-leg side of the steam generator and from 1C to 11C on the cold-leg side (refer to Figure 2-5). Byron 2 is authorized in the plant technical specifications to use Westinghouse laser-welded sleeves as a repair method.

During RFO 1 in 1989, approximately 48% of the tubes in each of the four steam generators were inspected full length with a bobbin coil. The remaining 52% of the tubes were inspected from the hot-leg tube end to the uppermost support on the cold-leg side (i.e., tube support 11C). There were 11 tubes plugged during this outage. Of these, one row 1 tube was plugged for a signal-to-noise indication in the U-bend region indicative of primary water stress corrosion cracking (PWSCC), one row 1 tube was plugged as a result of a large dent in the U-bend which was present in the preservice inspection (the tube was plugged to prevent possible PWSCC in the high-stressed area), two tubes were plugged as a result of wear at the AVBs (maximum depth was 36% throughwall), one tube was plugged as a result of a loose part (confirmed during RFO 5), three tubes were plugged for indications slightly above the hot-leg top of tubesheet as a result of throughwall indications in excess of the plugging criterion (the maximum depth was 83% throughwall, and one of these three was attributed to a confirmed loose part during RFO 5), three tubes were plugged as a result of narrow circumferential indications at the upper edge of the hot-leg tube support plates (one at 5H, two at 8H). With respect to the two tubes with narrow circumferential indications at 8H, subsequent inspections in RFO 5 confirmed the presence of a loose part in the vicinity of these indications. With respect to the tube with a narrow circumferential indication at 5H, subsequent inspections of adjacent tubes in RFO 5 indicated the possible presence of a loose part in the vicinity of this indication.

During RFO 2 in 1990, approximately 50% of the tubes in each of the four steam generators were inspected full length with a bobbin coil. The remaining 50% of the tubes were inspected from the hot-leg tube end to the uppermost support on the cold-leg side (i.e., tube support 11C). There were 21 tubes plugged during this outage.

Of the 21 tubes plugged during this outage, 19 tubes were plugged as a result of wear at the AVBs, 1 tube was removed from service due to a 53% throughwall indication that appeared to be caused by secondary side pitting at hot-leg tube support 8H, and one tube was removed from service due to a 47% throughwall indication above hot-leg tube support 9H. The maximum depth reported for the AVB wear indications was 63% throughwall.

During RFO 3 in 1992, approximately 49% of the tubes in each of the four steam generators were inspected full length with a bobbin coil. The remaining 51% of the tubes were inspected from the hot-leg tube end to the uppermost support on the cold-leg side. There were 29 tubes plugged during this outage.

Of the 29 tubes plugged, 25 were plugged as a result of wear at the AVBs, 1 tube was plugged as a result of outside-diameter-initiated indications above hot-leg tube support 10H and cold-leg tube support 10C, and 3 tubes were plugged as a result of outside-diameter-initiated indications indicative of manufacturing burnishing marks (one had indications above cold-leg tube support 6C and 9C, one tube had indications above hot-leg tube support 10H, and one tube had indications above hot-leg tube supports 9H and 11H). The maximum depth reported for the AVB wear indications was 49% throughwall.

During RFO 3, video probe inspections were performed verifying the existence of welded stub tube plugs in 8 locations in each steam generator (32 tubes in all). The stub tube plug locations are not considered tube locations in the D5 steam generator configuration.

During RFO 4 in 1993, approximately 49% of the tubes in each of the four steam generators were inspected full length with a bobbin coil. The remaining 51% of the tubes were inspected from the hot-leg tube end to the uppermost support on the cold-leg side. There were 36 tubes plugged during this outage.

Of the 36 tubes plugged, 33 were plugged as a result of wear at the AVBs and 3 tubes were plugged as a result of indications at the lower support edges, possibly due to pitting, intergranular attack, localized thinning, or other mechanisms (e.g., loose part wear) which result in small volumetric indications. These volumetric indications were located at hot-leg tube support 1H (two tubes) and 5H (one tube). Two of these three tubes were located near the periphery of the tube bundle. In addition to the 3 tubes plugged as a result of volumetric indications at tube supports, 12 other indications were reported. Five of these 12 indications were at hot-leg tube supports and the remainder were at cold-leg supports. One of these 12 indications was plugged since it was a tube that also contained an AVB wear indication in excess of the repair criteria. Of the 33 tubes plugged for AVB wear, 3 were plugged as a result of what was believed to be wear associated with an AVB stiffener strap. Based on an evaluation of the inspection data, the licensee reported that the AVB wear rate had slowed since the previous cycle; however, more indications were found during this inspection than in previous ones. The maximum depth reported for the AVB wear indications was 53% throughwall.

With respect to the three volumetric indications plugged at the tube supports, subsequent inspections of adjacent tubes in RFO 5 indicated the possible presence of a loose part in the vicinity of at least one of these indications (i.e., the degradation mechanism for one of these three indications is most likely wear from a loose part).

During RFO 5 in 1995, approximately 52% of the tubes in each of the four steam generators were inspected full length with a bobbin coil. The remaining 48% of the tubes were partially inspected from the hot-leg tube end to the uppermost support on the cold-leg side. There were 29 tubes plugged during this outage. In addition to the bobbin coil inspections, the rotating pancake coil probe was used to inspect the hot-leg expansion transition region in approximately 20% of tubes in steam generator B.

Of the 29 tubes plugged during this outage, 21 were plugged as a result of wear at the AVBs, 7 were plugged as a result of indications of possible loose parts, and 1 tube was plugged due to an "unusual" volumetric signal at the top of the tubesheet. The maximum depth reported for the AVB wear indications was 47% throughwall.

Based on the inspection results through RFO 5, the licensee reported that tube wear at the AVBs appears to be decreasing from outage to outage both in terms of the growth rate and the total number of indications observed.

There were two locations of suspected loose parts in steam generator B and two in steam generator C. In steam generator B, one location resulted in the plugging and stabilizing of five tubes for a possible loose part at the upper edge of hot-leg tube support 5H. These five tubes were near the periphery (columns 4 and 5). The second location of possible loose parts in steam generator B affected three tubes near the periphery of the T-slot. The part, a gasketlike material, was located at cold-leg tube support 2C and was removed from the steam generator and the tubes were left in service.

In steam generator C, one loose part location resulted in the plugging and stabilizing of two tubes as a result of a possible loose part at the upper edge of hot-leg tube support 5H. These tubes were near the periphery of the T-slot, and were plugged and stabilized. The tubes were not accessible, and the licensee could not perform a video inspection or retrieve the part. Two adjacent tubes had been plugged in previous outages. These tubes were deplugged and stabilized. The other location in steam generator C with possible loose parts had a volumetric indication at the upper edge of hot-leg tube support 8H. The tube was left in service after search and retrieval methods were used to remove a wedge-shaped object from the steam generator. Two tubes adjacent to this one were plugged in previous outages.

The tube with the "unusual" volumetric signal identified in RFO 5 was located in steam generator B at row 49 column 54 slightly above the hot-leg top of tubesheet. The indication was first identified as a result of a video inspection performed before and after sludge lancing. This tube is located near the periphery of the tube bundle and adjacent to the T-slot. Two adjacent tubes were plugged during RFO 1 as a result of a loose part which was removed during that outage. This tube was plugged during this outage after rotating pancake coil results indicated a volumetric indication at this location.

Byron 2 was shut down on August 8, 1996, due to a primary-to-secondary leak in steam generator A of approximately 120 gallons per day. Since the leak occurred near the end of the operating cycle, the licensee decided to enter the refueling outage early (i.e., RFO 6). During RFO 6, 100% of tubes in all four steam generators were inspected full length with a bobbin coil. In addition to the bobbin coil inspections, a rotating pancake coil probe was used to inspect the hot-leg expansion transition region for 25% of the tubes in each of the four steam generators. A rotating probe equipped with a plus-point coil was used to inspect the U-bend region of 25% of the row 1 and 2 tubes (57 tubes per steam generator) in each of the four steam generators. In addition, the rotating pancake coil probe was used to inspect the expanded portion of 25% of the tubes that were expanded in the preheater region (34 tubes per steam generator). Lastly, 25% of the tubes with dents greater than 5 volts (as measured with a bobbin coil) were inspected with a rotating pancake coil probe. There were 30 tubes plugged during this outage.

The tube that leaked was inspected with eddy current and video probes. It was determined that a foreign object had caused the leak. The foreign object was removed and was analyzed to determine its origin. The part affected four tubes, all of which were plugged. The object was 1.7-inches by 1.2-inches by 0.055 inches and had a triangular shape. The object was thermal-cutting debris from a 12- to 18-inch pipe. The loose part was located slightly above the cold-leg tubesheet in the periphery of the tube bundle.

An additional 26 tubes were plugged during this outage. Nineteen of these tubes were plugged as a result of wear at the AVBs. Four were plugged as a result of indications slightly above cold-leg tube support 2C (these tubes were inspected visually, revealing scale buildup on all four tubes; only one of these tubes had a volumetric indication based on rotating pancake coil examination). One of these 26 tubes was plugged due to a geometry change that resulted in the probe skipping over a section of the tube, preventing a complete exam (the geometry change was in the U-bend region of a row 1 tube). One tube was plugged as a result of a volumetric indication slightly above (or at) cold-leg tube support 2C (the indication originated from the outside diameter, and a historical review of the data indicated minimal growth both in phase and amplitude). One of these tubes was plugged as a result of a volumetric indication slightly above (or at) hot-leg tube support 1H (which originated from the outside diameter of the tube; a historical review showed minimal growth in both phase and amplitude). The maximum depth reported for the AVB wear indications was 46% throughwall.

During this outage, the licensee noticed that it had not inspected 26 tubes in steam generator D during RFO 3 (spring 92) and 4 tubes were not inspected during RFO 5 (spring 95) as a result of misencoding tubes (i.e., data from one tube was labeled as coming from another tube). The omissions were attributed to the operators inability to properly locate the inspection fixtures, moving the fixture without recalibration, or failure of the operator to use the "add cal point" feature of the data analysis software (which permits the operator to locate the fixture and the tubes to be inspected).

During RFO 7 in 1998, 100% of the tubes in each of the four steam generators were inspected full length with a bobbin coil. In addition to the bobbin coil inspections, a rotating probe equipped with a plus-point coil was used to inspect the hot-leg expansion transition region in 100% of the tubes in each of the steam generators, the U-bend region of 100% of the row 1 and 2 tubes in each steam generator, the preheater baffle plate expansions in 25% of the tubes in steam generator A (34 tubes containing 68 expansions), and 100% of the hot-leg dents with voltages greater than 5 volts. In addition to these eddy current inspections, a visual inspection of the secondary side of steam generator C (e.g., wedges, tie rod nuts, jacking studs) was performed, along with a visual inspection of the top of tubesheet region in all four steam generators and a visual inspection of all previously installed plugs. Thirty eight tubes were plugged during this outage.

During RFO 7, circumferential indications were identified at the hot-leg top of tubesheet region for the first time. A total of 29 indications were detected. Four of these tubes were in situ pressure-tested to verify structural integrity. No leakage was measured when the tube was pressurized to three times the normal operating differential pressure. Three of the in situ pressure tested tubes were also removed for destructive examination. Two tubes were cut 3 inches below the hot-leg tube support 3H and one tube was cut 3 inches below hot-leg tube support 5H. The destructive examinations indicated that the circumferential indications were not service-induced cracking or corrosion but shallow grooves that may have been caused during initial steam generator fabrication or the first few cycles of operation. Burst testing confirmed the indications had no impact on the structural integrity of the tubes. All 29 tubes with circumferential indications were stabilized and plugged.

Of the remaining nine tubes plugged, one was plugged as a result of wear at the AVBs, three were plugged due to confirmed loose parts which were visually identified and removed either during this outage or during a previous outage (these indications were plugged since a site-qualified depth sizing technique was not available), and five were plugged for other reasons, as discussed below. The maximum depth reported for the AVB wear indications was 43% throughwall.

Of the five tubes plugged for "other" reasons, four tubes had outside-diameter-initiated volumetric indications near the top edge of tube support plates. These indications were found with a bobbin coil and confirmed by plus-point coil examination. A review of previous inspection data and operating experience did not reveal the presence of foreign objects; however, the indications were considered to be very similar to wear scars left by foreign objects. These tubes were plugged. The last tube plugged for "other" reasons was plugged as a result of a large geometry distortion in the U-bend region. This tube was located in row 2, and no degradation was identified during the evaluation of the bobbin or plus-point coil data.

During RFO 8 in 1999, 100% of the tubes in each of the four steam generators were inspected full length with a bobbin coil. In addition to the bobbin coil inspections, a rotating probe equipped with a plus-point coil was used to inspect the hot-leg expansion transition region in 25% of the tubes in each of the steam generators, the U-bend region of 25% of the row 1 and 2 tubes in each steam generator, the preheater baffle plate expansions in 25% of the tubes in steam generator A (34 tubes containing 68 expansions), and 25% of the hot-leg dents with voltages greater than 5 volts. In addition to these eddy current inspections, visual inspections were performed on all previously installed welded plugs, 25% of previously installed mechanical plugs, 100% of newly installed tube plugs, and at the top of tubesheet region in all four steam generators. Fourteen tubes were plugged during this outage.

Of the 14 tubes plugged during the outage, 9 were plugged as a result of wear at the AVBs, 1 was plugged for wear in the preheater region, 2 were plugged for wear due to a foreign object, 1 was plugged as a result of a foreign object signal, and 1 was plugged for a volumetric indication near a support plate. Many of these indications are discussed in further detail below. The maximum depth reported for the AVB wear indications was 50% throughwall.

As discussed above, one tube was plugged as a result of preheater wear at cold-leg tube support 7C. This indication was estimated to be 28% throughwall and was preventatively removed from service. In addition to this tube, three adjacent tubes were plugged as a result of foreign objects. Two of these tubes had indications of tube wear (i.e., wall loss) and the third tube had a signal attributable to a foreign object with no wall loss. These indications were slightly above (or at) hot-leg tube support 5H. These tubes were in the periphery of the tube bundle and were stabilized prior to plugging. The one tube plugged as a result of a volumetric indication near a support plate had an outside-diameter-initiated signal near the top edge of cold-leg tube support 2C. The affected tube is near the periphery of the tube bundle.

During RFO 9 in 2001, only steam generator B was inspected. Steam generator B was chosen for inspection since it historically has had the most degradation. All the tubes in steam generator B were inspected full length with a bobbin coil and a visual inspection of all plugs was performed. Rotating probes equipped with a plus-point coil were only used to further characterize indications detected by the bobbin coil. Four tubes were plugged during this outage.

The indications in three of the four tubes plugged during this outage were attributed to wear associated with a foreign object, and the fourth tube was plugged because of an outside-diameter-initiated volumetric indication. Two of the three tubes plugged as a result of foreign object wear were adjacent to each other. These tubes were located in the periphery of the tube bundle and the wear occurred at (or near) hot-leg tube support 5H. These two tubes were stabilized and plugged. The third tube plugged for wear associated with a foreign object was located near the periphery of the tube bundle near the T-slot. The wear measured 9%

throughwall and was occurring near cold-leg tube support 2C. The foreign object was removed during a previous outage. The tube plugged for an outside-diameter-initiated volumetric indication had an eddy current signal slightly above cold-leg tube support 2C. The tube with this indication is located in the interior of the tube bundle.

During this outage, eight tubes were identified with preheater wear. The maximum reported depth for any of these indications was 13% throughwall. All indications were at cold-leg tube support 7C. The number of tubes with preheater wear went up slightly since the previous inspection.

As of December 2001, AVB wear is the dominant degradation mechanism at Byron 2, accounting for 58% of the plugged tubes. About 18% of the plugged tubes had manufacturing flaws, including the 29 tubes plugged in RFO 7 for circumferential indications at the hot-leg top of tubesheet which were confirmed through tube pulls to most likely be the result of manufacturing anomalies. Loose parts account for 12% of the tube plugging. A notable feature of the loose part indications is the active region in steam generator B at hot-leg tube support 5H bounded by rows 12 through 15 and columns 4 through 7. This region has accounted for 10 of the 27 tubes plugged as a result of loose parts. Another such active region is in column 56 of steam generator C between rows 38 and 41. This region has accounted for 4 of the 27 tubes plugged as a result of loose parts. The tubes in both these regions have been stabilized as the part has not been removed based on the information supplied to the NRC. For other tubes affected by loose parts, tubes were plugged several cycles after the part was removed. It is not clear from the information provided whether the plugging of these tubes was a result of continued degradation or was a preventive measure.

Lastly, one region in steam generator A was reported to have several indications in a region of scale/deposit buildup. This region is bounded by rows 44 through 49 and columns 66 through 74. All five tubes plugged in this region had indications near cold-leg tube support 2C.

3.2.3 Catawba 2

Tables 3-7, 3-8, and 3-9 summarize the information discussed below for Catawba 2. Table 3-7 provides the number of full-length bobbin inspections and the number of tubes plugged and deplugged during each outage for each of the four steam generators. Table 3-8 lists the reasons why the tubes were plugged. Table 3-9 lists of tubes plugged for reasons other than wear at the AVBs.

Catawba 2 has four Westinghouse model D5 steam generators. The licensee numbers its tube supports using the alternate naming convention in Figure 2-5. There are 141 tubes expanded at two tube support plate locations to prevent vibration in the preheater section of these steam generators. These tubes are located in the cold leg of the steam generators. The lowermost tube support (i.e., 1H) is a flow distribution baffle. It is 0.75 inch thick.

In August 1987, during the first cycle of operation, Catawba 2 shut down to repair a pump seal. During this outage, the licensee elected to inspect steam generators A and D to eliminate the need to do eddy current inspections of all four steam generators during the first refueling outage. No defective tubes were identified during these inspections.

During RFO 1, which began in December 1987, steam generator tube inspections were performed in steam generators B and C. Steam generators A and D were not scheduled to be inspected since they were inspected during the maintenance outage in August 1987. During the evaluation of the steam generator B eddy current data, a 77% throughwall defect initiating from the outside diameter of the tube at the top of tubesheet region was identified. The eddy current signal was indicative of degradation due to a loose part. As a result of this indication, visual inspections were performed on the secondary side of all four steam generators. These visual inspections identified foreign objects on the tubesheets of all four steam generators and exterior tube damage on one tube in steam generator B and one tube in steam generator D, as discussed below.

Visual inspections were performed on the secondary side of all four steam generators prior to and subsequent to sludge lancing. The pre-sludge-lancing visual inspections in steam generator A resulted in the identification of a 2-inch long nail and two pieces of wire. All of these foreign objects were removed. Post-sludge-lancing visual inspections in steam generator A resulted in the identification of a carbon steel block in the annulus area. After enlarging a 6-inch handhole, the block was removed and subsequently identified as a spacer block used during steam generator fabrication.

Pre-sludge-lancing visual inspections in steam generator B identified a nut and three large studs. Two of the studs were lying adjacent to the defective tube discussed above. The nut was removed with a magnet. The studs were identified as jacking studs that had apparently been left in the steam generator during fabrication. The studs were removed after enlarging an inspection port. Post-sludge-lancing visual inspections in steam generator B resulted in the identification of a carbon steel weld rod in the annulus region. This object was not removed because of difficulties in reaching and grasping it, but an analysis performed by the licensee indicated the part could be left in service for the next operating cycle.

Pre-sludge-lancing visual inspections in steam generator C revealed a small piece of wire and a piece of weld slag on the tubesheet. These were removed from the steam generator. No additional foreign objects were discovered in steam generator C during the post-sludge-lancing visual inspections.

Pre-sludge-lancing visual inspections in steam generator D resulted in the identification of a piece of metal, some small rocks, and a small piece of wire. The piece of metal was removed, but the other material was left in place because the licensee believed that subsequent sludge lancing would flush it into a more accessible area where it could be more easily removed. Post-sludge-lancing visual inspections in steam generator D were unable to locate the rocks and piece of wire; however, a badly damaged tube and another slightly damaged tube were discovered near where the debris had been.

As a result of identifying the visual damage to the tubes in steam generator D, the August 1987 eddy current data for these two tubes were reevaluated. This reevaluation revealed that the severely damaged tube had a 50% throughwall flaw that was not identified during the August 1987 data evaluation. Due to these findings, all steam generator A and D eddy current data from August 1987 was reevaluated. This reevaluation revealed that the severely damaged tube in steam generator D and one other tube in steam generator A had contained indications that exceeded the plant's repair criteria but were not identified during the original inspection. The tube in steam generator A had a 65% throughwall indication; however, the location of the wear on this tube was not considered indicative of damage due to loose parts. One of the reasons the licensee missed these indications in August 1987 was that the data was evaluated only by one analyst rather than by two analysts. The use of two analysts to evaluate the data had been approved by the licensee but not yet implemented.

Based upon the loose objects discovered in the steam generators and the defective tubes identified during the reevaluation of the August 1987 eddy current data, additional eddy current testing of the peripheral tubes in steam generators A and D was performed (the peripheral tubes in steam generators B and C were inspected during this outage as part of the initial eddy current testing sample). As a result of these inspections, three additional indications in steam generator A and one indication in steam generator D were identified that required plugging. These tubes had not been inspected in August 1987 and the location of the wear was not indicative of damage due to loose parts. In total, four tubes in A and two tubes in D were plugged during the first outage.

In summary, tube inspections were performed slightly before RFO 1 and during RFO 1. All four steam generators were inspected. The bobbin coil was used to inspect the full length of approximately 25% of the tubes in steam generator A, 12% of the tubes in steam generator B, 11% in steam generator C, and 26% in steam generator D. In addition to these full-length exams, partial-length inspections were performed on approximately 2.5% of the tubes in each of the four steam generators. Seven tubes were plugged as a result of the inspections. Of these, two were plugged due to wear associated with confirmed loose parts. The nature of the indications in the other five tubes was not specified, but one had an indication at the 3rd tube support plate, one had an indication at the 7th tube support plate, one had an indication in the freespan above the 12th tube support plate, one had two indications in the freespan above the 2nd and 5th tube support plates, and one had an indication in the freespan above the 3rd tube support plate.

During RFO 2 in 1989, approximately 32% of the tubes in each of the four steam generators were inspected full length with a bobbin coil. As a result of these inspections, eight tubes were plugged. The nature of the indications in these tubes was not specified; however, two adjacent tubes were plugged for indications at the 3rd tube support plate, two adjacent tubes had indications slightly above the 18th tube support plate, one tube had an indication slightly above the 17th tube support plate, one tube had an indication slightly above the 14th tube support plate, and one tube had an indication slightly below, or at, the 8th tube support plate. The eighth tube plugged was a row 1 tube for which no indication was reported.

During RFO 3 in 1990, approximately 71% of the tubes were inspected full length with a bobbin coil and the remaining 29% of the tubes received a partial inspection. In addition to the bobbin coil inspections, the rotating pancake coil probe was used to inspect the hot-leg expansion transition region in 100% of the tubes. As a result of these inspections, 19 tubes were plugged. Of the 19 tubes plugged, 14 were plugged as a result of wear at the AVBs, 3 were plugged for indications slightly above (or at) the 7th tube support plate, and no indications were reported for the other 2 tubes that were plugged. The maximum depth reported for the AVB wear indications was 59% throughwall.

During RFO 4 in 1991, 100% of the tubes in each of the four steam generators were inspected full length with a bobbin coil. In addition to the bobbin coil inspections, the rotating pancake coil probe was used to inspect the hot-leg expansion transition region in 100% of the tubes. Of the 12 tubes plugged during this outage, 6 tubes were plugged as a result of wear at the AVBs, 2 adjacent tubes were plugged as a result of outside-diameter-initiated indications slightly above or at the 5th tube support plate, 2 adjacent tubes were plugged as a result of outside-diameter-initiated indications slightly above (or at) the 7th tube support plate, 1 tube was plugged as a result of outside-diameter-initiated indications slightly above (or at) the 7th tube support plate, and one tube was plugged for outside-diameter-initiated indications above the 1st and 18th tube support plate. In addition to these 12 tubes, eight thimble (stub) tubes in each leg of each steam generator were plugged during this outage. These are not considered tubes in the model D5 steam generators. The maximum depth reported for the AVB wear indications was 44% throughwall.

During RFO 5 in 1993, 100% of the tubes in each of the four steam generators were inspected full length with a bobbin coil. In addition to the bobbin coil inspections, the rotating pancake coil probe was used to inspect the hot-leg expansion transition region in 100% of the tubes. Of the 43 tubes plugged during this outage, 2 tubes were plugged as a result of wear at the AVBs, 3 tubes were plugged for indications at the hot-leg expansion transition (2 classified as single axial indications, the other as an outside diameter indication), 30 tubes were plugged for indications in the freespan region (i.e., above various tube supports and the AVBs), 6 tubes were plugged for indications at the tube support plates (including 5 tubes with indications in the preheater region at the 18th tube support, some of which were classified as axial indications), and the reason for plugging 2 other tubes was not evident from the data submitted. The indications in the free span were located throughout the tube bundle. The maximum depth reported for the AVB wear indications was 43% throughwall.

During RFO 6 in 1994, 100% of the tubes in each of the four steam generators were inspected full length with a bobbin coil. In addition to the bobbin coil inspections, the rotating pancake coil probe was used to inspect the hot-leg expansion transition region in 100% of the tubes. Of the 31 tubes plugged, 1 was plugged as a result of wear at the AVBs, 4 tubes were plugged for indications at the hot-leg expansion transition (2 classified as nonquantifiable indications, 1 as a single axial indication, and 1 as an inside-diameter-initiated indication), 6 were plugged as a result of indications at the tube support plates, and 20 were plugged for indications in the freespan. These latter indications were on both the hot-leg and the cold-leg side of the steam generator and many were classified as volumetric or as outside diameter indications. The maximum depth reported for the AVB wear indications was 40% throughwall.

During RFO 7 in 1995, approximately 55% of the tubes in each of the four steam generators were inspected full length with a bobbin coil. In addition to the bobbin coil inspections, the licensee committed to perform rotating probe inspections in response to Generic Letter 95-03, "Circumferential Cracking of Steam Generator Tubes." These inspections were to be performed at the hot-leg expansion transition region in at least 50% of the tubes and the U-bend region of 20% of the row 1 and 2 tubes. Of the 23 tubes plugged during this outage, 1 tube was plugged as a result of wear at the AVBs, 2 tubes were plugged for indications at the hot-leg top of tubesheet (1 classified as a pit and 1 as volumetric), 10 tubes were plugged as a result of indications in the freespan, 5 tubes were plugged for indications at the tube support plates, and the reason for plugging 5 other tubes was not evident from the data submitted. The maximum depth reported for the AVB wear indications was 39% throughwall.

During RFO 8 in 1997, approximately 55% of the tubes in each of the four steam generators were inspected full length with a bobbin coil. Of the 10 tubes plugged during this outage, 2 tubes were plugged as a result of wear at the AVBs, 3 tubes were plugged as a result of indications at the hot-leg top of tubesheet attributed either to steam generator manufacture or loose parts wear, 1 tube was plugged for an indication in the freespan, and 4 tubes were plugged for inspection issues (2 for permeability variations, 1 for not obtaining rotating probe data, and 1 for general data quality issues). The maximum depth reported for the AVB wear indications was 43% throughwall.

During RFO 9 in 1998, approximately 52% of the tubes in each of the four steam generators were inspected full length with a bobbin coil. In addition to these full length inspections, approximately 4% of the tubes in each steam generator were partially inspected. A rotating probe equipped with a plus-point coil was used to inspect the hot-leg expansion transition region in 100% of the tubes and the U-bend region of 100% of the row 1 and 2 tubes. A rotating probe was also used to inspect a 20% sample of the tubes in the preheater region at tube supports 17 and 18. Of the 9 tubes plugged during the outage, 1 tube was plugged as a result of wear at the AVBs, 3 tubes were plugged as a result of wear at the tube support plates (2 on the hot-leg at tube supports 1H and 7H, 1 on the cold-leg at tube support 17C), 1 tube was plugged for an indication at a tube support plate attributed either to steam generator manufacture or loose parts wear, 2 tubes were plugged for indications at the hot-leg top of tubesheet attributed either to steam generator manufacture or loose parts wear, 1 row 1 tube was plugged for a dent signal change in the U-bend (classified as a multiple axial indication), and 1 tube was plugged for a permeability signal. The maximum depth reported for the AVB wear indications was 42% throughwall.

During RFO 10 in 2000, approximately 95% of the tubes in each of the four steam generators were inspected full length with a bobbin coil, and the remaining 5% were partially inspected. Of the seven tubes plugged during the outage, one tube was plugged as a result of wear at the AVBs, two tubes were plugged as a result of wear attributed to foreign objects (both at hot-leg tube support 1H, neither in the periphery), two tubes were plugged because the probe became lodged in the U-bend (both row 2 tubes), one tube was plugged because a rotating probe inspection was not performed in the U-bend (a row 1 tube), and one tube was plugged because a rotating probe inspection was not performed in the hot-leg top of tubesheet region. The maximum depth reported for the AVB wear indications was 42% throughwall.

During RFO 11 in 2001, approximately 44% of the tubes in each of the four steam generators were inspected full length with a bobbin coil and an additional 5% were partially inspected. A rotating probe equipped with a plus-point coil was also used to inspect the hot-leg expansion transition region in 100% of the tubes, the U-bend region of 100% of the row 1 and 2 tubes, 100% of the expansions in the preheater region (i.e., at tube supports 17 and 18), a 20% sample of dings/dents greater than 5 volts, and a 20% sample of dings/dents between 2 and 5 volts at tube support 8. No tubes were plugged as a result of these inspections.

As of December 2001, 183 tubes had been plugged at Catawba 2. The reason for plugging many of these tubes was not reported by the licensee (i.e., the reason for plugging 68% of the plugged tubes was not reported). Although the exact nature of the indications in these plugged tubes was not reported, the number of indications requiring plugging at Catawba 2 has declined since the early-to-mid 1990s.

3.2.4 Comanche Peak 2

Tables 3-10, 3-11, and 3-12 summarize the information discussed below for Comanche Peak 2. Table 3-10 provides the number of full-length bobbin inspections and the number of tubes plugged and deplugged during each outage for each of the four steam generators. Table 3-11 lists the reasons why the tubes were plugged. Table 3-12 lists tubes plugged for reasons other than wear at the AVBs.

Comanche Peak 2 has four Westinghouse model D5 steam generators. The licensee numbers its tube supports from 1H to 11H on the hot-leg side of the steam generator and from 1C to 11C on the cold-leg side (refer to Figure 2-5).

During RFO 1 in 1994, approximately 24% of the tubes in each of the four steam generators were inspected full length with a bobbin coil. In addition to the bobbin coil inspections, the licensee also used a rotating pancake coil to inspect the hot-leg expansion transition region in 359 tubes. These rotating pancake coil examinations were distributed between steam generators A, B, and D. No tubes were plugged as a result of these inspections.

During RFO 2 in 1996, approximately 47% of the tubes in steam generators A and D were inspected full length with a bobbin coil. In addition, the hot-leg expansion transition region in approximately 46% of the tubes in these two steam generators were inspected with a rotating pancake coil probe. The rotating pancake coil probe was also used to inspect the U-bend region of approximately 100 tubes in each of these two steam generators. No tubes were plugged as a result of these inspections.

During RFO 3 in 1997, the licensee inspected tubes in each of the four steam generators. The bobbin coil was used to inspect the full length of 85% of the tubes in steam generator A, 100% of the tubes in steam generators B and C, and 52% of the tubes in steam generator D. A rotating probe equipped with a plus-point coil was used to inspect the hot-leg expansion transition region in approximately 20% of the tubes, the U-bend region of 20% of the row 1 and 2 tubes (46 tubes), 20% of the expansions at preheater baffle plates B and D (28 tubes per steam generator), 100% of the dents greater than or equal to 5 volts at hot-leg tube support plate 3H, and a sampling of dents greater than or equal to 5 volts up through hot-leg tube support plate 11H.

As a result of the RFO 3 inspections, eight tubes were plugged. Five of these tubes were plugged as a result of wear at the AVB. The maximum depth reported for the AVB wear indications was 53% throughwall. Two of the eight tubes were plugged as a result of a confirmed loose part. The licensee removed the part from the steam generator after cutting an access port near the part. The part was at hot-leg tube support 8H in row 49 columns 53 and 54. One of the eight tubes was plugged as a result of a restriction approximately 3 inches above the top of the tubesheet on the cold-leg side of the steam generator. This tube was in row 14 column 67.

During RFO 4 in 1999, approximately 20% of the tubes in each of the four steam generators were inspected full length with a bobbin coil. In addition to the bobbin coil inspections, a rotating probe was used to inspect the hot-leg expansion transition region in approximately 20% of the tubes, the U-bend region of 20% of the row 1 and 2 tubes (46 tubes), 20% of the expansions at the preheater baffle plates, 100% of the dents greater than or equal to 5 volts at hot-leg tube support plate 3H, and 20% of the dings greater than or equal to 5 volts in the straight section of the hot leg.

Five tubes were plugged as a result of the inspections. Three of the five tubes were plugged for wear associated with possible loose parts. One of these possible loose parts was at the top of cold-leg tube support 6C; the other loose part, a faster nut affecting two tubes and lodged between them, was in the first inch above the top of the tubesheet. These latter two tubes were in column 59 rows 36 and 37. One of the five tubes was plugged for an obstruction in the tube 31 inches above hot-leg tube support plate 10H. This tube could not pass a 0.610-inch-diameter probe. In a previous inspection this tube passed a smaller bobbin coil probe, which detected a large dent at this location. One of the five tubes was plugged for a pitlike indication 6 inches above the hot-leg top of tubesheet. This indication had been tracked since RFO 2 (the first inservice inspection of the tube) and was attributed to a manufacturing artifact or loose part.

During RFO 5 in 2000, approximately 42% of the tubes in steam generator A and approximately 79% of the tubes in steam generator D were inspected full length with a bobbin coil. In addition to the bobbin coil inspections, a rotating probe equipped with a plus-point coil was used to inspect the hot-leg expansion transition region in approximately 43% of the tubes in steam generator A and 44% in steam generator D, the U-bend region of approximately 45% of the row 1 and 2 tubes in steam generator A (103 tubes) and 46% of the row 1 and 2 tubes in steam generator D (104 tubes), the expansions at the preheater baffle plates in approximately 42% of the expanded preheater tubes in steam generator A (59 tubes) and 40% of the expanded preheater tubes in steam generator D (55 tubes), and 100% of the dents greater than 5 volts at hot-leg tube support plate 3H. Steam generators B and C were not inspected.

During RFO 5, four tubes were plugged, all for indications of wear at the AVBs. The maximum depth reported for the AVB wear indications was 42% throughwall.

The licensee's historical tracking of AVB wear growth rate indicates that as the steam generators accumulate operating time, the AVB wear growth rates falls. The licensee has two possible explanations. The first is that the amplitude of vibration for each tube is finite, and tube wear eventually reaches a specific depth and then stops. The second explanation is that the volumetric wear rate is constant. As the depth and area of the wear increase, the volume affected decreases, and the rate of progression through the tube wall apparently falls.

Of the 37 tubes plugged at Comanche Peak as of December 2001, 54% were plugged prior to commencing commercial operation, 24% were plugged as a result of AVB wear, and 14% were plugged for loose parts. The extent of the steam generator inspections has been more limited at Comanche Peak than at the other plants with D5 steam generators.

3.3 Model F Steam Generator Operating Experience

Inspection results for Millstone 3, Seabrook, Vogtle 1, Vogtle 2, and Wolf Creek are provided in this section of the report. In addition, the results from inspections of the first 10 rows of tubes at Callaway are discussed. Although Salem 1 has model F steam generators and were the original steam generators to be used at the canceled Seabrook 2 facility, the summary of operating experience for Salem 1 is included in Section 3.4 on replacement steam generators because the flow conditions in the Salem steam generators could be significantly different than in other model F steam generators so that the experience may differ.

3.3.1 Callaway

Tables 3-13, 3-14, and 3-15 summarize the information discussed below for Callaway. Table 3-13 provides the number of full-length bobbin inspections and the number of tubes plugged and deplugged during each outage for each of the four steam generators. Table 3-14 lists the reasons why the tubes were plugged. Table 3-15 lists tubes plugged for reasons other than wear at the AVBs.

Callaway has four Westinghouse model F steam generators. The licensee numbers its tube supports from the hot-leg flow distribution baffle (FBH) to 7H on the hot-leg side of the steam generator and from cold-leg flow distribution baffle (FBC) to 7C on the cold-leg side (refer to Figure 2-8). Although Callaway has both thermally treated and mill-annealed Alloy 600 tubes, the following summarizes the inspections and repairs to the thermally treated tubes. Callaway is authorized in the plant technical specifications to use laser-welded sleeves and electrosleeves to repair defective tubes.

Prior to commercial operation, four thermally treated tubes were plugged in the Callaway steam generators. During RFO 1, no thermally treated tubes were plugged.

During a maintenance outage in April 1987, approximately 20% of the tubes in steam generators B and C were inspected with a bobbin coil. Presumably this sample included 20% of the thermally treated tubes. During RFO 2 in September 1987, approximately 60% of the tubes in steam generators A and D were inspected with a bobbin coil. Presumably this sample included 60% of the thermally treated tubes. One thermally treated tube was plugged as a result of these two inspections. This tube was plugged as a result of an eddy current indication at hot-leg tube support 7H.

During RFO 3 in 1989, 100% of the tubes in steam generators B and C were inspected full length with a bobbin coil. In addition to the bobbin coil inspections, the licensee also used a rotating probe to inspect the hot-leg expansion transition region in approximately 250 tubes, the area above and below hot-leg tube support 7H on an additional 250 tubes, and the U-bend region of approximately 10 row 1 tubes in steam generator B. The U-bend inspections were performed to obtain additional information on anomalies found in the U-bend region of row 1. No detectable discontinuities were found during the rotating probe inspections. One thermally treated tube was plugged as a result of a single axial indication at the cold-leg flow distribution baffle.

During RFO 4 in 1990, 100% of the tubes in steam generators A and D were inspected full length with a bobbin coil. No significant rotating probe testing was performed on the thermally treated tubes and no thermally treated tubes were plugged during this outage.

During RFO 5 in 1992, 100% of the tubes in steam generators B and C were inspected full length with a bobbin coil. In addition to the bobbin coil inspections, a rotating pancake coil probe was used to inspect the U-bend region of 100% of the row 1 and 2 tubes in steam generator C (244 tubes). One thermally treated tube was plugged as a result of the inspections. This tube (row 2 column 98) was removed from service due to an undefined indication just above cold-leg tube support 7C. This indication was not detected with the bobbin coil, and the eddy current analyst judged this indication to be a distorted signal (the distortion caused by its location in the U-bend transition). The hot-leg expansion transitions were shot-peened during this outage to limit the likelihood of PWSCC.

During RFO 6 in 1993, 100% of the tubes in steam generators A and D were inspected full length with a bobbin coil. In addition to the bobbin coil inspections, a rotating pancake coil probe was used to inspect the hot-leg expansion transition in 126 tubes in steam generator A and 482 tubes in steam generator D. No thermally treated tubes were removed from service during this outage.

During RFO 7 in 1995, 100% of the tubes in steam generators B and C were inspected full length with a bobbin coil. In addition to the bobbin coil inspections, a rotating pancake coil probe was used to inspect the hot-leg expansion transition region of 405 thermally treated tubes (8.3% of the thermally treated tube population). These inspections concentrated on the sludge deposition zones of steam generators A and C, where most of the crack indications were found in the mill-annealed tubes and where thermally treated tubes would most likely be affected. No indications were identified as a result of the rotating probe inspections of the thermally treated tubes; however, four thermally treated tubes were plugged during this outage. Of the four tubes plugged, two had indications approximately 4 inches above the tubesheet on the cold-leg side of steam generator B. These indications were 38% and 45% throughwall. The indications were attributed to loose parts wear damage since a large foreign object was later removed from steam generator B. In addition to these two tubes, two other thermally treated tubes were plugged. Although not specifically identified by the licensee, the staff believes these two tubes were located in row 1 column 1 in steam generators C and D and were damaged by improper installation of the chemical cleaning equipment. Chemical cleaning was performed during RFO 7 to reduce the potential for ODSCC and intergranular attack.

During RFO 8 in 1996, 100% of the tubes in steam generators A and D were inspected full length with a bobbin coil. In addition to the bobbin coil inspections, a rotating probe equipped with a plus-point coil was used to inspect the hot-leg expansion transition of 100% of the tubes in all four steam generators and the U-bend region of 113 tubes in row 1 of steam generator C. (The licensee originally planned to inspect the U-bend region of 100% of the unplugged row 1 tubes (i.e., 121 tubes), but eight tubes exhibited restrictions and were inspected with a bobbin probe.)

As a result of these inspections, five thermally treated tubes were plugged and three thermally treated tubes were sleeved with laser-welded sleeves. Of the five tubes plugged, three were plugged for volumetric indications, one was plugged for an axial indication, and one was plugged for a circumferential indication. All five of these indications were located on the hot-leg side of the steam generator near the top of the tubesheet. Of the three tubes sleeved, two were sleeved for circumferential indications and one was sleeved for a volumetric indication. These three indications were also located on the hot-leg side of the steam generator near the top of the tubesheet.

During RFO 9 in 1998, 100% of the tubes in steam generators B and C were inspected full length with a bobbin coil. In addition to the bobbin coil inspections, a rotating probe equipped with a plus-point coil was used to inspect the hot-leg expansion transition region of 100% of the tubes in all four steam generators, and the U-bend region of 121 of the row 1 tubes in steam generator A (i.e., 100% of the inservice row 1 tubes). No thermally treated tubes were plugged or repaired during this outage as a result of these inspections.

During RFO 10 in 1999, 100% of the tubes in steam generators A and D were inspected full length with a bobbin coil. In addition to the bobbin coil inspections, a rotating probe equipped with a plus-point coil was used to inspect the expansion transition of 100% of the tubes in all four steam generators and the U-bend region of 100% of the row 1 and 2 tubes in steam generator D. As a result of these inspections, three thermally treated tubes were electrosleeved. These tubes had volumetric indications slightly above the top of tubesheet on the hot-leg side of the steam generator.

During RFO 11 in 2001, 100% of the tubes in steam generators B and C were inspected full length with a bobbin coil. In addition to the bobbin coil inspections, a rotating probe equipped with a plus-point coil was used to inspect the hot-leg expansion transition region of 100% of the tubes in all four steam generators, the U-bend region of 100% of the row 1 and 2 tubes in steam generator B, and 20% of the dents and dings greater than 2 volts (as identified by the bobbin coil exam) in steam generators B and C. One thermally treated tube was plugged as a result of the inspections. This tube had an axial indication slightly above the top of the tubesheet on the hot-leg side of the steam generator.

3.3.2 Millstone 3

Tables 3-16, 3-17, and 3-18 summarize the information discussed below for Millstone 3. Table 3-16 provides the number of full-length bobbin inspections and the number of tubes plugged and deplugged during each outage for each of the four steam generators. Table 3-17 lists the reasons why the tubes were plugged. Table 3-18 lists tubes plugged for reasons other than wear at the AVBs.

Millstone 3 has four Westinghouse model F steam generators. The licensee numbers its tube supports using the alternate naming convention in Figure 2-8.

During RFO 1 in 1987, approximately 9% of the tubes in each of the four steam generators were inspected with a bobbin coil. The extent of the inspections was not specified (e.g., full length). As a result of the tube inspections performed during this outage, two tubes were plugged. Both tubes were plugged for wear at the AVBs. The maximum depth reported for the AVB wear indications was 34% throughwall.

During RFO 2 in 1989, approximately 42% of the tubes in steam generators A and C were inspected full length with a bobbin coil. In addition, approximately 2% of the tubes in steam generators A and C were partially inspected from the cold-leg tube end to the top support on the hot leg. As a result of these inspections, four tubes were plugged during this outage. Three tubes were plugged as a result of wear at the AVBs, and one row 1 tube was plugged due to a distorted signal above hot-leg tube support 8H. This indication was located at the hot-leg tangent point (i.e., the point where the tube starts to bend in the U-bend region--see Figure 2-3). The maximum depth reported for the AVB wear indications was 51% throughwall.

During RFO 3 in 1991, approximately 63% of the tubes in steam generators B and D were inspected full length with a bobbin coil except the row 1 tubes, which were inspected from the hot-leg tube end to the top tube support on the cold-leg side (i.e., tube support 8C). Five tubes were plugged during this outage. All five were plugged as a result of wear at the AVBs. The maximum depth reported for the AVB wear indications was 53% throughwall. The licensee considered the wear at the AVBs at Millstone 3 similar to the wear experienced in other model F steam generators. The wear was primarily observed at the AVBs in the tubes in row 20 and higher on the periphery and row 30 and greater in the middle of the tube bundle. The AVB wear flaws in the middle of the tube bundle tended to be shallower than those on the periphery.

As a result of extended shutdowns in 1991 and 1992, the NRC approved an extension of the steam generator tube inspection interval in August 1993. This extension extended the inspection interval during cycle 4 from 24 to 31 months. Up to this point, primary-to-secondary leakage in the steam generators had been below 0.08 gpd.

During RFO 4 in 1993, approximately 77% of the tubes in steam generator A and approximately 65% of the tubes in steam generator C were inspected full length with a bobbin coil. These inspections included all tubes in steam generators A and C which were not inspected during RFO 2. In addition to the bobbin coil inspections, a rotating probe was used to inspect the hot-leg expansion transition region in approximately 40 tubes. Seven tubes were plugged during this outage. All of these tubes were plugged as a result of wear at the AVBs. The maximum depth reported for the AVB wear indications was 61% throughwall.

During RFO 4, eight Westinghouse Alloy 600 mechanical plugs were removed and replaced. One unexpected finding of the plug replacement program was that one of the eight tubes (row 50 column 95), which was plugged in 1989 as a result of wear at the AVBs, had progressed in depth from 43% to 100% throughwall. To prevent the tube from severing and contacting adjacent tubes, the tube was stabilized.

During RFO 5 in 1995, approximately 75% of the tubes in steam generators B and D were inspected full length with a bobbin coil. In addition to the bobbin coil inspections, the Cecco 5 probe was used to inspect the hot-leg top of tubesheet region in approximately 11% of the tubes in steam generators B and D. The extent of inspection was from 12 inches above the hot-leg top of the tubesheet to the hot-leg tube end. These inspections were performed in response to the inspection results at Callaway, where circumferential cracking was identified near the top of the tubesheet. The Cecco 5 exams were performed in the high sludge region and also in tubes with excessive tube geometry variations caused by the hydraulic tubesheet expansion process. These geometry variations could increase the stress in the tubes at these locations, which are considered more susceptible than other locations to PWSCC. Eleven tubes were plugged during this outage, all for wear at the AVBs. The maximum depth reported for the AVB wear indications was 59% throughwall.

In the beginning of an extended shutdown period during cycle 6 in 1996, the licensee inspected the full length of 100% of the tubes in steam generator C with a bobbin coil. In addition to the bobbin coil inspections, a rotating probe equipped with a plus-point coil was used to inspect the hot-leg expansion transition region in approximately 10% of the tubes in steam generator C and the U-bend region of 25 row 1 tubes. Two tubes were plugged as a result of this inspection, for wear at the AVBs. The maximum depth reported for the AVB wear indications was 44% throughwall.

In September 1998, as a result of the extended midcycle maintenance outage from April 1996 through June 1998, the NRC authorized an extension to the 24-month steam generator tube inspection interval specified in the Millstone 3 technical specifications. This extension permitted the licensee to postpone the next inspection until the next refueling outage or July 1, 1999, whichever was earlier.

During RFO 6 in 1999, 100% of the tubes in steam generators A and C were inspected full length with a bobbin coil. In addition to the bobbin coil inspections, a rotating probe equipped with a plus-point coil was used to inspect various locations in steam generators A and C, including the hot-leg expansion transition region in approximately 48% of the tubes, the U-bend region of approximately 50% of the row 1 and 2 tubes, selected dents at hot-leg tube supports, and various tubesheet anomalies (153 tubes in steam generator A and 45 tubes in steam generator C). In addition to the inspections of steam generators A and C, limited bobbin inspections (42 tubes) and rotating probe inspections (2 tubes) were performed in steam generator D. These inspections were performed to address two flaw indications and several possible loose parts which were reported during the RFO 5 (1995) inspections.

Of the 14 tubes plugged during this outage, 13 tubes were plugged as a result of wear at the AVBs and 1 tube was plugged as a result of a single volumetric indication consistent with loose part damage. This latter tube was located in a high-flow region and the indication was at the top of the hot-leg tubesheet. The maximum depth reported for the AVB wear indications was 51% throughwall. During cycle 6, minimal (less than 1 gpd) primary-to-secondary leakage was observed.

With respect to the inspection of steam generator internal components, the licensee indicated that it planned to perform J-tube inspections during RFO 7.

During RFO 7 in 2001, 100% of the tubes in steam generators B and D were inspected full length with a bobbin coil. In addition to the bobbin coil inspections, a rotating probe was used to inspect various locations in steam generators B and D, including the hot-leg expansion transition region in approximately 50% of the tubes, the U-bend region of approximately 50% of the row 1 and 2 tubes, and all previously reported dents and dings in the hot-leg portion of the tube.

Of the 51 tubes plugged as a result of the inspections, 16 tubes were plugged as a result of wear at the AVBs, 29 tubes were plugged as a result of volumetric indications (one of which also had a pluggable AVB wear indication and is included in the 16 tubes discussed above), and 7 tubes were plugged because they were close to loose part indications (as identified by eddy current testing). The maximum depth reported for the AVB wear indications was 47% throughwall.

Of the 29 tubes plugged as a result of volumetric indications, 12 were at the cold-leg flow distribution baffle, 1 was at the hot-leg flow distribution baffle, 13 were at the top of the tubesheet on the hot-leg side, and 3 were at the top of the tubesheet on the cold-leg side. The licensee attributed most of these indications to foreign object wear based on the presence of adjacent loose part indications in many of the affected tubes and on the distribution of the indications within the tube bundle. Most, but not all, of these indications were at or near the periphery of the tube bundle. There was a cluster of 10 tubes with volumetric indications at the top of the tubesheet on the hot-leg side. The licensee attributed the cluster to steam generator fabrication since eddy current testing identified outside diameter axial scratches in the expanded portion of some of the tubes within the cluster (scratches the licensee considered to have been made during fabrication prior to tube expansion). These 10 tubes were all located in columns 23 or 24. Of the 29 indications, 16 were detected during the bobbin coil inspections, and the remaining 13 indications were detected as a result of rotating probe inspections of tubes adjacent to the 16 tubes with bobbin indications (i.e., during the expanded inspections done after the bobbin indications were identified).

Of the seven tubes plugged for indications of loose parts, six were in tubes adjacent to tubes with the volumetric indications discussed above, and one was isolated and in the interior of the bundle. For most of the 36 tubes with volumetric indications and/or loose part indications (attributed to loose parts or fabrication), no loose parts were visually confirmed since sludge lancing was performed concurrent with eddy current testing. Two machine curls were removed and a third part was identified visually but could not be removed. The licensee speculated that the loose parts were a result of an upper bundle flush in 1999 (i.e., the flush freed foreign objects that were previously stationary). None of these 36 tubes were stabilized.

3.3.3 Seabrook

Tables 3-19, 3-20, and 3-21 summarize the information discussed below for Seabrook. Table 3-19 provides the number of full-length bobbin inspections and the number of tubes plugged and deplugged during each outage for each of the four steam generators. Table 3-20 lists the reasons why the tubes were plugged. Table 3-21 lists tubes plugged for reasons other than wear at the AVBs.

Seabrook has four Westinghouse model F steam generators. The licensee numbers its tube supports using the alternate naming convention in Figure 2-8.

During the preservice inspection, six tubes exhibited indications of inadequate tube expansion in the tubesheet area. These tubes were subsequently reexpanded and satisfactorily reexamined prior to commercial operation.

During RFO 1 in 1991, approximately 32% of the tubes in each of the four steam generators were inspected full length with a bobbin coil. During this outage, 10 tubes were plugged: 4 were plugged as a result of wear at the AVBs, 4 to bound a loose part that could not be retrieved, and 2 for "high wall loss" indications. The maximum depth reported for the AVB wear indications was 38% throughwall. Of the high-wall-loss indications, one was considered a manufacturing burnishing mark and the other was a low-amplitude signal in the free span on the cold-leg side. In addition to these plugs, two bare holes were replugged in steam generator B. (A bare hole plug is a short piece of tubing closed at the top. It is installed like a normal tube. As a result it looks like a normal tube end when viewed from the steam generator channel head [i.e., from the primary face of the tubesheet]. Since bare hole plugs are exposed to primary coolant and potentially to secondary coolant, they can degrade with time.)

During RFO 2 in 1992, approximately 43% of the tubes in steam generators A and D were inspected full length with a bobbin coil. In addition to these full-length inspections, partial-length inspections were performed in a limited number of tubes (1% in steam generator A, less than 1% in steam generator D). No tubes were plugged as a result of these inspections.

During RFO 3 in 1994, approximately 41% of the tubes in steam generators B and C were inspected full length with a bobbin coil. In addition to these full-length inspections, partial-length inspections were performed in approximately 2% of the tubes in steam generators B and C. These partial length inspections were performed from the cold-leg tube end to the uppermost support on the hot-leg side since these tubes were only inspected on the hot-leg and through the U-bend during RFO 1 in 1991. One tube was plugged during this outage. This tube was plugged as a result of wear at the AVBs. The maximum depth reported for the AVB wear indications was 55% throughwall.

During RFO 4 in 1995, approximately 43% of the tubes in steam generators A and D were inspected full length with a bobbin coil. In addition to the bobbin coil inspections, a Cecco probe was used to inspect the hot-leg expansion transition region of approximately 9% of the tubes in steam generators A and D, and a rotating probe equipped with a plus-point coil was used to inspect the U-bend region of approximately 20% of the row 1 tubes in steam generators A and D. The rotating probe was also used to inspect dents and dings in 12 tubes in steam generators A and D.

During this outage, abnormal signal indications at the tube tangent point were reported. The tangent point is the point on the tube where the U-bend meets the straight tube length (i.e., the point where the tube begins to bend--refer to Figure 2-3). A review of the 1985 baseline data for a sample of these tubes confirmed the indications were present at that time and had not changed during operation. The indications are believed to be caused by geometry variations introduced during the bending process. Rotating probe inspections performed during previous inspections confirmed the tangent point signals to be non-flaw-like.

During this outage, 12 tubes were plugged. All 12 were plugged as a result of wear at the AVBs. The maximum depth reported for the AVB wear indications was 55% throughwall.

The licensee assessed the progression of wear at the AVBs from RFO 2 to RFO 4. The assessment included 172 AVB flaws which were greater than 20% throughwall in RFO 4. The licensee determined that (1) AVB flaws can initiate at any time, (2) the growth rate of AVB flaws is highest during the first cycle in which a flaw initiates, (3) for flaws greater than 10% throughwall in RFO 2, the average growth rate during subsequent cycles was 4.5% throughwall per cycle, and (4) the maximum growth rate observed over the two cycle period was 37%

throughwall (or 19% per cycle). This maximum growth rate was observed at both a newly initiated and a preexisting flaw location.

During RFO 5 in 1997, 100% of the tubes in steam generators B and C were inspected full length with the bobbin coil, except for the U-bend region of every other row 1 tube, which was tested with a rotating probe equipped with a plus-point coil. In addition to the bobbin coil inspections, a rotating probe equipped with a plus-point coil was used to inspect the hot- and cold-leg expansion transition regions in 100% of the tubes in steam generator B. In steam generator C, a rotating probe equipped with a plus-point coil was used to inspect the hot-leg expansion transition region in every other pair of columns. Hot-leg dents and dings at or below the fifth hot-leg tube support in steam generators B and C were also inspected with a rotating probe equipped with a plus-point coil.

Of the 13 tubes plugged during this outage, 7 were plugged as a result of wear at the AVBs, 4 as a result of wear associated with loose parts, and 2 as a result of a volumetric indication (wear) at cold-leg tube support 5C. The loose part that resulted in four tubes being plugged was verified visually at the top of the hot-leg tubesheet but attempts to retrieve the part were unsuccessful. The two tubes plugged for volumetric indications near cold-leg tube support 5C were believed to be associated with loose part wear; however, no indications of a loose part were still present at this location. The maximum depth reported for the AVB wear indications was 56% throughwall. An assessment of AVB wear rates between 1994 and 1997 (32 effective full-power months [EFPMs]) indicated an average growth of 6.3% for steam generator B and 4.2% for steam generator C over the 32 EFPM interval.

During RFO 6 in 1999, 100% of the tubes in steam generators A and D were inspected full length with a bobbin coil, except for the U-bend region of the row 1 and 2 tubes. In addition to the bobbin coil inspections, rotating probes equipped with a plus-point coil were used to inspect the hot-leg expansion transition region in 50% of the tubes, the U-bend region of 50% of the row 1 and 2 tubes, and 40% of all dents and dings in steam generators A and D.

During this outage, 25 tubes were plugged. All 25 tubes were plugged as a result of wear at the AVBs. The maximum depth reported for the AVB wear indications was 71% throughwall. The tube had not been inspected in four cycles. The structural limit for AVB wear is 75% throughwall. An assessment of AVB wear rates between 1995 and 1999 indicated an average growth of 5.3% for steam generator A and 8.3% for steam generator D.

During RFO 7 in 2000, 100% of the tubes in steam generators B and C were inspected full length with a bobbin coil, except for the U-bend region of the row 1 and 2 tubes. In addition to the bobbin coil inspections, rotating probes equipped with a plus-point coil were used to inspect the hot-leg expansion transition region in 50% of the tubes, the U-bend region of 50% of the row 1 and 2 tubes, and 40% of all hot-leg dents and dings with bobbin voltages greater than 5 volts in steam generators B and C. Additionally, visual inspections were performed to confirm the presence of loose parts at tube locations exhibiting possible loose part eddy current signals and to assess the condition of all installed tube plugs in the hot- and cold-leg of steam generators B and C.

Of the 16 tubes plugged during this outage, 13 were plugged as a result of wear at the AVBs and 3 were plugged as a result of possible loose part wear and/or the presence of a possible loose part. Two of these three plugged tubes were adjacent and had indications at the hot-leg top of tubesheet region. One of these two tubes had a volumetric indication while the other had a possible loose part signal (i.e., no tube degradation was noted). The presence of the part could not be confirmed. The third tube plugged on a count of a loose part was in row 1 and had a volumetric indication near hot-leg tube support 1H. The licensee speculated that the indication was caused by contact with an unknown object such as a foreign object or the tooling used during secondary-side cleaning. The maximum depth reported for the AVB wear indications was 57% throughwall.

Seabrook has experienced minor primary-to-secondary leakage (less than 2 gpd) since cycle 5 in steam generators B and D as discussed below. During cycle 6, Seabrook observed small amounts of leakage coming from steam generator D. During RFO 6, a tube with a 71% throughwall AVB wear scar was plugged in this steam generator. Subsequent to the outage, no primary-to-secondary leakage was observed in steam generator D; however, during cycle 7, Seabrook observed minor primary-to-secondary tube leakage in steam generator B. This leakage was less than 0.2 gpd. After startup from RFO 7, no leakage was observed; however, several months into cycle 8 minor steam generator leakage was once again observed in steam generator B. This leakage was less than 1 gpd.

3.3.4 Vogtle 1

Tables 3-22, 3-23, and 3-24 summarize the information discussed below for Vogtle 1. Table 3-22 provides the number of full-length bobbin inspections and the number of tubes plugged and deplugged during each outage for each of the four steam generators. Table 3-23 lists the reasons why the tubes were plugged. Table 3-24 lists tubes plugged for reasons other than wear at the AVBs.

Vogtle 1 has four Westinghouse model F steam generators. The licensee numbers its tube supports from the hot-leg flow distribution baffle (FBH or BPH) to 7H on the hot-leg side of the steam generator and from FBC/BPC to 7C on the cold-leg side (refer to Figure 2-8).

During the preservice inspection, 100% of the tubes in all four steam generators were inspected full length. No tubes required plugging as a result of the preservice inspection; however, the six tubes plugged by the manufacturer were verified as plugged during this inspection. Profilometry was performed for 100% of the tubes from the tube end to 2.5 inches above the top of the tubesheet. The tubes which were found to be underexpanded were reexpanded. No tubes were found to be overexpanded.

During RFO 1 in 1988, approximately 13% of the tubes in steam generators A and D were inspected full length with a bobbin coil. As a result of these inspections, one tube was plugged as a result of freespan degradation. The tube was plugged for indications above the fifth hot-leg tube support and the fourth cold-leg tube support. Both measured 39% throughwall.

During RFO 2 in 1990, approximately 27% of the tubes in steam generators A and D were inspected full length with a bobbin coil and approximately 42% of the tubes in steam generators B and C were inspected full length with a bobbin coil. In addition to these full-length inspections, the U-bend regions of approximately 43% of the tubes in steam generators A and

D and approximately 33% of the tubes in steam generators B and C were inspected with a bobbin coil.

During the inspection, several rotating pancake coil probe inspections were performed as a result of eddy current indications at the tangent point (refer to Figure 2-3). Specifically, rotating pancake coil probe inspections were performed as a result of indications at the cold-leg tangent point on the tubes in steam generator D and at the hot- and cold-leg tangent points in several tubes in steam generator C. These inspections did not confirm any flawlike indications. Of the four tubes plugged during the inspection, all were attributed to AVB wear. The maximum depth reported for the AVB wear indications was 45% throughwall.

During RFO 3 in 1991, approximately 20% of the tubes in each of the four steam generators were inspected full length with a bobbin coil. No tubes were plugged as a result of these inspections.

The licensee performed additional inspections during RFO 3 to verify what types of plugs had been installed prior to operation (i.e., at the factory). Two types of welded plugs were typically installed at the factory: a flush-welded plug and a bare-hole plug. The bare-hole plug is a short piece of tubing closed at the top. It is installed like a normal tube. As a result it looks like a normal tube end when viewed from the steam generator channel head (i.e., from the primary face of the tubesheet). The flush-welded plug, on the other hand, appears to be a blank spot on the tubesheet when viewed from the channel head. Since bare-hole plugs are exposed to primary coolant and potentially to secondary coolant, they could degrade with time. At Vogtle 1, steam generator C has four shop plugs installed (in two tubes) and steam generator D has eight shop plugs installed (in four tubes). All of the shop plugs were determined to be flush welded plugs.

During RFO 4 in 1993, approximately 52% of the tubes in steam generators B and C were inspected full length with a bobbin coil. All four tubes plugged during this outage were plugged as a result of wear at the AVBs. The maximum depth reported for the AVB wear indications was 47% throughwall.

During RFO 5 in 1994, approximately 75% of the tubes in each of the four steam generators were inspected full length with a bobbin coil. The licensee inspected all four steam generators as a result of a recommendation from the vendor concerning wear at the AVBs. The vendor's recommendation was based on operating experience at other plants that have changed their operating conditions as a result of a power uprate and/or T-hot reduction. The vendor recommended the inspection of 75% of the total tube population in each of the four steam generators and the inspection of 100% of the tube population in rows 25 and greater. All 12 tubes plugged during this outage were plugged as a result of wear at the AVBs. The maximum depth reported for the AVB wear indications was 52% throughwall. The inspection did not reveal any areas of concern as a result of the power uprate implemented at Vogtle during the preceding cycle.

During RFO 6 in 1996, approximately 60% of the tubes in steam generators A and D were inspected full length with a bobbin coil. In addition to the bobbin coil inspections, a rotating probe equipped with a plus-point coil was used to inspect the hot-leg expansion transition of approximately 20% of the tubes in steam generators A and D. All four tubes plugged during the outage were plugged as a result of wear at the AVBs. The maximum depth reported for the AVB wear indications was 42% throughwall.

In May 1996, shortly after starting up from RFO 6, Vogtle 1 was shut down in response to a possible loose part on the primary side of steam generator D. On entering the hot-leg channel head, licensee personnel found a support pin nut from a control rod guide tube assembly. The nut's locking device was wedged into the bottom of a tube. It was subsequently removed. Another object, believed to be a fragment from the support pin nut, was found on the cold-leg side of the steam generator. The lower tubesheet on the hot-leg side was impacted by the loose object and numerous indications were noted. The hot-legs of the other three steam generators did not exhibit any signs of damage. During the next (i.e., RFO 7) steam generator tube inspection, the shank of the broken support pin was found lodged in a tube. The shank was left in place and the tube was plugged. Damaged tube ends on the tubesheet were rerolled during RFO 7.

During RFO 7 in 1997, 100% of the tubes in steam generators B and C were inspected full length with a bobbin coil, and 100% of the tubes in steam generator D were inspected full length from the hot leg to ensure that the integrity of the tubes had not been compromised and that the tubes were not obstructed or damaged by loose parts from the broken pin. There were no tubesheet restrictions through which a probe could not be inserted.

In addition to the bobbin coil inspections, a rotating probe equipped with a plus-point coil was used to inspect the hot-leg expansion transition region of approximately 40% of the tubes in steam generators B and C and the U-bend region of approximately 40% of the row 1 and 2 tubes in steam generators B and C (98 tubes in B and 98 in C).

As a result of the RFO 7 inspections, 15 tubes were plugged: 12 as a result of wear at the AVBs, 2 due to obstructions/restrictions, and 1 for a loose part indication. The latter three tubes were subjected to a fiberoptic visual inspection. The inspection of the tube at row 4 column 3 revealed a foreign object that appeared to be a piece of fractured metal about the size and shape of the failed support pin. No attempt was made to retrieve the loose part. The other two tubes (R4C4 and R1C31) were restricted at the U-bend transition region preventing the passage of a 0.520-inch bobbin probe, and were subsequently removed from service (visual inspection attempts at these locations were unsuccessful). The maximum depth reported for the AVB wear indications was 44% throughwall.

During RFO 8 in 1999, 100% of the tubes in steam generators A and D were inspected full length with a bobbin coil. In addition to the bobbin coil inspections, a rotating probe equipped with a plus-point coil was used to inspect the hot-leg expansion transition of approximately 50% of the tubes, and the U-bend region of approximately 40% of the row 1 and 2 tubes in steam generators A and D (98 tubes in A and 98 in D). A visual inspection of previously installed plugs showed no signs of leakage. No tubes were plugged as a result of these inspections.

The licensee analyzed the RFO 8 inspection results using Wear Projection Technology. The analysis indicated that tubes with wear at the AVBs in steam generators A and D should not require stabilization for the foreseeable operating life of the plant. This analyses is believed to have included an evaluation of previously plugged tubes. The licensee stated that it was also tracking possible loose part indications at several locations in steam generator A (but none in steam generator D). One of these locations was near the top of the tubesheet; another was at the upper edge of the hot-leg baffle plate. Based on plus-point examination, this latter indication was characterized as a volumetric indication associated with wear from a loose part.

An analysis of tube wear rates for steam generators A and D based on the RFO 6 and RFO 8 results indicated that the two-cycle 95% cumulative distribution growth rates were 6.5% for steam generator A and 11.4% for steam generator D. The average growth rates over this period were 2.0% and 6.8%, respectively.

During RFO 9 in 2000, approximately 100% of the tubes in steam generators B and C were inspected full length with a bobbin coil. In addition to the bobbin coil inspections, a rotating probe equipped with a plus-point coil was used to inspect the hot-leg expansion transition of approximately 60% of the tubes, the U-bend region of approximately 50% of the row 1 and 2 tubes (122 tubes per steam generator), and approximately 20% of the hot-leg and U-bend freespan dings greater than 5 volts (as measured by the bobbin coil) in steam generators B and C.

Of the two tubes plugged during this outage, one was attributed to a volumetric indication and the other to wear at the AVBs. The volumetric indication was located slightly above the top of the tubesheet on the hot-leg side and was attributed to an artifact of fabrication; however, there was no historical rotating probe data to confirm this hypothesis so the tube was plugged. The maximum depth reported for the AVB wear indications was 41% throughwall.

The licensee stated it was tracking indications of possible loose parts in steam generators B and C. These loose parts are at, or just above, the tubesheet. Some are in the sludge zone rather than in the periphery. None of the loose parts are associated with tube wear. Attempts were made to retrieve the objects identified; where objects could not be removed, analyses were performed to verify that the objects would not challenge tube integrity during the next cycle.

An analysis of tube wear rates for steam generators B and C based on the RFO 7 and RFO 9 results indicated that the two-cycle 95% cumulative probability growth rate was 9.7% for steam generator B and 7.4% for steam generator C. The average growth rates over this period were 4.8% and 3.4%, respectively.

Prior to RFO 9, the licensee used the Wear Projection Technology to determine that one plugged tube in steam generator B with an AVB wear indication would need stabilization by RFO 11 (fall 2003) and two additional tubes in steam generator B would need stabilization by RFO 13 (spring 2005). Given these results, no tubes with wear indications were stabilized during RFO 9.

A visual inspection of tube plugs was performed. There were no visible signs of leakage from the plugged tubes.

3.3.5 Vogtle 2

Tables 3-25, 3-26, and 3-27 summarize the information discussed below for Vogtle 2. Table 3-25 provides the number of full-length bobbin inspections and the number of tubes plugged and deplugged during each outage for each of the four steam generators. Table 3-26 lists the reasons why the tubes were plugged. Table 3-27 lists tubes plugged for reasons other than wear at the AVBs.

Vogtle 2 has four Westinghouse model F steam generators. The licensee numbers its tube supports from the hot-leg flow distribution baffle (FBH or BPH) to 7H on the hot-leg side of the steam generator and from FBC/BPC to 7C on the cold-leg side (refer to Figure 2-8).

During the preservice inspection, 100% of the tubes in all four steam generators were inspected full length. In addition, 13 tubes that were plugged by the manufacturer were verified to be plugged during this inspection. Two additional tubes were plugged as a result of the tube inspections performed during the preservice inspection. Profilometry was performed for 100% of the tubes from the tube end to 2 inches above the top of the tubesheet.

During RFO 1 in 1990, approximately 20% of the tubes in each of the four steam generators were inspected full length with a bobbin coil. In addition to these full-length inspections, the U-bend region of approximately 46% of the tubes in each of the steam generators was inspected with a bobbin coil. No tubes were plugged as a result of these inspections. Several tubes had indications which appeared deep by the bobbin coil, but inspection with a rotating probe did not confirm degradation at these locations.

During RFO 2 in 1992, approximately 20% of the tubes in each of the four steam generators were inspected full length with a bobbin coil and several tubes in each of the four steam generators were inspected partially (e.g., from the uppermost cold-leg tube support to the end of the tube on the hot-leg side of the steam generator). Approximately 600 tubes in steam generator B were also inspected as part of a program investigating potential loose parts in the periphery of the tube bundle. No tubes were plugged as a result of these inspections.

Steam generators B, C, and D were inspected to verify the types of plugs installed during the fabrication of the steam generators. These inspections verified that the plugs installed after fabrication were flush-welded to the tube (rather than bare-hole plugs). The plugs in steam generator A were installed as a result of the preservice inspection, not during fabrication (i.e., no plugs were installed during fabrication in steam generator A).

During RFO 3 in 1993, approximately 53% of the tubes in steam generators A and D were inspected full length with a bobbin coil. A loose part was identified on the cold-leg baffle plate adjacent to the tube in row 57 column 68 in steam generator D. The loose part was removed and the tube was left in service since the extent of tube wear was less than the repair/plugging limit. An additional 12 bobbin coil inspections were performed around the tube with wear, and a rotating probe inspection of the tube in row 57 column 68 was performed. No tubes were plugged as a result of these inspections.

During RFO 4 in 1995, approximately 78% of the tubes in steam generators B and C were inspected full length with a bobbin coil. During this outage, the licensee implemented a recommendation from Westinghouse concerning AVB wear operating experience from plants that have changed their operating conditions as a result of a power uprate and/or T-hot reduction. Westinghouse recommended the inspection of 75% of the total tube population in each of the two steam generators and the inspection of 100% of the tube population in rows 25 and greater. All three tubes plugged during this outage were plugged as a result of wear at the AVBs. The maximum depth reported for the AVB wear indications was 60% throughwall. The inspection did not reveal any areas of concern as a result of the power uprate implemented at Vogtle during the preceding cycle.

During RFO 5 in 1996, 100% of the tubes in steam generators A and D were inspected full length with a bobbin coil. In addition to the bobbin coil inspections, a rotating probe was used to inspect the hot-leg expansion transition region of approximately 20% of the tubes in steam generators A and D. All six tubes plugged during this outage were plugged as a result of wear at the AVBs. The maximum depth reported for the AVB wear indications was 51% throughwall.

During RFO 6 in 1998, 100% of the tubes in steam generators B and C were inspected full length with a bobbin coil. In addition to the bobbin coil inspections, a rotating probe equipped with a plus-point coil was used to inspect the hot-leg expansion transition of approximately 40% of the tubes in steam generators B and C and the U-bend region of approximately 40% of the row 1 and 2 tubes in steam generators B and C (98 tubes in B and 98 in C). No tubes were plugged as a result of these inspections. A visual inspection of previously installed plugs in steam generators B and C did not reveal any visible signs of leakage.

An analysis of tube wear rates at the AVBs for steam generators B and C indicated that the two-cycle 95% cumulative distribution growth rate decreased from 13.1% (measured from RFO 2 to RFO 4) to 11.7% (measured from RFO 4 to RFO 6).

During RFO 7 in 1999, 100% of the tubes in steam generators A and D were inspected full length with the bobbin coil. In addition to the bobbin coil inspections, a rotating probe equipped with a plus-point coil was used to inspect the hot-leg expansion transition of approximately 53% of the tubes in steam generators A and D, the U-bend region of approximately 40% of the row 1 and 2 tubes in steam generators A and D, and 20% of the straight tube section dents greater than 5 volts in steam generators A and D. A visual inspection of previously installed plugs in steam generators A and D did not reveal any visible signs of leakage.

All five tubes plugged during this outage were plugged for wear at the AVBs. The maximum depth reported for the AVB wear indications was 40% throughwall.

The licensee evaluated the need to stabilize tubes in steam generators A and D as a result of AVB wear using the Wear Projection Technology. The licensee identified no tubes that would need stabilization during the foreseeable operating life of the plant.

An analysis of wear rates indicated the average wear rate for a two-cycle period was 4.1% for steam generator A and 3.8% for steam generator D. The 95% cumulative distribution growth rate for a two-cycle period was approximately 7.8% for steam generator A and 7.3% for steam generator D. Loose parrt signals were also analyzed following the outage. Many of the loose parts observed during the eddy current examination had not resulted in tube wear.

During RFO 8 in 2001, 100% of the tubes in steam generators B and C were inspected full length with a bobbin coil. In addition to the bobbin coil inspections, a rotating probe equipped with a plus-point coil was used to inspect the hot-leg expansion transition region of approximately 64% of the tubes in steam generators B and C, approximately 100% of hot-leg dents in the straight section which were greater than 5 volts as identified by the bobbin coil, 20% of the dents in the U-bend which were greater than 5 volts, and the U-bend region of approximately 60% of the row 1 and 2 tubes in steam generators B and C (146 tubes in steam generator B and 146 in C). No tubes were plugged as a result of these inspections. A visual inspection of previously installed plugs in steam generators B and C did not reveal any visible signs of leakage.

Based upon the results of the inspection, the licensee concluded that tube stabilization would not be required in either steam generator until after the end of plant life. An analysis of tube wear rates indicated that the 95% cumulative probability growth over two cycles was 3.5% for steam generator B and 2.1% for steam generator C. The average growth rates for these steam generators were slightly negative (based on RFO 6 and RFO 8 data), implying that there is little or no growth in the wear indications at the AVBs. This negative growth rate can also be attributed to slight differences (within tolerances) between the standards used in the inspections.

Several indications of loose parts are being tracked in steam generator C. Since none of these indications were expected to cause excessive wear, the affected tubes were left in service.

3.3.6 Wolf Creek

Tables 3-28, 3-29, and 3-30 summarize the information discussed below for Wolf Creek. Table 3-28 provides the number of full-length bobbin inspections and the number of tubes plugged and deplugged during each outage for each of the four steam generators. Table 3-29 lists the reasons why the tubes were plugged. Table 3-30 lists tubes plugged for reasons other than wear at the AVBs.

Wolf Creek has four Westinghouse model F steam generators. The licensee numbers its tube supports from the hot-leg flow distribution baffle (FBH or BPH) to 7H on the hot-leg side of the steam generator and from FBC/BPC to 7C on the cold-leg side (refer to Figure 2-8).

Before the steam generators were placed in service, 15 tubes were plugged. In addition, three holes had been drilled in the cold-leg tubesheet of steam generator A in locations where tubes were not supposed to exist and these three holes were also plugged.

During RFO 1 in 1986, approximately 7% of the tubes in steam generators B and C were inspected full length with a bobbin coil. In addition to these full-length inspections, a few partial-length inspections were performed with a bobbin coil. These partial-length inspections were performed in the U-bend region of the steam generator from the top tube support plate on the hot-leg side to the top tube support plate on the cold-leg side. No tubes were plugged as a result of these inspections.

During RFO 2, no steam generator tube inspections were performed; however, during RFO 3 in 1988, approximately 53% of the tubes in each of the four steam generators were inspected full length with a bobbin coil. This was the first inspection for steam generators A and D. During this outage a disproportionate number of indications were detected in steam generator D, and the licensee was unsuccessful in developing an explanation for this condition at that time.

During RFO 3, 22 tubes were plugged, 19 of them for wear at the AVBs. The maximum depth reported for the AVB wear indications was 73% throughwall. During RFO 7 in 1994, 6 of these 19 tubes were deplugged, inspected, and returned to service. All six of these tubes had AVB wear indications less than the plugging criterion both in RFO 7 as well as in RFO 3. The three other tubes plugged during this outage had eddy current indications in the freespan portion of the tube. One of these three tubes had an indication above the hot-leg baffle plate, another tube had an indication above the cold-leg baffle plate, and the third tube had an indication above hot-leg tube support 6H. The tube with an indication above the hot-leg baffle plate and the tube with an indication above the cold-leg baffle plate were returned to service during RFO 5 in 1991.

During RFO 4 in 1990, approximately 56% of the tubes in steam generators B and D were inspected full length with a bobbin coil. Both of the two tubes plugged during this outage were plugged as a result of wear at the AVBs. The maximum depth reported for the AVB wear indications was 42% throughwall.

During RFO 5 in 1991, approximately 28% of the tubes in steam generator A and approximately 22% of the tubes in steam generator C were inspected full length with a bobbin coil. In addition to these full-length inspections, approximately 4.5% of the tubes in steam generator C were inspected with a bobbin coil from the cold-leg tube end to the top cold-leg tube support (i.e., 7C). Two tubes were plugged during this outage, both as a result of wear at the AVBs. The maximum depth reported for the AVB wear indications was 43% throughwall.

Two tubes were unplugged and returned to service during RFO 5 after eddy current testing indicated that it was acceptable. These tubes had been plugged during RFO 3 in 1988. One of these tubes had an indication whose reported depth at the time of original plugging was less than the plugging criterion.

During RFO 6 in 1993, 100% of the tubes in steam generator B were inspected full length with a bobbin coil. All five tubes plugged during this outage were plugged as a result of wear at the AVBs. The maximum depth reported for the AVB wear indications was 50% throughwall. Four additional locations were plugged in steam generator B during this outage. These locations are referred to as "bare holes" and do not have tubes inserted into them. Bare holes are holes in the steam generator tubesheet which were capped internally by the manufacturer prior to steam generator delivery and installation. Bare holes can have either stub-type or bar-type plugs installed. The four locations in steam generator B had 26-inch stub-tube type plugs installed. These bare holes are not inspected as part of the inservice inspection program and were plugged to preclude the possibility of leakage.

During RFO 7 in 1994, 100% of the tubes in steam generators A and D were inspected full length with a bobbin coil. Of the 33 tubes plugged during this outage, 31 were plugged as a result of wear at the AVBs, 1 tube was plugged due to an indication slightly below (or at) hot-leg tube support 1H, and 1 tube was plugged for a volumetric indication slightly below (or at) hot-leg tube support 2C. The maximum depth reported for the AVB wear indications was 56% throughwall.

During RFO 7, 17 tubes with Alloy 600 mechanical plugs were deplugged and inspected as part of the plug replacement program in response to NRC Bulletin 89-01, "Failure of Westinghouse

Steam Generator Tube Mechanical Plugs." Of these 17 tubes, 6 were returned to service since the inspections indicated that the tubes were acceptable (they had been plugged for AVB wear in RFO 3 and the depth of the wear was less than the plugging criterion). The inspection of these 17 previously plugged tubes revealed that (1) some indications of AVB wear had progressed further through the tube wall despite being plugged, (2) some indications of AVB wear showed little or no change (zero or negative growth) between the time the tube was plugged and the time of this inspection, and (3) some AVB locations for which no degradation was reported at the time of plugging had indications of AVB wear.

During this outage, repairs and inspections were performed on bare holes in steam generator A. Five stub-type bare-hole plugs were mechanically plugged and one bar-type bare-hole plug was removed and replaced with a welded plug. Three other bar-type bare-hole plugs were inspected with a rotating pancake coil probe and left in service.

During RFO 8 in 1996, 100% of the tubes in steam generators B and C were inspected full length with a bobbin coil. In addition to the bobbin coil inspections, a rotating probe equipped with a plus-point coil was used to inspect the hot-leg expansion transition region in 20% of the tubes in steam generators B and C and the U-bend region of 20% of the row 1 tubes in steam generators B and C. All 16 tubes plugged during this outage were plugged as a result of wear at the AVBs. The maximum depth reported for the AVB wear indications was 60% throughwall.

During RFO 9 in 1997, 100% of the tubes in steam generators A and D were inspected full length with a bobbin coil. In addition to the bobbin coil inspections, a rotating probe equipped with a plus-point coil was used to inspect the hot-leg expansion transition region in approximately 55% of the tubes in steam generators A and D and the U-bend region of 50% of the row 1 and 2 tubes in steam generators A and D. All 19 indications plugged during this outage were plugged as a result of wear at the AVBs. The maximum depth reported for the AVB wear indications was 60% throughwall.

During RFO 10 in 1999, 100% of the tubes in steam generators B and C were inspected full length with a bobbin coil. In addition to the bobbin coil inspections, a rotating probe was used to inspect the hot-leg expansion transition region in 55% of the tubes in steam generators B and C and the U-bend region of 50% of the row 1 and 2 tubes in steam generators B and C. All six tubes plugged during this outage were plugged as a result of wear at the AVBs. The maximum depth reported for the AVB wear indications was 57% throughwall.

During the RFO 10 inspections of steam generators B and C, tube wear at the AVB intersections and wear due to prior loose parts were observed. No loose parts were detected near the location of the worn tubes. In addition, a number of distorted signals were identified at the flow distribution baffle plate, primarily on the cold-leg side of the steam generator. The licensee considered the location of these signals atypical with regard to any potential corrosion degradation. A review of the 1996 inspection data for these indications showed no change in the shape or size of these signals. All of the signals were inspected with a rotating probe. Seven signals were confirmed as wear indications with the rotating probe and were sized with a bobbin coil and left in service. In addition to the flow distribution baffle plate indications, several indications, which were sized, were reported at (or near) the top of the hot-leg tubesheet and one indication was reported above hot-leg tube support 7H (this indication may be near the first AVB).

During RFO 11 in 2000, 100% of the tubes in steam generators A and D were inspected full length with a bobbin coil. In addition to the bobbin coil inspections in steam generators A and D, a rotating probe was used to inspect the hot-leg expansion transition region in 55% of the tubes and the U-bend region of 50% of the row 1 and 2 tubes. Of the 32 tubes plugged during this outage, 30 were plugged as a result of wear at the AVBs. The maximum depth reported for the AVB wear indications was 65% throughwall. The other two tubes were plugged for volumetric indications at the hot-leg top of tubesheet and at hot-leg tube support 4H. Rotating probe inspections of these tubes led the licensee to conclude that the indication at the top of tubesheet was most likely a result of manufacture and the indication at the hot-leg tube support was a benign indication, having been present in the prior two inspections with essentially no change.

3.4 Replacement Model Steam Generator Operating Experience

This section of the report provides inspection results for Indian Point 2, Point Beach 1, Robinson 2, Salem 1, Surry 1 and 2, and Turkey Point 3 and 4. Salem 1 has model F steam generators but is included here since the flow conditions in the Salem steam generators could be different than in the other model F steam generators.

3.4.1 Indian Point 2

Tables 3-31, 3-32, and 3-33 summarize the information discussed below for Indian Point 2. Table 3-31 provides the number of full-length bobbin inspections and the number of tubes plugged and deplugged during each outage for each of the four steam generators. Table 3-32 lists the reasons why the tubes were plugged. Table 3-33 lists tubes plugged for reasons other than wear at the AVBs.

Indian Point 2 has four Westinghouse model 44F steam generators. These steam generators were installed at the plant in December 2000. The tube supports are numbered as shown in Figure 2-10.

Prior to operation, two tubes were plugged in the replacement steam generators. These tubes were plugged because they were expanded above the top of the tubesheet. In addition, one tubesheet was misdrilled during fabrication, resulting in an extra hole on one side of the steam generator. This hole was plugged with a welded plug. During the preservice inspection, 100% of the tubes in each of the four steam generators were inspected full length with a bobbin coil. In addition to the bobbin coil inspections, a rotating probe equipped with a plus-point coil was used to inspect the hot-leg expansion transition region of 100% of the tubes in all four steam generators and the U-bend region of 100% of the row 1 and 2 tubes in all four steam generators.

The first inservice inspection of the replacement steam generators is not planned until the fall of 2002.

3.4.2 Point Beach 1

Tables 3-34, 3-35, and 3-36 summarize the information discussed below for Point Beach 1. Table 3-34 provides the number of full-length bobbin inspections and the number of tubes plugged and deplugged during each outage for each of the two steam generators. Table 3-35 lists the reasons why the tubes were plugged. Table 3-36 lists tubes plugged for reasons other than wear at the AVBs.

Point Beach 1 has two Westinghouse model 44F steam generators. These steam generators were installed at the plant during RFO 11 in 1984. The tube supports are numbered as shown in Figure 2-10.

Prior to the preservice inspection in 1984, three tubes in steam generator A were plugged with welded shop plugs. No tubes in steam generator B were plugged. During the preservice inspection in January 1984, 100% of the active tubes in both steam generators were inspected full length with a bobbin coil. As a result of the preservice inspection, one tube was plugged in steam generator B. The tube had a 60% throughwall defect approximately 25 inches above the hot-leg tubesheet.

During RFO 12 in 1985, approximately 3% of the tubes in steam generators A and B were inspected full length with a bobbin coil. In addition to these full-length inspections, approximately 0.6% of the tubes in each steam generator were inspected from the hot-leg tube end through the U-bend region. No tubes were plugged as a result of these inspections.

During RFO 13 in 1986, approximately 3.8% of the tubes in steam generator A and approximately 4.5% of the tubes in steam generator B were inspected full length with a bobbin coil. In addition to these full-length inspections, a number of partial-length inspections were performed. In steam generator A, "U-bend tests" were performed in 0.6% of the tubes. In steam generator B, 0.6% of the tubes received U-bend tests, 0.3% of the tubes were inspected through the fourth tube support, and approximately 7.7% of the tubes were inspected through the third tube support. Presumably these latter inspections were from the hot-leg tube end to the third or fourth hot-leg tube support. No tubes were plugged as a result of these inspections.

During RFO 14 in 1987, no steam generator tube inspections were performed.

During RFO 15 in 1988, approximately 4.0% of the tubes in steam generator A and approximately 3.5% of the tubes in steam generator B were inspected full length with a bobbin coil. The initial inspections showed no indications in either steam generator; however, two tubes were damaged in the cold leg of steam generator B as a result of a project to remove tube-lane-blocking-devices. As a result of this damage, the tubes were plugged and five tubes in this steam generator received partial-length inspections. A loose parts concern was raised during the closeout inspection following the blocking device removal project in steam generator A. As a result of this concern, approximately 5.6% of the tubes in steam generator A were inspected through the first tube support plate.

During RFO 16 in 1989, approximately 18% of the tubes in steam generator A and approximately 19% of the tubes in steam generator B were inspected full-length with a bobbin coil. In addition to these full length inspections, approximately 2% of the tubes in each steam generator were inspected from the hot-leg tube end to the uppermost support on the cold-leg side of the steam generator (i.e., the sixth cold-leg tube support), and approximately 0.6% of the tubes in steam generator B were inspected as a result of manufacturing burnishing marks. Manufacturing burnishing marks appear randomly throughout the tube bundle and are a result of attempts to dress or buff scratches made in the tubes during the fabrication of the tube bundle. No tubes were plugged as a result of these inspections.

During RFO 17 in 1990, no steam generator tube inspections were performed; however, the plugs in the three tubes in steam generator B were repaired as a result of concerns with stress corrosion cracking in Alloy 600 plugs.

During RFO 18 in 1991, approximately 18% of the tubes in each of the two steam generators were inspected full length with a bobbin coil. In addition to these full-length inspections, a number of partial-length exams were performed in both steam generators. These partial-length inspections included inspections in the periphery of the tube bundle to address loose parts concerns and to address the degradation found in steam generator A (discussed below). In addition to the bobbin coil inspections, a rotating pancake coil probe was used to inspect a number of manufacturing burnishing marks.

Two tubes were plugged during this outage. One tube in steam generator A was plugged for a 68% throughwall flaw located approximately 0.6-inch below hot-leg tube support 5H and attributed to wear from interaction with the tube support. The other tube plugged during this outage was in steam generator B. It was plugged as a result of a 38% throughwall AVB wear indication.

During RFO 18, remote video equipment was used to inspect up through the second tube support plate region in both steam generators. During these inspections, the annular region, the tube lanes, the baffle plates, and a few tubes into the tube bundle were inspected. In addition, in steam generator A, the inspection port at the sixth tube support plate was removed to allow access for inspection. The tube bundle was found to be in very good condition. A sample of boiler scale found throughout the steam generator was removed for analysis to determine a method for removal and also to attempt to quantify its thermal properties. Sludge lancing was performed on both steam generators. Post-cleaning examination was performed and verified the effectiveness of the cleaning.

During RFO 19 in 1992, approximately 18% of the tubes in both steam generators were inspected full length with a bobbin coil. In addition to these full-length inspections, a number of tubes in the periphery were inspected partially to address loose parts concerns. No tubes were plugged as a result of these inspections. However, one tube (in row 38 column 69) was reported as not being expanded in the hot-leg tubesheet.

During RFO 20 in 1993, approximately 18% of the tubes in both steam generators were inspected full length with a bobbin coil. In addition to these full-length inspections, a number of tubes in the periphery were inspected partially to address loose parts concerns. No tubes were plugged as a result of these inspections.

During RFO 21 in 1994, no steam generator tube inspections were performed, although a loose parts inspection was performed in steam generator A and sludge lancing was performed in both steam generators. Presumably the loose parts inspection was performed visually.

During RFO 22 in 1995, 100% of the tubes in both steam generators were inspected full length with a bobbin coil. In addition to the bobbin coil inspections, a rotating pancake coil probe was used to inspect the portion of the tube within the tubesheet for approximately 20 tubes. One tube was plugged as a result of a 45% throughwall AVB wear indication discovered during these inspections.

During RFO 23 in 1996, no steam generator tube inspections were performed. The plant was shut down for most of 1997.

During RFO 24 in 1998, 100% of the tubes in both steam generators were inspected full length with a bobbin coil with the exception of the U-bend region of the row 1 and 2 tubes. In addition to the bobbin coil inspections, a rotating probe equipped with a plus-point coil was used to inspect the hot-leg expansion transition region of 20% of the tubes, the U-bend region of 100% of the row 1 and 2 tubes, and a sample of dented locations (55 tubes in steam generator A and 68 tubes in steam generator B). No tubes were plugged as a result of these inspections. At this point, the steam generators had been operating for approximately 11.5 EFPY.

During RFO 25 in 1999, no steam generator tube inspections were performed.

In February 2000, the licensee shut down the plant to investigate an indication of a loose part. After a thorough investigation and inspection found no loose parts, the unit was restarted. The scope and method of inspection were not provided.

During RFO 26 in 2001, 100% of the tubes in both steam generators were inspected full length with a bobbin coil. In addition to the bobbin coil inspections, a rotating probe equipped with a plus-point coil was used to inspect the hot-leg expansion transition region of approximately 40% of the tubes and the U-bend region of approximately 20% of the row 1 tubes. One tube was plugged during this outage as a result of a 39% throughwall AVB wear indication.

3.4.3 Robinson 2

Tables 3-37, 3-38, and 3-39 summarize the information discussed below for Robinson 2. Table 3-37 provides the number of full-length bobbin inspections and the number of tubes plugged and deplugged during each outage for each of the three steam generators. Table 3-38 lists the reasons why the tubes were plugged. Table 3-39 lists tubes plugged for reasons other than wear at the AVBs.

Robinson 2 has three Westinghouse model 44F steam generators. These steam generators were installed at the plant in 1984. At the time of the replacement, the water chemistry program was changed from phosphate to all-volatile treatment (AVT). The tube supports are numbered as shown in Figure 2-10 (although the AVBs are numbered 01A, 02A, 03A, and 04A rather than AVB1, AVB2, AVB3, and AVB4, respectively).

The first steam generator inservice inspection after the steam generator replacement in 1984 was performed during RFO 10 in 1986. During RFO 10, approximately 9% of the tubes in each of the three steam generators were inspected full length with a bobbin coil. In addition to these full-length inspections, approximately 0.8% of the tubes were inspected from the hot-leg tube end through the U-bend to the uppermost (i.e., sixth) support plate on the cold-leg side. These partial-length inspections were performed primarily on the tubes in rows 1 through 4. No tubes were plugged as a result of these inspections.

During RFO 11 in 1987, approximately 9% of the tubes in each of the three steam generators were inspected full length with a bobbin coil. In addition to these full-length inspections, approximately 0.7% of the tubes in each of the three steam generators received a partial-length examination, typically from the hot-leg tube end to the sixth (uppermost) tube support plate on the cold-leg side. No tubes were plugged as a result of these inspections. One tube in steam generator C was found to have been expanded above the top of the secondary face of the tubesheet. This tube was not plugged.

During RFO 12 in 1988, approximately 20% of the tubes in each of the three steam generators were inspected full length with a bobbin coil. In addition, approximately 0.5% of the tubes in each of the three steam generators received a partial-length examination, typically from the hot-leg tube end to the sixth (uppermost) tube support plate on the cold-leg side. As a result of these inspections, one tube was plugged. This tube had a 76% throughwall indication near the hot-leg tubesheet. The indication was characterized as a gouge indicative of a defect caused by debris. The last time this tube had been inspected was during the 1984 preservice inspection. No indication had been reported at this location. A secondary side inspection of the affected steam generator in 1988 did not reveal any debris. As a result of identifying the degradation in this tube, the licensee inspected approximately 20 tubes from the hot-leg tube end through the first or second hot-leg tube support in the vicinity of the affected tube. No similar indications were observed during these inspections.

In April 1989, Robinson 2 was shut down to investigate alarms from the loose part monitoring system. The alarms indicated the possibility of a loose part in the hot-leg channel head of steam generator C. Upon investigation, the alarm was attributed to a control rod guide tube support pin nut (i.e., a split pin nut). The nut was removed. It had damaged the hot-leg tubesheet and tube ends in steam generator C. Some of the tubesheet face markings used to identify tubes on the hot leg were obliterated, and the damage to the hot-leg tube ends resulted in limitations on the ability to insert inspection probes at these locations. As a result of this event, in 1990 the licensee for Robinson 2 submitted a request to modify its technical specifications in 1990 to permit tube inspection from either the hot- or the cold-leg side of the steam generator.

During RFO 13 in 1990, approximately 20% of the tubes in each of the three steam generators were inspected full length with a bobbin coil. In addition to the bobbin coil inpections, a rotating pancake coil probe was used to inspect the hot-leg expansion transition region of approximately 3% of the tubes in each of the three steam generators. Indications of copper deposits were noted both in the bobbin and the rotating probe data. The rotating pancake coil inspections were focused on the sludge pile region. One row 2 tube was plugged for an indication above the cold-leg tubesheet as a result of the inspections. The licensee speculated that this indication was from a loose part, possibly the same loose part which resulted in the plugging of the tube during RFO 12 in 1988 (although the degradation identified during 1988 was on the hot-leg side of the steam generator). No surrounding tubes had indications of tube damage.

During RFO 14 in 1992, approximately 20% of the tubes in each of the three steam generators were inspected full length with a bobbin coil. The row 1 tubes were only examined from the hot-leg tube end to the sixth support plate on the cold-leg side of the steam generator. No random rotating pancake coil inspections were performed during this outage, unlike the previous outage. One tube was plugged as a result of the bobbin coil inspections. This tube, located in row 1 column 29 in steam generator A, was plugged because a 0.580-inch diameter probe could not pass through the tube at the sixth (uppermost) hot-leg tube support plate. A review of historical data showed that an indentation was present in the tube in 1984 (i.e., during the baseline inspection). This indentation prevented the passage of a 0.720-inch diameter probe in 1984, but the tube was left in service. Sludge height measurements made during this outage indicated that the sludge height did not exceed 3 inches. As was the case during RFO 13, indications of copper were observed in the eddy current data.

During RFO 15 in 1993, approximately 35% of the tubes in each of the three steam generators were inspected full length with a bobbin coil. The row 1 tubes were only examined from the hot-leg tube end to the sixth support plate on the cold-leg side of the steam generator. The bobbin coil inspection included all tubes which had not been inspected since the 100% baseline inspection in 1984. In addition to the bobbin coil inspections, a rotating pancake coil probe was used to inspect approximately 20% of the hot-leg manufacturing buff marks in each of the three steam generators (approximately 80 tubes total). Tubes inspected with a rotating pancake coil probe at buff mark locations were also inspected with this probe at the hot-leg expansion transition region.

As a result of these inspections, one tube was plugged. This tube, located in row 2 column 6 of steam generator A, was plugged because neither a 0.610-inch diameter probe nor a 3/8-inch diameter poly shaft could be passed through the tube. During the baseline inspection performed in 1984, a 0.720-inch probe could not pass through this tube, but the tube was left in service.

In February 1994, Robinson 2 was shut down for repairs to an emergency diesel generator. During this shutdown, a loose-parts-monitor alarm from steam generator C was investigated. The investigation revealed two strips of metal resting on the tubesheet, one near the periphery of the tube bundle and the other by a handhole. Their composition was similar to that of welding electrodes believed to have been used to fabricate the replacement steam generator shell welds. The metal strips were removed from the steam generators, and two tubes (row 1 column 90 and row 3 column 90) were plugged because of localized wear where the metal strips contacted the tubes. One of the metal strips was observed laying across the tube lane, wedged between columns 90 and 91 and leaning against three rows of tubes in column 90. The tube in row 1 column 90 exhibited a 33% throughwall indication on the hot-leg side of the steam generator and a 57% throughwall indication on the cold-leg side. The tube in row 3 column 90 exhibited a 26% throughwall indication on the cold-leg side. These tubes had been examined during RFO 13 in 1991 and found to be free of degradation. Two nearby tubes had been plugged in prior outages due to either outside diameter wear or manufacturing marks. These tubes located in row 2 column 90 and row 7 column 92 were plugged in 1990 and 1988, respectively. The row 2 tube indication was on the cold-leg side and the row 7 indication was on the hot-leg side of the steam generator. These indications may have been related to the loose part. A total of 484 tubes were inspected during this unplanned outage.

As of June 29, 1994, Robinson 2 had only six tubes plugged (not including the 28 tubes plugged prior to operation) and had accumulated only 6.5 effective full-power years on its steam generators.

During RFO 16 in 1995, 100% of the tubes in steam generator C were inspected full length with a bobbin coil. In addition to the bobbin coil inspections, a rotating pancake coil probe was used to examine the remaining 80% of the hot-leg manufacturing buff marks in steam generator C not inspected during the 20% RFO 15 (1993) sample. These examinations were performed to ensure that these indications were manufacturing related rather than flaws. In all, 101 steam generator C hot-leg buff marks were inspected in RFOs 15 and 16. No tubes were plugged as a result of these inspections.

Visual inspections were performed in all three steam generators during this outage. These inspections included a detailed foreign object search and retrieval (FOSAR) inspection at the top of the tubesheet. Although some collar scaling was found in all three steam generators, no significant detrimental conditions were identified.

As of 1995, Robinson 2 had performed sludge lancing five times since the steam generator replacement, including the sludge lancing during the 1995 outage. Analysis of sludge samples showed a declining trend in the amount of copper in the sludge. Excessive copper deposits on the outside diameter of the steam generator tubing can often mask defects, making eddy current detection more difficult. In 1986, copper levels ranged from 30% to 35%. In 1993, copper levels ranged from 11% to 15%. This downward trend in copper is attributed to the replacement of the condenser and feedwater heater tubing (presumably with non-copper alloys), the use of full-flow condensate polishing, and the sludge lancing.

During RFO 17 in 1996, 100% of the tubes in steam generator A were inspected full length with a bobbin coil. In addition to the bobbin coil inspections, a rotating pancake coil probe was used to inspect the steam generator A hot-leg manufacturing buff marks not inspected during RFO 15 in 1993 (i.e., the remaining 80% of the population) and all new hot-leg buff marks identified during RFO 17. The rotating pancake coil probe was also used to inspect hot-leg dented intersections, the U-bend region of 20% of the row 1 and 2 tubes, and the hot-leg expansion transition region of 40% of the tubes in steam generator A. During this outage, one tube was plugged as a result of a 38% throughwall indication believed to be caused by a loose part.

During RFO 18 in 1998, approximately 63% of the tubes in steam generator B and approximately 50% of the tubes in steam generator C were inspected full length with a bobbin coil. In addition to the bobbin coil inspections, a rotating probe equipped with a plus-point coil was used to inspect approximately 50% of the hot-leg side manufacturing buff marks, 50% of the dents greater than 2 volts in amplitude at tube supports, the hot-leg expansion transition region of approximately 50% of the tubes, and the U-bend region of approximately 50% of the row 1 and 2 tubes in steam generators B and C.

As a result of these inspections, no tubes were plugged; however, two tubes had signal responses indicative of a loose part. Visual inspection in the vicinity of these tubes indicated a piece of wire adhering to the two tubes. Attempts to retrieve the wire were unsuccessful. The affected tubes did not exhibit any signs of degradation (i.e., there was a signal of a loose part but no wear signal associated with a loose part). Dents in the free span and at tube supports were also reported during this outage. Most of these dents were attributed to initial manufacture, but a few were attributed to transient loose parts based on their location, the signals for the latter dents generally being lower in amplitude than for dents that are manufacturing related.

During RFO 19 in 1999, approximately 50% of the tubes in steam generator A were inspected full length with a bobbin coil. In addition to the bobbin coil inspections, a rotating probe equipped with a plus-point coil was used to inspect the hot-leg expansion transition region of approximately 60% of the tubes, approximately 20% of the hot-leg manufacturing buff marks, dents, and benign indications (50 exams in 42 tubes), and the U-bend region of 100% of the row 1 and 2 tubes. No tubes were plugged as a result of these inspections.

During the inspection, five tubes were considered to have imperfections due to manufacturing irregularities at the tubesheet interface. In addition, three tubes contained indications detected with the low-frequency channel indicating the presence of a loose part. No degradation was associated with the loose part.

The licensee identified 54 indications in 34 tubes with the plus-point coil. These indications were located in the periphery of the tube bundle on both the hot- and the cold-leg sides of the steam generator. These indications were small in volume and were dispositioned as being the result of either maintenance equipment contact or transient loose parts. The indications were sized with a site-qualified sizing technique and left in service. The indications were attributed to maintenance equipment contact based on the location/height of the indications, the eddy current response, the limited number of loose parts observed, video tapes with evidence of wear marks on the secondary side of tubes, and the absence of wear growth for a few previously identified indications.

In addition to these tubes, one tube in the cold-leg was reported as having no tube expansion in the tubesheet, and one tube was reported as having a slight overexpansion at the tubesheet interface. The unexpanded tube was left in service since the portion of the tube within the tubesheet did not exhibit any degradation during a full-length inspection with a rotating probe and since the tube end weld is the pressure boundary and no credit was taken for the expansion of the tube within the tubesheet. The overexpanded tube was also left in service.

During RFO 20 in 2001, approximately 50% of the tubes in steam generators B and C were inspected full length with a bobbin coil. In addition to the bobbin coil inspections, a rotating probe equipped with a plus-point coil was used to inspect 20% of the hot-leg manufacturing buff marks, 20% of the dents, the U-bend region of 50% of the row 1 and 2 tubes, and the hot-leg expansion transition region of 50% of the tubes in steam generators B and C. There was no primary-to-secondary leakage at the time RFO 20 was entered.

As a result of these inspections, four tubes were plugged. One of these tubes was plugged because a dent, present since steam generator fabrication, prevented an examination by a qualified bobbin probe and the use of a rotating probe resulted in poor-quality data. A second tube was plugged for a 43% throughwall wear indication at the hot-leg flow distribution baffle. The wear was attributed to a transient loose part. This tube is located in the periphery of the tube bundle and no indication was present during the previous inspection of this tube in 1998. A third tube was plugged for wear near the top of the hot-leg tubesheet. This tube also had a wear indication (approximately 32% throughwall) attributed to a transient loose part. Ultrasonic testing performed on this tube led the licensee to attribute the indication to wear. This tube is not in the periphery of the tube bundle. A fourth tube was plugged for an obstruction in the tube above the sixth hot-leg tube support plate. This tube would not permit the passage of a 0.650-inch diameter rotating probe, but did permit the passage of a 3/8-inch poly shaft. The obstruction was attributed to foreign material lodged in the tube, although visual examinations were not performed to confirm this. The obstruction is not located near a tube support (i.e., it is midspan). This tube was previously examined during RFOs 15 and 16 with no obstruction noted (i.e., a 0.720-inch probe passed through the tube).

Secondary side visual inspections have been performed at Robinson 2. This inspection involves inspection of the tube support plates up through the flow slots to the bottom of the top tube support plate. No upper bundle fouling or corrosion product buildup in the tube support plate areas was identified. Minor deposition was observed in the land area of the quatrefoil support with no bridging of the deposits between the lands.

The licensee refers to a number of tubes as "wrapper MOD tubes." These tubes were damaged during a wrapper modification in which a small piece of the wrapper was cut out at the handhole to allow access for in-bundle lancing. The vendor inadvertently scratched a number of tubes while cutting out the wrapper. The licensee identified the scratches and used a rotating probe equipped with a plus-point coil to examine each affected tube in the area of concern.

During the first 10 years of operation of the replacement steam generators, a sample of tubes was inspected in all three steam generators during each outage at Robinson 2. In subsequent years, a subset of steam generators was inspected each outage, with one steam generator being examined one outage and the other two steam generators being examined the following outage.

3.4.4 Salem 1

Tables 3-40, 3-41, and 3-42 summarize the information discussed below for Salem 1. Table 3-40 provides the number of full-length bobbin inspections and the number of tubes plugged and deplugged during each outage for each of the four steam generators. Table 3-41 lists the reasons why the tubes were plugged. Table 3-42 lists tubes plugged for reasons other than wear at the AVBs.

Salem 1 has four Westinghouse model F steam generators. These steam generators were installed at the plant in 1997. The steam generators at Unit 1 were replaced with the steam generators from the canceled Seabrook 2 plant. The licensee numbers its tube supports from the hot-leg flow distribution baffle (FBH or BPH) to 7H on the hot-leg side of the steam generator and from FBC/BPC to 7C on the cold-leg side (refer to Figure 2-8).

During RFO 13 in 1999, the first inservice inspection of the replacement steam generators, 100% of the tubes in each of the four steam generators were inspected full length with a bobbin coil. In addition to the bobbin coil inspections, a rotating probe equipped with a plus-point coil was used to inspect the U-bend region of 20% of the row 1 and 2 tubes in steam generators A and C (100 tubes in all), the hot-leg expansion transition region of 20% of the tubes in steam generators A and C, and 20% of the dents at the tube support plates with magnitudes greater than 5 volts and 20% of freespan dings with magnitudes greater than 5 volts up to 2 inches above hot-leg tube support 7H in each steam generator. In 2001, it was noted that one tube in steam generator C had not been inspected with a bobbin probe because the tube locationwas misencoded.

Of the 10 tubes plugged during this outage, 8 were plugged for AVB wear and 2 were plugged because they were not properly expanded into the tubesheet (i.e., the tube was not hydraulically expanded the full depth of the tubesheet). Wear at the AVBs was observed in all four steam generators, and the growth rates were within expectations for the first cycle of operation of model F steam generators. The licensee indicated it expected the growth rates to decrease during subsequent inspections. The maximum depth reported for the AVB wear indications was 54% throughwall. For the two unexpanded tubes, the licensee performed an evaluation demonstrating the design requirements were met for all analyzed conditions. During this outage, one loose part was identified in steam generator D. The part did not cause wear on any of the tubes and attempts to remove it were unsuccessful.

During RFO 14 in 2001, 100% of the tubes in each of the four steam generators were inspected full length with a bobbin coil. In addition to the bobbin coil inspections, a rotating probe equipped with a plus-point coil was used to inspect the U-bend region of 100% of the row 1 and 2 tubes in each steam generator, the hot-leg expansion transition region of 50% of the tubes in steam generators B and D, and 100% of the dents at the hot-leg tube support plates with magnitudes greater than or equal to 5 volts and 100% of hot-leg freespan dings with magnitudes greater than 5 volts in each steam generator.

As a result of these inspections, 35 tubes were plugged. Of the 35 tubes plugged during this outage, 29 were plugged as a result of wear at the AVBs, 2 were plugged for loose part indications, and 4 were plugged for unacceptable data quality. The maximum depth reported for the AVB wear indications was 64% throughwall. The two loose part indications were detected in the U-bend region near the seventh cold-leg tube support. One of these indications was in a row 1 tube of steam generator A and one was in a row 2 tube in steam generator B. The indication in the row 1 tube was above the seventh cold-leg tube support and was aligned with one of the tube support contact points (i.e., one of the four tube support lands). The indication in the row 2 tube was below the seventh cold-leg tube support and was between two of the tube support contact points. Of the four tubes plugged for unacceptable data quality, one was plugged due to a permeability variation, two were plugged because they would not permit the passage of a 0.520-inch diameter plus-point probe (although they were inspected with a bobbin coil), and one was plugged because the 0.520-inch diameter plus-point probe skipped or stalled in the U-bend region.

A visual inspection of installed steam generator tube plugs was performed to verify that the plugs were installed in the proper location and to identify signs of leakage. No anomalies were noted during this inspection.

3.4.5 Surry 1

Tables 3-43, 3-44, and 3-45 summarize the information discussed below for Surry 1. Table 3-43 provides the number of full-length bobbin inspections and the number of tubes plugged and deplugged during each outage for each of the three steam generators. Table 3-44 lists the reasons why the tubes were plugged. Table 3-45 lists tubes plugged for reasons other than wear at the AVBs.

Surry 1 has three Westinghouse model 51F steam generators. These steam generators were installed at the plant in 1981. The tube supports are numbered as shown in Figure 2-12.

During the first refueling outage following replacement (RFO 1) in 1983, approximately 9% of the tubes in steam generator B and approximately 11% of the tubes in steam generator C were inspected with a bobbin coil from the hot-leg tube end through the top tube support on the cold-leg side (i.e., 7C). No tubes were plugged as a result of these inspections.

During RFO 2 (i.e., the second refueling outage following replacement) in 1984, approximately 26% of the tubes in steam generator A and approximately 17% of the tubes in steam generator B were inspected full-length with a bobbin coil. In addition to these full length inspections, approximately 6% of the tubes in steam generator A and approximately 4% of the tubes in steam generator B were inspected with a bobbin coil from the hot-leg tube-end to the uppermost cold-leg tube support (i.e., 7C).

Three of the four tubes plugged during RFO 2 were plugged for indications at (or near) the hot-leg tube support plates and one was plugged for an indication at (or near) the hot-leg tubesheet. The depths for the defects in these tubes were estimated at the time to be 44%, 60%, 89%, and 96% throughwall, respectively. No additional details were provided.

During RFO 3 in 1986, approximately 86% of the tubes in steam generator A, approximately 46% of the tubes in steam generator B, and approximately 86% of the tubes in steam generator C were inspected full length with a bobbin coil. In addition to these full-length inspections, the remaining 14% of the tubes in steam generator A, 2% of the tubes in steam generator B, and the remaining 14% of the tubes in steam generator C were inspected with a bobbin coil, primarily from the hot-leg tube-end to the uppermost cold-leg tube support (i.e., 7C).

Of the four tubes plugged during this outage, one tube was plugged as a result of multiple indications between hot-leg tube supports 2H and 4H, one tube was plugged for an indication at cold-leg tube support 2C, one tube (i.e., row 2 column 7) was plugged for a restriction, and one tube location was plugged because the tube was removed to destructively examine an indication at (or near) hot-leg tube support 7H.

During RFO 4 in 1988, approximately 24% of the tubes in steam generators B and C were inspected full length with a bobbin coil. In addition to these full-length inspections, approximately 3% of the tubes in steam generators B and C were inspected with a bobbin coil from the hot-leg tube-end to the uppermost cold-leg tube support (i.e., 7C).

No tubes were plugged as a result of these inspections. From the results of the 1986 tube pull, the licensee concluded that many of the distorted indications or undefined signals in steam generator tubes were insignificant indications (either less than 20% throughwall or not relevant). These indications were recorded for future tracking and trending purposes.

During RFO 5 in 1990, approximately 4% of the tubes in steam generator A, approximately 26% of the tubes in steam generator B, and approximately 37% of the tubes in steam generator C were inspected full length with a bobbin coil. In addition to these full-length inspections, approximately 2% of the tubes in steam generator A, approximately 1% of the tubes in steam generator B, and approximately 2% of the tubes in steam generator C were partially inspected along various lengths of the tube with the bobbin coil. These partial-length exams were primarily on the hot-leg side of the steam generator. In addition to the bobbin coil inspections, a rotating pancake coil probe was used to inspect the hot-leg expansion transition region of 100% of the tubes in each of the three steam generators.

As a result of these inspections, portions of two tubes were pulled for destructive examination and the tube locations were plugged. The tubes were pulled to examine axial and circumferential anomalies at the top of the tubesheet. The examination found no operationally induced degradation of the tube wall.

During RFO 6 in 1992, approximately 35% of the tubes in steam generators A and B were inspected full length with a bobbin coil. One of the two tubes plugged during this outage was plugged for a dent and an associated indication at hot-leg tube support 4H and the other tube was plugged as a result of wear at the AVBs. The maximum depth reported for the AVB wear indications was 35% throughwall.

During RFO 7 in 1994, approximately 100% of the tubes in steam generator B were inspected full length with a bobbin coil. In addition to the bobbin coil inspections, a rotating pancake coil probe was used to inspect the hot-leg expansion transition region of approximately 9% of the tubes in steam generator B. Of the four tubes plugged during the outage, all were plugged as a result of wear at the AVBs. The maximum depth reported for the AVB wear indications was 24% throughwall.

During RFO 8 in 1995, 100% of the tubes in steam generator C were inspected full length with a bobbin coil. In addition to the bobbin coil inspections, a rotating pancake coil probe was used to inspect the hot-leg expansion transition region of 9% of the tubes in steam generator C. As a result of these inspections, one tube was plugged for wear at the AVBs. The maximum depth reported for the AVB wear indications was 29% throughwall.

During RFO 9 in 1997, 100% of the tubes in steam generator A were inspected full length with the bobbin coil. In addition to the bobbin coil inspections, a rotating pancake coil probe was used to inspect the hot-leg expansion transition region of approximately 22% of the tubes in steam generator A.

Of the five tubes plugged during this outage, three were plugged because tube restrictions prevented the bobbin probe from passing through the tube, one was plugged due to wear at the AVBs, and one was plugged for a permeability signal. The restricted tubes were all in row 1 and would not allow the passage of a probe through the cold-leg tube end. The tube with a permeability signal was considered unsuitable for inspection. The maximum depth reported for the AVB wear indications was 25% throughwall.

During RFO 10 in 1998, 100% of the tubes in steam generator B were inspected full length with a bobbin coil. In addition to the bobbin coil inspections, a rotating pancake coil probe was used to inspect the hot-leg expansion transition region of approximately 20% of the tubes and the U-bend region of 20% (19) of the row 1 tubes in steam generator B. Ultrasonic testing (UT) was performed on five tubes to characterize anomalous signals.

Of the six tubes plugged during the outage, three tubes in row 1 were plugged because restrictions at the hot-leg tubesheet prevented a complete inspection, and three tubes were plugged for indications at the hot-leg side baffle plate attributed to a foreign object. These latter indications were inspected with a rotating probe and characterized as volumetric indications.

During RFO 11 in 2000, approximately 100% of the tubes in steam generator C were inspected full length with a bobbin coil. In addition to the bobbin coil inspections, a rotating probe was used to inspect the hot-leg expansion transition region of approximately 20% of the tubes and the U-bend region of 100% of the row 1 tubes (94 tubes) in steam generator C.

Of the eight tubes plugged during this outage, seven were plugged as a result of wear at the AVBs and one was plugged for a volumetric indication between AVB 2 and AVB 3. Inspection of this latter tube with a rotating probe indicated that the indication was on one side of the tube ("one-sided wear"). The AVBs are V-shaped bars which extend into the bundle to row 8 and row 11. The wear indication on this latter tube (in row 11 column 38) appeared to correspond to the bottom of the AVB (i.e., the V section) rather than to the leg of the AVB. There was no indication at this location in 1995, the last time this tube was inspected. The maximum depth reported for the AVB wear indications was 33% throughwall. The average growth rate per cycle for AVB wear indications since the last inspection of steam generator C was 4.1% and the maximum growth rate per cycle was 8.0%. These growth rates were twice the rates observed following prior inspections.

During this outage, several dents at the sixth and seventh tube supports were detected. Of the 46 dents reported at the sixth tube support plate, 17 were greater than 5 volts and did not appear in previous inspection data and were therefore inspected with a rotating probe equipped with a plus-point coil. The plus-point coil confirmed that the bobbin coil indications were low-level dents corresponding to the edge of the tube support plate. No cracklike or other forms of tube degradation were noted. Some locations had multiple dent indications corresponding to the quatrefoil lands.

During RFO 12 in 2001, 100% of the tubes in steam generator A were inspected full length with a bobbin coil. In addition to the bobbin coil inspections, a rotating probe equipped with a plus-point coil was used to inspect the hot-leg expansion transition region of approximately 20% of the tubes and the U-bend region of 100% of the row 1 tubes in steam generator A.

Of the five tubes plugged during this outage, one tube was plugged as a result of wear at the AVBs, one tube (in row 10 column 44) was plugged as a result of a wear indication that was attributed to the tip (i.e., the V section) of the AVB contacting the tube, and three tubes were plugged as a result of wear indications caused by sludge lancing equipment used during RFO 11 in 2000. Attempts to characterize the indication in the tube at row 10 column 44 associated with the wear indication at the tip of the AVB were unsuccessful because the 0.680-inch rotating probe equipped with a plus-point coil could not pass through either the hot-leg or the cold-leg tangent point of the U-bend. The maximum depth reported for the AVB wear indications was 30% throughwall. The average growth rate per cycle for AVB wear indications since the last inspection of steam generator A was 1.5% and the maximum growth rate per cycle was 5.3%. These growth rates were consistent with prior performance of this steam generator.

During this outage, approximately 40 tubes were identified with dent indications at the sixth and seventh tube supports. The licensee stated these dent indications appeared to be concentrated in the periphery of the tube bundle near the wedge regions and were at (or near) the edges of the support plate. Altogether 507 tubes with dent indications (located throughout the tube bundle) were recorded this outage. Most of these dents were less than 5 volts.

During the preceding cycle, there was a small (0.5 gpd) primary-to-secondary leak in steam generator B.

At the completion of RFO 12 in 2001, the replacement steam generators at Surry 1 had operated for approximately 15.5 EFPYs. Only 43 tubes had been plugged as of this outage. Approximately 15 were plugged for wear at the AVBs, 2 for wear associated with the tip of the AVB, 7 for restrictions, 3 for loose parts, 8 for manufacturing flaws or mechanical damage during maintenance, 1 for data quality, and 7 for other reasons.

3.4.6 Surry 2

Tables 3-46, 3-47, and 3-48 summarize the information discussed below for Surry 2. Table 3-46 provides the number of full-length bobbin inspections and the number of tubes plugged and deplugged during each outage for each of the three steam generators. Table 3-47 lists the reasons why the tubes were plugged. Table 3-48 lists tubes plugged for reasons other than wear at the AVBs.

Surry 2 has three Westinghouse model 51F steam generators. These steam generators were installed at the plant in 1980. The tube supports are numbered as shown in Figure 2-12.

During the first refueling outage following replacement (RFO 1) in 1981, the tubes in steam generators A and B were inspected. No tubes were plugged as a result of these inspections.

During RFO 2 (the second refueling outage following replacement) in 1983, approximately 1% of the tubes in steam generator A were inspected full length with a bobbin coil. In addition to these full-length inspections, approximately 20% of the tubes in steam generator A and approximately 17% of the tubes in steam generator C were inspected with a bobbin coil from the hot-leg tube-end to the uppermost cold-leg tube support (i.e., 7C). No tubes were plugged as a result of these inspections.

During RFO 3 in 1985, approximately 16% of the tubes in steam generators A and B were inspected full length with a bobbin coil. In addition to these full-length inspections, approximately 6% of the tubes in steam generator A and approximately 5% of the tubes in steam generator B were inspected with a bobbin coil from the hot-leg tube-end to the uppermost cold-leg tube support (i.e., 7C). No tubes were plugged as a result of these inspections.

In June 1986, Surry 2 was shut down, in part because of a primary-to-secondary leak in steam generator A. A pressure test revealed a leak on the cold-leg side of a tube in the periphery (row 41 column 28). A video inspection in the region between the tubes and the steam generator wrapper revealed several loose objects lying on the tubesheet and against or between adjacent tubes in the vicinity of the leaking tube. The loose object was identified as a grinding burr and was removed. Altogether 23 tubes were inspected during this outage. In addition to the leaking tube, eddy current signals were observed in two neighboring tubes, and an eddy current signal suggesting the presence of a loose object was observed in another tube. All the signals were attributed to the grinding burr. Only the leaking tube was plugged.

During RFO 4 in 1986, approximately 18% of the tubes in steam generator B and approximately 17% of the tubes in steam generator C were inspected full length with a bobbin coil. In addition to these full-length inspections, approximately 4% of the tubes in steam generators B and C were inspected with a bobbin coil from the hot-leg tube-end to the uppermost cold-leg tube support (i.e., 7C). No tubes were plugged as a result of these inspections.

During RFO 5 in 1988, approximately 24% of the tubes in steam generator A and approximately 23% of the tubes in steam generator C were inspected full length with a bobbin coil. In addition to these full length inspections, approximately 3% of the tubes in steam generators A and C were inspected from the hot-leg tube-end to either cold-leg tube support 6C or 7C. No tubes were plugged as a result of these inspections.

In 1989, no steam generator tube inspections were performed at Surry Unit 2. However, the plugs in one tube in steam generator A were removed and replaced as a result of industry experience with mechanical tube plug failures. During this replugging operation, an adjacent tube (in row 41 column 27) was inadvertently plugged on the hot-leg side only. This plug was subsequently removed during RFO 6 in 1991.

During RFO 6 in 1991, approximately 35% of the tubes in steam generators A and C were inspected full length with a bobbin coil. No tubes were plugged as a result of these inspections. As discussed above, the plug installed in 1989 in the hot leg of the tube in row 41 column 27 in 1989 was removed. The tube was subsequently inspected and returned to service.

During RFO 7 in 1993, 100% of the tubes in steam generator B were inspected full length with a bobbin coil. In addition to the bobbin coil inspections, a rotating pancake coil probe was used to inspect the hot-leg expansion transition region of approximately 9% of the tubes in steam generator B. As a result of these inspections, two tubes were plugged for wear at the AVBs. The maximum depth reported for the AVB wear indications was 20% throughwall.

During RFO 8 in 1995, 100% of the tubes in steam generator A were inspected full length with a bobbin coil. In addition to the bobbin coil inspections, a rotating pancake coil probe was used to inspect the hot-leg expansion transition region of approximately 9% of the tubes in steam generator A.

Four of the five tubes plugged during this outage were plugged for axially oriented indications at the top of tubesheet on the cold-leg side and the fifth tube was plugged for a restriction at the tubesheet on the hot-leg side. The axially oriented indications were attributed to pitting.

During RFO 9 in 1996, 100% of the tubes in steam generator C were inspected full length with a bobbin coil. In addition to the bobbin coil inspections, a rotating pancake coil probe was used to inspect the hot-leg expansion transition region of approximately 20% of the tubes in steam generator C.

Of the eight tubes plugged during this outage, three tubes were plugged as a result of wear at the AVBs, two tubes were plugged for single axial anomalies in the hot leg at the top of the tubesheet, two row 1 tubes were plugged for restrictions (one at the hot-leg tube end and the other at the cold-leg tube end), and one tube was plugged for a multiple axial anomaly and distorted roll indication at the top of the tubesheet on the hot-leg side. The maximum depth reported for the AVB wear indications was 42% throughwall.

During RFO 10 in 1997, approximately 100% of the tubes in steam generator B were inspected full length with a bobbin coil. In addition to the bobbin coil inspections, a rotating pancake coil probe was used to inspect the hot-leg expansion transition region of approximately 20% of the tubes and the U-bend region of approximately 20 row 1 tubes in steam generator B.

Five tubes were plugged during this outage. Two row 1 tubes were plugged because they did not allow passage of a 0.720-inch diameter probe (although they did allow passage of a 0.680-inch diameter probe), and three tubes were plugged as a result of wear at the AVBs. The maximum depth reported for the AVB wear indications was 25% throughwall.

During RFO 11 in 1999, 100% of the tubes in steam generator A were inspected full length with a bobbin coil. In addition to the bobbin coil inspections, a rotating pancake coil probe was used to inspect the hot-leg expansion transition region of approximately 20% of the tubes and the U-bend region of approximately 20% (19) of the row 1 tubes in steam generator A.

Eight of the nine tubes plugged during this outage were plugged for pitlike indications near the top of the tubesheet on the cold-leg side and one row 1 tube was plugged because it would not allow passage of a 0.720-inch diameter probe (although it did allow passage of a 0.680-inch diameter probe). One of the eight tubes plugged for pitlike indications was in steam generator C. The pitlike indication in this tube was reported to be 26% throughwall in 1995/1996.

Prior to this outage the licensee had been tracking six cold-leg pit indications above the tubesheet secondary face in four tubes in the Surry 2 steam generators. Copper deposits, which are a potential contributor to the development of steam generator tube pits in Alloy 600 material, were present on the tubing prior to chemical cleaning in 1994, and the pitting is believed to have initiated prior to the chemical cleaning. During the 1999 outage, the licensee inspected all but one of these tubes by UT and removed all four tubes from service because of concerns with nondestructive examination sizing uncertainty. The results of the inspections supported the licensee's conclusion that the indications were volumetric corrosion-induced degradation. However, no tubes have been removed to confirm pitting as the degradation mechanism.

Over the last few outages, a number of tubes had been plugged due to restrictions in the row 1 tubes. The concern with the "dinged" row 1 tubes was considered closed as a result of this inspection because all steam generators had been inspected since the phenomenon was judged to have begun. All identified tubes exhibiting this phenomenon have been removed from service. The nature of the dings on the row 1 tubes was not described; however, they are believed to have been made by maintenance equipment used during outages.

The maximum growth rate per cycle for AVB wear indications in steam generator A was 3.7%.

During RFO 12 in 2000, 100% of the tubes in steam generator C were inspected full length with a bobbin coil. In addition to the bobbin coil inspections, a rotating pancake coil probe was used to inspect the hot-leg expansion transition region of approximately 20% of the tubes and a rotating probe equipped with a plus-point coil was used to inspect the U-bend region of 100% of the row 1 tubes (92 tubes) in steam generator C.

All seven tubes plugged during this outage were plugged as a result of wear at the AVBs. The maximum depth reported for the AVB wear indications was 43% throughwall. The average growth rate per cycle for AVB wear indications since the last inspection of steam generator C was 3.8% and the maximum growth rate per cycle was 7.0%. These growth rates are approximately twice the rates documented from prior inspections although they are similar to the rates seen in steam generator C of Surry 1.

During this outage, several dents were detected at the sixth and seventh tube support. These dent signals appear to be associated with contact between the tubes and the quatrefoil land, not with contact between the tube and corrosion products (as was observed at plants with carbon steel tube support plates). Altogether 251 dented locations were identified with voltages greater than or equal to 2.0 volts. The number of reported dent indications increased during this inspection as a result of lowering the reporting threshold for dents from 5 volts to 2 volts. The inspection guidelines at Surry 2 require dents greater than or equal to 5 volts to be inspected with a rotating probe unless a review of historical data confirms that the signal voltage and phase attributes are essentially unchanged from previous inspections. A total of 74 dent locations (28 hot-leg and 46 cold-leg) had to be inspected with the rotating probe. These inspections confirmed the dent signals and most of the signals corresponded to the edge of the tube support plate and were in line with the quatrefoil lands. No crack-like or other forms of tube degradation were noted at any of the dent locations. Some support plate locations had two or more dents that corresponded with the quatrefoil lands.

At the completion of RFO 12 in 2000, the replacement steam generators at Surry 2 had operated for approximately 15.2 EFPYs. Only 39 tubes had been plugged as of this outage, 15 for wear at the AVBs, 12 for pitlike indications, 1 for a foreign object, 6 for restrictions, 3 for anomalous indications at the top of hot-leg tubesheet, and 2 for manufacturing flaws.

3.4.7 Turkey Point 3

Tables 3-49, 3-50, and 3-51 summarize the information discussed below for Turkey Point 3. Table 3-49 provides the number of full-length bobbin inspections and the number of tubes plugged and deplugged during each outage for each of the three steam generators. Table 3-50 lists the reasons why the tubes were plugged. Table 3-51 lists tubes plugged for reasons other than wear at the AVBs.

Turkey Point 3 has three Westinghouse model 44F steam generators. They were installed at the plant in 1982. The tube supports are numbered as shown in Figure 2-10. Minor denting occurred at the upper tube support plates during manufacturing of these steam generators. The denting affects no more than 341 intersections in each steam generator hot leg. In addition, overexpanison of the tubesheet joint occurred on a maximum of 300 tubes in each hot leg when the hydraulic expansion tool was set at a depth exceeding the thickness of the tubesheet. The tool made a slight bulge in the tube at the top of the tubesheet. This anomalous condition produces residual stresses in the affected locations, making them more susceptible to cracking than nonoverexpanded areas. Based on accident analysis considerations, a maximum of 20% of the tubes in the three steam generators can be plugged.

During RFO 8 in 1983, the first refueling outage following replacement, approximately 10% of the tubes were inspected (the actual numbers of tubes and steam generators inspected were not readily available). No tubes were plugged as a result of these inspections.

During RFO 9 in 1985, approximately 8.6% of the tubes in steam generator A, approximately 13.1% of the tubes in steam generator B, and approximately 6.2% of the tubes in steam generator C were inspected full length with a bobbin coil. Of the four tubes plugged during this outage, one exceeded the plant technical specification plugging criterion and the other three were plugged as a preventive measure. Three of the indications were near the top of the hot-leg tubesheet and the other indication was at tube support 4H. The maximum depth reported for these indications was 56% throughwall.

During RFO 10 in 1987, approximately 10.1% of the tubes in steam generator A, approximately 10.3% of the tubes in steam generator B, and approximately 11.6% of the tubes in steam generator C were inspected full length with a bobbin coil. One tube was plugged during this outage as a result of a 48% throughwall indication in the cold-leg sludge pile. The nature of this indication was not provided. In addition, two stub tubes (i.e., non-full-length tubes) with shop plugs in steam generator C were plugged. Stub tubes are not considered tube locations.

During RFO 11 in 1990, 100% of the tubes in each of the steam generators were inspected full length with a bobbin coil. Of the 11 tubes plugged during this outage, 7 were plugged as a result of wear at the AVBs, 2 were plugged for indications near the top of the tubesheet (1 above the hot-leg tubesheet, 1 above the cold-leg tubesheet), and 2 were plugged for indications at the tube support plates. The nature of these four indications was not provided. The maximum depth reported for the AVB wear indications was 39% throughwall. In addition, four stub tubes with shop plugs, two in steam generator A and two in steam generator B were plugged.

During RFO 12 in 1992, 100% of the tubes in each of the three steam generators were inspected full length with a bobbin coil. Of the seven tubes plugged during this outage, three were plugged as a result of wear at the AVBs, one was plugged for an indication above hot-leg tube support 6H (the uppermost tube support), one was plugged for an indication above cold-leg tube support 2C, one was plugged for an indication above the cold-leg tubesheet, and one was plugged for an indication above cold-leg tube support 6C (the uppermost tube support). The maximum depth reported for the AVB wear indications was 35% throughwall. During this outage, the secondary side of each of the three steam generators was visually inspected. Debris was found inside steam generator B, and the areas with debris were cleaned. No other reportable indications were found during the secondary side inspections.

During RFO 13 in 1994, 100% of the tubes in each of the three steam generators were inspected full length with a bobbin coil. In addition to the bobbin coil inspections, a rotating pancake coil probe was used to inspect the hot-leg expansion transition region of the overexpanded tubes in two of the three steam generators and approximately 2% of the dents on the hot-leg side in one steam generator. Of the four tubes plugged during this outage, three were plugged as a result of wear at the AVBs, and one was plugged for an indication at (or near) hot-leg tube support 1H. The maximum depth reported for the AVB wear indications was 41% throughwall. In addition, one tube was replugged because the original welded plug was leaking.

During RFO 14 in 1995, 100% of the tubes in each of the three steam generators were inspected full length with a bobbin coil. In addition to the bobbin coil inspections, a rotating pancake coil probe was used to inspect the hot-leg expansion transition region of 100% of the overexpanded tubes (approximately 300 tubes) and 20% of the dented tube support intersections in one steam generator. One of the two tubes plugged during this outage was plugged as a result of wear at the AVBs and the other as a result of an indication slightly above the top of tubesheet on the hot-leg side of the steam generator. The maximum depth reported for the AVB wear indications was 42% throughwall.

During RFO 15 in 1997, 100% of the tubes in each of the three steam generators were inspected full length with a bobbin coil. In addition to the bobbin coil inspections, a rotating probe was used to inspect the hot-leg expansion transition region of 100% of the overexpanded tubes (approximately 300 tubes) in steam generators A and B, the U-bend region of 20% of the row 1 tubes, 20% of the dented tube support intersections in steam generator A, and 10% of the dented tube support intersections in steam generator B.

Of the 14 tubes plugged during this outage, 8 were plugged for indications slightly above the hot-leg top of tubesheet, 1 was plugged for an indication at (or near) hot-leg tube support 5H, 1 was plugged for an indication at (or near) hot-leg tube support 6H, 1 was plugged for an indication at (or near) cold-leg tube support 3C, 2 were plugged because they were adjacent to a foreign object, and 1 was plugged as a result of wear at the AVBs. The maximum depth reported for the AVB wear indications was 37% throughwall.

During RFO 16 in 1998, 100% of the tubes in each of the three steam generators were inspected full length with a bobbin coil. In addition to the bobbin coil inspections, a rotating probe equipped with a plus-point coil was used to inspect the hot-leg expansion transition region of 20% of the overexpanded tubes in two of the three steam generators (approximately 68 tubes), the U-bend region of 20% of the row 1 tubes in two of the three steam generators, and 20% of the dented tube support intersections in two of the three steam generators. This was the first outage in which a plus-point coil was used. Previously, a three coil rotating probe had been used. One tube was plugged during this outage as a result of wear at the AVBs. The maximum depth reported for the AVB wear indications was 39% throughwall. During this outage the licensee performed secondary side cleaning and inspections. These inspections included a visual inspection of the feed ring and moisture separating equipment and ultrasonic thickness measurements of the feed ring. No adverse findings were reported.

During RFO 17 in 2000, approximately 50% of the tubes in each of the three steam generators were inspected full length with a bobbin coil. In addition to the bobbin coil inspections, a rotating probe equipped with a plus-point coil was used to inspect the hot-leg expansion transition region of 100% of the tubes, the U-bend region of 20% of the row 1 and 2 tubes, and 20% of the hot-leg dents in each steam generator. This was the first outage in which extensive rotating probe inspections were performed at the hot-leg expansion transition area. This inspection was the 10th inspection of the current steam generators, which at the start of RFO 17 had operated for approximately 12.2 effective full power years (EFPYs).

Of the 69 tubes plugged during this outage, 5 were plugged as a result of wear at the AVBs and the remaining 64 were plugged for reasons given below. The maximum depth reported for the AVB wear indications was 43% throughwall.

During the outage, 64 tubes were identified as having possible corrosion degradation or original manufacturing indications. Both volumetric and circumferential indications were detected. All 41 volumetric indications initiated from the outside diameter of the tube. Of the 23 circumferential indications, 15 initiated from the inside diameter of the tube and 8 initiated from the outside diameter of the tube. All of these indications were detected with the rotating probe. Generally they were not detectable with the bobbin probe due to their proximity to tube geometry changes at the top of the tubesheet. All of these indications were plugged and the circumferential indications were stabilized.

During RFO 17 in 2000, the licensee conducted an investigation to determine the cause of the indications detected at the hot-leg top of tubesheet. This investigation included a review of the steam generator design features, manufacturing information, inspection techniques, and historical and current chemistry programs. Due to the lack of prior rotating probe inspection data and the limited number of defects identified in thermally treated Alloy 600 tubing, the results were inconclusive for the circumferential and volumetric indications. The licensee suggested two potential causes: (1) the indications were true indications generated by stress corrosion cracking and intergranular attack, or (2) the indications were false positive indications produced by manufacturing anomalies or deposits at the top of the tubesheet or introduced by the inspection technique.

Based on the review of applicable industry experience and subsequent inspection data from Turkey Point 4, the licensee reevaluated the circumferential and volumetric indications detected at Unit 3 during RFO 17 in March 2000 was performed. After the Unit 3 March 2000 inspection, an eddy current inspection of the Turkey Point 4 steam generators (which have the same design as Turkey Point 3 steam generators) was performed in October 2000, and similar indications were reported near the top of the tubesheet. Based on ultrasonic investigation of several of these circumferential indications in Unit 4, the licensee concluded that the circumferential indications detected in Unit 3 during RFO 17 in March 2000 were a result of minor geometric variations associated with the tube-to-tubesheet joint fabrication process and were not due to degradation. The licensee also determined that tubes removed from steam generators of similar design contained similar minor geometric variations. These variations resulted from the tube-to-tubesheet joint fabrication process and produced circumferential indications such as those observed at Turkey Point 3 and 4.

The licensee also concluded that the volumetric indications reported during March 2000 were a result of an overly conservative analysis of the inspection data. This conclusion was based on a post-outage review by various industry experts, a reanalysis of the data, and the ultrasonic examination of two similar volumetric indications in the Turkey Point 4 steam generators in October 2000. The ultrasonic examination at Unit 4 showed that one indication was a result of minor wall loss consistent with wear from a prior foreign object and the other indication was a single pitlike indication (although it was sharper and more defined than pit indications examined by ultrasonic techniques in another model F steam generator). On this basis, the licensee concluded that the volumetric indications were not due to corrosion-induced degradation. This conclusion was supported by the Unit 3 RFO 18 inspection (discussed below), in which no additional circumferential, volumetric, or pitlike indications were detected.

As a result of this effort, the licensee concluded that of the 64 volumetric and circumferential indications originally identified, only 26 tubes contained volumetric or pitlike indications (possibly due to manufacturing and installation artifacts) and the remaining 38 tubes contained no degradation (13 had circumferential geometric anomalies, 23 had dings or dents, and 2 had manufacturing buff marks).

During RFO 18 in 2001, 100% of the tubes in each of the three steam generators were inspected full length with a bobbin coil. In addition to the bobbin coil inspections, a rotating probe was used to inspect the hot-leg expansion transition region of approximately 50% of the tubes, the U-bend region of some of the row 1 and 2 tubes, and selected hot-leg dents in each steam generator.

Of the 14 tubes plugged during this outage, 12 were plugged as a result of indications of mechanical wear at the broached tube support plates, 1 was plugged as a result of wear at the AVBs, and 1 was plugged because of a restriction in the U-bend region prevented an inspection of the tube. The maximum depth reported for the AVB wear indications was 34% throughwall. One of the 12 tubes plugged for mechanical wear at the tube support plates also had an indication attributed to a loose part. One of the indications on this tube exceeded the technical specification repair limit of 40% throughwall; however, the depth of the indication was not provided. During this outage, the licensee examined the secondary side of steam generator A for debris and damage. No reportable indications were identified. Additional visual inspections of the inner bundle regions of the hot-leg tubesheet in steam generator C revealed several small objects (small wires, scale deposits). The objects were inaccessible and could not be retrieved.

3.4.8 Turkey Point 4

Tables 3-52, 3-53, and 3-54 summarize the information discussed below for Turkey Point 4. Table 3-52 provides the number of full-length bobbin inspections and the number of tubes plugged and deplugged during each outage for each of the three steam generators. Table 3-53 lists the reasons why the tubes were plugged. Table 3-54 lists tubes plugged for reasons other than wear at the AVBs.

Turkey Point 4 has three Westinghouse model 44F steam generators. These steam generators were installed at the plant in 1983. The tube supports are numbered as shown in Figure 2-10. Minor denting occurred at the upper tube support plates during manufacturing of these steam generators. The denting affects no more than 341 intersections in each steam generator hot leg. In addition, overexpansion of the tubesheet joint occurred on a maximum of 300 tubes in each hot leg when the hydraulic expansion tool was set at a depth exceeding the thickness of the tubesheet. The tool made a slight bulge in the tube at the top of the tubesheet. This anomalous condition produces residual stresses in the affected locations, making them more susceptible to cracking than nonoverexpanded areas. Based on accident analysis considerations, a maximum of 20% of the tubes in the three steam generators can be plugged.

-84-

According to steam generator fabrication records, nine tubes (one in one of the steam generators and eight in another) were plugged in the steam generators before the preservice inspection. Based on information submitted following the 1993 steam generator tube inspections, 15 tubes in steam generator A, 7 tubes in steam generator B, and 9 tubes in steam generator C were plugged before the steam generators were placed in service.

During RFO 9 in 1984, the first refueling outage following replacement, the licensee inspected approximately 6.5% of the tubes in steam generator A, approximately 5.0% of the tubes in steam generator B, and approximately 15.6% of the tubes in steam generator C. The inspections in steam generator C included some partial-length examinations of bulged regions at the top of the tubesheet. No additional details on these bulged regions were provided. No tubes were plugged as a result of these inspections.

During RFO 10 in 1986, approximately 10.2% of the tubes in steam generator A, approximately 9.9% of the tubes in steam generator B, and approximately 10.7% of the tubes in steam generator C were inspected. Presumably these were full-length inspections performed with a bobbin coil. No tubes were plugged as a result of these inspections.

During RFO 11 in 1988, 100% of the tubes in each of the three steam generators were inspected full length with a bobbin coil. One tube was plugged as a result of these inspections. The tube was plugged because a piece of a hose clamp was caught inside the portion of the tube expanded into the hot-leg tubesheet. Attempts to remove the clamp were unsuccessful.

During RFO 12 in 1991, 100% of the tubes in each of the three steam generators were inspected full length with a bobbin coil. In addition to the bobbin coil inspections, a rotating pancake coil probe was used to inspect the hot-leg expansion transition region of 74% of the tubes that were overexpanded above the top of the tubesheet in one steam generator. One tube was plugged during this outage. The tube was plugged due to a restriction approximately 2 inches below the secondary face of the hot-leg tubesheet. This tube was inspected with a 0.720-inch diameter probe during the preservice inspection and a 0.650-inch diameter probe in 1988, and permitted the passage of a 0.5-inch diameter wand during this outage. A Welch-Allyn video probe inspection showed that no foreign object was present in the tube and revealed minor irregularities of the inside surface.

During RFO 13 in 1993, 100% of the tubes in each of the three steam generators were inspected full length with a bobbin coil. In addition to the bobbin coil inspections, a rotating pancake coil probe was used to inspect the hot-leg expansion transition region of 85% of the tubes that were overexpanded above the top of the tubesheet in one steam generator. No tubes were plugged as a result of these inspections. During this outage, the secondary side of all three steam generators was visually inspected with no reportable indications noted.

During RFO 14 in 1994, 100% of the tubes in each of the three steam generators were inspected full length with a bobbin coil. In addition to the bobbin coil inspections, a rotating pancake coil probe was used to inspect the hot-leg expansion transition region of 85% of the tubes that were overexpanded above the top of the tubesheet in one steam generator and 54% of the hot-leg dents in one steam generator. No tubes were plugged as a result of these inspections.

During RFO 15 in 1996, no steam generator tube inspections were performed.

During RFO 16 in 1997, 100% of the tubes in each of the three steam generators were inspected full length with a bobbin coil. In addition to the bobbin coil inspections, a rotating probe was used to inspect the hot-leg expansion transition region of 20% of the tubes that were overexpanded above the top of the tubesheet, the U-bend region of 20% of the row 1 tubes, and 20% of the hot-leg dents in two of the steam generators. No tubes were plugged as a result of these inspections.

During RFO 17 in 1999, no steam generator tube inspections were performed.

During RFO 18 in 2000, approximately 50% of the tubes in each of the three steam generators were inspected full length with a bobbin coil. In addition to the bobbin coil inspections, a rotating probe equipped with a plus-point coil was used to inspect the hot-leg expansion transition region of 100% of the tubes, the U-bend region of 20% of the row 1 and 2 tubes, and 20% of the hot-leg dented locations in each of the three steam generators. This was the first large-scale inspection of the hot-leg top of tubesheet region with a rotating probe at Turkey Point 4. Of the 10 tubes plugged during this outage, 1 tube was plugged as a result of wear at the AVBs, 1 tube was plugged for wear at the hot-leg baffle plate, 1 tube was plugged for a permeability signal at the hot-leg expansion transition region, and 7 tubes were plugged as a result of possible corrosion degradation. These latter tubes had volumetric and pitlike eddy current indications. The maximum depth reported for the AVB wear indications was 36% throughwall.

Table 3-1: Braidwood 2: Summary of Bobbin Inspections and Tube Plugging

Outage	Completion Date	Cumul. EFPY	SG A Insp.	SG A Plug	SG A DePl	SG B Insp.	SG B Plug	SG B DePl	SG C Insp.	SG C Plug	SG C DePl	SG D Insp.	SG D Plug	SG D DePl	Total Plug	Total DePl	Cumul. Plugged	Percent Plugged	Notes
Pre-op				1			2			0			3		6	0	6	0.03	
RFO 1	04/26/90	1.162	4569	0		4568	0		4570	2		4567	0		2	0	8	0.04	
RFO 2	11/11/91	2.288	2285	4		2284	0		2284	7		2284	0		11	0	19	0.10	1
RFO 3	04/13/93	3.405	2440	6		2374	1	1	2370	8		2430	1		16	1	34	0.19	1
RFO 4	10/25/94	4.566				4568	0		4553	6					6	0	40	0.22	
RFO 5	04/12/96	5.838	4559	17		4568	2		4547	4		4566	12		35	0	75	0.41	
RFO 6	10/20/97		4542	7		4566	3		4543	12		4554	6		28	0	103	0.56	
RFO 7	05/05/99		4535	0		4563	1		4531	4		4548	1		6	0	109	0.60	
RFO 8	10/28/00		4535	8		4562	1		4527	1		4547	1		11	0	120	0.66	2
Totals:				43	0		10	1		44	0		24	0	121	1			

Plant Data
Model: D5
T-hot (approximate):
Tubes per steam generator: 4570
Number of steam generators: 4

Acronyms
Pre-op = prior to operation
Cumul. = cumulative
Insp. = number of tubes inspected
Plug = number of tubes plugged
DePl = number of tubes deplugged
RFO = refueling outage

Notes
1. All tubes in each steam generator were examined through the U-bend
2. Cycle 8 expected to be 1.425 EFPY.

Table 3-2: Braidwood 2 Causes of Tube Plugging

Cause of Tube Plugging/Outage		Pre-Op	1990 RFO 1	1991 RFO 2	1993 RFO 3	1994 RFO 4	1996 RFO 5	1997 RFO 6	1999 RFO 7	2000 RFO 8	Totals	Totals
Wear	AVB		2	11	16	6	29	12	6	10	92	92
	Pre-heater TSP (D5)										0	
	TSP										0	
Loose Parts	Confirmed						2				2	2
	Not confirmed, periphery										0	
	Not confirmed, not periphery										0	
Obstruction Restriction	From PSI, no progression										0	0
	Service-induced										0	
Manufacturing Flaws	Preservice	6			-1						5	20
	Other							15			15	
Inspection Issues	Probe lodged										0	1
	Data quality										0	
	Dent/geometry										0	
	Permeability									1	1	
	Not inspected										0	
Other	Top of tubesheet						1				1	5
	Free span						1	1			2	
	TSP						2				2	
	Other/not reported										0	
SCC	ID										0	0
	OD										0	
TOTALS		6	2	11	15	6	35	28	6	11	120	120
Notes:					1			2				

Notes
1. One tube deplugged during RFO 3   Assumed it was a tube plugged prior to commercial operation.
2. Fifteen tubes plugged with circumferential indications at hot-leg top of tubesheet reclassified as manufacturing anomalies based on tube pulls from Byron 2.

Table 3-3: Braidwood 2: Tubes Plugged for Indications Other Than AVB Wear

STEAM GENERATOR A				
Tube	Location	RFO #	Characterization	Stabilized[1]
31-53	1H	5	Volumetric	

STEAM GENERATOR B				
Tube	Location	RFO #	Characterization	Stabilized[1]
1-45	U-bend	8	Permeability	
48-29	FS (2C)	6	Volumetric	

STEAM GENERATOR C				
Tube	Location	RFO #	Characterization	Stabilized[1]

STEAM GENERATOR D				
Tube	Location	RFO #	Characterization	Stabilized[1]
1-11	U-bend	5	Single axial indication	
30-48	1H	5	Volumetric	
36-60	TSH	5	Volumetric	
43-72	8H	5	Confirmed Loose Part (CLP) (part could not be retrieved)	
43-73	8H	5	CLP (part could not be retrieved)	

[1]An empty cell indicates that it was not reported whether the tube was stabilized or not

Table 3-4: Byron 2: Summary of Bobbin Inspections and Tube Plugging

Outage	Completion Date	Cumul. EFPY	SG A			SG B			SG C			SG D			Total Plug	Total DePl	Cumul. Plugged	Percent Plugged	Notes
			Insp.	Plug	DePl	Insp.	Plug	DePl	Insp.	Plug	DePl	Insp.	Plug	DePl					
Pre-op				4			2			4			1		11	0	11	0.06	
RFO 1	01/01/89		2278	2		2277	6		2279	3		2284	0		11	0	22	0.12	1
RFO 2	09/01/90		2270	1		2268	17		2272	1		2273	2		21	0	43	0.24	1
RFO 3	03/01/92		2252	9		2215	9		2235	5		2223	6		29	0	72	0.39	1
RFO 4	10/02/93		2259	6		2239	23		2260	7		2264	0		36	0	108	0.59	1
RFO 5	03/01/95		2398	9		2386	8		2456	7		2448	5		29	0	137	0.75	1
RFO 6	09/01/96		4539	11		4505	10		4543	6		4556	3		30	0	167	0.91	1
RFO 7	05/05/98		4528	7		4495	26		4537	5		4553	0		38	0	205	1.12	2
RFO 8	11/04/99		4521	1		4469	8		4532	3		4553	2		14	0	219	1.20	3
RFO 9	04/13/01					4461	4								4	0	223	1.22	4
Totals:				50	0		113	0		41	0		19	0	223	0			

Plant Data
Model: D5
T-hot (approximate):
Tubes per steam generator: 4570
Number of steam generators: 4

Acronyms
Pre-op = prior to operation
Cumul. = cumulative
Insp. = number of tubes inspected
Plug = number of tubes plugged
DePl = number of tubes deplugged
RFO = refueling outage

Notes
1. All tubes in each steam generator were examined through the U-bend.
2. Forced outage due to leakage.
3. Cycle 8 expected to be 1.412 EFPY.
4. Cycle 9 expected to be 1.4 EFPY.

Table 3-5: Byron 2 Causes of Tube Plugging

Cause of Tube Plugging/Outage		Pre-Op	1989 RFO 1	1990 RFO 2	1992 RFO 3	1993 RFO 4	1995 RFO 5	1996 RFO 6	1998 RFO 7	1999 RFO 8	2001 RFO 9	Totals	Group Totals
Wear	AVB		2	19	25	33	21	19	1	9		129	130
	Pre-heater TSP (D5)									1		1	
	TSP											0	
Loose Parts	Confirmed		4				1	4	3		1	13	27
	Not confirmed, periphery		1			1	7			3	2	14	
	Not confirmed, not periphery											0	
Obstruction Restriction	From PSI, no progression											0	0
	Service-Induced											0	
Manufacturing Flaws	Preservice	11										11	40
	Other								29			29	
Inspection Issues	Probe lodged											0	4
	Data quality		1									1	
	Dent/geometry		1					1	1			3	
	Permeability											0	
	Not inspected											0	
Other	Top of tubesheet		2									2	22
	Free span			1	3			4			1	9	
	TSP			1	1	2		2	4	1		11	
	Other/not reported											0	
SCC	ID											0	0
	OD											0	
TOTALS		11	11	21	29	36	29	30	38	14	4	223	223
Notes:		1,2,3			4	4	5	6	7	8			

Notes

1. Data quality: signal-to-noise Indication indicative of SCC in U-bend of row 1 tube.
2. Dent/Geometry: Large dent in U-bend of row 1 tube from PSI.
3. Loose part in B at TSH in R49C55 and R49C56 was confirmed as was loose part in C at 8H in R49C54 and R49C55. Suspect part in C at 5H in R38C56. Refer to RFO [5]
4. Loose Part: Loose part in C at 5H R39C56, stabilized in RFO 5.
5. Loose Parts: Confirmed presence with magnet in B at R12C4, R12C5, R13C4, R13C5, R14C5. Suspect part in C at 5H in R40C56 and R41C56. All 7 plugged.
6. Leaker outage. Stabilized A-R16C110 in CL.
7. 3 tubes pulled with circumferential indications at top of tubesheet Indicated the 29 circumferential indications were manufacturing related indications. All 29 were stabilize[d]
8. 3 tubes with PLPs were stabilized. B-R15C5, R15C6, R14C6. Stabilized tube with pre-heater wear B-R49C51.
9. Stabilized tubes with PLPs in B-R14C7 and B-R15C7. Plugged tube with confirmed loose part since part was removed in B-R20C56.

Table 3-6: Byron 2: Tubes Plugged for Indications Other Than AVB Wear

STEAM GENERATOR A				
Tube	Location	RFO #	Charactenzation	Stabilized[1]
1-87	U-bend	RFO 1	Large dent	
1-110	U-bend	RFO 1	Signal to noise indication indicative of PWSCC	
15-109	TSC	RFO 6	CLP (part removed)	
15-110	TSC	RFO 6	CLP (part removed)	
15-111	TSC	RFO 6	CLP (part removed)	
16-110	TSC	RFO 6	CLP (part removed) - leaker	Y (cold)
44-67	2C	RFO 7	OD volumetnc	
46-67	FS (2C)	RFO 6	Scale/deposits	
47-66	FS (2C)	RFO 6	Scale/deposits	
48-74	FS (2C)	RFO 6	Scale/deposits	
49-74	FS (2C)	RFO 6	Scale/deposits	

[1]An empty cell indicates that it was not reported whether the tube was stabilized or not

Table 3-6: Byron 2: Tubes Plugged for Indications Other Than AVB Wear (cont'd)

	STEAM GENERATOR B			
Tube	Location	RFO #	Characterization	Stabilized[1]
1-2	U-bend	RFO 6	Geometry change	
2-57	U-bend	RFO 7	Geometry change	
12-4	5H	RFO 5	Possible loose part (PLP) (orientation by magnet)	Y
12-5	5H	RFO 5	PLP (orientation by magnet)	Y
13-4	5H	RFO 5	PLP (orientation by magnet)	Y
13-5	5H	RFO 5	PLP (orientation by magnet)	Y
14-5	5H	RFO 5	PLP (orientation by magnet)	Y
14-6	5H	RFO 8	PLP	Y
14-7	5H	RFO 9	PLP	Y
15-5	5H	RFO 8	PLP	Y
15-6	5H	RFO 8	PLP	Y
15-7	5H	RFO 9	PLP	Y
20-56	2C	RFO 9	CLP (removed in RFO 5)	N
20-57	2C	RFO 6	OD volumetric (CLP removed in RFO 5)	
21-55	2C	RFO 7	CLP removed in RFO 5	
25-7	TSH	RFO 1	Mechanism not reported	
27-8	TSH	RFO 1	Mechanism not reported	
28-25	1H	RFO 7	CLP (removed - outage not specified)	
28-26	1H	RFO 4	Volumetric	
37-67	FS (2C)	RFO 9	OD volumetric	
47-76	2C	RFO 8	OD volumetric	
49-51	7C	RFO 8	Preheater wear	Y
49-54	TSH	RFO 5	CLP (removed in RFO 1)	
49-55	TSH	RFO 1	Not reported (CLP in RFO 5, part removed in RFO 1)	
49-56	TSH	RFO 1	PLP (CLP in RFO 5, part removed in RFO 1)	

[1]An empty cell indicates that it was not reported whether the tube was stabilized or not

Table 3-6: Byron 2: Tubes Plugged for Indications Other Than AVB Wear (cont'd)

Tube	Location	RFO #	Characterization	Stabilized[1]
STEAM GENERATOR C				
9-39	FS (10C) FS (10H)	RFO 3	ODI	
18-25	1H	RFO 7	OD volumetric	
19-27	1H	RFO 7	OD volumetric	
21-29	1H	RFO 4	Volumetric	
22-29	1H	RFO 6	OD volumetric	
33-66	8H	RFO 2	Pit	
34-66	8H	RFO 7	OD volumetric	
38-56	5H	RFO 1	Narrow circumferential indication (PLP in RFO 5)	Y RFO 5
39-56	5H	RFO 4	PLP	Y RFO 5
40-56	5H	RFO 5	PLP	Y
41-56	5H	RFO 5	PLP	Y
49-53	8H	RFO 7	CLP (part removed in RFO 5)	
49-54	8H	RFO 1	Narrow circ (CLP removed in RFO 5)	
49-55	8H	RFO 1	Narrow circ (CLP removed in RFO 5)	

Tube	Location	RFO #	Characterization	Stabilized[1]
STEAM GENERATOR D				
20-34	FS (6C) FS (9C)	RFO 3	Outside diameter indication (ODI) -manufacturing burnishing mark (MBM)	
22-37	10H	RFO 3	ODI - MBM	
37-17	FS (9H) FS (11H)	RFO 3	ODI	
44-74	FS (5H) FS (9H)	RFO 2	ODI	

[1]An empty cell indicates that it was not reported whether the tube was stabilized or not.

Table 3-7: Catawba 2: Summary of Bobbin Inspections and Tube Plugging

Outage	Completion Date	Cumul. EFPY	SG A Insp.	SG A Plug	SG A DePl	SG B Insp.	SG B Plug	SG B DePl	SG C Insp.	SG C Plug	SG C DePl	SG D Insp.	SG D Plug	SG D DePl	Total Plug	Total DePl	Cumul. Plugged	Percent Plugged	Notes
Pre-op				1			7			1			5		14	0	14	0.08	1
Mid-Cycle	08/26/87			0						0			0		0	0	14	0.08	2
RFO 1	02/12/88		1133	4		546	1		515	0		1215	2		7	0	21	0.11	
RFO 2	04/01/89		1456	2		1519	5		1443	1		1542	0		8	0	29	0.16	
RFO 3	07/01/90		3274	9		3230	1		3243	2		3265	7		19	0	48	0.26	
RFO 4	11/20/91		4554	7		4556	0		4566	4		4556	1		12	0	60	0.33	
RFO 5	03/01/93		4547	14		4556	6		4562	13		4555	10		43	0	103	0.56	
RFO 6	06/01/94	5.62	4533	6		4550	11		4549	5		4545	9		31	0	134	0.73	
RFO 7	11/01/95		2569	10		2476	2		2419	5		2596	6		23	0	157	0.86	
RFO 8	04/01/97	7.93	2624	1		2520	5		2447	0		2628	4		10	0	167	0.91	
RFO 9	09/01/98		2501	1		2317	5		2273	1		2485	2		9	0	176	0.96	
RFO 10	03/01/00		4303	0		4401	4		4313	2		4309	1		7	0	183	1.00	
RFO 11	10/15/01		2210	0		1890	0		1807	0		2071	0		0	0	183	1.00	
Totals:				55	0		47	0		34	0		47	0	183	0			

Plant Data
Model: D5
T-hot (approximate): 618 F
Tubes per steam generator: 4570
Number of steam generators: 4

Acronyms
Pre-op = prior to operation
Cumul. = cumulative
Insp. = number of tubes inspected
Plug = number of tubes plugged
DePl = number of tubes deplugged
RFO = refueling outage

Notes
1. Assumed based on other information.
2. Licensee elected to inspect 2 of the steam generators during an unplanned maintenance outage to limit the inspections during the subsequent refueling outage.

Table 3-8: Catawba 2 Causes of Tube Plugging

Cause of Tube Plugging/Outage		Pre-Op	1988 RFO 1	1989 RFO 2	1990 RFO 3	1991 RFO 4	1993 RFO 5	1994 RFO 6	1995 RFO 7	1997 RFO 8	1998 RFO 9	2000 RFO 10	2001 RFO 11	Totals
Wear	AVB				14	6	2	1	1	2	1	1		28
	Pre-heater TSP (D5)										1			1
	TSP										2			2
Loose Parts	Confirmed		2											2
	Not confirmed, periphery													0
	Not confirmed, not periphery											2		2
Obstruction Restriction	From PSI, no progression													0
	Service-induced													0
Manufacturing Flaws	Preservice	14												14
	Other													0
Inspection Issues	Probe lodged											2		2
	Data quality									1				1
	Dent/geometry										1			1
	Permeability									2	1			3
	Not inspected									1		2		3
Other	Top of tubesheet						3	4	2	3	2			14
	Free span		3	4		1	30	20	10	1				69
	TSP		2	3	3	5	6	6	5		1			31
	Other/not reported			1	2		2		5					10
SCC	ID													0
	OD													0
TOTALS		14	7	8	19	12	43	31	23	10	9	7	0	183

Notes:

1. Since no tubes were plugged during the 1987 mid-cycle outage, reference is just made to RFO 1 in this table.

-96-

Table 3-9: Catawba 2: Tubes Plugged for Indications Other Than AVB Wear

STEAM GENERATOR A				
Tube	Location	RFO #	Characterization	Stabilized[1]
1-5	FS(12); 4+ 9	7	ODI, volumetric	
1-6	4+ 8	7	ODI, volumetric	
1-7	4+ 6	7	ODI, volumetric	
3-9	FS(12,13,15-19), 15+1.5, 16-1.0, TSC, 19+1.5	7	Absolute drift indication (ADI), non-quantifiable indication (NQI), volumetric, ODI	
7-12	?	5	?	
8-107	FS(7,8,10)	6	NQI, ODI, volumetric	
15-50	FS(10)	8	Bobbin indication greater than 40% through-wall, no degradation found (NDF) with rotating probe	
15-77	FS(2,5)	1	ODI, location not indicative of PLP	
16-72	TSH	6	IDI	
19-102	?	7	?	
21-105	FS(10)	5	ODI, volumetric	
24-104	FS(10)	5	ODI, NQI	
24-108	FS(7,8), 8-1 4	6	NQI, ODI, volumetric	
24-67	3	1	ODI, location not indicative of PLP	
24-68	3	2	OD	
24-69	3	2	OD	
25-19	FS(3,5,6,7,9,10)	7	NQI, volumetric, ODI	
25-86	?	7	?	
25-100	FS(4,11,17)	5	ODI, volumetric, NQI	
28-102	FS (3, 7)	5	ODI, volumetric, NQI	
29-24	FS(7)	6	NQI, ODI	
29-70	FS (2)	5	ODI, volumetric	
29-96	FS (10)	5	ODI, volumetric	
34-91	?	7	?	
40-72	TSH	6	NQI	
43-68	FS(10)	9	Permeability	
44-49	FS (5,6,7,10)	7	NQI, ODI, volumetric	
48-43	18+.4	5	ODI, preheater	
48-44	18+ 5	5	ODI, preheater	
49-38	7+/-.1	3	OD	
49-39	7	1	ODI, location not indicative of PLP	

STEAM GENERATOR A				
Tube	Location	RFO #	Characterization	Stabilized[1]
49-40	7+.1	3	OD	
49-41	7+ 65	5	ODI, NQI	
49-42	7+ 6	4	OD	
49-44	18+ 8	5	ODI, preheater	
49-54	FS (12)	1	ODI, location not indicative of PLP	
49-64	7+ 6	4	OD	
49-65	7+ 7	4	OD	
49-66	7+ 1	3	OD	
49-68	18-.02	5	Multiple axial indication (MAI), Single axial indication (SAI), preheater	
49-77	18+ 03	5	MAI, preheater	

[1] An empty cell indicates that it was not reported whether the tube was stabilized or not.

-98-

Table 3-9: Catawba 2: Tubes Plugged for Indications Other Than AVB Wear (cont'd)

Tube	Location	RFO #	Characterization	Stabilized[1]
			STEAM GENERATOR B	
1-61	FS(9)	9	Dent signal change	
2-99	U-bend	10	Plus-point lodged in U-bend	
8-31	FS (1, 16)	5	ODI, volumetric	
16-29	1H+ 5	10	Wear, no size available - PLP	
17-90	14+1 4	2	OD	
20-104	TSH	9	MBM/PLP wear	
21-62	8- 3	2	OD	
25-40	FS(18)	5	ODI	
26-26	FS(3)	5	ODI, volumetric	
28-106	TSH	5	ODI, volumetric	
29-23	FS(9,11)	5	ODI, volumetric	
29-87	FS(7)	6	ODI, volumetric	
29-105	TSH	8	MBM/PLP wear	
30-90	FS(4)	6	ODI, volumetric	
31-89	17- 1, 17+2 2	2	OD	
33-68	8+1 63	6	ODI	
33-74	8+1 52	6	ODI	
33-78	8+1 41	6	ODI	
34-42	1H+ 5	10	Wear, no size available - PLP	
35-38	FS(11)	7	ODI, volumetric	
35-41	1H+ 5	9	MBM/PLP wear	
36-36	FS(10)	5	ODI	
36-56	TSH	7	NQI, volumetric, prt	
37-35	FS(10)	6	ODI, NQI	
38-82	FS(2,3), AVB	6	NQI, ODI, volumetric, wear	
39-85	FS(10,11,17)	8	Lack of RPC data	
39-97	U-bend	8	Permeability	
40-19	TSH	8	MBM/PLP wear	
40-64	1+0 56	6	ODI, volumetric	
41-20	TSH	1	CLP (removed)	
41-64	1+0 57	6	ODI, volumetric	
43-22	TSH	8	MBM/PLP wear	
45-37	19+0 43	6	ODI, volumetric	
46-54	1H+ 5	9	Wear, no size available	
47-80	FS(8)	6	ODI	
48-39	17C+ 15	9	Wear, no size available	
48-67	18+1.7	2	OD	
49-67	18+1 3, 18+2 5	2	OD	

[1] An empty cell indicates that it was not reported whether the tube was stabilized or not

-99-

Table 3-9: Catawba 2: Tubes Plugged for Indications Other Than AVB Wear (cont'd)

Tube	Location	RFO #	Characterization	Stabilized[1]
	STEAM GENERATOR C			
1-5	?	2	?	
1-22	U-bend	10	No plus-point exam in U-bend	
2-30	U-bend	10	Probe lodged in U-bend	
9-35	TSH	6	SAI	
13-15	10-1 7	7	ODI, volumetric	
18-45	TSH	7	ODI, volumetric	
19-85	?	7	?	
20-109	?	7	?	
27-16	FS(1)	5	ODI, volumetric	
31-77	TSH	5	SAI	
32-79	9-1 34	7	ODI, volumetric	
33-24	FS(4,10,12); 9-0 86; 9-2.96	6	ODI, volumetric	
39-20	FS(9,12,13,15)	6	NQI, ODI, volumetric	
39-47	FS(11,13)	6	NQI, volumetric	
39-67	FS(9,10,11,13) 9+1 47	5	NQI, ODI, volumetric	
39-71	8+1 4, FS(12)	5	ODI, volumetric, ADS	
39-75	U-bend, FS(12)	5	ODI, NQI	
39-87	FS(1), 18+ 4	4	OD	
41-65	16+.9, 16+1 4; FS(8,10,18)	5	NQI, ODI, volumetric	
42-61	FS(6); 9+1.6	5	ODI	
42-92	18+ 8; 18+2 4	5	ODI, volumetric	
42-93	?	5	?	
43-34	U-bend, FS(2,5,13)	5	ODI, absolute drift signal (ADS)	
43-91	FS(10)	5	ODI	
46-59	FS(1,13)	5	ODI, volumetric	
46-87	FS(10)	6	ODI	
49-61	5+ 7	4	OD	
49-62	5+.7	4	OD	

[1]An empty cell indicates that it was not reported whether the tube was stabilized or not

Table 3-9: Catawba 2: Tubes Plugged for Indications Other Than AVB Wear (cont'd)

Tube	Location	RFO #	Characterization	Stabilized[1]
	STEAM GENERATOR D			
2-1	FS(14)	7	ODI, volumetric	
2-46	FS(16)	5	NQI, volumetric	
4-43	FS(3,15)	6	ADI, ODI, volumetric	
6-19	FS(8,10)	7	NQI, volumetric	
6-81	FS(12)	8	Data quality	
7-26	FS(7,10,12,13,14)	7	NQI, ODI, volumetric	
9-2	9+1.1, FS(7,10)	5	NQI, ODI	
14-4	FS(7,10)	5	ADS, ODI	
15-29	FS(12)	7	ADI, volumetric	
15-108	TSH	6	NQI	
16-62	8-1.1, FS(7,10)	6	ADI, ODI, volumetric	
17-103	FS(1,4,13)	5	NQI, ODI, volumetric	
19-65	TSH	10	No RPC exam at TTS	
20-40	FS(12)	7	ODI, volumetric	
20-46	FS(12)	7	ODI, volumetric	
20-89	FS(18)	5	ODI	
21-107	FS(18)	5	ODI, volumetric	
21-110	FS(18)	6	ODI, volumetric	
25-43	FS(11,12,13,16)	5	ADS, NQI, volumetric	
25-44	FS(7,10)	5	ODI	
28-81	9-1.2, 9-2 4, FS(10)	6	ODI, volumetric	
29-96	?	3	?	
30-59	9-0 6, FS(7)	6	ODI	
33-16	7H+ 3	9	Wear, no sizing	
33-48	10+/-1.1, 10+0 7, FS(10)	6	ODI, volumetric	
35-93	U-bend	8	Permeability in U-bend	
40-67	FS(8,10)	6	ODI, volumetric	
41-43	U-bend, FS(9,11)	6	NQI, ODI, volumetric	
42-24	FS(10)	5	ODI, volumetric	
43-62	FS(3)	1	ODI, location not indicative of PLP	
48-75	TSH	9	MBM, PLP wear	
49-34	?	3	?	
49-63	TSH	5	SAI	
49-64	TSH	1	CLP (loose part washed away)	

[1]An empty cell indicates that it was not reported whether the tube was stabilized or not

Table 3-10: Comanche Peak 2: Summary of Bobbin Inspections and Tube Plugging

Outage	Completion Date	Cumul. EFPY	SG A Insp.	SG A Plug	SG A DePl	SG B Insp.	SG B Plug	SG B DePl	SG C Insp.	SG C Plug	SG C DePl	SG D Insp.	SG D Plug	SG D DePl	Total Plug	Total DePl	Cumul. Plugged	Percent Plugged	Notes
Pre-op				5			3			3			9		20	0	20	0.11	
RFO 1	11/01/94		1104	0	0	1078	0	0	1062	0	0	1125	0	0	0	0	20	0.11	
RFO 2	03/15/96		2149	0	0							2161	0	0	0	0	20	0.11	
RFO 3	11/14/97		3867	3		4567	5		4567	0		2389	0		8	0	28	0.15	
RFO 4	04/09/99		914	1		914	0		914	0		914	4		5	0	33	0.18	
RFO 5	10/09/00		1927	3								3609	1		4	0	37	0.20	1
Totals:				12	0		8	0		3	0		14	0	37	0			

Plant Data
Model. D5
T-hot (approximate). 618 F
Tubes per steam generator: 4570
Number of steam generators. 4

Acronyms
Pre-op = prior to operation
Cumul. = cumulative
Insp. = number of tubes inspected
Plug = number of tubes plugged
DePl = number of tubes deplugged
RFO = refueling outage

Notes
1. Cycle 5 was 1.433 EFPY.

-102-

Table 3-11: Comanche Peak 2 Causes of Tube Plugging

Cause of Tube Plugging/Outage		Pre-Op	1994 RFO 1	1996 RFO 2	1997 RFO 3	1999 RFO 4	2000 RFO 5	Totals	Totals
Wear	AVB				5		4	9	9
	Pre-heater TSP (D5)							0	
	TSP							0	
Loose Parts	Confirmed				2			2	5
	Not confirmed, periphery					2		2	
	Not confirmed, not periphery					1		1	
Obstruction Restriction	From PSI, no progression							0	2
	Service-induced				1	1		2	
Manufacturing Flaws	Preservice	20						20	20
	Other							0	
Inspection Issues	Probe lodged							0	0
	Data quality							0	
	Dent/geometry							0	
	Permeability							0	
	Not inspected							0	
Other	Top of tubesheet					1		1	1
	Free span							0	
	TSP							0	
	Other/not reported							0	
SCC	ID							0	0
	OD							0	
TOTALS		20	0	0	8	5	4	37	37

Notes:

Table 3-12: Comanche Peak 2: Tubes Plugged for Indications Other Than AVB Wear

STEAM GENERATOR A				
Tube	Location	RFO #	Characterization	Stabilized[1]
34-96	TSH	4	Pit, manufacturing artifact, PLP	
49-53	8H	3	CLP	
49-54	8H	3	CLP	

STEAM GENERATOR B				
Tube	Location	RFO #	Characterization	Stabilized[1]
14-67	TSC	3	Restricted tube	

STEAM GENERATOR C				
Tube	Location	RFO #	Characterization	Stabilized[1]

STEAM GENERATOR D				
Tube	Location	RFO #	Characterization	Stabilized[1]
12-92	6C	4	PLP	
20-106	10H	4	Restricted tube/dent	
36-59	TTS	4	PLP	
37-59	TTS	4	PLP	

[1]An empty cell indicates that it was not reported whether the tube was stabilized or not

Table 3-13: Callaway: Summary of Bobbin Inspections and Tube Plugging (TT Tubes Only)

Outage	Completion Date	Cumul. EFPY	SG A Insp.	SG A Plug	SG A DePl	SG B Insp.	SG B Plug	SG B DePl	SG C Insp.	SG C Plug	SG C DePl	SG D Insp.	SG D Plug	SG D DePl	Total Plug	Total DePl	Cumul. Plugged	Percent Plugged	Notes
Pre-op				2			0			0			2		4	0	4	0.08	
RFO 1	04/07/87														0	0	4	0.08	1
Mid-Cycle	10/02/87					243	0	0	243	0	0				0	0	4	0.08	2
RFO 2			728	1	0							728	0	0	1	0	5	0.10	3
RFO 3	04/24/89		1211	0	0	1214	0	0	1214	1	0	1212	0	0	1	0	6	0.12	
RFO 4	10/23/90														0	0	6	0.12	
RFO 5	04/28/92		1211	0	0	1214	0	0	1213	1	0	1212	0	0	1	0	7	0.14	
RFO 6	10/28/93														0	0	7	0.14	
RFO 7	05/01/95		1211	0	0	1214	2	0	1212	1	0	1211	1	0	4	0	11	0.23	4
RFO 8	11/11/96			1			2			2					5	0	16	0.33	4,5
RFO 9	04/01/98		1210	0	0	1210	0	0	1210	0	0	1210	0	0	0	0	16	0.33	4
RFO 10	11/05/99														0	0	16	0.33	4,6
RFO 11	05/21/01					1210	0	0	1210	1	0		1		1	0	17	0.35	4
Totals:				4	0		4	0		5	0		4	0	17	0			

Plant Data
Model: F
T-hot (approximate): 618 F
Tubes per steam generator: 5626 (1214 are TT)
Number of steam generators: 4

Acronyms
Pre-op = prior to operation
Cumul. = cumulative
Insp. = number of tubes inspected
Plug = number of tubes plugged
DePl = number of tubes deplugged
RFO = refueling outage
TT = thermally treated

Notes
1. Inspection reports for RFO 1 could not be readily located. Based on information contained in other reports, no TT tubes were plugged.
2. Assumed 20% of TT tubes were inspected since 20% of steam generator (SG) was inspected.
3. Assumed 60% of TT tubes were inspected since 60% of steam generator was inspected. Licensee elected to perform SG inspections during a planned maintenance outage.
4. Various portions of tubes in all steam generators were inspected with a rotating probe.
5. 3 tubes were repaired with laser welded sleeves: 1 in steam generator A, 2 in steam generator C.
6. 3 tubes in steam generator C were repaired by electrosleeving.

Table 3-14: Callaway Causes of Tube Plugging (Thermally Treated Tubes Only)

Cause of Tube Plugging/Outage		Pre-Op	1987 RFO 1	1987 Mid-Cyc	1987 RFO 2	1989 RFO 3	1990 RFO 4	1992 RFO 5	1993 RFO 6	1995 RFO 7	1996 RFO 8	1998 RFO 9	1999 RFO 10	2001 RFO 11	Totals
Wear	AVB														0
	Pre-heater TSP (D5)														0
	TSP														0
Loose Parts	Confirmed														2
	Not confirmed, periphery									2					
	Not confirmed, not periphery														0
Obstruction Restriction	From PSI, no progression														0
	Service-induced														0
Manufacturing Flaws	Preservice	4													4
	Other														0
Inspection Issues	Probe lodged														0
	Data quality														0
	Dent/geometry														0
	Permeability														0
	Not inspected														0
Other	Top of tubesheet										3			1	4
	Free span					1				2	2				5
	TSP				1			1							2
	Other/not reported														0
SCC	ID														0
	OD														0
TOTALS		4	0	0	1	1	0	1	0	4	5	0	0	1	17
Notes:										1		2		

Notes

1. 3 thermally treated tubes were repaired by inserting laser welded sleeves. These tubes are not reflected in the totals
2. 3 thermally treated tubes were repaired by electrosleeving These tubes are not reflected in the totals.

Table 3-15: Callaway: Tubes Plugged for Indications Other Than AVB Wear
(Thermally Treated Tubes only)

STEAM GENERATOR A				
Tube	Location	RFO #	Characterization	Stabilized[1]
2-87	TSH+3 47	8	Single volumetric indication	N
3-44	7H	2	45% through-wall indication	
8-115	TSH-0 06	8	Tube sleeved, single circumferential indication	

STEAM GENERATOR B				
Tube	Location	RFO #	Characterization	Stabilized[1]
1-100	TSH-0 11	8	Single circumferential indication	Y
1-119	TSH+3 89	8	Single volumetric indication	N
1-120	TSC+4 02	7	38% wall thinning, PLP	N
1-121	TSC+3 66	7	45% wall thinning, PLP	N

[1]An empty cell indicates that it was not reported whether the tube was stabilized or not

Table 3-15 Callaway: Tubes Plugged for Indications Other Than AVB Wear (cont'd)
(Thermally Treated Tubes only)

STEAM GENERATOR C				
Tube	Location	RFO #	Charactenzation	Stabilized[1]
1-1	1C	7	Obstruction, damage due to chemical cleaning equipment	N
2-6	TSH+0 07	8	Single axial indication	N
2-10	TSH-0.01	11	Single axial indication	N
2-98	7C+1.5	5	Undefined indication 1 5 inches above 7th cold-leg tube support	
4-11	FBC	3	Single axial indication	
1-5	TSH+0 12	10	Tube electrosleeved (8"), single volumetric indication	
9-64	TSH+0 24	10	Tube electrosleeved (8"), single volumetric indication	
10-48	TSH+0.17	8	Tube sleeved (laser welded), single volumetric indication	
10-70	TSH-0 08	8	Tube sleeved (laser welded), single circumferential indication	
10-93	TSH+0 23 to 0 91	10	Tube electrosleeved (8"), single volumetric indication	

STEAM GENERATOR D				
Tube	Location	RFO #	Characterization	Stabilized[1]
1-1	TSC+17 25	7	Dent, damage due to chemical cleaning equipment	N
7-102	TSH+0.18	8	Single volumetric indication	N

[1]An empty cell indicates that it was not reported whether the tube was stabilized or not

Table 3-16: Millstone 3: Summary of Bobbin Inspections and Tube Plugging

Outage	Completion Date	Cumul. EFPY	SG A Insp.	SG A Plug	SG A DePl	SG B Insp.	SG B Plug	SG B DePl	SG C Insp.	SG C Plug	SG C DePl	SG D Insp.	SG D Plug	SG D DePl	Total Plug	Total DePl	Cumul. Plugged	Percent Plugged	Notes
Pre-op				3			3			3			1		10	0	10	0.04	
RFO 1	11/24/87		543	1		501	0		506	0		504	1		2	0	12	0.05	
RFO 2	05/29/89		2431	4					2358	0					4	0	16	0.07	
RFO 3	02/21/91					3555	0					3546	5		5	0	21	0.09	
RFO 4	08/21/93		4350	6					3660	1					7	0	28	0.12	
RFO 5	05/09/95					4237	1					4236	10		11	0	39	0.17	
Mid-Cycle	10/01/96								5622	2					2	0	41	0.18	1
RFO 6	05/17/99		5612	12					5620	2		42	0		14	0	55	0.24	
RFO 7	02/18/01					5622	0					5609	51		51	0	106	0.47	
Totals:				26	0		4	0		8	0		68	0	106	0			

Plant Data
Model: F
T-hot (approximate): 617 F
Tubes per steam generator: 5626
Number of steam generators: 4

Acronyms
Pre-op = prior to operation
Cumul. = cumulative
Insp. = number of tubes inspected
Plug = number of tubes plugged
DePl = number of tubes deplugged
RFO = refueling outage

Notes
1. Licensee elected to perform steam generator tube inspections during an extended shutdown period.

Table 3-17: Millstone 3 Causes of Tube Plugging

Cause of Tube Plugging/Outage		Pre-Op	1987 RFO 1	1989 RFO 2	1991 RFO 3	1993 RFO 4	1995 RFO 5	1996 Mid-Cyc	1999 RFO 6	2001 RFO 7	Totals	Totals
Wear	AVB		2	3	5	7	11	2	13	15	58	58
	Pre-heater TSP (D5)										0	
	TSP										0	
Loose Parts	Confirmed											8
	Not confirmed, periphery								1	6	7	
	Not confirmed, not periphery									1	1	
Obstruction Restriction	From PSI, no progression										0	0
	Service-induced										0	
Manufacturing Flaws	Preservice	10									10	10
	Other										0	
Inspection Issues	Probe lodged										0	0
	Data quality										0	
	Dent/geometry										0	
	Permeability										0	
	Not inspected										0	
Other	Top of tubesheet									13	13	30
	Free span			1						3	4	
	TSP									13	13	
	Other/not reported										0	
SCC	ID										0	0
	OD										0	
TOTALS		10	2	4	5	7	11	2	14	51	106	106
Notes:										1		

Notes

1. One tube had both a volumetric indication at the top of the tubesheet and an AVB wear indication The tube was included under "Other, Top of Tubesheet."

Table 3-18: Millstone 3: Tubes Plugged for Indications Other Than AVB Wear

STEAM GENERATOR A				
Tube	Location	RFO #	Characterization	Stabilized[1]
1-122	8H+10 56	2	36% throughwall, distorted eddy current signal	
20-6	TSH+0 07	6	Volumetric - possible loose part	

STEAM GENERATOR B				
Tube	Location	RFO #	Characterization	Stabilized[1]

STEAM GENERATOR C				
Tube	Location	RFO #	Characterization	Stabilized[1]

[1]An empty cell indicates that it was not reported whether the tube was stabilized or not.

Table 3-18: Millstone 3: Tubes Plugged for Indications Other Than AVB Wear (cont'd)

Tube	Location	RFO #	Characterization	Stabilized[1]
			STEAM GENERATOR D	
1-119	TSH+13 94	7	Volumetric	N
1-120	TSH+14.11	7	Volumetric	N
1-121	TSH+14 09	7	Volumetric	N
15-18	TSH+0 27	7	Possible loose part (not in periphery of bundle)	N
35-23	TSH+0 09	7	Volumetric - possibly manufacturing related	N
37-23	TSH+0 15	7	Volumetric - possibly manufacturing related	N
37-24	TSH+0.15	7	Volumetric - possibly manufacturing related	N
38-107	1C+1 45	7	Volumetric - possible loose part	N
39-107	1C+1 52	7	Volumetric - possible loose part	N
42-23	TSH+0 16	7	Volumetric - possibly manufacturing related	N
43-23	TSH+0.11	7	Volumetric - possible manufacturing related and AVB wear	N
43-24	TSH+0.14	7	Volumetric - possibly manufacturing related	N
44-23	TSH+0.13	7	Volumetric - possibly manufacturing related	N
44-24	TSH+0 14	7	Volumetric - possibly manufacturing related	N
45-23	TSH+0.15	7	Volumetric - possibly manufacturing related	N
45-24	TSH+0.13	7	Volumetric - possibly manufacturing related	N
52-53	TSC+0 81	7	Volumetric (not in periphery of bundle)	N
52-54	TSC+0 25	7	Volumetric (not in periphery of bundle)	N
53-54	TSC+0 01	7	Volumetric (not in periphery of bundle)	N
53-79	1C+0 9	7	Volumetric - possible loose part	N
54-45	1C+0 5	7	Volumetric	N
54-79	1C+0 51	7	Possible loose part	N
54-80	1C+0 43	7	Volumetric - possible loose part	N
54-81	1C+0.48	7	Possible loose part	N
55-45	1C+0 58	7	Volumetric	N
55-46	1C+0 77	7	Volumetric	N
57-74	1C+1 01	7	Volumetric - possible loose part	N
57-75	1C+0 58	7	Possible loose part	N
57-79	1H+0 91	7	Volumetric - possible loose part	N
58-54	1C+0 56	7	Volumetric	N
58-55	1C+0 70	7	Volumetric - possible loose part	N
58-56	1C+0 69	7	Volumetric	N
58-74		7	Possible loose part	N
58-75	1C+0 64	7	Volumetric - possible loose part	N
59-55	1C+0 68	7	Possible loose part	N
59-56	1C+0 61	7	Possible loose part	N

[1]An empty cell indicates that it was not reported whether the tube was stabilized or not.

Table 3-19: Seabrook: Summary of Bobbin Inspections and Tube Plugging

Outage	Completion Date	Cumul. EFPY	SG A			SG B			SG C			SG D			Total Plug	Total DePI	Cumul. Plugged	Percent Plugged	Notes
			Insp.	Plug	DePI	Insp.	Plug	DePI	Insp.	Plug	DePI	Insp.	Plug	DePI					
Pre-op				4			4			5			0		13	0	13	0.06	1
RFO 1	08/28/91		1797	0		1761	1		1747	8		1884	1		10	0	23	0.10	
RFO 2	10/01/92		2409	0		2327	1		2337	0		2400	0		0	0	23	0.10	
RFO 3	05/12/94					2327	1			0			0		1	0	24	0.11	
RFO 4	11/27/95		2424	8								2443	4		12	0	36	0.16	
RFO 5	06/10/97					5620	9		5613	4					13	0	49	0.22	2
RFO 6	04/20/99		5614	5								5621	20		25	0	74	0.33	
RFO 7	11/09/00					5611	7		5609	9					16	0	90	0.40	
Totals:				17	0		22	0		26	0		25	0	90	0			

Plant Data
Model: F
T-hot (approximate):
Tubes per steam generator: 5626
Number of steam generators: 4

Notes
1. Based on data contained in RFO 4 reports.
2. Between RFO 3 and 5, the plant operated for 32 EFPM

Acronyms
Pre-op = prior to operation
Cumul. = cumulative
Insp. = number of tubes inspected
Plug = number of tubes plugged
DePI = number of tubes deplugged
RFO = refueling outage

Table 3-20: Seabrook Causes of Tube Plugging

Cause of Tube Plugging/Outage		Pre-Op	1991 RFO 1	1992 RFO 2	1994 RFO 3	1995 RFO 4	1997 RFO 5	1999 RFO 6	2000 RFO 7	Totals	Totals
Wear	AVB		4		1	12	7	25	13	62	62
	Pre-heater TSP (D5)									0	
	TSP									0	
Loose Parts	Confirmed		4				4			8	13
	Not confirmed, periphery								1	1	
	Not confirmed, not periphery						2		2	4	
Obstruction Restriction	From PSI, no progression									0	0
	Service-induced									0	
Manufacturing Flaws	Preservice	13								13	13
	Other									0	
Inspection Issues	Probe lodged									0	0
	Data quality									0	
	Dent/geometry									0	
	Permeability									0	
	Not inspected									0	
Other	Top of tubesheet									0	2
	Free span		2							2	
	TSP									0	
	Other/not reported									0	
SCC	ID									0	0
	OD									0	
TOTALS		13	10	0	1	12	13	25	16	90	90

Notes:

Notes

Table 3-21: Seabrook: Tubes Plugged for Indications Other Than AVB Wear

STEAM GENERATOR A				
Tube	Location	RFO #	Characterization	Stabilized[1]

STEAM GENERATOR B				
Tube	Location	RFO #	Characterization	Stabilized[1]
27-24	FS (6H)	1	37% throughwall, high wall loss indication - MBM	
43-97	TSH	5	Confirmed loose part - part not removed	
43-98	TSH	5	Confirmed loose part - part not removed	
43-99	TSH	5	Confirmed loose part - part not removed	
43-100	TSH	5	Confirmed loose part - part not removed	

STEAM GENERATOR C				
Tube	Location	RFO #	Characterization	Stabilized[1]
1-11	TSH + 19 06	7	Volumetric - possible loose part	
11-120	FS (7C)	1	High wall loss	
22-12	5C	5	Volumetric - possible loose part (not in periphery of bundle)	
22-13	5C	5	Volumetric - possible loose part (not in periphery of bundle)	
31-12		1	Confirmed loose part - part not removed	
31-13		1	Confirmed loose part - part not removed	
32-12		1	Confirmed loose part - part not removed	
32-13		1	Confirmed loose part - part not removed	
43-28	TSH + 0.04	7	Volumetric - possible loose part (not in periphery of bundle)	
44-28	TSH + 0 06	7	Possible loose part (not in periphery of bundle)	

STEAM GENERATOR D				
Tube	Location	RFO #	Characterization	Stabilized[1]

[1]An empty cell indicates that it was not reported whether the tube was stabilized or not

-115-

Table 3-22: Vogtle 1: Summary of Bobbin Inspections and Tube Plugging

Outage	Completion Date	Cumul. EFPY	SG A Insp.	SG A Plug	SG A DePl	SG B Insp.	SG B Plug	SG B DePl	SG C Insp.	SG C Plug	SG C DePl	SG D Insp.	SG D Plug	SG D DePl	Total Plug	Total DePl	Cumul. Plugged	Percent Plugged	Notes
Pre-op				0				0		2			4		6	0	6	0.03	
RFO 1	10/22/88		754	1		821						821	0		1	0	7	0.03	
RFO 2	03/11/90		1514	0		2357	4		2403	0		1471	0		4	0	11	0.05	
RFO 3	10/08/91		1067	0		1050	0		1078	0		1011	0		0	0	11	0.05	
RFO 4	04/03/93					2951	0		2934	4					4	0	15	0.07	
RFO 5	10/01/94		4224	0		4213	4		4231	5		4220	3		12	0	27	0.12	
RFO 6	03/22/96		3387	4								3395	0		4	0	31	0.14	
RFO 7	10/05/97					5618	3		5615	6		5619	6		15	0	46	0.20	
RFO 8	03/15/99	10.06	5621	0								5613	0		0	0	46	0.20	1
RFO 9	10/11/00					5615	0		5609	2					2	0	48	0.21	2
																			3
Totals:				5	0		11	0		19	0		13	0	48	0			

Plant Data
Model: F
T-hot (approximate) 618 F
Tubes per steam generator: 5626
Number of steam generators 4

Acronyms
Pre-op = prior to operation
Cumul. = cumulative
Insp. = number of tubes inspected
Plug = number of tubes plugged
DePl = number of tubes deplugged
RFO = refueling outage

Notes
1. 949 EFPD between RFO 6 and RFO 8
2. 2.9 EFPY between RFO 7 and RFO 9.
3. RFO 8 to RFO 10 projected to be 2.77 EFPY, Expect cumulative time to be 12.83 EFPY

Table 3-23: Vogtle 1 Causes of Tube Plugging

Cause of Tube Plugging/Outage		Pre-Op	1988 RFO 1	1990 RFO 2	1991 RFO 3	1993 RFO 4	1994 RFO 5	1996 RFO 6	1997 RFO 7	1999 RFO 8	2000 RFO 9	Totals
Wear	AVB											
	Pre-heater TSP (D5)			4		4	12	4	12		1	37
	TSP											
Loose Parts	Confirmed											
	Not confirmed, periphery								1			1
	Not confirmed, not periphery											
Obstruction Restriction	From PSI, no progression											
	Service-Induced								2			2
Manufacturing Flaws	Preservice	6										6
	Other											
Inspection Issues	Probe lodged											
	Data quality											
	Dent/geometry											
	Permeability											
	Not Inspected											
Other	Top of tubesheet										1	1
	Free span		1									1
	TSP											
	Other/not reported											
SCC	ID											
	OD											
TOTALS		6	1	4	0	4	12	4	15	0	2	48

Notes:

<u>Notes</u>

Table 3-24: Vogtle 1: Tubes Plugged for Indications Other Than AVB Wear

STEAM GENERATOR A				
Tube	Location	RFO #	Characterization	Stabilized[1]
28-37	5H+7 0 4C+38 0	1	39% throughwall indication	

STEAM GENERATOR B				
Tube	Location	RFO #	Characterization	Stabilized[1]

STEAM GENERATOR C				
Tube	Location	RFO #	Characterization	Stabilized[1]
21-13	TSH+0 21	9	Volumetric	

STEAM GENERATOR D				
Tube	Location	RFO #	Characterization	Stabilized[1]
1-31	U-bend	7	Obstruction to a 0 520-inch probe	
4-3	TSH	7	Confirmed loose part - part not removed	
4-4	U-bend	7	Obstruction to a 0 520-inch probe	

[1]An empty cell indicates that it was not reported whether the tube was stabilized or not

Table 3-25: Vogtle 2: Summary of Bobbin Inspections and Tube Plugging

Outage	Completion Date	Cumul. EFPY	SG A Insp.	SG A Plug	SG A DePl	SG B Insp.	SG B Plug	SG B DePl	SG C Insp.	SG C Plug	SG C DePl	SG D Insp.	SG D Plug	SG D DePl	Total Plug	Total DePl	Cumul. Plugged	Percent Plugged	Notes
Pre-op				2			4			1			8		15	0	15	0.07	
RFO 1	10/03/90		1143	0	0	1130	0	0	1139	0	0	1135	0	0	0	0	15	0.07	
RFO 2	03/30/92		1056	0	0	1570	0	0	1066	0	0	1061	0	0	0	0	15	0.07	
RFO 3	10/02/93		2984	0								3008	0		0	0	15	0.07	
RFO 4	03/16/95					4382	3		4576	0					3	0	18	0.08	
RFO 5	09/30/96		5624	1								5618	5		6	0	24	0.11	
RFO 6	04/02/98					5619	0		5625	0					0	0	24	0.11	1
RFO 7	10/22/99		5623	1								5613	4		5	0	29	0.13	
RFO 8	04/24/01					5619	0		5625	0					0	0	29	0.13	2
Totals:				4	0		7	0		1	0		17	0	29	0			

Acronyms
Pre-op = prior to operation
Cumul. = cumulative
Insp. = number of tubes inspected
Plug = number of tubes plugged
DePl = number of tubes deplugged
RFO = refueling outage

Plant Data
Model: F
T-hot (approximate): 618 F
Tubes per steam generator: 5626
Number of steam generators: 4

Notes
1. 1015 EFPD between RFO 4 to RFO 6.
2. 2.7 EFPY between RFO 5 to RFO 7.

Table 3-17: Millstone 3 Causes of Tube Plugging

Cause of Tube Plugging/Outage		Pre-Op	1987 RFO 1	1989 RFO 2	1991 RFO 3	1993 RFO 4	1995 RFO 5	1996 Mid-Cyc	1999 RFO 6	2001 RFO 7	Totals	Totals
Wear	AVB		2	3	5	7	11	2	13	15	58	58
	Pre-heater TSP (D5)										0	
	TSP										0	
Loose Parts	Confirmed										0	8
	Not confirmed, periphery								1	6	7	
	Not confirmed, not periphery									1	1	
Obstruction Restriction	From PSI, no progression										0	0
	Service-induced										0	
Manufacturing Flaws	Preservice	10									10	10
	Other										0	
Inspection Issues	Probe lodged										0	0
	Data quality										0	
	Dent/geometry										0	
	Permeability										0	
	Not inspected										0	
Other	Top of tubesheet									13	13	30
	Free span			1						3	4	
	TSP									13	13	
	Other/not reported										0	
SCC	ID										0	0
	OD										0	
TOTALS		10	2	4	5	7	11	2	14	51	106	106

Notes:	1

Notes
1. One tube had both a volumetric indication at the top of the tubesheet and an AVB wear indication. The tube was included under "Other, Top of Tubesheet."

Table 3-19: Seabrook: Summary of Bobbin Inspections and Tube Plugging

Outage	Completion Date	Cumul. EFPY	SG A Insp.	SG A Plug	SG A DePI	SG B Insp.	SG B Plug	SG B DePI	SG C Insp.	SG C Plug	SG C DePI	SG D Insp.	SG D Plug	SG D DePI	Total Plug	Total DePI	Cumul. Plugged	Percent Plugged	Notes
Pre-op				4			4			5			0		13	0	13	0.06	1
RFO 1	08/28/91		1797	0	0	1761	1	1	1747	8		1884	1	0	10	0	23	0.10	
RFO 2	10/01/92		2409	0	0							2400	0	0	0	0	23	0.10	
RFO 3	05/12/94					2327	1		2337	0					1	0	24	0.11	
RFO 4	11/27/95		2424	8								2443	4		12	0	36	0.16	
RFO 5	06/10/97					5620	9		5613	4					13	0	49	0.22	2
RFO 6	04/20/99		5614	5								5621	20		25	0	74	0.33	
RFO 7	11/09/00					5611	7		5609	9					16	0	90	0.40	
Totals:				17	0		22	0		26	0		25	0	90	0			

Plant Data
Model: F
T-hot (approximate):
Tubes per steam generator: 5626
Number of steam generators: 4

Notes
1. Based on data contained in RFO 4 reports.
2. Between RFO 3 and 5, the plant operated for 32 EFPM

Acronyms
Pre-op = prior to operation
Cumul. = cumulative
Insp. = number of tubes inspected
Plug = number of tubes plugged
DePI = number of tubes deplugged
RFO = refueling outage

Table 3-20: Seabrook Causes of Tube Plugging

Cause of Tube Plugging/Outage		Pre-Op	1991 RFO 1	1992 RFO 2	1994 RFO 3	1995 RFO 4	1997 RFO 5	1999 RFO 6	2000 RFO 7	Totals	Totals
Wear	AVB		4		1	12	7	25	13	62	62
	Pre-heater TSP (D5)									0	
	TSP									0	
Loose Parts	Confirmed		4				4			8	13
	Not confirmed, periphery								1	1	
	Not confirmed, not periphery						2		2	4	
Obstruction Restriction	From PSI, no progression									0	0
	Service-induced									0	
Manufacturing Flaws	Preservice	13								13	13
	Other									0	
Inspection Issues	Probe lodged									0	0
	Data quality									0	
	Dent/geometry									0	
	Permeability									0	
	Not inspected									0	
Other	Top of tubesheet									0	2
	Free span		2							2	
	TSP									0	
	Other/not reported									0	
SCC	ID									0	0
	OD									0	
TOTALS		13	10	0	1	12	13	25	16	90	90

Notes:

Notes

Table 3-22: Vogtle 1: Summary of Bobbin Inspections and Tube Plugging

Outage	Completion Date	Cumul. EFPY	SG A Insp.	SG A Plug	SG A DePl	SG B Insp.	SG B Plug	SG B DePl	SG C Insp.	SG C Plug	SG C DePl	SG D Insp.	SG D Plug	SG D DePl	Total Plug	Total DePl	Cumul. Plugged	Percent Plugged	Notes
Pre-op				0			0			2			4		6	0	6	0.03	
RFO 1	10/22/88		754	1								821	0		1	0	7	0.03	
RFO 2	03/11/90		1514	0		2357	4		2403	0		1471	0		4	0	11	0.05	
RFO 3	10/08/91		1067	0		1050	0		1078	0		1011	0		0	0	11	0.05	
RFO 4	04/03/93					2951	0		2934	4					4	0	15	0.07	
RFO 5	10/01/94		4224	0		4213	4		4231	5		4220	3		12	0	27	0.12	
RFO 6	03/22/96		3387	4								3395	0		4	0	31	0.14	
RFO 7	10/05/97					5618	3		5615	6		5619	6		15	0	46	0.20	
RFO 8	03/15/99	10.06	5621	0								5613	0		0	0	46	0.20	1
RFO 9	10/11/00					5615	0		5609	2					2	0	48	0.21	2
																			3
Totals:				5	0		11	0		19	0		13	0	48	0			

Acronyms
Pre-op = prior to operation
Cumul. = cumulative
Insp. = number of tubes inspected
Plug = number of tubes plugged
DePl = number of tubes deplugged
RFO = refueling outage

Plant Data
Model: F
T-hot (approximate) 618 F
Tubes per steam generator: 5626
Number of steam generators 4

Notes
1. 949 EFPD between RFO 6 and RFO 8
2. 2.9 EFPY between RFO 7 and RFO 9.
3. RFO 8 to RFO 10 projected to be 2.77 EFPY. Expect cumulative time to be 12.83 EFPY

Table 3-23: Vogtle 1 Causes of Tube Plugging

Cause of Tube Plugging/Outage		Pre-Op	1988 RFO 1	1990 RFO 2	1991 RFO 3	1993 RFO 4	1994 RFO 5	1996 RFO 6	1997 RFO 7	1999 RFO 8	2000 RFO 9	Totals
Wear	AVB			4		4	12	4	12		1	37
	Pre-heater TSP (D5)											0
	TSP											0
Loose Parts	Confirmed								1			1
	Not confirmed, periphery											0
	Not confirmed, not periphery											0
Obstruction Restriction	From PSI, no progression											0
	Service-Induced								2			2
Manufacturing Flaws	Preservice	6										6
Inspection Issues	Other											0
	Probe lodged											
	Data quality											
	Dent/geometry											
	Permeability											
	Not inspected											
Other	Top of tubesheet											
	Free span		1								1	2
	TSP											
	Other/not reported											
SCC	ID											0
	OD											0
TOTALS		6	1	4	0	4	12	4	15	0	2	48

Totals summary:

Totals	Totals
37	37
0	
0	
1	1
0	
0	
0	2
2	
6	6
0	0
0	
0	
0	
0	
0	
1	2
1	
0	
0	0
0	
48	**48**

Notes:

Notes

Table 3-25: Vogtle 2: Summary of Bobbin Inspections and Tube Plugging

Outage	Completion Date	Cumul. EFPY	SG A Insp.	SG A Plug	SG A DePl	SG B Insp.	SG B Plug	SG B DePl	SG C Insp.	SG C Plug	SG C DePl	SG D Insp.	SG D Plug	SG D DePl	Total Plug	Total DePl	Cumul. Plugged	Percent Plugged	Notes
Pre-op				2			4			1			8		15	0	15	0.07	
RFO 1	10/03/90		1143	0		1130	0		1139	0		1135	0		0	0	15	0.07	
RFO 2	03/30/92		1056	0		1570	0		1066	0		1061	0		0	0	15	0.07	
RFO 3	10/02/93		2984	0								3008	0		0	0	15	0.07	
RFO 4	03/16/95					4382	3		4576	0					3	0	18	0.08	
RFO 5	09/30/96		5624	1		5619	0		5625	0		5618	5		6	0	24	0.11	
RFO 6	04/02/98														0	0	24	0.11	1
RFO 7	10/22/99		5623	1		5619	0		5625	0		5613	4		5	0	29	0.13	2
RFO 8	04/24/01														0	0	29	0.13	
Totals:				4	0		7	0		1	0		17	0	29	0			

Plant Data
Model: F
T-hot (approximate): 618 F
Tubes per steam generator: 5626
Number of steam generators: 4

Notes
1. 1015 EFPD between RFO 4 to RFO 6.
2. 2.7 EFPY between RFO 5 to RFO 7.

Acronyms
Pre-op = prior to operation
Cumul. = cumulative
Insp. = number of tubes inspected
Plug = number of tubes plugged
DePl = number of tubes deplugged
RFO = refueling outage

Table 3-26: Vogtle 2 Causes of Tube Plugging

Cause of Tube Plugging/Outage		Pre-Op	1990 RFO 1	1992 RFO 2	1993 RFO 3	1995 RFO 4	1996 RFO 5	1998 RFO 6	1999 RFO 7	2001 RFO 8	Totals	Totals
Wear	AVB											14
	Pre-heater TSP (D5)					3	6		5		14	
	TSP										0	
Loose Parts	Confirmed										0	0
	Not confirmed, periphery										0	
	Not confirmed, not periphery										0	
Obstruction Restriction	From PSI, no progression										0	0
	Service-induced										0	
Manufacturing Flaws	Preservice	15									15	15
	Other										0	
Inspection Issues	Probe lodged										0	0
	Data quality										0	
	Dent/geometry										0	
	Permeability										0	
	Not inspected										0	
Other	Top of tubesheet										0	0
	Free span										0	
	TSP										0	
	Other/not reported										0	
SCC	ID										0	0
	OD										0	
TOTALS		15	0	0	0	3	6	0	5	0	29	29

Notes:

Notes

Table 3-27: Vogtle 2: Tubes Plugged for Indications Other Than AVB Wear

STEAM GENERATOR A				
Tube	Location	RFO #	Characterization	Stabilized[1]

STEAM GENERATOR B				
Tube	Location	RFO #	Characterization	Stabilized[1]

STEAM GENERATOR C				
Tube	Location	RFO #	Characterization	Stabilized[1]

STEAM GENERATOR D				
Tube	Location	RFO #	Characterization	Stabilized[1]

[1]An empty cell indicates that it was not reported whether the tube was stabilized or not.

Table 3-28: Wolf Creek: Summary of Bobbin Inspections and Tube Plugging

Outage	Completion Date	Cumul. EFPY	SG A Insp.	SG A Plug	SG A DePl	SG B Insp.	SG B Plug	SG B DePl	SG C Insp.	SG C Plug	SG C DePl	SG D Insp.	SG D Plug	SG D DePl	Total Plug	Total DePl	Cumul. Plugged	Percent Plugged	Notes
Pre-op				8			3			4					15	0	15	0.07	
RFO 1	10/27/86	0.68				393	0		384	0					0	0	15	0.07	
RFO 2		1.66													0	0	15	0.07	1
RFO 3	11/18/88	2.33	2969	1		2972	1		2973	3		2975	17		22	0	37	0.16	
RFO 4	04/04/90	3.47				3205	0					3169	2		2	0	39	0.17	
RFO 5	10/24/91	4.69	1565	0					1227	2	2				2	2	39	0.17	
RFO 6	03/31/93	5.71				5623	5								5	0	44	0.20	
RFO 7	10/11/94	6.98	5617	9								5607	24	6	33	6	71	0.32	
RFO 8	03/05/96					5617	12		5619	4					16	0	87	0.39	
RFO 9	11/06/97		5608	5								5589	14		19	0	106	0.47	
RFO 10	04/24/99					5605	1		5615	5					6	0	112	0.50	
RFO 11	10/20/00		5603	3								5575	29		32	0	144	0.64	
Totals:				26	0		22	0		18	2		86	6	152	8			

Plant Data
Model: F
T-hot (approximate): 618 F
Tubes per steam generator: 5626
Number of steam generators: 4

Acronyms
Pre-op = prior to operation
Cumul = cumulative
Insp = number of tubes inspected
Plug = number of tubes plugged
DePl = number of tubes deplugged
RFO = refueling outage

Notes
1. No tube inspections were performed during RFO 2.

-122-

Table 3-29: Wolf Creek Causes of Tube Plugging

Cause of Tube Plugging/Outage		Pre-Op	1986 RFO 1	RFO 2	1988 RFO 3	1990 RFO 4	1991 RFO 5	1993 RFO 6	1994 RFO 7	1996 RFO 8	1997 RFO 9	1999 RFO 10	2000 RFO 11	Totals	Totals
Wear	AVB				19	2	2	5	25	16	19	6	30	124	124
	Pre-heater TSP (D5)													0	
	TSP													0	
Loose Parts	Confirmed													0	0
	Not confirmed, periphery													0	
	Not confirmed, not periphery													0	
Obstruction Restriction	From PSI, no progression													0	0
	Service-induced													0	
Manufacturing Flaws	Preservice	15												15	15
	Other													0	
Inspection Issues	Probe lodged													0	0
	Data quality													0	
	Dent/geometry													0	
	Permeability													0	
	Not inspected													0	
Other	Top of tubesheet												1	1	5
	Free span				3		-2							1	
	TSP								2				1	3	
	Other/not reported													0	
SCC	ID													0	0
	OD													0	
TOTALS		15	0	0	22	2	1	5	27	16	19	6	32	144	144
Notes:							1		2						

Notes
1. Deplugged 2 Free Span indications originally plugged during RFO 3 (R28C56, R28C76)
2. Deplugged 6 previously plugged AVB wear indications. Plugged 31 other AVB wear indications for a net total of 25 tubes plugged for AVB wear.

Table 3-30: Wolf Creek: Tubes Plugged for Indications Other Than AVB Wear

STEAM GENERATOR A				
Tube	Location	RFO #	Characterization	Stabilized[1]
15-68	1H-0 81	7	55% throughwall indication	
45-91	TSH-0 07	11	Volumetric	

STEAM GENERATOR B				
Tube	Location	RFO #	Characterization	Stabilized[1]

STEAM GENERATOR C				
Tube	Location	RFO #	Characterization	Stabilized[1]
14-17	6H+9 26	3	36% throughwall	
28-56	FBH+16 75	3	37% throughwall indication, deplugged in RFO 5	
28-76	FBC+14 28	3	45% throughwall indication, deplugged in RFO 5	

STEAM GENERATOR D				
Tube	Location	RFO #	Characterization	Stabilized[1]
7-88	4H+0 54	11	Volumetric	
19-93	2C+0 08	7	Volumetric	

[1]An empty cell indicates that it was not reported whether the tube was stabilized or not.

Table 3-31: Indian Point 2: Summary of Bobbin Inspections and Tube Plugging

Outage	Completion Date	Cumul. EFPY	SG A Insp.	SG A Plug	SG A DePl	SG B Insp.	SG B Plug	SG B DePl	SG C Insp.	SG C Plug	SG C DePl	SG D Insp.	SG D Plug	SG D DePl	Total Plug	Total DePl	Cumul. Plugged	Percent Plugged	Notes
Pre-op					0		0	0		0	0		2	2	2	0	2	0.02	
																		0.00	
																		0.00	
																		0.00	
																		0.00	
																		0.00	
																		0.00	
																		0.00	
																		0.00	
																		0.00	
Totals:			0	0	0	0	0	0	0	0	0	2	2	0	2	0			

Plant Data
Model: 44F
T-hot (approximate)
Tubes per steam generator: 3214
Number of steam generators: 4

Notes

Acronyms
Pre-op = prior to operation
Cumul = cumulative
Insp. = number of tubes inspected
Plug = number of tubes plugged
DePl = number of tubes deplugged
RFO = refueling outage

-125-

Table 3-32: Indian Point 2 Causes of Tube Plugging

Cause of Tube Plugging/Outage		Year Pre-Op	Totals	Totals
Wear	AVB		0	0
	Pre-heater TSP (D5)		0	
	TSP		0	
Loose Parts	Confirmed		0	0
	Not confirmed, periphery			
	Not confirmed, not periphery		0	
Obstruction Restriction	From PSI, no progression		0	0
	Service-induced		0	
Manufacturing Flaws	Preservice	2	2	2
	Other		0	
Inspection Issues	Probe lodged		0	0
	Data quality		0	
	Dent/geometry		0	
	Permeability		0	
	Not inspected		0	
Other	Top of tubesheet		0	0
	Free span		0	
	TSP		0	
	Other/not reported		0	
SCC	ID		0	0
	OD		0	
TOTALS		2	2	2

Notes:

Notes

-126-

Table 3-33: Indian Point 2: Tubes Plugged for Indications Other Than AVB Wear

STEAM GENERATOR A				
Tube	Location	RFO #	Characterization	Stabilized[1]

STEAM GENERATOR B				
Tube	Location	RFO #	Characterization	Stabilized[1]

STEAM GENERATOR C				
Tube	Location	RFO #	Characterization	Stabilized[1]

STEAM GENERATOR D				
Tube	Location	RFO #	Characterization	Stabilized[1]

[1] An empty cell indicates that it was not reported whether the tube was stabilized or not.

Table 3-34: Point Beach 1: Summary of Bobbin Inspections and Tube Plugging

Outage	Completion Date	Cumul. EFPY	SG A Insp.	SG A Plug	SG A DePI	SG B Insp.	SG B Plug	SG B DePI	Total Plug	Total DePI	Cumul. Plugged	Percent Plugged	Notes
Pre-op	04/09/84		3211	3		3214	1		4	0	4	0.06	
RFO 12	04/13/85		101	0		101	0		0	0	4	0.06	
RFO 13	04/19/86		122	0		146	0		0	0	4	0.06	
RFO 14	1987										4	0.06	
RFO 15	05/06/88		129	0		112	2		2	0	6	0.09	
RFO 16	04/11/89		592	0		610	0		0	0	6	0.09	
RFO 17	04/09/90										6	0.09	
RFO 18	04/18/91		576	1		584	1		2	0	8	0.12	
RFO 19	04/18/92		591	0		592	0		0	0	8	0.12	
RFO 20	04/17/93		588	0		591	0		0	0	8	0.12	
RFO 21	1994										8	0.12	
RFO 22	03/25/95		3210	0		3210	1		1	0	9	0.14	
RFO 23	1996										9	0.14	
RFO 24	03/31/98		3210	0		3209	0		0	0	9	0.14	
RFO 25	12/09/99										9	0.14	
Mid-Cycle	03/05/00										9	0.14	
RFO 26	04/24/01	13.5	3210	0		3209	1		1	0	10	0.16	1

Totals: SG A Plug 4, SG A DePI 0, SG B Plug 6, SG B DePI 0, Total Plug 10, Total DePI 0

Plant Data
Model: 44F
T-hot (approximate)
Tubes per steam generator: 3214
Number of steam generators: 2

Acronyms
Pre-op = prior to operation
Cumul = cumulative
Insp = number of tubes inspected
Plug = number of tubes plugged
DePl = number of tubes deplugged
RFO = refueling outage

Notes
1. Plant was shut down to investigate an indication of a possible loose part

-128-

Table 3-35: Point Beach 1 Causes of Tube Plugging

Cause of Tube Plugging/Outage		Pre-Op	1985 RFO 12	1986 RFO 13	1987 RFO 14	1988 RFO 15	1989 RFO 16	1990 RFO 17	1991 RFO 18	1992 RFO 19	1993 RFO 20	1994 RFO 21	1995 RFO 22	1996 RFO 23	1996 RFO 24	1999 RFO 25	2000 Mid-Cycle	2001 RFO 26	Totals
Wear	AVB								1				1					1	3
	Pre-heater TSP (D5)																		0
	TSP								1										1
Loose Parts	Confirmed																		0
	Not confirmed, periphery																		0
	Not confirmed, not periphery																		0
Obstruction Restriction	From PSI, no progression																		0
	Service-induced																		0
Manufacturing Flaws	Preservice	4																	4
	Other					2													2
Inspection Issues	Probe lodged																		0
	Data quality																		0
	Dent/geometry																		0
	Permeability																		0
	Not inspected																		0
Other	Top of tubesheet																		0
	Free span																		0
	TSP																		0
	Other/not reported																		0
SCC	ID																		0
	OD																		0
TOTALS		4	0	0	0	2	0	0	2	0	0	0	1	0	0	0	0	1	10
Notes									1								1		

Notes
1. Mid-cycle outage due to an indication of a possible loose part

-129-

Table 3-36: Point Beach 1: Tubes Plugged for Indications Other Than AVB Wear

STEAM GENERATOR A				
Tube	Location	RFO #	Characterization	Stabilized[1]
21-63	5H-O 65	18	68% throughwall wear indication	

STEAM GENERATOR B				
Tube	Location	RFO #	Characterization	Stabilized[1]
1-1	TSC+18"	15	Damaged during tube lane blocking device removal	
2-1	TSC+18"	15	Damaged during tube lane blocking device removal	

[1]An empty cell indicates that it was not reported whether the tube was stabilized or not.

Table 3-37: Robinson 2: Summary of Bobbin Inspections and Tube Plugging

Outage	Completion Date	Cumul. EFPY	SG A Insp.	Plug	DePl	SG B Insp.	Plug	DePl	SG C Insp.	Plug	DePl	Total Plug	Total DePl	Cumul. Plugged	Percent Plugged	Notes
Pre-op				15			4			9		28	0	28	0.29	
RFO 10	02/01/86		306	0	0	305	0	0	287	0	0	0	0	28	0.29	
RFO 11	05/01/87		301	0	0	301	0	0	296	0	0	0	0	28	0.29	
RFO 12	12/05/88		630	0	0	631	0	0	633	1	0	1	0	29	0.30	
Mid-Cycle	04/15/89											0	0	29	0.30	1
RFO 13	11/01/90		654	0	0	655	0	0	653	1	0	1	0	30	0.31	
RFO 14	04/28/92		661	1	0	659	0	0	667	0	0	1	0	31	0.32	2
RFO 15	10/05/93		1084	1	0	1187	0	0	1083	0	0	1	0	32	0.33	
Mid-Cycle	03/20/94								484	2	0	2	0	34	0.35	3
RFO 16	06/21/95		3197	0	0				3201	0	0	0	0	34	0.35	
RFO 17	09/27/96			1								1	0	35	0.36	
RFO 18	04/14/98					2025	0	0	1607	0	0	0	0	35	0.36	
RFO 19	10/24/99		1610	0	0							0	0	35	0.36	
RFO 20	04/27/01					1619	1	0	1697	3	0	4	0	39	0.40	
Totals:				18	0		5	0		16	0	39	0			

Plant Data
Model: 44F
T-hot (approximate): 604 F
Tubes per steam generator: 3214
Number of steam generators: 3

Acronyms
Pre-op = prior to operation
Cumul = cumulative
Insp = number of tubes inspected
Plug = number of tubes plugged
DePl = number of tubes deplugged
RFO = refueling outage

Notes
1 Mid-cycle outage to investigate an indication of a possible loose part on the primary side of the steam generator. No tube inspections performed.
2 Cycle 13 (RFO 12 to RFO 13) planned for 347 EFPD
3 Mid-cycle outage to investigate an indication of a possible loose part on the secondary side of the steam generator.

Table 3-38: Robinson 2 Causes of Tube Plugging

Cause of Tube Plugging/Outage		Pre-Op	1986 RFO 10	1987 RFO 11	1988 RFO 12	1989 Mid-Cyc	1990 RFO 13	1992 RFO 14	1993 RFO 15	1994 Mid-Cyc	1995 RFO 16	1996 RFO 17	1998 RFO 18	1999 RFO 19	2001 RFO 20	Totals
Wear	AVB															0
	Pre-heater TSP (D5)															0
	TSP															0
Loose Parts	Confirmed									2						2
	Not confirmed, periphery				1	1						1			1	4
	Not confirmed, not periphery														1	1
Obstruction Restriction	From PSI, no progression							1	1							2
	Service-induced														1	1
Manufacturing Flaws	Preservice	28														28
	Other															0
Inspection Issues	Probe lodged															0
	Data quality														1	1
	Dent/geometry															0
	Permeability															0
	Not inspected															0
Other	Top of tubesheet															0
	Free span															0
	TSP															0
	Other/not reported															0
SCC	ID															0
	OD															0
TOTALS		28	0	0	1	1	0	1	1	2	0	1	0	0	4	39

Notes¹

Notes
1 Mid-cycle outage due to an indication of a possible loose part

-132-

Table 3-39: Robinson 2: Tubes Plugged for Indications Other Than AVB Wear

STEAM GENERATOR A				
Tube	Location	RFO #	Characterization	Stabilized[1]
1-29	6H	14	Restriction at 6H (since preservice inspection)	
2-6	6H	15	Restriction at 6H (since preservice inspection)	
37-73	Cold-leg	17	Possible loose part in periphery (38% throughwall indication)	

STEAM GENERATOR B				
Tube	Location	RFO #	Characterization	Stabilized[1]
43-55		20	Dent (since manufacture) resulting in poor data quality	

STEAM GENERATOR C				
Tube	Location	RFO #	Characterization	Stabilized[1]
1-90	TSH, TSC	1994	57% throughwall confirmed loose part indication	
2-90	TSC+0 6"	13	44% throughwall possible loose part indication	
3-90	TSC	1994	33% throughwall confirmed loose part indication	
7-92	TSH	12	76% throughwall gouge-like indication indicative of a debris related defect	
32-26	TSH+0 28"	20	32% throughwall wear indication attributed to transient loose part	
33-34	6H	20	Obstruction above 6H	
44-56	FBH+0 45"	20	Flow distribution baffle wear indication attributed to transient loose part	

[1]An empty cell indicates that it was not reported whether the tube was stabilized or not.

Table 3-40: Salem 1: Summary of Bobbin Inspections and Tube Plugging

Outage	Completion Date	Cumul. EFPY	SG A Insp.	Plug	DePl	SG B Insp.	Plug	DePl	SG C Insp.	Plug	DePl	SG D Insp.	Plug	DePl	Total Plug	Total DePl	Cumul. Plugged	Percent Plugged	Notes
Pre-op				0	0		3	0		9	0		1	0	13	0	13	0.06	
RFO 13	10/15/99		5626	3	0	5623	0	0	5617	4	0	5625	3	0	10	0	23	0.10	
RFO 14	05/03/01		5623	6		5623	12		5613	11		5622	6		35	0	58	0.26	
Totals:				9	0		15	0		24	0		10	0	58	0			

Plant Data
Model: F
T-hot (approximate):
Tubes per steam generator: 5626
Number of steam generators: 4

Notes

Acronyms
Pre-op = prior to operation
Cumul = cumulative
Insp = number of tubes inspected
Plug = number of tubes plugged
DePl = number of tubes deplugged
RFO = refueling outage

-134-

Table 3-41: Salem 1 Causes of Tube Plugging

Cause of Tube Plugging/Outage		Pre-Op	1999 RFO 13	2001 RFO 14	Totals	Totals
Wear	AVB		8	29	37	37
	Pre-heater TSP (D5)				0	
	TSP				0	
Loose Parts	Confirmed					2
	Not confirmed, periphery			2	2	
	Not confirmed, not periphery				0	
Obstruction Restriction	From PSI, no progression				0	0
	Service-induced				0	
Manufacturing Flaws	Preservice	13			13	15
	Other		2		2	
Inspection Issues	Probe lodged				0	4
	Data quality			3	3	
	Dent/geometry				0	
	Permeability			1	1	
	Not Inspected				0	
Other	Top of tubesheet				0	0
	Free span				0	
	TSP				0	
	Other/not reported				0	
SCC	ID				0	0
	OD				0	0
TOTALS		13	10	35	58	58

| Notes: | | | 1 | 2 | | |

Notes
1. 2 tubes were not fully expanded into the tubesheet.
2. The 2 possible loose parts indications were in the U-bend region of the tube bundle.

Table 3-42: Salem 1: Tubes Plugged for Indications Other Than AVB Wear

STEAM GENERATOR A				
Tube	Location	RFO #	Characterization	Stabilized[1]
1-3	Above 7C	14	Possible loose part indication aligned with one of tube support lands	
58-48	5H+6 69 to 5H+32 09"	14	Permeability	

STEAM GENERATOR B				
Tube	Location	RFO #	Characterization	Stabilized[1]
1-43	7H+2 17"	14	Data quality/obstruction	

STEAM GENERATOR C				
Tube	Location	RFO #	Characterization	Stabilized[1]
1-4	7H+5 81	14	Data quality - probe skipping/stalling	
46-64	Tubesheet	13	Tube not fully expanded into tubesheet	
54-60	Tubesheet	13	Tube not fully expanded into tubesheet	

STEAM GENERATOR D				
Tube	Location	RFO #	Characterization	Stabilized[1]
1-79	7H+5 74"	14	Data quality/obstruction	
2-23	Below 7C	14	Possible loose part indication aligned between 2 tube support lands	

[1]An empty cell indicates that it was not reported whether the tube was stabilized or not

Table 3-43: Surry 1: Summary of Bobbin Inspections and Tube Plugging

Outage	Completion Date	Cumul. EFPY	SG A Insp.	Plug	DePl	SG B Insp.	Plug	DePl	SG C Insp.	Plug	DePl	Total Plug	Total DePl	Cumul. Plugged	Percent Plugged	Notes
Pre-op				1			1			0		2	0	2	0.02	
RFO 1	03/01/83	1.3				316	0		378	0		0	0	2	0.02	1
RFO 2	11/01/84	2.3	858	3		562	1					4	0	6	0.06	
RFO 3	06/01/86	3.4	2869	0		1553	2		2874	2		4	0	10	0.10	
RFO 4	04/01/88	4.7				788	0		788	0		0	0	10	0.10	
RFO 5	10/01/90	6.0	152	0		881	0		1246	2		2	0	12	0.12	
RFO 6	03/01/92	7.1	1170	2		1170	0					2	0	14	0.14	
RFO 7	02/01/94	8.7				3339	4					4	0	18	0.18	
RFO 8	10/01/95	10.0							3338	1		1	0	19	0.19	
RFO 9	03/01/97	11.3	3336	5								5	0	24	0.24	
RFO 10	10/01/98	12.7				3334	6					6	0	30	0.30	
RFO 11	04/01/00	14.0							3337	8		8	0	38	0.38	
RFO 12	10/01/01	15.5	3331	5								5	0	43	0.43	
Totals:				16	0		14	0		13	0	43	0			

Plant Data
Model 51F
T-hot (approximate):
Tubes per steam generator 3342
Number of steam generators 3

Acronyms
Pre-op = prior to operation
Cumul = cumulative
Insp = number of tubes inspected
Plug = number of tubes plugged
DePl = number of tubes deplugged
RFO = refueling outage

Notes
1. Inspections were from hot-leg tube end through uppermost tube support on cold-leg (i e , no full length inspections)

Table 3-44: Surry 1 Causes of Tube Plugging

Cause of Tube Plugging/Outage		Pre-Op	1983 RFO 1	1984 RFO 2	1986 RFO 3	1988 RFO 4	1990 RFO 5	1992 RFO 6	1994 RFO 7	1995 RFO 8	1997 RFO 9	1998 RFO 10	2000 RFO 11	2001 RFO 12	Totals	Totals
Wear	AVB							1	4	1	1		7	1	15	15
	Pre-heater TSP (D5)														0	
	TSP														0	
Loose Parts	Confirmed														0	3
	Not confirmed, periphery											3			3	
	Not confirmed, not periphery														0	
Obstruction Restriction	From PSI, no progression														0	7
	Service-induced				1						3	3			7	
Manufacturing Flaws	Preservice	2													2	8
	Other				1		2							3	6	
Inspection Issues	Probe lodged														0	1
	Data quality														0	
	Dent/geometry														0	
	Permeability										1				1	
	Not Inspected														0	
Other	Top of tubesheet			1											1	9
	Free span				1			1					1	1	4	
	TSP			3	1										4	
	Other/not reported														0	
SCC	ID														0	0
	OD														0	
TOTALS		2	0	4	4	0	2	2	4	1	5	6	8	5	43	43
Notes:					1,2		3				4		4	4,5		

Notes

1. Assumed tube plugged for a restriction was service-induced.
2. A tube pulled for destructive examination was classified as a manufacturing flaw.
3. Two tubes pulled for destructive examination revealed manufacturing flaws.
4. One tube plugged for indication in U-bend attributed to interaction with (wear from) the tip of the AVB was classified as a free span indication
5. Three tubes plugged as a result of mechanical damage from the sludge lancing equipment were classified as manufacturing flaws.

Table 3-45: Surry 1: Tubes Plugged for Indications Other Than AVB Wear

STEAM GENERATOR A				
Tube	Location	RFO #	Characterization	Stabilized[1]
1-9	TSC+16"	12	Mechanical damage due to sludge lancing equipment	
1-28	TSC, TSH+16"	12	Mechanical damage due to sludge lancing equipment	
1-35	TSC	9	Restriction	
1-36	TSC	9	Restriction	
1-37	TSC	9	Restriction	
1-67	TSH+16"	12	Mechanical damage due to sludge lancing equipment	
10-44	U-bend Freespan	12	Wear caused by tip of AVB	
13-20	4H	6	31% throughwall indication associated with a dent	
14-85		9	Permeability	
36-58	TSH	2	60% throughwall indication	
37-20	7H	2	89% throughwall indication	
39-60	5H	2	96% throughwall indication	

STEAM GENERATOR B				
Tube	Location	RFO #	Characterization	Stabilized[1]
1-58	TSH	10	Restriction	
1-59	TSH	10	Restriction	
1-60	TSH	10	Restriction	
11-14	2H to 4H	3	Multiple indications between 2H and 4H ranging from 33% to 53% throughwall	
32-14	FBH	10	22% throughwall possible loose part wear indication	
32-16	FBH	10	21% throughwall possible loose part wear indication	
33-16	FBH	10	26% throughwall possible loose part wear indication	
33-43	2C	3	59% throughwall indication	
46-46	3H	2	44% throughwall indication	

[1]An empty cell indicates that it was not reported whether the tube was stabilized or not

Table 3-45: Surry 1: Tubes Plugged for Indications Other Than AVB Wear (cont'd)

STEAM GENERATOR C				
Tube	Location	RFO #	Characterization	Stabilized[1]
2-7		3	Restriction	
10-53	Tubesheet	5	Tube pulled - no service induced degradation	
11-38	U-bend Freespan	11	Wear caused by tip of AVB	
25-57	Tubesheet	5	Tube pulled - no service induced degradation	
40-70	7H	3	Tube pulled - no service induced degradation	

[1]An empty cell indicates that it was not reported whether the tube was stabilized or not

Table 3-46: Surry 2: Summary of Bobbin Inspections and Tube Plugging

Outage	Completion Date	Cumul. EFPY	SG A Insp.	SG A Plug	SG A DePl	SG B Insp.	SG B Plug	SG B DePl	SG C Insp.	SG C Plug	SG C DePl	Total Plug	Total DePl	Cumul. Plugged	Percent Plugged	Notes
Pre-op		0		1						1		2	0	2	0.02	
RFO 1	12/01/81	1.1					0				1	0	0	2	0.02	1
RFO 2	06/01/83	2.4	701	0					572	0		0	0	2	0.02	2
RFO 3	04/01/85	3.6	535	0		534	0					0	0	2	0.02	
Mid-Cycle	06/01/86	4.5	23	1								1	0	3	0.03	3
RFO 4	10/01/86	4.7				586	0		580	0		0	0	3	0.03	
RFO 5	10/01/88	5.9	786	0					781	0		0	0	3	0.03	
RFO 6	03/01/91	7.2	1180	0					1175	0		0	0	3	0.03	
RFO 7	03/01/93	8.7				3342	2					2	0	5	0.05	
RFO 8	02/01/95	10.2	3340	5								5	0	10	0.10	
RFO 9	04/01/96	11.2							3341	8		8	0	18	0.18	
RFO 10	10/01/97	12.5				3340	5					5	0	23	0.23	
RFO 11	04/01/99	13.9	3335	8					0	1		9	0	32	0.32	
RFO 12	10/01/00	15.2							3332	7		7	0	39	0.39	
Totals:				15	0		7	0		17	0	39	0			

Plant Data
Model: 51F
T-hot (approximate):
Tubes per steam generator: 3342
Number of steam generators: 3

Acronyms
Pre-op = prior to operation
Cumul. = cumulative
Insp = number of tubes inspected
Plug = number of tubes plugged
DePl = number of tubes deplugged
RFO = refueling outage

Notes
1. Number of tubes inspected was not readily available. Inspections only performed in steam generators A and B
2. Most inspections are from the hot-leg tube end and through uppermost tube support on cold-leg (i.e., limited full-length inspections)
3. During a plant shutdown, a 21 gpd primary-to-secondary leak was investigated and 23 tubes were inspected.

Table 3-47: Surry 2 Causes of Tube Plugging

Cause of Tube Plugging/Outage		Year →	1981	1983	1985	1986	1986	1988	1991	1993	1995	1996	1997	1999	2000	Totals
		Outage →	Pre-Op	RFO 1	RFO 2	RFO 3	Mid-Cyc	RFO 4	RFO 5	RFO 6	RFO 7	RFO 8	RFO 9	RFO 10	RFO 11	RFO 12	Totals
Wear	AVB										2		3	3		7	15
	Pre-heater TSP (D5)																0
	TSP																0
Loose Parts	Confirmed						1										1
	Not confirmed, periphery																0
	Not confirmed, not periphery																0
Obstruction Restriction	From PSI, no progression																0
	Service-induced											1	2	2	1		6
Manufacturing Flaws	Preservice		2														2
	Other																0
Inspection Issues	Probe lodged																0
	Data quality																0
	Dent/geometry																0
	Permeability																0
	Not inspected																0
Other	Top of tubesheet																0
	Free span											4	3		8		15
	TSP																0
	Other/not reported																0
SCC	ID																0
	OD																0
TOTALS			2	0	0	0	1	0	0	0	2	5	8	5	9	7	39
Notes:								1					2			2	

Notes

1. During a plant shutdown, a 21 gpd primary-to-secondary leak was investigated
2. Top of tubesheet indications attributed to "pitlike" indications.

-142-

Table 3-48: Surry 2: Tubes Plugged for Indications Other Than AVB Wear

STEAM GENERATOR A				
Tube	Location	RFO #	Characterization	Stabilized[1]
1-36		8	Restriction	
1-59	TSH	8	Restriction	
4-36	TSC	8	Axially oriented anomaly - pitlike indication	
4-43	TSC+2 44	11	Pitlike indication	
4-45	TSC+2 3 TSC+3 2	11	Pitlike indication	
6-38	TSC+3 8 TSC+4 2	11	Pitlike indication	
6-39	TSC	8	Axially oriented anomaly - pitlike indication	
7-36	TSC+4 7	11	Pitlike indication	
7-39	TSC	8	Axially oriented anomaly - pitlike indication	
7-49	TSC+4 27 TSC+5 47	11	Pitlike indication	
7-50	TSC	8	Axially oriented anomaly - pitlike indication	
7-57	TSC+3 06	11	Pitlike indication	
9-51	TSC+3 19	11	Pitlike indication	
41-28	TSC	1986	Confirmed loose part - part removed	

STEAM GENERATOR B				
Tube	Location	RFO #	Characterization	Stabilized[1]
1-34		10	Restriction - -	
1-35		10	Restriction	

STEAM GENERATOR C				
Tube	Location	RFO #	Characterization	Stabilized[1]
1-36	TEH	9	Restriction	
1-59	TEC	9	Restriction	
25-13	TSC+2 2	11	Pitlike indication	
31-27	TSH	9	Single axial anomaly	
34-73	TSH	9	Single axial anomaly	
35-68	TSH	9	Multiple axial anomaly	

[1]An empty cell indicates that it was not reported whether the tube was stabilized or not.

Table 3-49: Turkey Point 3: Summary of Bobbin Inspections and Tube Plugging

Outage	Completion Date	Cumul. EFPY	SG A Insp.	SG A Plug	SG A DePl	SG B Insp.	SG B Plug	SG B DePl	SG C Insp.	SG C Plug	SG C DePl	Total Plug	Total DePl	Cumul. Plugged	Percent Plugged	Notes
Pre-op	10/01/83			13			7			19		39	0	39	0.40	1
RFO 8	06/01/85			0			0			0		0	0	39	0.40	2
RFO 9	06/13/87		276	0		420	4		199	0		4	0	43	0.45	
RFO 10	03/13/90		324	0		332	0		373	1		1	0	44	0.46	
RFO 11	10/18/92		3203	2		3205	3		3194	6		11	0	55	0.57	
RFO 12	04/25/94		3199	1		3200	1		3188	5		7	0	62	0.64	
RFO 13	09/19/95		3198	1		3199	1		3183	2		4	0	66	0.68	
RFO 14	03/19/97		3197	0		3198	2		3181	0		2	0	68	0.71	
RFO 15	10/08/98		3197	3		3196	9		3181	2		14	0	82	0.85	
RFO 16	03/15/00	10.7	3194	0		3187	1		3179	0		1	0	83	0.86	
RFO 17	10/13/01	12.2	1609	25		1601	28		1627	16		69	0	152	1.58	
RFO 18		13.6	3169	1		3158	11		3163	2		14	0	166	1.72	
Totals:				46	0		67	0		53	0	166	0			

Plant Data
Model: 44F
T-hot (approximate):
Tubes per steam generator: 3214
Number of steam generators: 3

Acronyms
Pre-op = prior to operation
Cumul = cumulative
Insp. = number of tubes inspected
Plug = number of tubes plugged
DePl = number of tubes deplugged
RFO = refueling outage

Notes
1. Number of tubes plugged inferred from other inspection results
2. Extent of inspections not readily available. No tubes were plugged during this outage.

Table 3-50: Turkey Point 3 Causes of Tube Plugging

Cause of Tube Plugging/Outage		Pre-Op	1983 RFO 8	1985 RFO 9	1987 RFO 10	1990 RFO 11	1992 RFO 12	1994 RFO 13	1995 RFO 14	1997 RFO 15	1998 RFO 16	2000 RFO 17	2001 RFO 18	Totals	Totals
Wear	AVB					7	3	3	1	1	1	5	1	22	34
	Pre-heater TSP (D5)													0	
	TSP												12	12	
Loose Parts	Confirmed													0	2
	Not confirmed, periphery									2				2	
	Not confirmed, not periphery													0	
Obstruction Restriction	From PSI, no progression	.												0	1
	Service-induced												1	1	
Manufacturing Flaws	Preservice	39												39	39
	Other													0	
Inspection Issues	Probe lodged													0	0
	Data quality													0	
	Dent/geometry													0	
	Permeability													0	
	Not inspected													0	
Other	Top of tubesheet			3	1	2			1	8		64		79	90
	Free span			1		2	4	1						8	
	TSP									3				3	
	Other/not reported													0	
SCC	ID													0	0
	OD													0	
TOTALS		39	0	4	1	11	7	4	2	14	1	69	14	166	166

Notes:

Notes
1 Volumetric and circumferential indications were detected in 64 tubes. Many of these indications were reclassified after the outage as not service induced degradation

-145-

Table 3-51: Turkey Point 3: Tubes Plugged for Indications Other Than AVB Wear

Tube	Location	RFO #	Characterization	Stabilized[1]
STEAM GENERATOR A				
3-80	TSH-0 08	17	Circumferential indication (reclassified as no service-related degradation)	Y
9-32	4H	11	≥40-percent throughwall indication	
10-31	TSH-0 15	17	Circumferential indication (reclassified as no service-related degradation)	Y
13-5	TSH+3 8	15	No characterization provided	
16-64	TSH-0 09	17	Circumferential indication (reclassified as no service-related degradation)	Y
17-15	TSH+0 05	17	Circumferential indication (reclassified as no service-related degradation)	Y
17-33	TSH+0.15	17	Circumferential indication (reclassified as no service-related degradation)	Y
18-83	TSH+0.11	17	Volumetric indication (reclassified as a pit)	
18-84	TSH+0 16	17	Volumetric indication (reclassified as a pit)	
19-84	TSH+0 91 TSH+0 46	17	Volumetric indication (reclassified as a pit)	
21-32	6H+2.3	12	44-percent throughwall indication	
21-87	TSH+0 68	17	Volumetric indication (reclassified as no service-related degradation)	
28-75	TSH+0 15	17	Volumetric indication (reclassified as a pit)	
29-75	TSH+0 14	17	Volumetric	
30-65	TSH+0 24	17	Volumetric indication (reclassified as no service-related degradation)	
31-18	6H+1 1	15	Volumetric	
31-77	TSH+0 1	17	Volumetric indication (reclassified as a pit)	
32-15	1H-0 45	18	Wear	
32-23	TSH-0 05	17	Circumferential indication (reclassified as no service-related degradation)	Y
32-63	TSH+0 05	17	Circumferential indication (reclassified as a volumetric indication)	Y
32-64	TSH-0 01	17	Circumferential indication (reclassified as no service-related degradation)	Y
33-35	TSH-0 02	17	Circumferential indication (reclassified as a pit)	Y
33-78	TSH+0.65	17	Volumetric indication (reclassified as no service-related degradation)	
34-25	TSH-0 08	17	Circumferential indication (reclassified as no service-related degradation)	Y
35-65	TSH+0 98	17	Volumetric indication (reclassified as no service-related degradation)	
36-69	TSH+0 21	17	Volumetric	
38-66	TSH+0.23	17	Volumetric indication (reclassified as no service-related degradation)	
39-67	TSH-0 05	17	Volumetric indication (reclassified as no service-related degradation)	
44-36	TSH+0 7	15	Volumetric	

[1]An empty cell indicates that it was not reported whether the tube was stabilized or not

Table 3-51: Turkey Point 3: Tubes Plugged for Indications Other Than AVB Wear (cont'd)

	STEAM GENERATOR B			
Tube	Location	RFO #	Characterization	Stabilized[1]
1-3		18	Restriction in U-bend	
1-14	TSH-0 28	17	Circumferential indication (reclassified as no service-related degradation)	Y
7-92	TSH+0 57	17	Volumetric indication (reclassified as no service-related degradation)	
8-8	1H+0 7	13	44-percent throughwall indication	
15-17	TSH-0.06	17	Circumferential indication (reclassified as no service-related degradation)	Y
15-76	3H-0.7	18	Wear	
19-10	TSH+0 24	17	Volumetric indication (reclassified as a pit)	
19-12	TSH+0 54	17	Volumetric indication (reclassified as a pit)	
19-13	TSH+0 25	17	Volumetric indication (reclassified as a pit)	
19-14	TSH+0 29	17	Volumetric indication (reclassified as a pit)	
20-10	TSH+0 03	17	Volumetric indication (reclassified as a pit)	
20-12	TSH+0 21	17	Volumetric indication (reclassified as a pit)	
20-13	TSH+0 03	17	Volumetric indication (reclassified as a pit)	
21-56	TSH+0 43	17	Volumetric indication (reclassified as no service-related degradation)	
22-53	TSH+0 58	17	Volumetric indication (reclassified as no service-related degradation)	
23-7	TSH+0 58	17	Volumetric indication (reclassified as no service-related degradation)	
23-41	3C+0 5	15	Volumetric	
25-32	4H+0 0	9	31-percent throughwall indication	
25-34	TSH+0 2	17	Volumetric indication (reclassified as no service-related degradation)	
26-71	TSH+0 12	17	Volumetric indication (reclassified as no service-related degradation)	
26-77	2H-0 48	18	Wear	
27-41	3C+0 59	18	Wear	
27-42	3C+0 59	18	Wear	
28-41	3C+0 69 3C+0 61	18	Wear	
30-17	2C+0 56	18	Wear	
32-19	2H-0 61	18	Wear	
32-66	2H-084	18	Wear	
33-70	TSH-0 06	17	Circumferential indication (reclassified as no service-related degradation)	Y
34-57	TSH+0.1	17	Volumetric indication (reclassified as a pit)	
37-20	TSH+0 4	15	Volumetric	
37-46	TSH+0 04	17	Volumetric indication (reclassified as a pit)	
38-39	TSH+0	17	Circumferential indication (reclassified as a volumetric)	Y

STEAM GENERATOR B				
Tube	Location	RFO #	Characterization	Stabilized[1]
38-45	TSH+0.16	17	Circumferential indication (reclassified as a pit)	Y
38-46	TSH+0 59	17	Volumetric indication (reclassified as a pit)	
38-69	2H+0.99	18	Wear	
39-39	5H+0 8	15	Volumetric	
39-59	TSH+0 19	17	Volumetric indication (reclassified as no service-related degradation)	
40-39	5H	11	≥40-percent throughwall indication	
41-43	TSH+0 04	17	Volumetric indication (reclassified as no service-related degradation)	
41-44	TSH+0 6	15	Volumetric	
41-65	TSH+0 63	17	Volumetric indication (reclassified as no service-related degradation)	
42-30	TSH+0 4	9	36-percent throughwall indication	
42-37	TSH+0.7	14	44-percent throughwall indication	
42-38	TSH+1 5	15	Volumetric	
43-33	TSH+0 14	17	Volumetric indication (reclassified as a pit)	
44-40	TSH+0 3 TSH+1.8	15	82-percent throughwall volumetric indication, pit	
44-41	TSH+0 2 TSH+0 4 TSH+0 5	15	Volumetric	
44-42	TSH+0 4	17	Volumetric indication (reclassified as a pit)	
45-41	TSH+0 6	15	Adjacent to a loose part so tube was plugged	
45-42	TSH+1.3	15	Adjacent to a loose part so tube was plugged	
45-43	TSH+0 6 TSH+0 8	9	56-percent throughwall indication	
45-44	TSH+3 6 TSH+3 8	9	39-percent throughwall indication Tube was replugged in RFO13 since plug was leaking	
45-47	TSH+0 64	17	Volumetric indication (reclassified as no service-related degradation)	

[1]An empty cell indicates that it was not reported whether the tube was stabilized or not.

Table 3-51: Turkey Point 3: Tubes Plugged for Indications Other Than AVB Wear (cont'd)

	STEAM GENERATOR C			
Tube	Location	RFO #	Characterization	Stabilized[1]
1-20	TSH-0 12	17	Circumferential indication (reclassified as no service-related degradation)	Y
2-55	TSC+24 1	12	60-percent throughwall indication	
2-70	2C+0 7	12	45-percent throughwall indication	
3-46	TSH-0 08	17	Circumferential indication (reclassified as no service-related degradation)	Y
7-3	TSH+0 09	17	Volumetric indication (reclassified as no service-related degradation)	
13-89	TSC	11	≥40-percent throughwall indication	
14-6	TSH	11	≥40-percent throughwall indication	
14-89	CL	10	48-percent throughwall indication in sludge pile	
15-44	TSH+0 03	17	Circumferential indication (reclassified as no service-related degradation)	Y
19-85	2H-0 78	18	Wear	
20-66	6C+2 4	12	41-percent throughwall indication	
22-7	TSH+0.55	17	Volumetric indication (reclassified as no service-related degradation)	
23-7	TSH+0 59	17	Volumetric indication (reclassified as no service-related degradation)	
30-69	TSH-0 03	17	Circumferential indication (reclassified as no service-related degradation)	Y
31-24	TSH+0.16	17	Circumferential indication (reclassified as a volumetric indication)	Y
32-64	2H-0 59	18	Wear	
33-66	TSH+0 6	15	58-percent throughwall indication	
34-40	TSH-0 08	17	Circumferential indication (reclassified as no service-related degradation)	Y
34-66	TSH+0 23	17	Volumetric indication (reclassified as no service-related degradation)	
36-74	TSH-0 07	17	Circumferential indication (reclassified as no service-related degradation)	Y
39-49	TSH-0 01	17	Volumetric	
40-49	TSH+0 06	17	Circumferential indication (reclassified as a volumetric indication)	Y
45-49	TSH+2 89	17	Volumetric indication (reclassified as no service-related degradation)	

[1]An empty cell indicates that it was not reported whether the tube was stabilized or not

Table 3-52: Turkey Point 4: Summary of Bobbin Inspections and Tube Plugging

Outage	Completion Date	Cumul. EFPY	SG A Insp.	SG A Plug	SG A DePl	SG B Insp.	SG B Plug	SG B DePl	SG C Insp.	SG C Plug	SG C DePl	Total Plug	Total DePl	Cumul. Plugged	Percent Plugged	Notes
Pre-op				15			7			9		31	0	31	0.32	1
RFO 9	05/15/84		211	0		162	0		502	0		0	0	31	0.32	
RFO 10	03/16/86		328	0		318	0		345	0		0	0	31	0.32	
RFO 11	11/15/88		3199	1		3207	0		3205	0		1	0	32	0.33	
RFO 12	05/13/91		3198	0		3207	1		3205	0		1	0	33	0.34	
RFO 13	04/28/93		3198	0		3206	0		3205	0		0	0	33	0.34	
RFO 14	10/17/94		3198	0		3206	0		3205	0		0	0	33	0.34	
RFO 15	03/01/96											0	0	33	0.34	
RFO 16	09/22/97		3198	0		3206	0		3205	0		0	0	33	0.34	
RFO 17	03/01/99											0	0	33	0.34	
RFO 18	10/09/00		1602	3		1604	5		1607	2		10	0	43	0.45	
Totals:				19	0		13	0		11	0	43	0			

Plant Data
Model. 44F
T-hot (approximate)
Tubes per steam generator: 3214
Number of steam generators. 3

Acronyms
Pre-op = prior to operation
Cumul = cumulative
Insp = number of tubes inspected
Plug = number of tubes plugged
DePl = number of tubes deplugged
RFO = refueling outage

Notes
1. Number of tubes plugged was deduced based on information provided in various reports

-150-

Table 3-53: Turkey Point 4 Causes of Tube Plugging

Cause of Tube Plugging/Outage		Pre-Op	1984 RFO 9	1986 RFO 10	1988 RFO 11	1991 RFO 12	1993 RFO 13	1994 RFO 14	1996 RFO 15	1997 RFO 16	1999 RFO 17	2000 RFO 18	Totals	Totals
Wear	AVB											1	1	2
	Pre-heater TSP (D5)												0	
	TSP											1	1	
Loose Parts	Confirmed												0	0
	Not confirmed, periphery												0	
	Not confirmed, not periphery												0	
Obstruction Restriction	From PSI, no progression												0	2
	Service-Induced				1	1							2	
Manufacturing Flaws	Preservice	31											31	31
	Other												0	
Inspection Issues	Probe lodged												0	1
	Data quality												0	
	Dent/geometry												0	
	Permeability											1	1	
	Not inspected												0	
Other	Top of tubesheet											7	7	7
	Free span												0	
	TSP												0	
	Other/not reported												0	
SCC	ID												0	0
	OD												0	
TOTALS		31	0	0	1	1	0	0	0	0	0	10	43	43

Notes:

Notes

-151-

Table 3-54: Turkey Point 4: Tubes Plugged for Indications Other Than AVB Wear

STEAM GENERATOR A				
Tube	Location	RFO #	Characterization	Stabilized[1]
2-5	HL Tubesheet	11	Clamp stuck inside tube. Attempts to retrieve were unsuccessful	
12-25		18	Permeability signal in expansion transition area	
26-80	TSH+2.27	18	Pit	
33-73	TSH+0 17	18	Volumetric indication	

STEAM GENERATOR B				
Tube	Location	RFO #	Characterization	Stabilized[1]
2-90	FBH-0 46	18	Wear	
8-81	TSH-2.0	12	Restriction	
20-80	TSH	18	Pit	
21-80	TSH+0 05	18	Pit	
29-62	TSH+0 12	18	Pit	
43-51	TSH-0 04	18	Pit	

STEAM GENERATOR C				
Tube	Location	RFO #	Characterization	Stabilized[1]
3-91	TSH+0	18	Pit	

[1]An empty cell indicates that it was not reported whether the tube was stabilized or not.

4 SUMMARY

The following sections summarize the operating experience presented in Section 3. Summaries are provided for each of the three groupings of plants (i.e., model D5, model F, and replacement models). There is also a combined summary. The combined summary includes a discussion on tubes removed for destructive examination, discussion on unscheduled steam generator outages (i.e., forced outages), and observations regarding the results from the inspections.

4.1 Model D5 Summary

There are a total of 73,120 thermally treated tubes in the four plants with model D5 steam generators. Cumulatively, these four plants have operated for 51 calendar years (as of December 2001), and have commercially operated for an average of 13 calendar years (as of December 2001). Of the 73,120 tubes in these steam generators, only 563 tubes (0.8%) have been plugged. This information is summarized in Table 4-1.

Table 4-2 summarizes the number of tubes plugged in the model D5 steam generators as a function of the degradation mechanism. The information in this table is graphically depicted in Figure 4-1. As can be seen from the figure, approximately 53% of the tubes were plugged as a result of tube wear. This wear occurred predominantly at the antivibration bars (AVBs), although some occurred at tube support plates and near loose parts. With only a few tubes being plugged for wear in the preheater region, it appears that the tube expansion at the preheater baffle plates (as discussed in Section 2.2) was successful in mitigating this phenomenon. In addition to tube wear, many (17%) of the tubes were plugged as a result of flaws attributed to manufacturing.

Figures 4-2 and 4-3 depict the number of tubes plugged at each plant as a function of year and refueling outage, respectively. These figures indicate, for the most part, that the four plants are operating similarly. The information in Figure 4-2 is summarized in Tables 4-3 and 4-4. The information in Figure 4-3 is summarized in Table 4-5.

Figure 4-4 depicts the fraction of tubes plugged for a specific mechanism as a function of year. This figure was developed from the data provided in Tables 4-6, 4-7, and 4-8. In this figure, tubes plugged prior to commercial operation were treated as being plugged during the year the plant began commercial operation (in previous tables and figures in this report, tubes plugged prior to operation were treated as a distinct group independent of the actual year/outage in which they were plugged).

Tables 3-1, 3-4, 3-7, and 3-10 indicate that plants with D5 steam generators typically performed bobbin coil inspections in all four steam generators during each refueling outage in the 1990s. In addition, with the exception of Comanche Peak 2, these inspections usually involved a large percentage of the tubes (i.e., greater than 50%). In 2000 and 2001, these plants began reducing the number of steam generators inspected and/or the number of tubes inspected during the refueling outage. For example, in 2000 Comanche Peak 2 only inspected two steam generators, and in 2001 Byron 2 only inspected one steam generator.

4.2 Model F Summary

There are a total of 117,376 thermally treated tubes in the six plants that originally installed model F steam generators in their plants. Cumulatively, these six plants have operated for approximately 88 calendar years as of December 2001, and have commercially operated for an average of 15 calendar years (as of December 2001). Of the 117,376 tubes in these steam generators, only 434 tubes (0.4%) have been plugged. This information is summarized in Table 4-9.

Table 4-10 summarizes the number of tubes plugged in the model F steam generators as a function of degradation mechanism. The information in this table is graphically depicted in Figure 4-5. As can be seen from the figure, approximately 74% of the tubes were plugged as a result of tube wear. This wear occurred predominantly at the AVBs, although some occurred near loose parts. No (or a very limited number of) tubes have been plugged for wear at the tube support plates. In addition to tube wear, many (14%) of the tubes were plugged as a result of manufacturing flaws.

The wear at the AVBs in model F steam generators is primarily observed in the tubes in row 20 and higher on the periphery and row 30 and higher in the middle of the tube bundle. At least one licensee has reported that the AVB wear flaws in the middle of the tube bundle tend to be shallower than those on the periphery. In addition, several licensees reported that the average AVB wear rate generally decreases with time.

Figures 4-6 and 4-7 depict the number of tubes plugged at each plant as a function of year and refueling outage, respectively. These figures indicate, for the most part, that the six plants are operating similarly. The information in Figure 4-6 is summarized in Tables 4-11 and 4-12. The information in Figure 4-7 is summarized in Table 4-13.

Figure 4-8 depicts the fraction of tubes plugged for a specific mechanism as a function of year. This figure was developed from the data provided in Tables 4-14, 4-15, and 4-16. In this figure, tubes plugged prior to commercial operation were treated as being plugged during the year the plant began commercial operation (in previous tables and figures in this report, tubes plugged prior to operation were treated as a distinct group independent of the actual year/outage in which they were plugged).

Tables 3-13, 3-16, 3-19, 3-22, 3-25, and 3-28 indicate that plants with model F steam generators typically inspect 100% of the tubes in two of the four steam generators each refueling outage. Of particular note, however, is that the majority of the tubes at Callaway are mill-annealed.

4.3 Replacement Model Summary

There are a total of 90,766 tubes in the eight plants with replacement steam generators that contain thermally treated Alloy 600 tubes. Cumulatively, these eight plants have operated for approximately 120 calendar years as of December 2001, and have commercially operated for an average of 15 calendar years (as of December 2001). Of the 90,766 tubes in these steam generators, only 400 tubes (0.4%) have been plugged. This information is summarized in Table 4-17.

-154-

Table 4-18 summarizes the number of tubes plugged in the replacement model steam generators as a function of degradation mechanism. The information in this table is graphically depicted in Figure 4-9. As can be seen from the figure, approximately 31% of the tubes were plugged as a result of tube wear. This wear occurred predominantly at the AVBs although some occurred near loose parts. No (or a very limited number of) tubes have been plugged for wear at the tube support plates. Replacement steam generators appear to be less susceptible to wear at the AVBs than the model F steam generators as evidenced by operating experience and evaluations. In addition to tube wear, many (33%) of the tubes were plugged as a result of manufacturing flaws.

Figures 4-10 and 4-11 depict the number of tubes plugged at each plant as a function of year and refueling outage, respectively. These figures indicate, for the most part, that the eight plants are operating similarly with the possible exception of Salem 1, which has Model F steam generators, and Turkey Point 3, which has plugged significantly more tubes than the other plants. The information in Figure 4-10 is summarized in Tables 4-19 and 4-20. The information in Figure 4-11 is summarized in Table 4-21.

Figure 4-12 depicts the fraction of tubes plugged for a specific mechanism as a function of year. This figure was developed from the data provided in Tables 4-22, 4-23, and 4-24. In this figure, tubes plugged prior to commercial operation were treated as being plugged during the year the plant began commercial operation (in previous tables and figures in this report, tubes plugged prior to operation were treated as a distinct group independent of the actual year/outage in which they were plugged).

Tables 3-31, 3-34, 3-37, 3-40, 3-43, 3-46, 3-49, and 3-52 indicate that plants with replacement steam generators with thermally treated Alloy 600 tubes have a variety of strategies for inspecting their steam generators. Several plants inspect a subset of steam generators each refueling outage (e.g., one of three steam generators is inspected each outage). This is referred to as "skip steam generator." Others inspect all steam generators every other outage (i.e., no tube inspections are performed during one refueling outage but all steam generators are inspected the next refueling outage). This schedule is referred to as "skip-cycle." Yet others inspect all steam generators every outage. Plants that skip cycles or skip steam generators typically inspect 100% of the tubes in the steam generators inspected.

4.4 Overall Summary

4.4.1 Forced Outages

As of December 2001, the steam generator operating experience of plants with thermally treated Alloy 600 has been favorable. These plants account for approximately 25% of the currently operating PWRs. A historical review identified only six unplanned outages as a result of steam generator issues in plants with thermally treated Alloy 600 tubes: two due to primary-to-secondary leakage and four due to indications of loose parts (e.g., loose parts monitor alarms). These six outages are discussed below. (During the preparation of this report in the first half of 2002, two additional unplanned outages attributed to steam generator issues occurred. One of these was attributed to leakage and one was attributed to an indication of a loose part. These are briefly discussed below.)

Only two plants with thermally treated Alloy 600 tubes have experienced any significant primary-to-secondary leakage. One of these plants, Byron 2, entered a refueling outage early as a result of a 120-gallon-per-day primary-to-secondary leak in 1996. The cause of the leak was a foreign object attributed to thermal-cutting debris from a pipe whose diameter was somewhere between 12 and 18 inches. The foreign object was located on the secondary side of the steam generator. This object damaged four tubes and the tubes were plugged. One tube had a 100% throughwall indication, one had a 56% throughwall indication, and the remaining two tubes were plugged as the result of nonquantifiable volumetric indications found by a rotating pancake coil probe. The other plant, Surry 2, shut down in June 1986 as a result of a leak in an expansion joint on the service water return line from a recirculation spray heat exchanger and to identify the source of a steam generator tube leak. Similar to Byron 2, the source of the Surry 2 leak was a tube affected by a foreign object. One steam generator tube was plugged as a result of this outage. Other plants (e.g., Seabrook) have experienced amounts of leakage (< 5 gallons per day) too small to necessitate a plant shutdown. The sources of such small amounts of leakage are usually never conclusively identified. (As mentioned in the Executive Summary, Byron 2 shut down in June 2002 as a result of a 75- to 80- gpd primary-to-secondary leak. Preliminary investigations indicate the cause of the leak was a loose part.)

In February 2000, the licensee for Point Beach 1 shut down the unit to investigate indications of loose parts in the steam generator. A thorough inspection found no loose parts and the unit was restarted.

In May 1996, Vogtle 1 was shut down in response to a possible loose part on the primary side of steam generator 4. Upon entering the hot-leg channel head, licensee personnel found a support pin nut from a control rod guide tube assembly. The nut's locking device was found wedged into the bottom of a tube and was subsequently removed. Another object, believed to be a fragment of the support pin nut, was found on the cold-leg side of the steam generator. The loose object impacted the lower tubesheet on the hot-leg side and numerous indications were noted. The hot-legs of the other three steam generators did not exhibit any signs of damage. During a subsequent steam generator tube inspection, the shank of the broken support pin was found lodged in a tube. The shank was left in place and the tube was plugged. Damaged tube ends on the tubesheet were rerolled during this outage.

In February 1994, the licensee for Robinson 2 shut down the facility for repairs to an emergency diesel generator. During this shutdown, the licensee also investigated a loose parts monitor alarm. The investigation revealed two strips of metal resting on the tubesheet. Their composition was similar to that of welding electrodes believed to have been used to fabricate the replacement steam generator shell welds. The pieces of metal were removed from the steam generators and two tubes were plugged because of localized wear where the metal objects contacted the tubes. Two nearby tubes had been plugged in prior outages due to either outside diameter wear or manufacturing marks. These indications may have been related to the loose part.

On April 3, 1989, the licensee for Robinson 2 shut down the unit as a result of audio signals indicating a loose part in the hot-leg channel head of steam generator C. When the licensee opened the steam generator manway, a loose part fell out. The part was a split pin nut from a control rod guide tube support. Examination of the tubesheet, tube ends, tube-to-tubesheet welds, and divider plate welds did not reveal conditions that required immediate repair. However, this examination did reveal damage to the tubesheet and tube ends on the hot-leg side of steam generator C. This damage obliterated some of the tubesheet face markings used to identify tubes on the hot leg, complicating the insertion of inspection probes through the hot-leg tube end.

(As briefly discussed in the Executive Summary, Wolf Creek was shut down in May 2002 as a result of a loose part located on the primary side of the steam generator. The part was a control rod guide tube support pin nut and locking device.)

4.4.2 Tube Pulls

To characterize eddy current indications found during steam generator tube inservice inspections, portions of a few tubes have been removed from steam generators with thermally treated Alloy 600 tubes. Based on information supplied to the NRC, tubes have only been removed from two such plants as of December 2001: Surry 1 and Byron 2. The results of these examinations are discussed below. (During the preparation of this report in the first half of 2002, portions of two tubes were removed from Seabrook as discussed below.)

- In 1998, Byron 2 removed portions of three tubes with circumferential indications at the hot-leg expansion transition region for destructive examination. A total of 29 tubes with circumferential indications were identified and plugged and stabilized during this outage. According to the preliminary tube pull results, the circumferential indications were not service-induced cracking or corrosion but shallow grooves that may have been introduced during initial steam generator fabrication or the first few cycles of operation. Burst testing of the indications showed that the indications did not affect the structural integrity of the tubes. Final results from these examinations were not readily available.

- In 1990, portions of two tubes were removed from Surry 1 to examine axial and circumferential anomalies at the top of the tubesheet and were subsequently plugged. The examination found no operationally induced degradation of the tube wall on either of these tubes. Field nondestructive examination results suggested the presence of circumferentially oriented degradation. Upon further review of the nondestructive examination results for one of the pulled tubes, the licensee concluded that the poorly defined rotating pancake coil signal was similar to that of a ding or mechanical deformation. For the other pulled tube, a 70° groove, mechanical in nature, was found on the outside diameter of the tube and attributed to the interaction of the tube with the edge of the tubesheet during the expansion process. Although the hydraulic expansion process used was designed to position the transition slightly below the top of the tubesheet, the licensee concluded that this tube was overexpanded above the top of the tubesheet. In summary, destructive examination of the pulled tube segments detected no corrosion. The nondestructive examination indications were attributed to probe liftoff in the expansion transition and to the tube installation process.

- Portions of one tube were removed from steam generator C at Surry 1 in 1986 to examine an eddy current indication near the uppermost (seventh) tube support plate. The indication was thought to be caused by conductive deposits on the outside surface of the tubes. The tube pull confirmed the absence of degradation where eddy current testing had suggested degradation.

Although tube wear (from support structures and loose parts) is the dominant degradation mechanism, no tubes have been pulled from plants with thermally treated Alloy 600 to characterize these indications.

(As discussed in the Executive Summary, portions of two tubes were pulled from Seabrook in May 2002 to investigate the nature of axial-crack-like indications which were observed at the hot- and cold-leg tube support plates. All of the indications were on the portion of the tube within the thickness of the tube support plate and opposite the broached tube hole lands. In all 15 tubes were found to have indications at 42 tube support plate intersections. The maximum depth of the indications was estimated to be 62% throughwall and the lengths ranged from 0.3 to 0.75 inch. The NRC issued Information Notice 2002-21, "Axial Outside-Diameter Cracking Affecting Thermally Treated Alloy 600 Steam Generator Tubing," on June 25, 2002, describing the nondestructive examination results from Seabrook. The destructive examination confirmed the presence of cracks in these tubes, representing the first confirmed instance of cracking in thermally treated Alloy 600 tubes. The root cause evaluation, including the destructive examination of these two pulled tubes, confirmed that the indications were axially oriented outside diameter stress corrosion cracking, and also identified unusually high levels of residual stress in the straight leg sections of both the hot and cold legs. Nonoptimal tube processing during steam generator manufacturing was strongly suspected to be the primary cause of the high residual stresses and the principal factor increasing the susceptibility of the affected tubes to stress corrosion cracking. The precise processing steps responsible for the adverse stress state could not be conclusively determined from a review of the tube processing records.)

4.4.3 Selected Inspection Findings

Some of the more noteworthy findings from inspections of thermally treated Alloy 600 tubes are summarized below. Except as noted, the tubes discussed below were plugged. In addition, none of these tubes were removed for destructive examination except for two of the tubes at Seabrook (as discussed in Section 4.4.2).

- As briefly discussed in the Executive Summary, axial crack-like indications were detected at 42 tube-to-tube-support-plate intersections in 15 tubes at Seabrook in May 2002. Two tubes were pulled to characterize the nature of the degradation. The destructive examination confirmed the presence of cracks in these tubes, representing the first confirmed instance of cracking in thermally treated Alloy 600 tubes. The root cause evaluation, including the destructive examination of these two pulled tubes, confirmed that the indications were axially oriented outside diameter stress corrosion cracking, and also identified unusually high levels of residual stress in the straight leg sections of both the hot and cold legs. Nonoptimal tube processing during steam generator manufacturing was strongly suspected to be the primary cause of the high residual stresses and the principal factor increasing the susceptibility of the affected tubes to stress corrosion cracking. The precise processing steps responsible for the adverse stress state could not be conclusively determined from a review of the tube processing records.

- At Millstone 3 in February 2001, 29 single volumetric indications at the top of the tubesheet and flow distribution baffle were identified. These indications were attributed to wear due to loose parts and to fabrication-related defects.

- At Turkey Point 3 in 2001, 12 tubes were plugged as a result of indications of mechanical wear at the broached tube support plates. Plugging of tubes for wear at tube support plates is fairly rare in plants with thermally treated Alloy 600 tubes.

- At Turkey Point 3 in the spring of 2000, 41 volumetric pitlike indications, 15 inside-diameter-initiated circumferential indications, and 8 outside-diameter-initiated circumferential indications were identified. Most of these indications were in the hot-leg hydraulic-expansion transition region at the top of the tubesheet. The volumetric and circumferential indications were detected with rotating probes. This was the first time rotating probes were extensively used at Turkey Point 3. As a result of these findings, the licensee began a review of historical data and industry experience, during the outage, to assess the root causes of the tube degradation. Because of the lack of prior rotating probe inspection data for Turkey Point 3 and the limited number of defects identified by the industry in thermally treated Alloy 600 tubes, the results, at the time of the inspection, were inconclusive for the circumferential and volumetric indications. Based on subsequent investigation, the licensee concluded that of the 64 volumetric and circumferential indications originally identified, only 26 tubes contain volumetric or pitlike indications (possibly due to manufacturing and installation artifacts), while the remaining 38 tubes contain no degradation (13 had circumferential geometric anomalies, 23 had dings or dents, and 2 had manufacturing buff marks).

- In an outage at Turkey Point 4 in the fall of 2000, the licensee detected seven tubes with possible corrosion degradation and plugged these tubes since a qualified depth-sizing technique was not available. Based on the eddy current and ultrasonic examination results of this inspection, the licensee reanalyzed the spring 2000 Unit 3 data (discussed above). The licensee's judgment is that the indications at Unit 3 were false positives and caused by manufacturing anomalies or deposits at the top of tubesheet or by the inspection techniques associated with the rotating probe. These results are discussed in NRC Information Notice 2001-016, "Recent Foreign and Domestic Experience With Degradation of Steam Generator Tubes and Internals."

- At Surry 1 in 2000 and 2001, denting of tubes at the sixth and seventh tube supports was detected. These dents corresponded to the quatrefoil lands. The dents are concentrated in the periphery of the tube bundle near the wedge regions and are located at (or near) the edges of the support plate.

- At Braidwood 2 in 1996, one axial indication was detected in a small-radius tube (in row 1). The licensee concluded at that time that the most likely cause for this indication was primary water stress corrosion cracking (PWSCC).

- At Callaway in 1996, axial, circumferential, and volumetric indications were detected at the hot-leg expansion transition. Additional indications were detected near the top of the tubesheet (i.e., the expansion transition region) in subsequent outages.

- At Millstone 3 in August 1993, a tube was deplugged in order to replace the plug with a more corrosion-resistant material. This tube had been plugged in 1989 as a result of a 43% throughwall wear indication at the fifth anti-vibration bar. During the 4 years the tube was plugged, the defect had apparently grown from 43% to 100% throughwall. To prevent the tube from severing at the defect and contacting adjacent tubes, a stabilizer was inserted before the tube was replugged.

- At Callaway in 1992, one undefined indication was detected in a row 2 tube. The indication, located just above the seventh cold-leg support plate, was not identified with the bobbin coil. The licensee concluded that this indication was an anomaly since no degradation mechanism had been identified in this region. In addition, a senior eddy current analyst judged this indication to be a distorted signal caused by its location in the U-bend transition.

- At Surry 2 in the mid-1990s, the licensee began detecting a limited number of pitlike indications above the tubesheet on the cold-leg side of the steam generator. The licensee used the rotating pancake coil terrain plot display as the primary basis for classifying the signals as pitlike indications. The indications were nearly round and were located in the cold leg above the tubesheet expansion transition, where pitting might be expected given the chemistry conditions. Some of these tubes with pitlike indications were initially left in service. The pitting is believed to have initiated before the chemical cleaning which was performed in 1994. New pits are unlikely to initiate in future cycles because the licensee removes copper-rich sludge, the major contributor to pitting, and has improved its chemistry control program. The licensee eventually plugged all 12 tubes with pitlike indications due to the uncertainty in nondestructive sizing estimates.

4.4.4 Summary and Observations

As depicted in Figure 4-13, there were 281,262 thermally treated Alloy 600 tubes placed in service at 18 plants between 1980 and 2001. Cumulatively, these 18 plants have operated for approximately 260 calendar years (as of December 2001) and have commercially operated for an average of 14 calendar years (as of December 2001). Of these 281,262 tubes, only 1397 tubes (0.5%) have been plugged. The number and percentage of tubes plugged at the 18 plants with thermally treated tubes are summarized in Table 4-25. Figure 4-14 depicts the total number and percentage of tubes plugged in plants with thermally treated Alloy 600 tubes as a function of model/grouping (i.e., model D5, model F, replacement models).

Tables 4-26 and 4-27 summarize the causes of tube plugging for Model D5, Model F, and replacement steam generators. In addition, these tables summarize the causes of tube plugging for all steam generators with thermally treated Alloy 600 tubes. The information in these tables is graphically depicted in Figure 4-15. As can be seen from the tables and figure, the dominant degradation mode of thermally treated Alloy 600 tubes is wear. Of the approximately 1400 tubes plugged, approximately 53% of the tubes were plugged as a result of tube wear. Tube wear occurs as a result of contact between the tube and a support structure (e.g., an anti-vibration bar) or a foreign object (e.g., a loose part). Loose parts can be introduced during steam generator fabrication, during maintenance activities, or as a result of corrosion degradation of other components in the primary or secondary side of the steam generator (e.g., a split pin nut). The rate of tube wear from support structures is generally predictable and is readily managed. Wear from loose parts is usually unexpected and can only be detected by inspection, loose parts monitoring systems, or primary-to-secondary leakage. The wear in thermally treated tubes has occurred predominantly at the AVBs although some occurred near loose parts. A very limited number of tubes have been plugged for wear at the tube support plates.

The percentage of tubes plugged for wear is greater for the Model F steam generators than for the Model D5 or replacement model steam generators. Manufacturing flaws also accounted for a significant percentage of tube plugging, accounting for 21% of the tubes plugged. The plugging of 23% of the tubes was attributed to "other" degradation mechanisms. Several tubes have been plugged due to restrictions. The nature and causes of many of these restrictions have not been provided.

Plants with replacement steam generators with thermally treated Alloy 600 tubes have a variety of strategies for inspecting their steam generators. Several plants inspect a subset of steam generators each refueling outage (e.g., one of three steam generators is inspected each outage). This is referred to as "skip steam generator." Others inspect all steam generators every other outage (i.e., no tube inspections are performed during one refueling outage but all steam generators are inspected the next refueling outage). This schedule is referred to as "skip-cycle." Yet others inspect all steam generators every outage. Plants that skip cycles or skip steam generators typically inspect 100% of the tubes in the steam generators inspected. In general, licensees with thermally treated Alloy 600 tubes inspect a subset of the total number of steam generators during an outage (e.g., two of four steam generators are inspected during one outage and the remaining two steam generators are inspected during the next outage). Such inspection programs result in an inspection frequency for thermally treated Alloy 600 tubes of every two cycles. At a few plants, steam generators are inspected every three operating cycles (e.g., at intervals of 48 effective full-power months).

Based on a review of inspection summary reports, tube inspections in plants with thermally treated Alloy 600 have become more comprehensive since the early 1980s. The inspections today focus on ensuring tube integrity for the interval between inspections consistent with Nuclear Energy Institute 97-06, "Steam Generator Program Guidelines." There have been no reported instances in which a thermally treated Alloy 600 tube did not satisfy the structural performance criterion (e.g., three times the normal operating differential pressure).

Figure 4-16 depicts the number of tubes plugged for each type of thermally treated Alloy 600 steam generator (e.g., Model D5) as a function of year. Similarly, Figure 4-17 provides the percentage of tubes plugged for each type of thermally treated Alloy 600 steam generator (e.g., Model D5) as a function of year. The percentage of tubes plugged each year has been relatively constant since the early 1990s. The data used to compile these figures is summarized in Table 4-28.

Figure 4-18 depicts the fraction of tubes plugged for a specific mechanism as a function of year. This figure was developed from the data provided in Tables 4-29, 4-30, and 4-31. In this figure, tubes plugged prior to commercial operation were treated as being plugged during the year the plant began commercial operation (in previous tables and figures in this report, tubes plugged prior to operation were treated as a distinct group independent of the actual year/outage in which they were plugged).

-161-

As a result of reviewing the operating experience with thermally treated Alloy 600 steam generator tubes, the following observations are made:

- A number of plants with mill-annealed Alloy 600 tubes stabilize tubes as a result of finding circumferential indications. Stabilization is intended to prevent a plugged tube from contacting neighboring tubes in the event that it severs. A tube could sever as a result of tube degradation that continues to progress following plugging. Some plants assess the need to stabilize forms of degradation (e.g., wear) other than circumferential indications and preventively stabilize tubes when indications reach or are projected to reach certain limits.

- At least one plant identified a tube that continued to wear following plugging. The wear indication proceeded throughwall after being plugged four years earlier with a 43% throughwall indication. The potential for tubes to continue to degrade following plugging raises questions about the need for tube stabilization in the future.

- Plugging of tubes for wear at tube support plates is fairly uncommon in plants with thermally treated Alloy 600 tubes. Recently plants have reported plugging tubes for this form of degradation. In addition, plants have been observing denting at tube supports corresponding to the quatrefoil lands.

- Some plants cut out access ports in the steam generator shell in order to remove loose parts. Plants remove the loose parts to prevent the initiation or continuation of wear degradation to tubes and/or to avoid preventively plugging and stabilizing tubes that may potentially be affected by these loose parts.

- Several plants, if not all, plug stub tubes since these locations are not routinely inspected during the inservice inspection.

- Several plants have reported tube expansion anomalies in the tubesheet. These areas are locations where degradation is likely to occur. These anomalies include tubes that were not expanded, tubes that were not expanded for the full length of the tubesheet, and tubes that were expanded above the top of the secondary face of the tubesheet. For tubes that were not expanded, some plants have plugged these tubes while others have reexpanded the tubes to avoid inspecting these tubes every outage (presumably with a rotating probe). Tubes that were not expanded do not appear to be found until well after the start of operation. When a tube was not fully expanded for the full length of the tubesheet, the expansion transition occurs below the secondary face of the tubesheet, resulting in an open crevice region where sludge deposits can accumulate. The expansion of a tube above the top of the secondary face of the tubesheet is an anomaly which results in an area of higher stress. Some plants inspect all identified expansion anomalies with a rotating probe.

- Performing tube inspections concurrent or after maintenance activities (e.g., sludge lancing) may make it difficult to assess the cause of indications since the maintenance activities may cause the loose parts to move . On the other hand, performing tube inspections before maintenance activities may result in missing indications of degradation induced during these activities and/or result in missing opportunities to find loose parts introduced as a result of these activities.

- Manufacturing buff marks (MBMs) and free span differential (FSD) signals are the result of a light buffing of the tubes to remove small imperfections of the tubing outside diameter. The two types of signals are generally analogous, except that the FSDs are readily discernable in the differential channels of the eddy current data, whereas MBMs are called in the absolute channel. Historical reviews are frequently performed for MBMs and FSD signals to determine if they have changed phase angle and/or voltage since the baseline. If the signal changes, supplemental rotating probe testing is typically performed.

- The few tubes pulled for destructive examination suggest that manufacturing anomalies or some other phenomena are producing eddy current signals indicative of degradation. The ability of the nondestructive examination techniques to distinguish true flaw signals from these anomalous inspection signals may become important as the second-generation steam generators age (and the potential for corrosion increases). Performing comprehensive baseline inspections before the steam generators are placed in service could provide confidence that "anomalous" nondestructive examination signals are truly signals from manufacturing marks rather than from service-induced conditions.

- Plants initially identify manufacturing flaws well after placing the steam generators in service. This is attributed to many factors including more stringent calling criteria, improvements in analyst performance, and improvements in inspection technology.

- Plants have found a number of indications (volumetric and linear) for which no definitive root cause was identified (although plausible explanations for the indications were put forward). The frequency of finding such indications appears to be increasing.

- A number of volumetric indications attributed to tube wear have been detected in the midspan of tubes and/or in the interior of the tube bundle. Material reviewed during the development of this report contained no insights on how a foreign object moves deep into the interior of the tube bundle without damaging other tubes on its path. In addition, no information was available on whether an object was found or retrieved near the location of the tube wear in many of these cases.

- Obstructions to the passage of bobbin coil probes have been identified in a few tubes. These obstructions were often identified only after a number of years of operation. The causal mechanism for these obstructions was not readily ascertainable. Obstructed tubes were reported at Callaway in 1996 (in a tube inspected in 1992), Comanche Peak in 1997, Surry 1 and 2 in the mid-1990s as well as in 1986, Vogtle 1 in 1997, and Robinson 2 in 2001.

- Volumetric indications have been detected at several plants. The cause of these indications has not been determined through removal of tubes for destructive examination. Destructive examination might provide insights on the nature of the indications. Volumetric indications have been reported at a number of plants, including Braidwood 2 in 1996 (1H), Byron 2 in 1996 (2C and 1H), Byron 2 in 2001 (above 2C), and at Wolf Creek in various years.

Far fewer tubes have been plugged in the steam generators with second-generation tube materials (i.e., thermally treated alloy 600) than in earlier steam generators with comparable operating times. Improvements in the design and operation of the second-generation steam generators appear to have increased the corrosion resistance of the tubes, as evidenced by the general lack of any significant amounts of corrosion degradation. The enhanced corrosion resistance is largely due to the thermal treatment process that has superseded the mill annealing process used in earlier steam generator designs.

The relatively good operating experience for plants with thermally treated Alloy 600 steam generator tubes can be attributed to several factors in addition to the heat treatment the tubes received: hydraulic expansion of the tubes into the tubesheet, the quatrefoil design of the tube support plates, and the stainless steel material used to fabricate the plates. The residual stress levels at the expansion transition in tubes hydraulically expanded into the tubesheet are lower than observed in plants whose tubes were expanded mechanically or explosively. Since crack growth rate and time to crack initiation depend, in part, on the stress level, lower stresses may result in lower crack growth rates and/or longer times before crack initiation.

This historical review has identified a number of issues which may warrant additional investigation in the future.

Although the operating experience with thermally treated Alloy 600 tubes has been favorable to date, there is a continued need to monitor the tubes to detect the onset of tube degradation (including cracking) and to assure the structural and leakage integrity of the tubes during the intervals between inspections. A better understanding of the nature of a number of these findings would be useful in determining appropriate intervals for future monitoring of tube degradation.

Table 4-1: Model D5: Total Number and Percentage of Tubes Plugged (12/01)

Plant	Number of Tubes Plugged[1]	Percent Plugged	Operating Time[2]
Braidwood 2	120	0.66	13
Byron 2	223	1.22	14
Catawba 2	183	1.00	15
Comanche Peak 2	37	0.20	8
TOTALS:	563	0.77	

[1]As of 12/31/01
[2]Operating Time = calendar years of operation as of 12/31/01

Table 4-2: Model D5: Number of Tubes Plugged as a Function of Mechanism (Detailed) (12/01)

Cause of Tube Plugging		Tubes Plugged	Percentage of Plugs	Tubes Plugged	Percentage of Plugs
Wear	AVB	258	45.8%	262	46.5%
	Pre-heater TSP (D5)	2	0.4%		
	TSP	2	0.4%		
Loose Parts	Confirmed	19	3.4%	38	6.7%
	Not Confirmed, Periphery	16	2.8%		
	Not Confirmed, Not Periphery	3	0.5%		
Obstruction Restriction	From PSI - no progression	0	0.0%	2	0.4%
	Service Induced	2	0.4%		
Manufacturing Flaws	Preservice	50	8.9%	94	16.7%
	Other	44	7.8%		
Inspection Issues	Probe Lodged	2	0.4%	15	2.7%
	Data Quality	2	0.4%		
	Dent/Geometry	4	0.7%		
	Permeability	4	0.7%		
	Not Inspected	3	0.5%		
Other	Top of Tubesheet	18	3.2%	152	27.0%
	Free Span	80	14.2%		
	TSP	44	7.8%		
	Other/Not Reported	10	1.8%		
SCC	ID	0	0.0%	0	0.0%
	OD	0	0.0%		
TOTALS		563	100.0%	563	100.0%

Total Tubes: 73120
Fraction Plugged: 0.77%

Table 4-3: Model D5: Cumulative Plugging Per Year

Year	Braidwood 2	Byron 2	Catawba 2	Comanche Peak 2
Pre-Op	6	11	14	20
1986				
1987			14	
1988			21	
1989		22	29	
1990	8	43	48	
1991	19		60	
1992		72		
1993	34	108	103	
1994	40		134	20
1995		137	157	
1996	75	167		20
1997	103		167	28
1998		205	176	
1999	109	219		33
2000	120		183	37
2001		223	183	

Table 4-4: Model D5: Plugging Per Year

Year	Braidwood 2	Byron 2	Catawba 2	Comanche Peak 2	Model D5 Totals
Pre-Op	6	11	14	20	51
1986					0
1987			0		0
1988			7		7
1989		11	8		19
1990	2	21	19		42
1991	11		12		23
1992		29			29
1993	15	36	43		94
1994	6		31	0	37
1995		29	23		52
1996	35	30		0	65
1997	28		10	8	46
1998		38	9		47
1999	6	14		5	25
2000	11		7	4	22
2001		4	0		4
Totals:	120	223	183	37	563

Table 4-5: Model D5: Cumulative Plugging Per RFO

Outage	Braidwood 2	Byron 2	Catawba 2	Comanche Peak 2
Pre-Op	6	11	14	20
RFO 1	8	22	21	20
RFO 2	19	43	29	20
RFO 3	34	72	48	28
RFO 4	40	108	60	33
RFO 5	75	137	103	37
RFO 6	103	167	134	
RFO 7	109	205	157	
RFO 8	120	219	167	
RFO 9		223	176	
RFO 10			183	
RFO 11			183	

Table 4-6: Model D5: Number of Tubes Plugged As a Function of Mechanism Per Year (Detailed)

Cause of Tube Plugging/Outage		1980	1981	1982	1983	1984	1985	1986	1987	1988	1989	1990	1991	1992	1993	1994	1995	1996	1997	1998	1999	2000	2001	Totals
Wear	AVB										2	35	17	25	51	7	22	48	19	2	15	15		258
	Pre-heater TSP (D5)																				1	1		2
	TSP																		1				1	2
Loose Parts	Confirmed									2	4						1	6	2	3			1	19
	Not Confirmed, Periphery											1			1		7				5			16
	Not Confirmed, Not Periphery										1										1		2	3
Obstruction Restriction	From PSI - no progression																							0
	Service Induced																		1		1			2
Manufacturing Flaws	Preservice							14	11	6					19									50
	Other																		15	29				44
Inspection Issues	Probe Lodged																					2		2
	Data Quality																			1		1		2
	Dent/Geometry										1								1	2				4
	Permeability																		2	1	1			4
	Not Inspected										1								1			1	2	3
Other	Top of Tubesheet										2				3	4	2	1	3	2	1			18
	Free Span									3	4	4	1	3	30	20	10	5	5	2				80
	TSP									2	3	4	5	1	8	6	5	4	2	5	1		1	44
	Not Reported										1	2			2		5							10
SCC	ID																							0
	OD																							0
TOTALS		0	0	0	0	0	0	14	11	13	19	42	23	29	114	37	52	65	46	47	25	22	4	563

Notes

Notes

Table 4-7: Model D5: Number of Tubes Plugged As a Function of Mechanism Per Year (Summary)

Year / Cause	1980	1981	1982	1983	1984	1985	1986	1987	1988	1989	1990	1991	1992	1993	1994	1995	1996	1997	1998	1999	2000	2001	Totals
Wear										2	35	17	25	51	7	22	48	19	5	16	15		262
Loose Parts									2	5				1		8	6	2	3	6	2	3	38
Restrictions																		1		1			2
Manufacturing							14	11	6					19				15	29				94
Inspection issues										2							1	4	3		5		15
Other									5	10	7	6	4	43	30	22	10	5	7	2		1	152
SCC																							0
	0	0	0	0	0	0	14	11	13	19	42	23	29	114	37	52	65	46	47	25	22	4	563

Notes

Notes

-171-

Table 4-8: Model D5: Fraction of Tubes Plugged As a Function of Mechanism Per Year (Summary)

Cause	1980	1981	1982	1983	1984	1985	1986	1987	1988	1989	1990	1991	1992	1993	1994	1995	1996	1997	1998	1999	2000	2001	Totals
Wear										0.11	0.83	0.74	0.86	0.45	0.19	0.42	0.74	0.41	0.11	0.64	0.68		0.47
Loose Parts									0.15	0.26				0.01		0.15	0.09	0.04	0.06	0.24	0.09	0.75	0.07
Restrictions																		0.02		0.04			0.00
Manufacturing							1.00	1.00	0.46					0.17				0.33	0.62				0.17
Inspection issues										0.11								0.09					0.03
Other																	0.02		0.06		0.23		0.27
SCC									0.38	0.53	0.17	0.26	0.14	0.38	0.81	0.42	0.15	0.11	0.15	0.08		0.25	
	0.00	0.00	0.00	0.00	0.00	0.00	1.00	1.00	1.00	1.00	1.00	1.00	1.00	1.00	1.00	1.00	1.00	1.00	1.00	1.00	1.00	1.00	1.00

Notes

Notes

Table 4-9: Model F: Total Number and Percentage of Tubes Plugged (12/01)

Plant	Number of Tubes Plugged[1]	Percent Plugged	Operating Time[2]
Callaway[3]	17	0.35	17
Millstone 3	106	0.47	16
Seabrook 1	90	0.40	11
Vogtle 1	48	0.21	15
Vogtle 2	29	0 13	13
Wolf Creek 1	144	0 64	16
TOTALS:	434	0.37	

[1]As of 12/31/01
[2]Operating Time = calendar years of operation as of 12/31/01
[3]Thermally Treated Tubes only

Table 4-10: Model F: Number of Tubes Plugged as a Function of Mechanism (Detailed) (12/01)

Cause of Tube Plugging		Tubes Plugged	Percentage of Plugs	Tubes Plugged	Percentage of Plugs
Wear	AVB	295	68.0%	295	68.0%
	Pre-heater TSP (D5)	0	0.0%		
	TSP	0	0.0%		
Loose Parts	Confirmed	9	2.1%	24	5.5%
	Not Confirmed, Periphery	10	2.3%		
	Not Confirmed, Not Periphery	5	1.2%		
Obstruction Restriction	From PSI - no progression	0	0.0%	2	0.5%
	Service Induced	2	0.5%		
Manufacturing Flaws	Preservice	63	14.5%	63	14.5%
	Other	0	0.0%		
Inspection Issues	Probe Lodged	0	0.0%	0	0.0%
	Data Quality	0	0.0%		
	Dent/Geometry	0	0.0%		
	Permeability	0	0.0%		
	Not Inspected	0	0.0%		
Other	Top of Tubesheet	19	4.4%	50	11.5%
	Free Span	13	3.0%		
	TSP	18	4.1%		
	Other/Not Reported	0	0.0%		
SCC	ID	0	0.0%	0	0.0%
	OD	0	0.0%		
TOTALS		434	100.0%	434	100.0%

Total Tubes: 117376
Fraction Plugged   0.37%

Table 4-11: Model F: Cumulative Plugging Per Year

Outage	Callaway	Millstone 3	Seabrook	Vogtle 1	Vogtle 2	Wolf Creek
Pre-Op	4	10	13	6	15	15
1986	4					15
1987	5	12				
1988				7		37
1989	6	16				
1990	6			11	15	39
1991		21	23	11		39
1992	7		23		15	
1993	7	28		15	15	44
1994			24	27		71
1995	11	39	36		18	
1996	16	41		31	24	87
1997			49	46		106
1998	16				24	
1999	16	55	74	46	29	112
2000			90	48		144
2001	17	106			29	

Table 4-12: Model F: Plugging Per Year

Outage	Callaway	Millstone 3	Seabrook	Vogtle 1	Vogtle 2	Wolf Creek	Model F Totals
Pre-Op	4	10	13	6	15	15	63
1986	0					0	0
1987	1	2					3
1988				1		22	23
1989	1	4					5
1990	0			4	0	2	6
1991		5	10	0		0	15
1992	1		0		0		1
1993	0	7		4	0	5	16
1994			1	12		27	40
1995	4	11	12		3		30
1996	5	2		4	6	16	33
1997			13	15		19	47
1998	0				0		0
1999	0	14	25	0	5	6	50
2000			16	2		32	50
2001	1	51			0		52
Totals:	17	106	90	48	29	144	434

Table 4-13: Model F: Cumulative Plugging Per RFO

Outage	Callaway	Millstone 3	Seabrook	Vogtle 1	Vogtle 2	Wolf Creek
Pre-Op	4	10	13	6	15	15
RFO 1	4	12	23	7	15	15
RFO 2	5	16	23	11	15	15
RFO 3	6	21	24	11	15	37
RFO 4	6	28	36	15	18	39
RFO 5	7	39	49	27	24	39
RFO 6	7	55	74	31	24	44
RFO 7	11	106	90	46	29	71
RFO 8	16			46	29	87
RFO 9	16			48		106
RFO 10	16					112
RFO 11	17					144

Table 4-14: Model F: Number of Tubes Plugged As a Function of Mechanism Per Year (Detailed)

Cause of Tube Plugging/Outage		1980	1981	1982	1983	1984	1985	1986	1987	1988	1989	1990	1991	1992	1993	1994	1995	1996	1997	1998	1999	2000	2001	Totals	Totals
Wear	AVB								2	19	3	6	11		16	38	26	28	38		49	44	15	295	295
	Pre-heater TSP (D5)																							0	
	TSP																							0	
Loose Parts	Confirmed												4						5					9	24
	Not Confirmed, Periphery																				1	1	6	10	
	Not Confirmed, Not Periphery																2		2			2	1	5	
Obstruction Restriction	From PSI - no progression																							0	2
	Service Induced																		2					2	
Manufacturing Flaws	Presence					4	15	10	6		15	13												63	63
	Other																							0	
Inspection Issues	Probe Lodged																							0	0
	Data Quality																							0	
	Dent/Geometry																							0	
	Permeability																							0	
	Not Inspected																							0	
Other	Top of Tubesheet									4	1							3				2	14	19	50
	Free Span										1	1						2				1	3	13	
	TSP								1					1		2	2						13	18	
	Not Reported																							0	
SCC	ID																							0	0
	OD																							0	
	TOTALS	0	0	0	0	4	15	10	9	23	20	19	15	1	16	40	30	33	47	0	50	50	52	434	434

Notes

-178-

Table 4-15: Model F: Number of Tubes Plugged As a Function of Mechanism Per Year (Summary)

Cause \ Year	1980	1981	1982	1983	1984	1985	1986	1987	1988	1989	1990	1991	1992	1993	1994	1995	1996	1997	1998	1999	2000	2001	Totals
Wear								2	19	3	6	11		16	38	26	28	38		49	44	15	295
Loose Parts												4				2		7		1	3	7	24
Restrictions																		2					2
Manufacturing					4	15	10	6		15	13												63
Inspection Issues																							0
Other								1	4	2			1		2	2	5				3	30	50
SCC																							0
	0	0	0	0	4	15	10	9	23	20	19	15	1	16	40	30	33	47	0	50	50	52	434

Notes*

Notes

-179-

Table 4-16: Model F: Fraction of Tubes Plugged As a Function of Mechanism Per Year (Summary)

Cause	1980	1981	1982	1983	1984	1985	1986	1987	1988	1989	1990	1991	1992	1993	1994	1995	1996	1997	1998	1999	2000	2001	Totals
Wear								0.22	0.83	0.15	0.32	0.73		1.00	0.95	0.87	0.85	0.81		0.98	0.88	0.29	0.68
Loose Parts												0.27				0.07		0.15		0.02	0.06	0.13	0.06
Restrictions																		0.04					0.00
Manufacturing					1.00	1.00	1.00	0.67		0.75	0.68												0.15
Inspection Issues																							
Other								0.11	0.17	0.10			1.00		0.05	0.07	0.15				0.06	0.58	0.12
SCC																							
	0.00	0.00	0.00	0.00	1.00	1.00	1.00	1.00	1.00	1.00	1.00	1.00	1.00	1.00	1.00	1.00	1.00	1.00	0.00	1.00	1.00	1.00	1.00

Notes

Notes

Table 4-17: Replacement Models: Total Number and Percentage of Tubes Plugged (12/01)

Plant	Number of Tubes Plugged[1]	Percent Plugged	Operating Time[2]
Indian Point 2	2	0.02	1
Point Beach 1	10	0.16	18
Robinson 2	39	0.40	17
Salem 1	58	0.26	4
Surry 1	43	0.43	20
Surry 2	39	0.39	21
Turkey Point 3	166	1.72	20
Turkey Point 4	43	0.45	19
TOTALS:	400	0.44	

[1]As of 12/31/01
[2]Operating Time = calendar years of operation as of 12/31/01

Table 4-18: Replacement Models: Number of Tubes Plugged as a Function of Mechanism (Detailed) (12/01)

Cause of Tube Plugging		Tubes Plugged	Percentage of Plugs	Tubes Plugged	Percentage of Plugs
Wear	AVB	93	23.3%	107	26.8%
	Pre-heater TSP (D5)	0	0.0%		
	TSP	14	3.5%		
Loose Parts	Confirmed	3	0.8%	15	3.8%
	Not Confirmed, Periphery	11	2.8%		
	Not Confirmed, Not Periphery	1	0.3%		
Obstruction Restriction	From PSI - no progression	2	0.5%	19	4.8%
	Service Induced	17	4.3%		
Manufacturing Flaws	Preservice	121	30.3%	131	32.8%
	Other	10	2.5%		
Inspection Issues	Probe Lodged	0	0.0%	7	1.8%
	Data Quality	4	1.0%		
	Dent/Geometry	0	0.0%		
	Permeability	3	0.8%		
	Not Inspected	0	0.0%		
Other	Top of Tubesheet	102	25.5%	121	30.3%
	Free Span	12	3.0%		
	TSP	7	1.8%		
	Other/Not Reported	0	0.0%		
SCC	ID	0	0.0%	0	0.0%
	OD	0	0.0%		
TOTALS		400	100.0%	400	100.0%

Total Tubes: 90766
Fraction Plugged 0.44%

Table 4-19: Replacement Models: Cumulative Plugging Per Year

Outage	Indian Point 2	Point Beach 1	Robinson 2	Salem 1	Surry 1	Surry 2	Turkey Point 3	Turkey Point 4
Pre-Op	2	4	28	13	2	2	39	31
1980								
1981								
1982						2		
1983		4			2	2	39	31
1984		4			6			
1985		4				2	43	
1986		4	28		10	3		31
1987		4	28				44	
1988		6	29		10	3		32
1989		6	29					
1990		6	30		12		55	
1991		8	31			3		33
1992		8	32		14		62	
1993		8	34			5		33
1994		8	34		18		66	33
1995		9	34		19	10	68	
1996		9	35			18		33
1997		9			24	23	82	33
1998		9	35		30		83	
1999		9	35	23		32		33
2000		9			38	39	152	43
2001		10	39	58	43		166	

Table 4-20: Replacement Models: Plugging Per Year

Outage	Indian Point 2	Point Beach 1	Robinson 2	Salem 1	Surry 1	Surry 2	Turkey Point 3	Turkey Point 4	Replacement Totals
Pre-Op	2	4	28	13	2	2	39	31	121
1980									0
1981						0			0
1982									0
1983		0			0	0	0		0
1984		0			4			0	4
1985		0				0	4		4
1986		0	0		4	1		0	5
1987		1	0			0			1
1988		2	1		0			1	4
1989		0	0						0
1990		0	1		2		11		14
1991		2	0			0		1	3
1992		0	1		2		7		10
1993		0	1			2		0	3
1994		0	2		4		4	0	10
1995		1	0		1	5	2		9
1996		0	1			8		0	9
1997		0	0		5	5	14	0	24
1998		0	0		6		1		7
1999		0	4		5	9	1	0	19
2000		0	0	10	8	7	69		94
2001		1		35			14	10	59
Totals:	2	10	39	58	43	39	166	43	400

Table 4-21: Replacement Models: Cumulative Plugging Per RFO

Outage	Indian Point 2	Point Beach 1	Robinson 2	Salem 1	Surry 1	Surry 2	Turkey Point 3	Turkey Point 4
Pre-Op	2	4	28	13	2	2	39	31
RFO 1		4	28	23	2	2	39	31
RFO 2		4	28	58	6	2	43	31
RFO 3		4	29		10	2	44	32
RFO 4		6	30		10	3	55	33
RFO 5		6	31		12	3	62	33
RFO 6		6	32		14	3	66	33
RFO 7		8	34		18	5	68	33
RFO 8		8	35		19	10	82	33
RFO 9		8	35		24	18	83	33
RFO 10		8	35		30	23	152	43
RFO 11		9	39		38	32	166	
RFO 12		9			43	39		
RFO 13		9						
RFO 14		9						
RFO 15		10						
RFO 16								
RFO 17								
RFO 18								
RFO 19								
RFO 20								
RFO 21								
RFO 22								

Table 4-22: Replacement Models: Number of Tubes Plugged As a Function of Mechanism Per Year (Detailed)

Cause of Tube Plugging/Outage		1980	1981	1982	1983	1984	1985	1986	1987	1988	1989	1990	1991	1992	1993	1994	1995	1996	1997	1998	1999	2000	2001	Totals	Totals
Wear	AVB											7	1	4	2	7	3	3	5	1	8	20	32	93	107
	Pre heater TSP (D5)																							0	
	TSP												1									1	12	14	
Loose Parts	Confirmed							1								2								3	15
	Not Confirmed, Periphery									1		1						1	2	3			3	11	
	Not Confirmed, Not Periphery																						1	1	
Obstruction Restriction	From PSI - no progression													1	1									2	19
	Service Induced						1	1		1		1						2	5	3	1		2	17	
Manufacturing Flaws	Preservice	2	2	39	31	32						2							13					121	131
	Other							1		2		2						2			2		3	10	
Inspection Issues	Probe Lodged																							0	7
	Data Quality																						4	4	
	Dent/Geometry																							0	
	Permeability																		1		1		1	3	
	Not Inspected																							0	
Other	Top of Tubesheet					1	3		1			2		5			5	3	8		8	71	1	102	121
	Free Span					3	1									3	1		3			1		12	
	TSP					3	1					2				1								7	
	Not Reported																							0	
SCC	ID																							0	0
	OD																							0	
TOTALS		2	2	39	31	36	4	5	1	4	0	14	3	10	10	10	9	9	37	7	19	96	59	400	400

Notes

Notes

Table 4-23: Replacment Models: Number of Tubes Plugged As a Function of Mechanism Per Year (Summary)

Cause \ Year	1980	1981	1982	1983	1984	1985	1986	1987	1988	1989	1990	1991	1992	1993	1994	1995	1996	1997	1998	1999	2000	2001	Totals
Wear											7	2	4	2	7	3	3	5	1	8	21	44	107
Loose Parts							1		1		1				2		1	2	3			4	15
Restrictions							1		1			1	1	1		1	2	5	3	1		2	19
Manufacturing	2	2	39	31	32		1		2		2							13		2	2	3	131
Inspection Issues																		1			1	5	7
Other					4	4	2	1			4		5		1	5	3	11		8	72	1	121
SCC																							0
	2	2	39	31	36	4	5	1	4	0	14	3	10	3	10	9	9	37	7	19	96	59	400

Notes

Notes

-187-

Table 4-24: Replacement Models: Fraction of Tubes Plugged As a Function of Mechanism Per Year (Summary)

Cause \ Year	1980	1981	1982	1983	1984	1985	1986	1987	1988	1989	1990	1991	1992	1993	1994	1995	1996	1997	1998	1999	2000	2001	Totals
Wear							0.20		0.25		0.50	0.67	0.40	0.67	0.70	0.33	0.33	0.14	0.14	0.42	0.22	0.75	0.27
Loose Parts							0.20		0.25		0.07				0.20		0.11	0.05	0.43			0.07	0.04
Restrictions												0.33	0.10	0.33		0.11	0.22	0.14	0.43	0.05		0.03	0.05
Manufacturing	1.00	1.00	1.00	1.00	0.89		0.20		0.50		0.14							0.35		0.11	0.02	0.05	0.33
Inspection Issues																		0.03			0.01	0.08	0.02
Other					0.11																		
SCC						1.00	0.40	1.00			0.29		0.50		0.10	0.56	0.33	0.30		0.42	0.75	0.02	0.30
	1.00	1.00	1.00	1.00	1.00	1.00	1.00	1.00	1.00	0.00	1.00	1.00	1.00	1.00	1.00	1.00	1.00	1.00	1.00	1.00	1.00	1.00	1.00

Notes

Notes

Table 4-25: All Models: Total Number and Percentage of Tubes Plugged (12/01)

Plant	Number of Tubes Plugged[1]	Percent Plugged	Operating Time[2]
Braidwood 2	120	0.66	13
Byron 2	223	1.22	14
Callaway	17	0.35	17
Catawba 2	183	1.00	15
Comanche Peak 2	37	0.20	8
Indian Point 2	2	0.02	1
Millstone 3	106	0.47	16
Point Beach 1	10	0.16	18
Robinson 2	39	0.40	17
Salem 1	58	0.26	4
Seabrook 1	90	0.40	11
Surry 1	43	0.43	20
Surry 2	39	0.39	21
Turkey Point 3	166	1.72	20
Turkey Point 4	43	0.45	19
Vogtle 1	48	0.21	15
Vogtle 2	29	0.13	13
Wolf Creek 1	144	0.64	16
TOTALS:	1397	0.50	

[1]As of 12/31/01
[2]Operating Time = calendar years of operation as of 12/31/01

Table 4-26: All Models: Number of Tubes Plugged As a Function of Mechanism (Detailed) (12/01)

Cause of Tube Plugging		Model D5		Model F		Replacement Models		All Models	
		Tubes Plugged	Percentage of Plugs	Tubes Plugged	Percentage of Plugs	Tubes Plugged	Percentage of Plugs	Tubes Plugged	Percentage of Plugs
Wear	AVB	258	45.8%	295	68.0%	93	23.3%	646	46.2%
	Pre-heater TSP (D5)	2	0.4%	0	0.0%	0	0.0%	2	0.1%
	TSP	2	0.4%	0	0.0%	14	3.5%	16	1.1%
Loose Parts	Confirmed	19	3.4%	9	2.1%	3	0.8%	31	2.2%
	Not Confirmed, Periphery	16	2.8%	10	2.3%	11	2.8%	37	2.6%
	Not Confirmed, Not Periphery	3	0.5%	5	1.2%	1	0.3%	9	0.6%
Obstruction Restriction	From PSI - no progression	0	0.0%	0	0.0%	2	0.5%	2	0.1%
	Service Induced	2	0.4%	2	0.5%	17	4.3%	21	1.5%
Manufacturing Flaws	Preservice	50	8.9%	63	14.5%	121	30.3%	234	16.8%
	Other	44	7.8%	0	0.0%	10	2.5%	54	3.9%
Inspection Issues	Probe Lodged	2	0.4%	0	0.0%	0	0.0%	2	0.1%
	Data Quality	2	0.4%	0	0.0%	4	1.0%	6	0.4%
	Dent/Geometry	4	0.7%	0	0.0%	0	0.0%	4	0.3%
	Permeability	4	0.7%	0	0.0%	3	0.8%	7	0.5%
	Not Inspected	3	0.5%	0	0.0%	0	0.0%	3	0.2%
Other	Top of Tubesheet	18	3.2%	19	4.4%	102	25.5%	139	9.9%
	Free Span	80	14.2%	13	3.0%	12	3.0%	105	7.5%
	TSP	44	7.8%	18	4.1%	7	1.8%	69	4.9%
	Other/Not Reported	10	1.8%	0	0.0%	0	0.0%	10	0.7%
SCC	ID	0	0.0%	0	0.0%	0	0.0%	0	0.0%
	OD	0	0.0%	0	0.0%	0	0.0%	0	0.0%
TOTALS		563	100.0%	434	100.0%	400	100.0%	1397	100.0%

	Model D5	Model F	Replacement Models	All Models
Total Tubes:	73120	117376	90766	281262
Fraction Plugged:	0.77%	0.37%	0.44%	0.50%
Average Age (years):	12.8	14.6	15.1	14.4

Table 4-27: All Models: Number of Tubes Plugged as a Function of Mechanism (Summary) (12/01)

Cause of Tube Plugging		Model D5 Tubes Plugged	Model D5 Percentage of Plugs	Model F Tubes Plugged	Model F Percentage of Plugs	Replacement Models Tubes Plugged	Replacement Models Percentage of Plugs	All Models Tubes Plugged	All Models Percentage of Plugs
Wear	AVB Pre-heater TSP (D5) TSP	262	46.5%	295	68.0%	107	26.8%	664	47.5%
Loose Parts	Confirmed Not Confirmed, Periphery Not Confirmed, Not Periphery	38	6.7%	24	5.5%	15	3.8%	77	5.5%
Obstruction Restriction	From PSI - no progression Service Induced	2	0.4%	2	0.5%	19	4.8%	23	1.6%
Manufacturing Flaws	Preservice Other	94	16.7%	63	14.5%	131	32.8%	288	20.6%
Inspection Issues	Probe Lodged Data Quality Dent/Geometry Permeability Not Inspected	15	2.7%	0	0.0%	7	1.8%	22	1.6%
Other	Top of Tubesheet Free Span TSP Other/Not Reported	152	27.0%	50	11.5%	121	30.3%	323	23.1%
SCC	ID OD	0	0.0%	0	0.0%	0	0.0%	0	0.0%
TOTALS		563	100.0%	434	100.0%	400	100.0%	1397	100.0%

	Model D5	Model F	Replacement Models	All Models
Total Tubes:	73120	117376	90766	281262
Fraction Plugged:	0.77%	0.37%	0.44%	0.50%
Average Age (years):	12.8	14.6	15.1	14.4

Table 4-28: All Models: Plugging Per Year

Year	Model D5	Model F	Replacement Models	All Models	Tubes in TT SGs
Pre-Op	51	63	121	235	281262
1980			0	0	10026
1981			0	0	20052
1982			0	0	29694
1983			0	0	39336
1984			4	4	60262
1985			4	4	82766
1986	0	0	5	5	123550
1987	0	3	1	4	164334
1988	7	23	4	34	182614
1989	19	5	0	24	205118
1990	42	6	14	62	227622
1991	23	15	3	41	227622
1992	29	1	10	40	227622
1993	94	16	3	113	245902
1994	37	40	10	87	245902
1995	52	30	9	91	245902
1996	65	33	9	107	245902
1997	46	47	24	117	268406
1998	47	0	7	54	268406
1999	25	50	19	94	268406
2000	22	50	94	166	281262
2001	4	52	59	115	281262
Totals:	563	434	400	1397	

Table 4-29: All Models: Number of Tubes Plugged As a Function of Mechanism Per Year (Detailed)

Cause of Tube Plugging/Outage	Mechanism	1980	1981	1982	1983	1984	1985	1986	1987	1988	1989	1990	1991	1992	1993	1994	1995	1996	1997	1998	1999	2000	2001	Totals	Totals
Wear	AVB								2	19	5	48	29	29	69	52	51	79	62	3	72	79	47	646	664
	Pre-heater TSP (D5)																			1	1			2	
	TSP												1							2		1	12	16	
Loose Parts	Confirmed							1		2	4						1	6	7	3	6		1	31	77
	Not Confirmed, Periphery									1	1	1	4			2	9	1	2	3	1	1	11	37	
	Not Confirmed, Not Periphery																		3			4	2	9	
Obstruction Restriction	From PSI - no progression													1	1									2	23
	Service Induced							1					1		1		1		8	3	2		2	21	
Manufacturing Flaws	Preservice	2	2	39	31	36	15	24	17	6	15	13			19			2	13					234	288
	Other							1		2									15	29	2	2	3	54	
Inspection Issues	Probe Lodged																					2		2	22
	Data Quality																							6	
	Dent/Geometry																						4	4	
	Permeability																		3	2		2		7	
	Not Inspected										1							1	1	1		2	1	3	
Other	Top of Tubesheet					1	3	1	1	7	2	2	1	9	3	4	7	7	11	2	9	73	14	139	323
	Free Span										5	5	5	1	30	21	12	7	5			1	5	105	
	TSP					3	1	1	1	2	4	4			8	8	5	4		5	1	1	13	69	
	Not Reported										1	1			2		5							10	
SCC	ID																							0	0
	OD																							0	
	TOTALS	2	2	39	31	40	19	29	21	40	39	75	41	40	133	87	91	107	130	54	94	168	115	1397	1397

Notes

Notes

-193-

Table 4-30: All Models: Number of Tubes Plugged As a Function of Mechanism Per Year (Summary)

Year / Cause	1980	1981	1982	1983	1984	1985	1986	1987	1988	1989	1990	1991	1992	1993	1994	1995	1996	1997	1998	1999	2000	2001	Totals
Wear								2	19	5	48	30	29	69	52	51	79	62	6	73	80	59	664
Loose Parts							1		3	5	1	4		1	2	10	7	11	6	7	5	14	77
Restrictions							1		1			1	1	1		1	2	8	3	2	5	2	23
Manufacturing	2	2	39	31	36	15	25	17	8	15	15			19				28	29				288
Inspection issues										2							1	5	3	2	6	5	22
Other					4	4	2	2	9	12	11	6	10	43	33	29	18	16	7	10	75	32	323
SCC																							0
	2	2	39	31	40	19	29	21	40	39	75	41	40	133	87	91	107	130	54	94	168	115	1397

Notes*

Notes

-194-

Table 4-31: All Models: Fraction of Tubes Plugged As a Function of Mechanism Per Year (Summary)

Cause \ Year	1980	1981	1982	1983	1984	1985	1986	1987	1988	1989	1990	1991	1992	1993	1994	1995	1996	1997	1998	1999	2000	2001	Totals
Wear								0.10	0.48	0.13	0.64	0.73	0.73	0.52	0.60	0.56	0.74	0.48	0.11	0.78	0.48	0.51	0.48
Loose Parts							0.03		0.08	0.13	0.01	0.10		0.01	0.02	0.11	0.07	0.08	0.11	0.07	0.03	0.12	0.06
Restrictions							0.03		0.03			0.02	0.03	0.01		0.01	0.02	0.06	0.06	0.02		0.02	0.02
Manufacturing	1.00	1.00	1.00	1.00	0.90	0.79	0.86	0.81	0.20	0.38	0.20							0.22	0.54		0.01	0.03	0.21
Inspection Issues										0.05				0.14			0.01	0.04	0.06	0.02	0.04	0.04	0.02
Other					0.10	0.21	0.07	0.10	0.23	0.31	0.15	0.15	0.25	0.32	0.38	0.32	0.17	0.12	0.13	0.11	0.45	0.28	0.23
SCC																							
	1.00	1.00	1.00	1.00	1.00	1.00	1.00	1.00	1.00	1.00	1.00	1.00	1.00	1.00	1.00	1.00	1.00	1.00	1.00	1.00	1.00	1.00	1.00

Notes:

Notes

-195-

Figure 4-1: Model D5: Causes of Tube Plugging

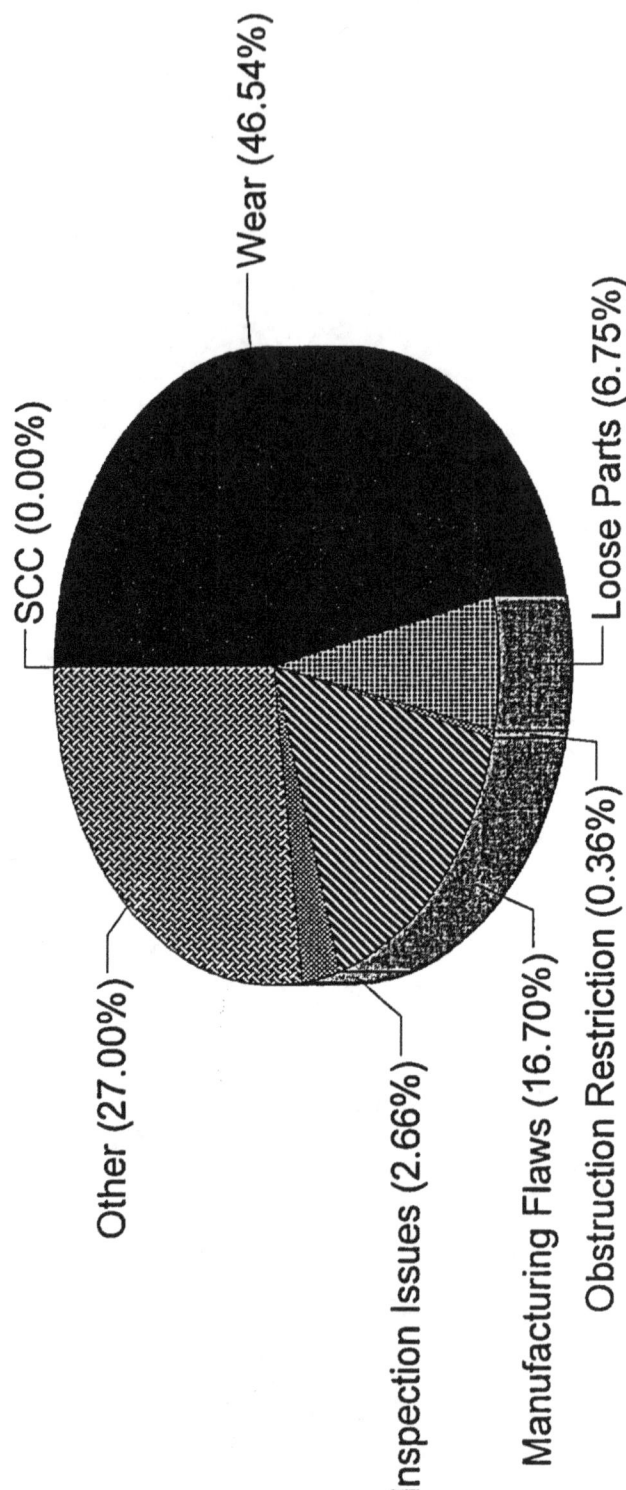

Wear (46.54%)

SCC (0.00%)

Loose Parts (6.75%)

Other (27.00%)

Inspection Issues (2.66%)

Manufacturing Flaws (16.70%)

Obstruction Restriction (0.36%)

Figure 4-2: Model D5: Plugging Per Year

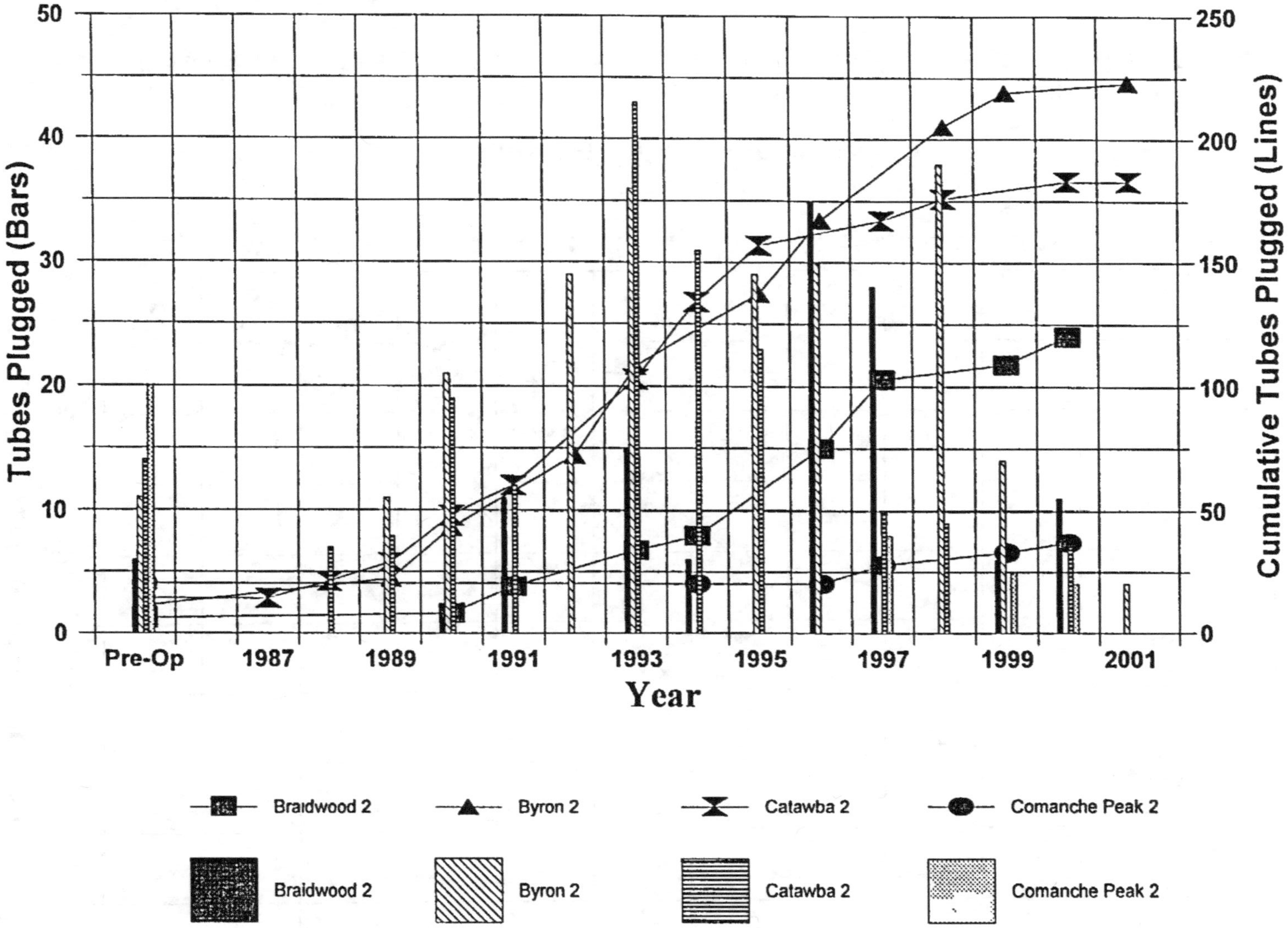

-197-

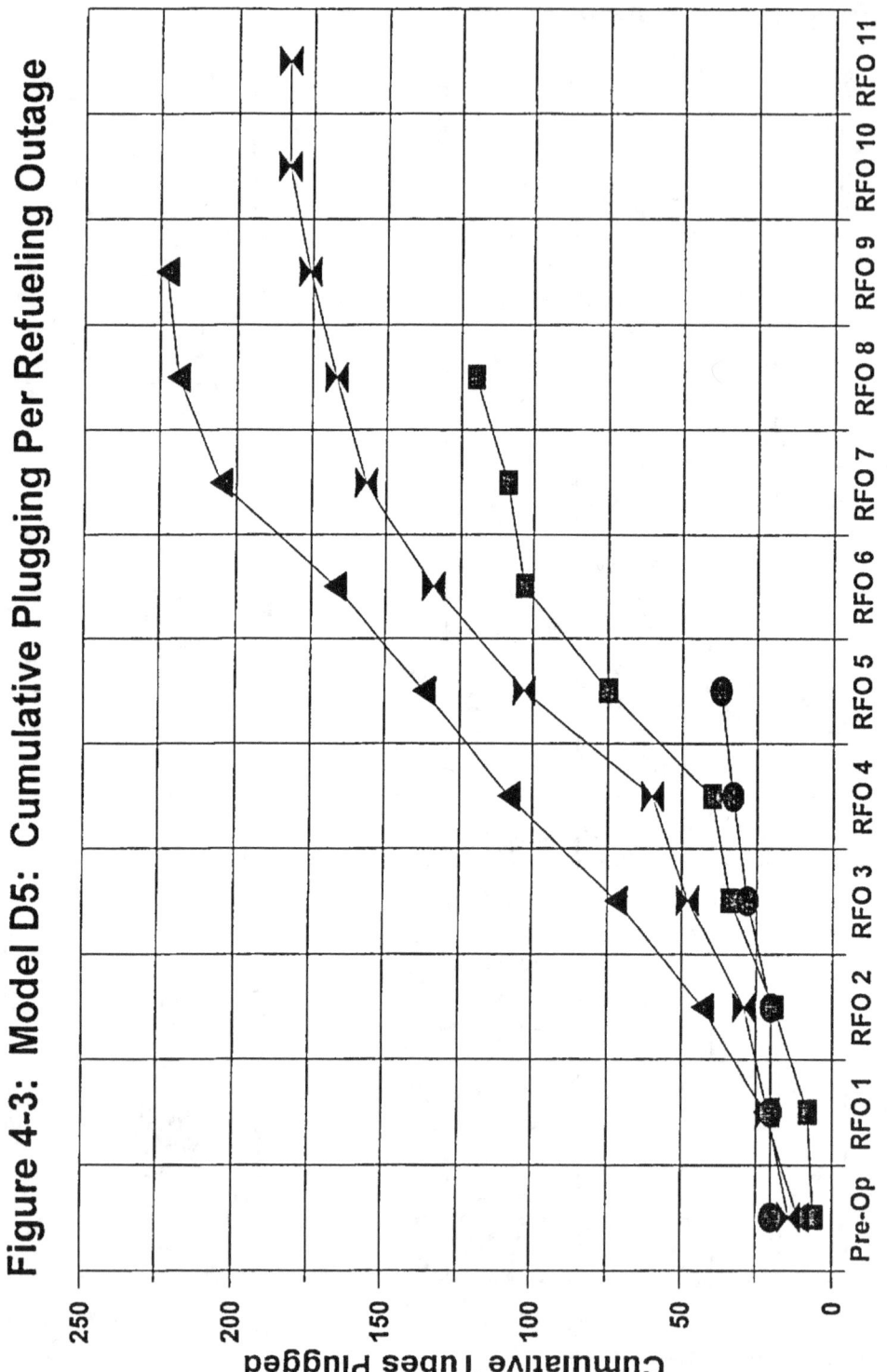

Figure 4-3: Model D5: Cumulative Plugging Per Refueling Outage

Refueling Outage Number (RFO)

-198-

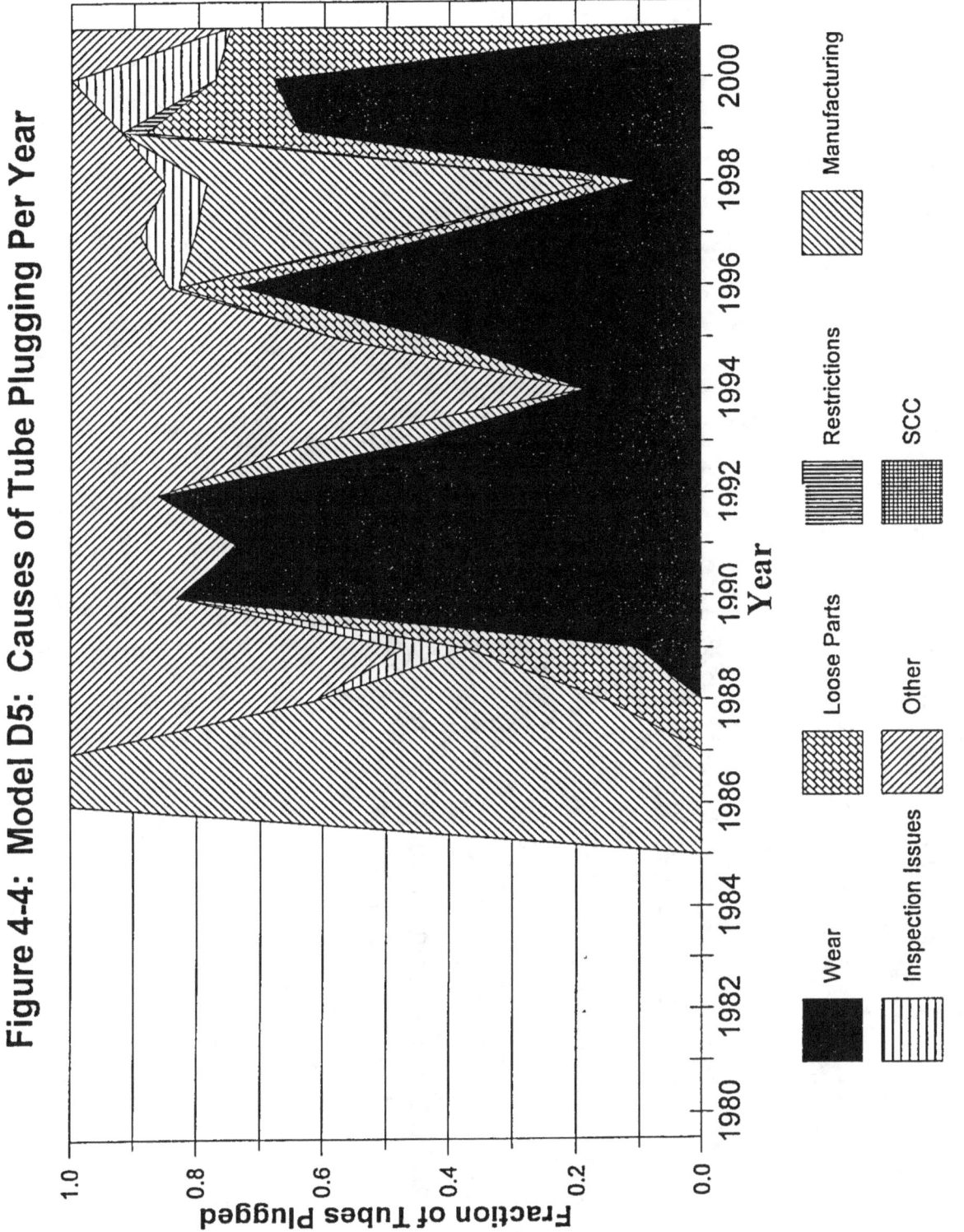

Figure 4-4: Model D5: Causes of Tube Plugging Per Year

Figure 4-5: Model F: Causes of Tube Plugging (12/01)

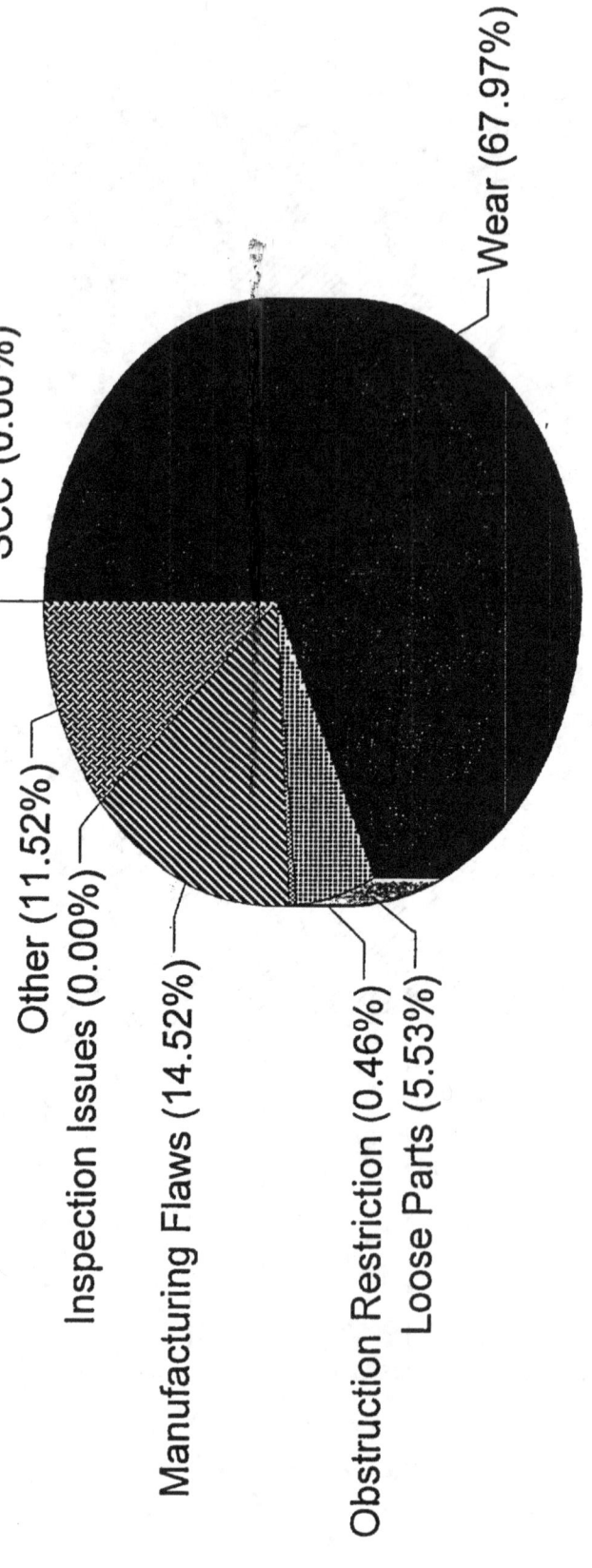

SCC (0.00%)

Wear (67.97%)

Other (11.52%)

Inspection Issues (0.00%)

Manufacturing Flaws (14.52%)

Obstruction Restriction (0.46%)

Loose Parts (5.53%)

Figure 4-6: Model F: Plugging Per Year

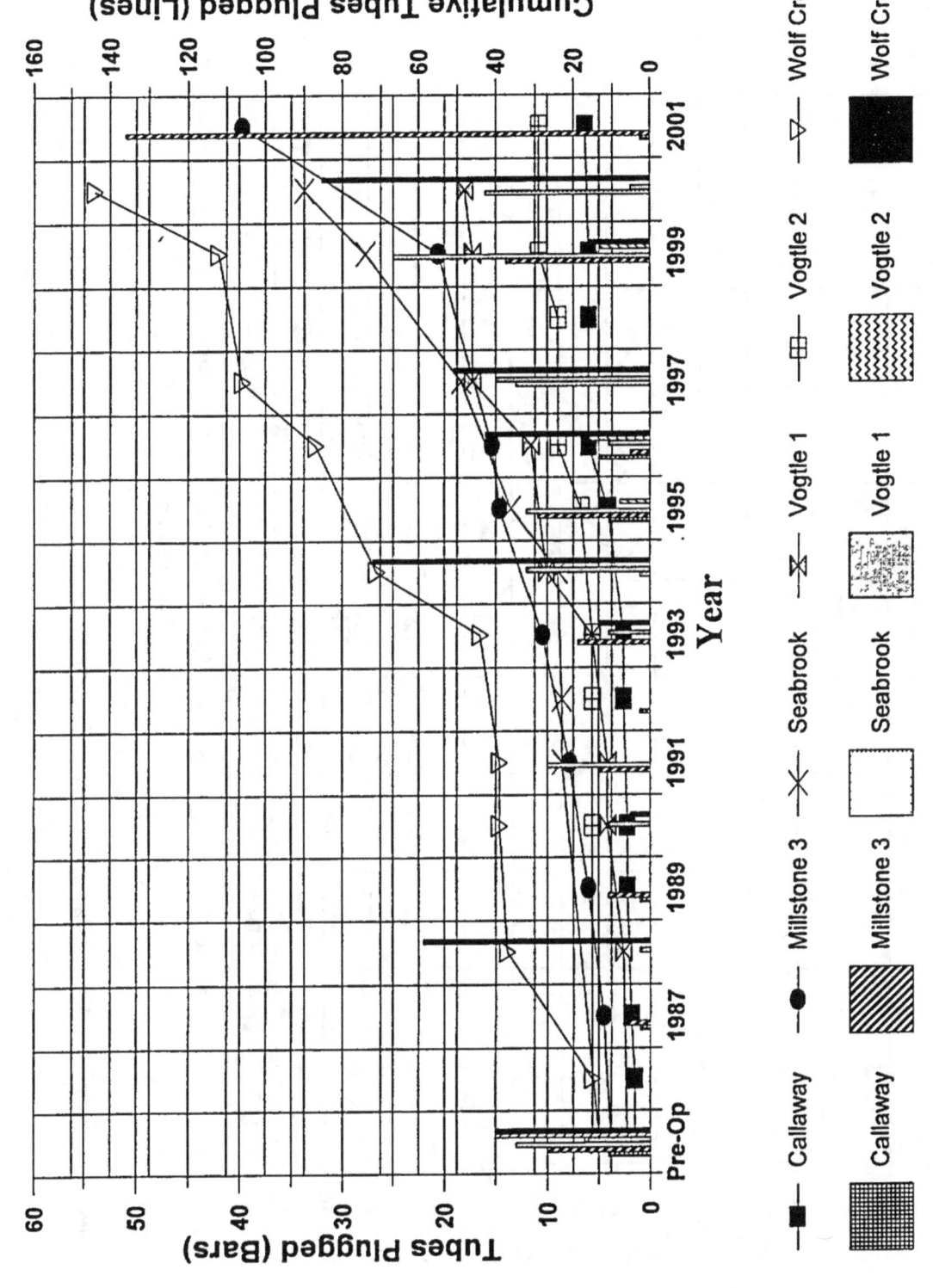

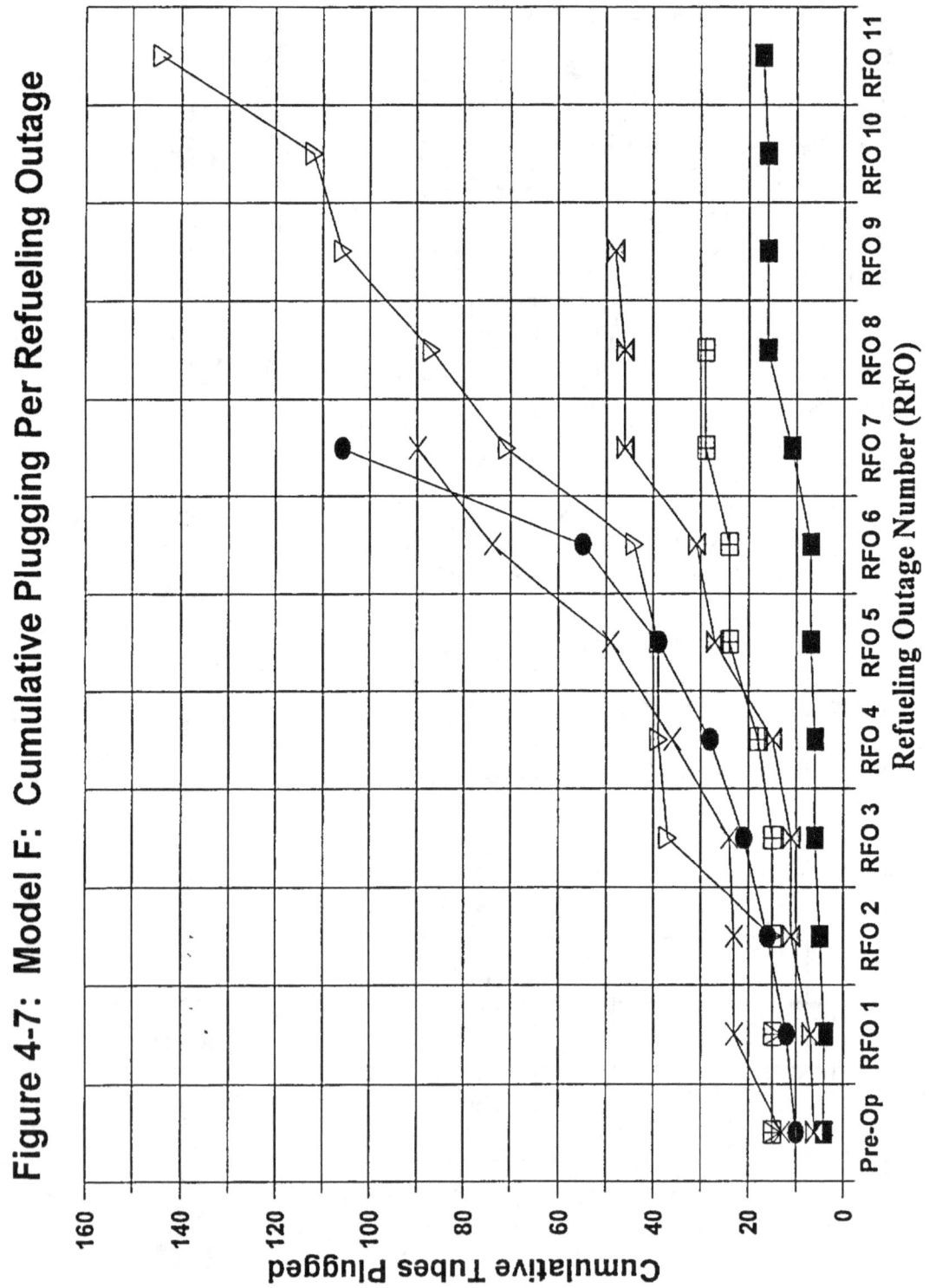

Figure 4-7: Model F: Cumulative Plugging Per Refueling Outage

Cumulative Tubes Plugged

Refueling Outage Number (RFO)

■— Callaway   ●— Millstone 3   ✕— Seabrook   ⋈— Vogtle 1   ⊞— Vogtle 2   ▽— Wolf Creek

-202-

Figure 4-8: Model F: Causes of Tube Plugging Per Year

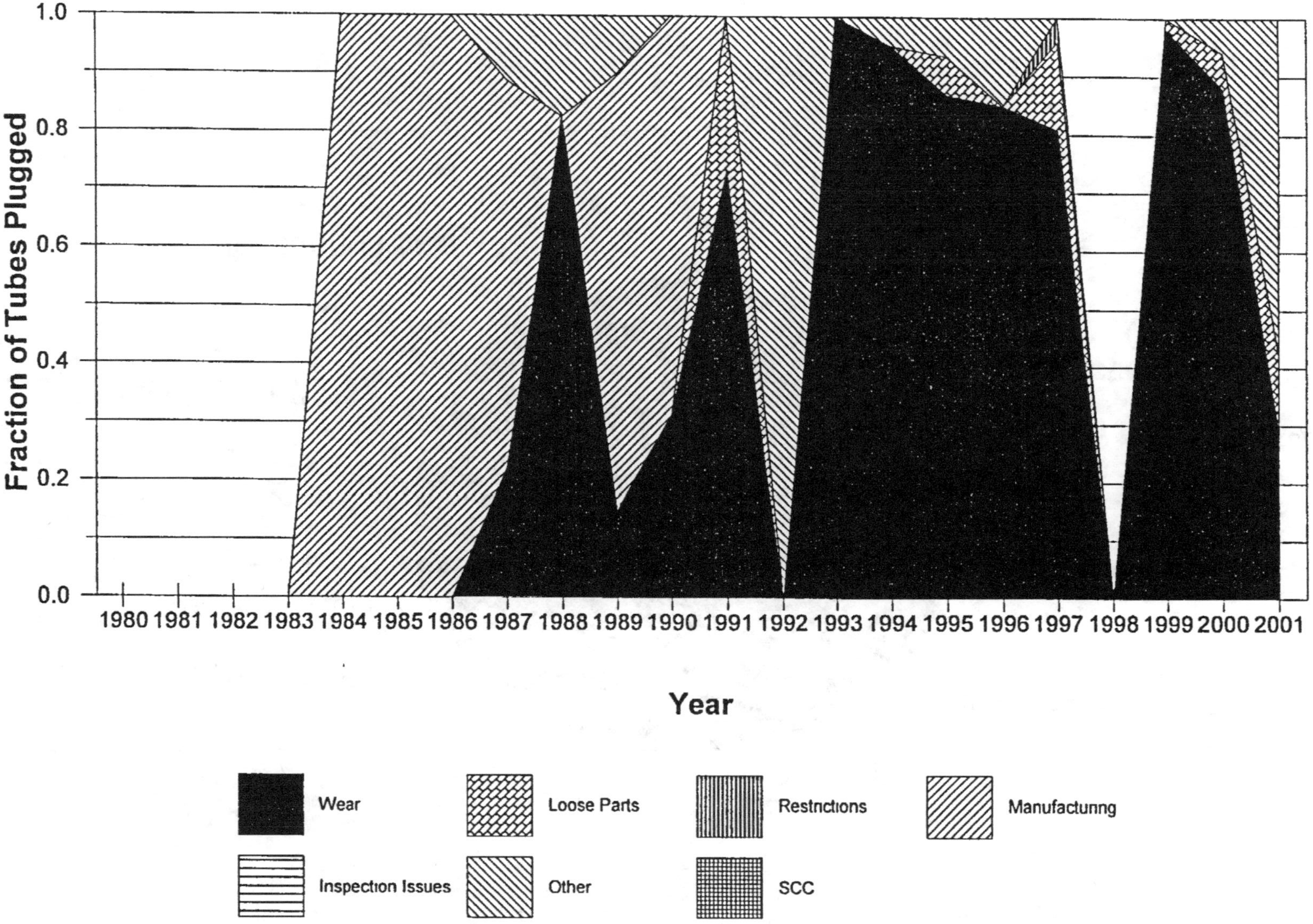

Figure 4-9: Replacement Models: Causes of Tube Plugging (12/01)

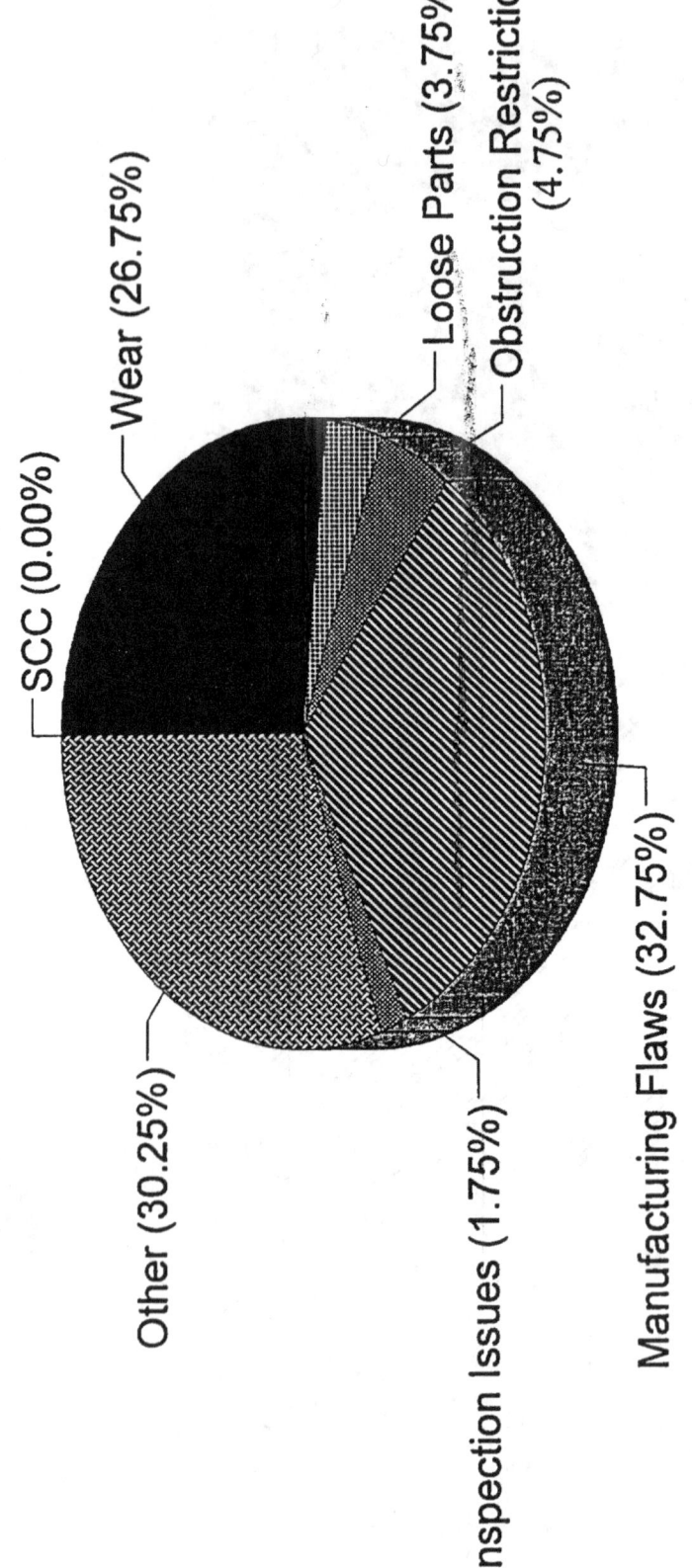

Figure 4-10: Replacement Models: Plugging Per Year

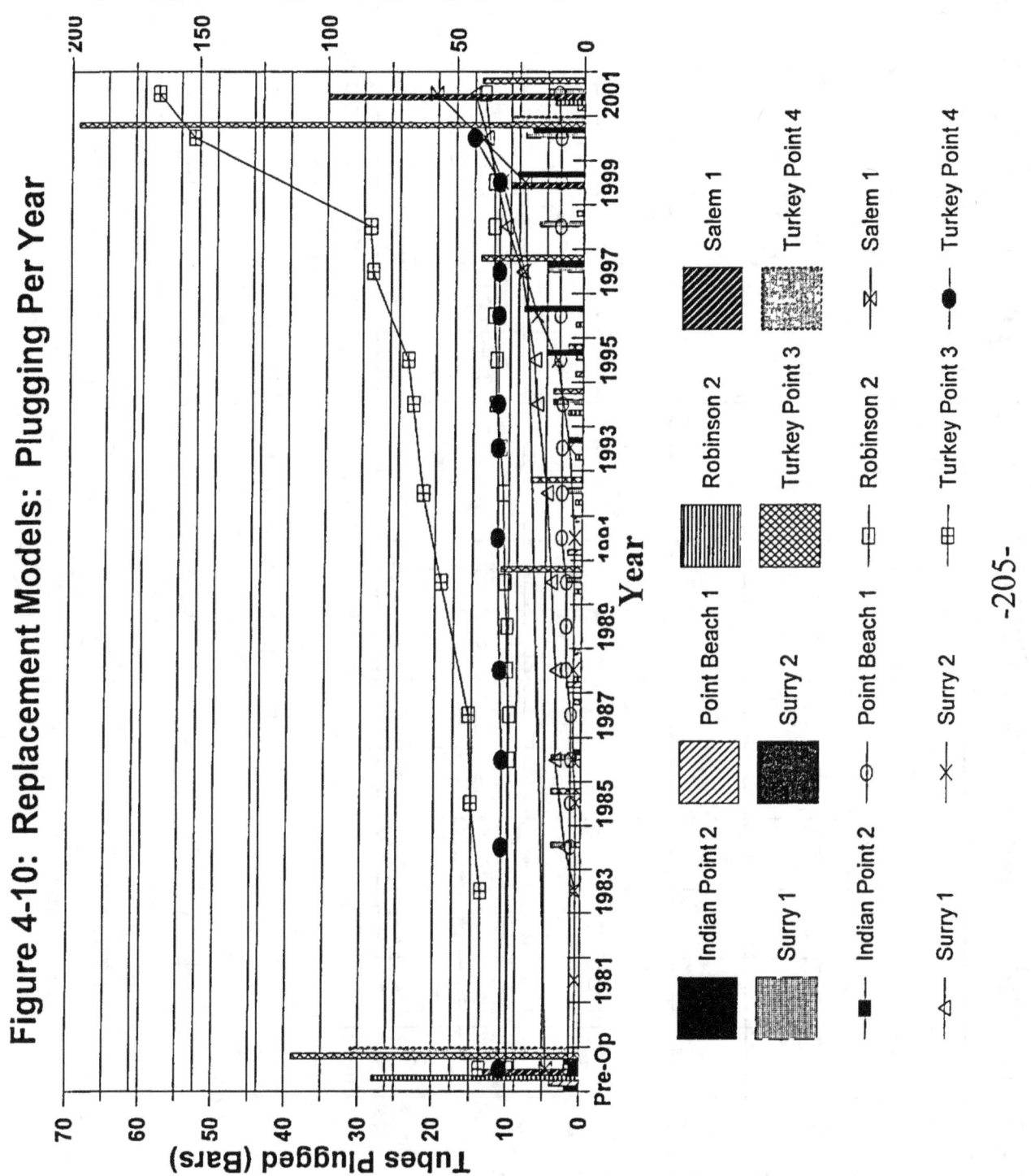

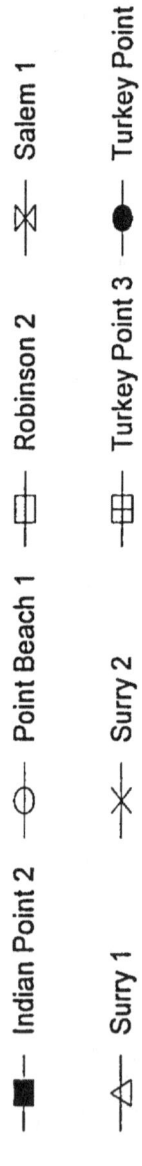

Figure 4-11: Replacement Models: Cumulative Plugging Per Refueling Outage

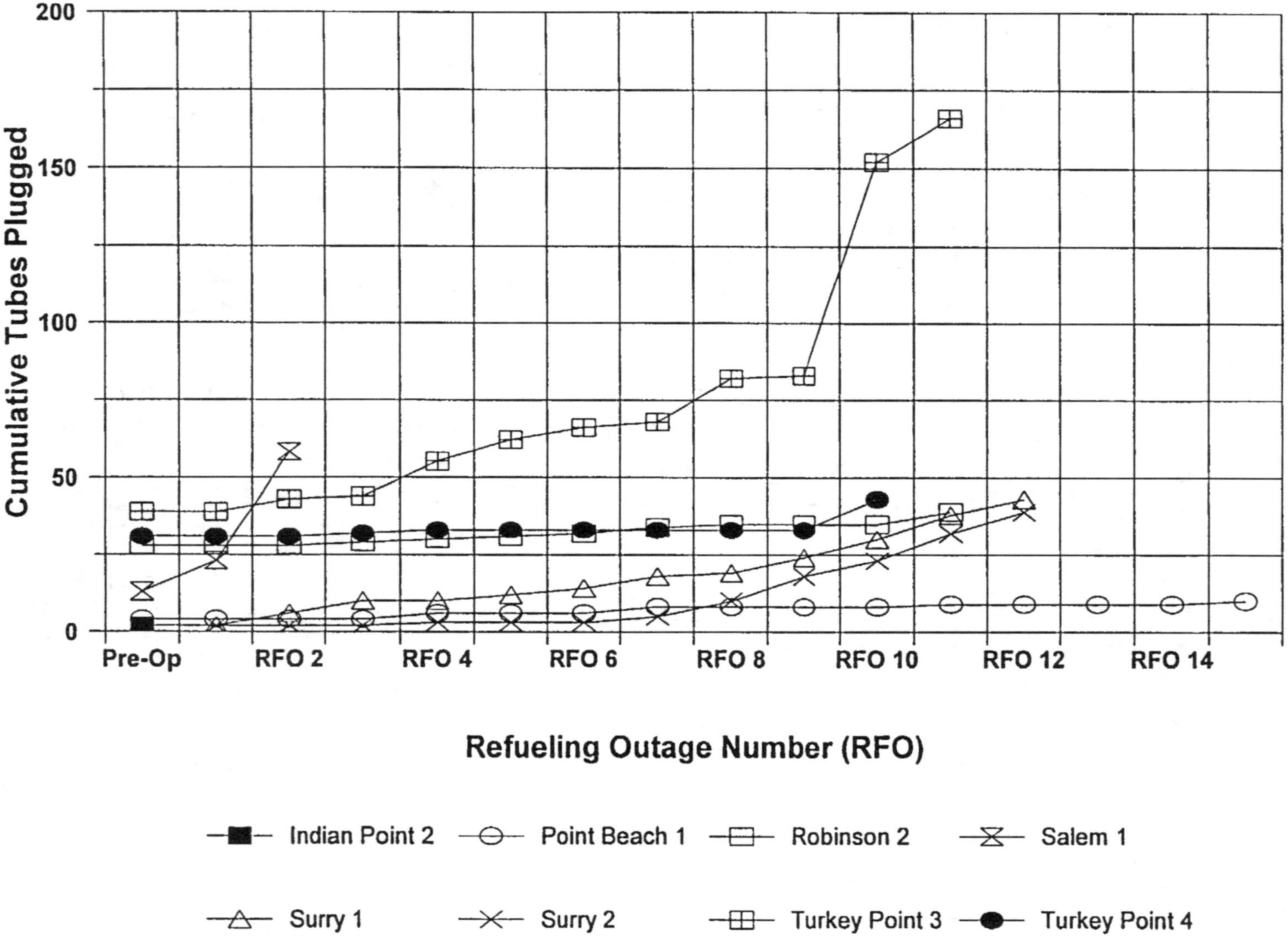

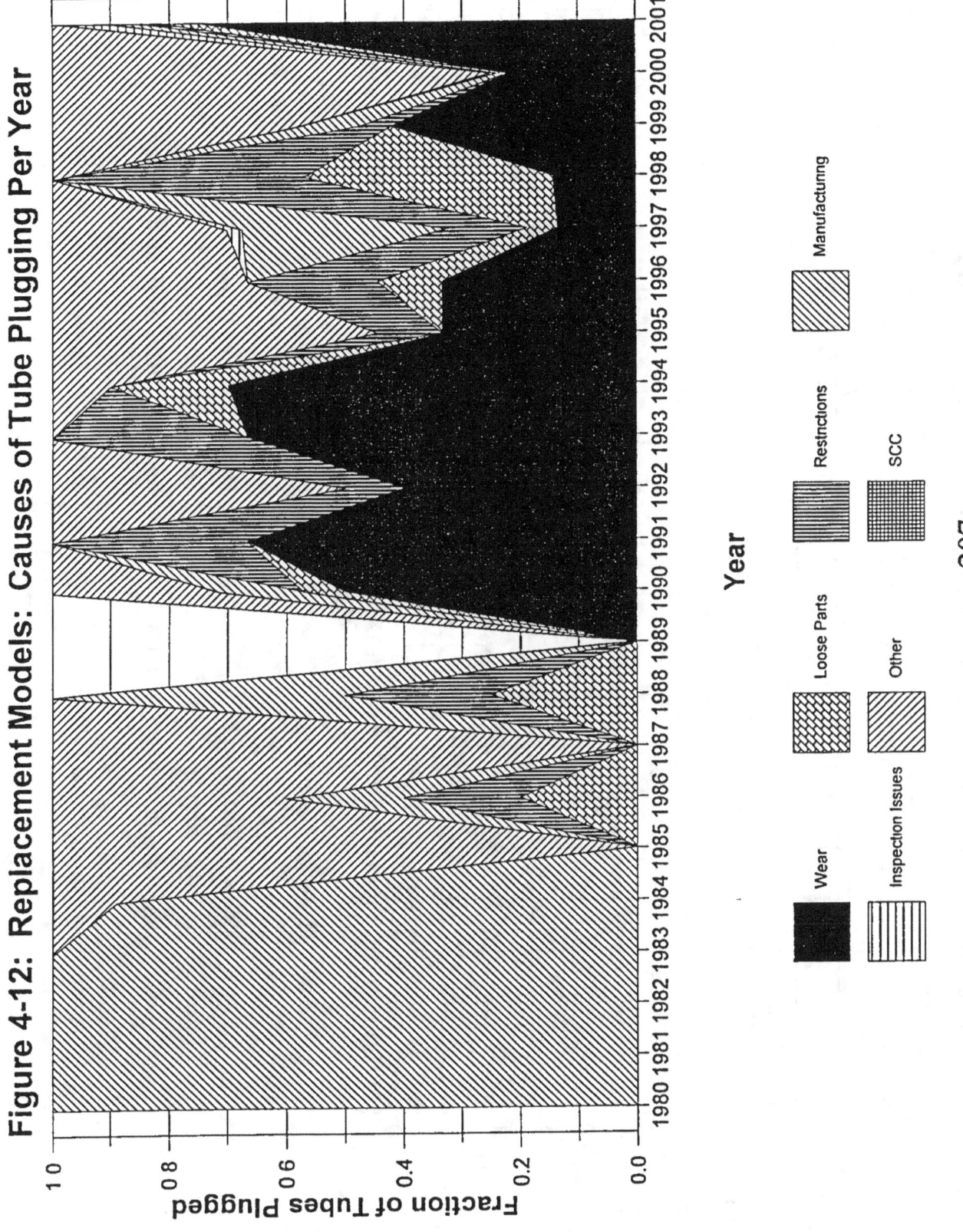

Figure 4-12: Replacement Models: Causes of Tube Plugging Per Year

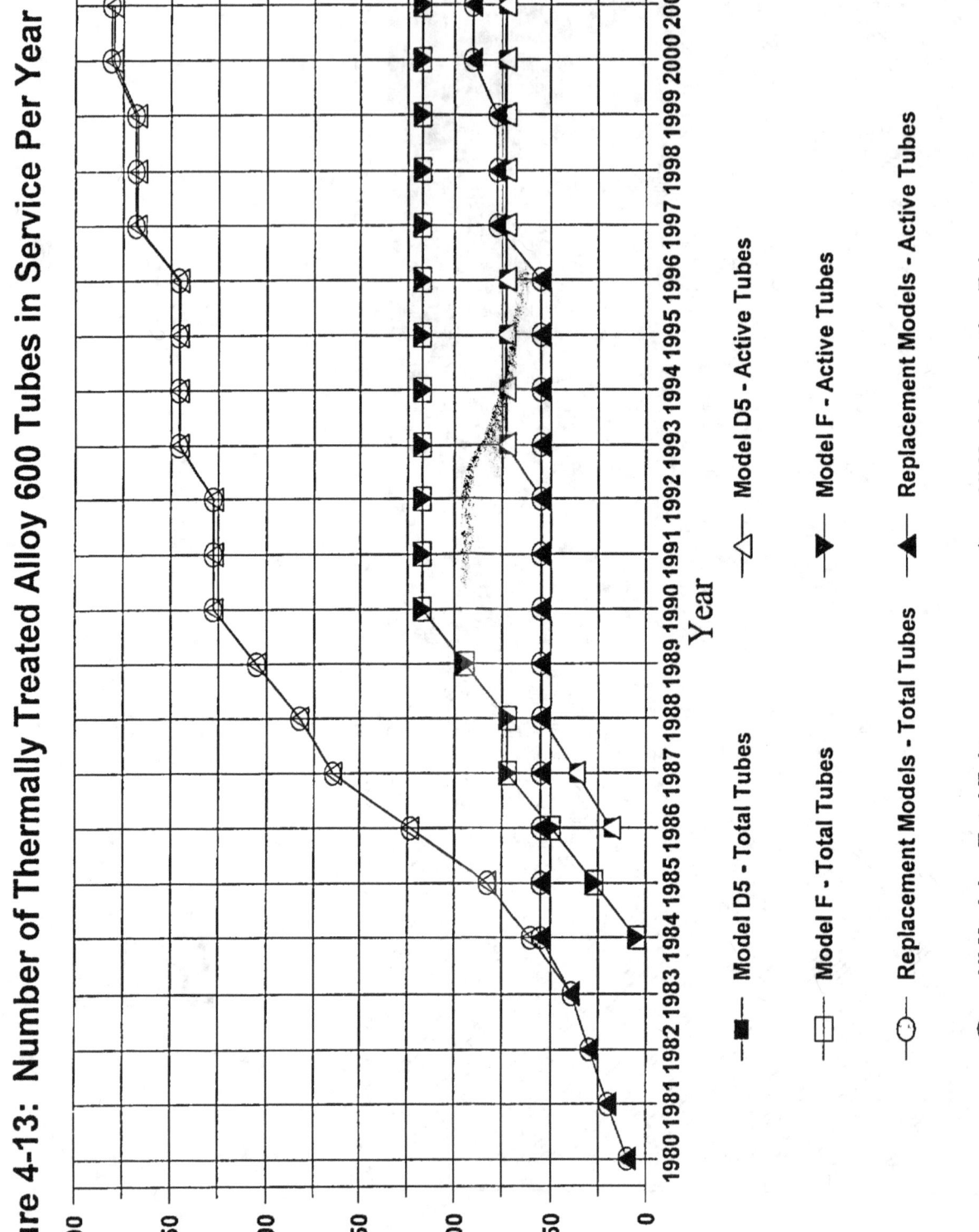

Figure 4-13: Number of Thermally Treated Alloy 600 Tubes in Service Per Year

Number of Tubes
Thousands

Year

- Model D5 - Total Tubes
- Model F - Total Tubes
- Replacement Models - Total Tubes
- All Models - Total Tubes
- Model D5 - Active Tubes
- Model F - Active Tubes
- Replacement Models - Active Tubes
- All Models - Active Tubes

Figure 4-14: All Models: Tubes Plugged Per Grouping/Model (12/01)

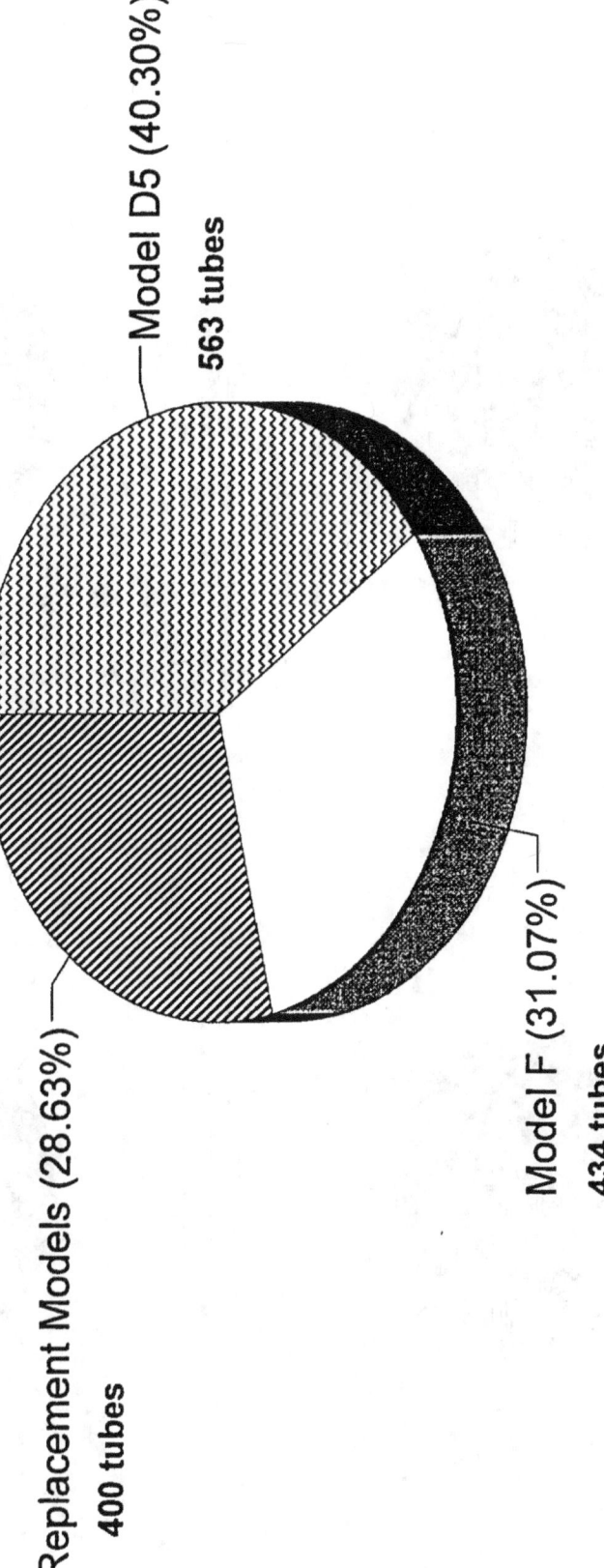

Model D5 (40.30%)
563 tubes

Model F (31.07%)
434 tubes

Replacement Models (28.63%)
400 tubes

Model 4-15: All Models: Causes of Tube Plugging (12/01)

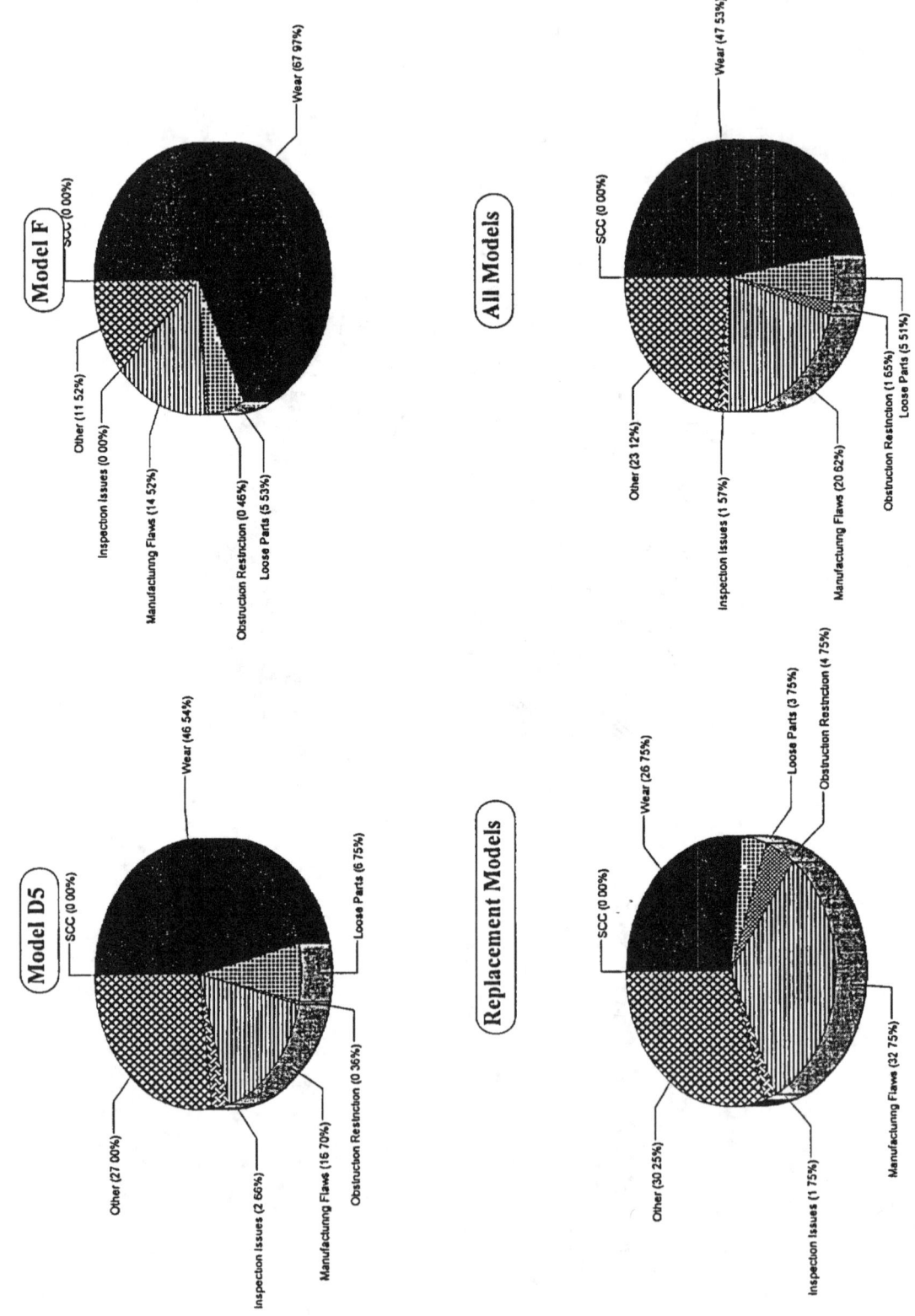

Model F

SCC (0 00%)
Wear (67 97%)
Other (11 52%)
Inspection Issues (0 00%)
Manufacturing Flaws (14 52%)
Obstruction Restriction (0 46%)
Loose Parts (5 53%)

All Models

SCC (0 00%)
Wear (47 53%)
Other (23 12%)
Inspection Issues (1 57%)
Manufacturing Flaws (20 62%)
Obstruction Restriction (1 65%)
Loose Parts (5 51%)

Model D5

SCC (0 00%)
Wear (46 54%)
Other (27 00%)
Inspection Issues (2 66%)
Manufacturing Flaws (16 70%)
Obstruction Restriction (0 36%)
Loose Parts (6 75%)

Replacement Models

SCC (0 00%)
Wear (26 75%)
Loose Parts (3 75%)
Obstruction Restriction (4 75%)
Other (30 25%)
Inspection Issues (1 75%)
Manufacturing Flaws (32 75%)

-210-

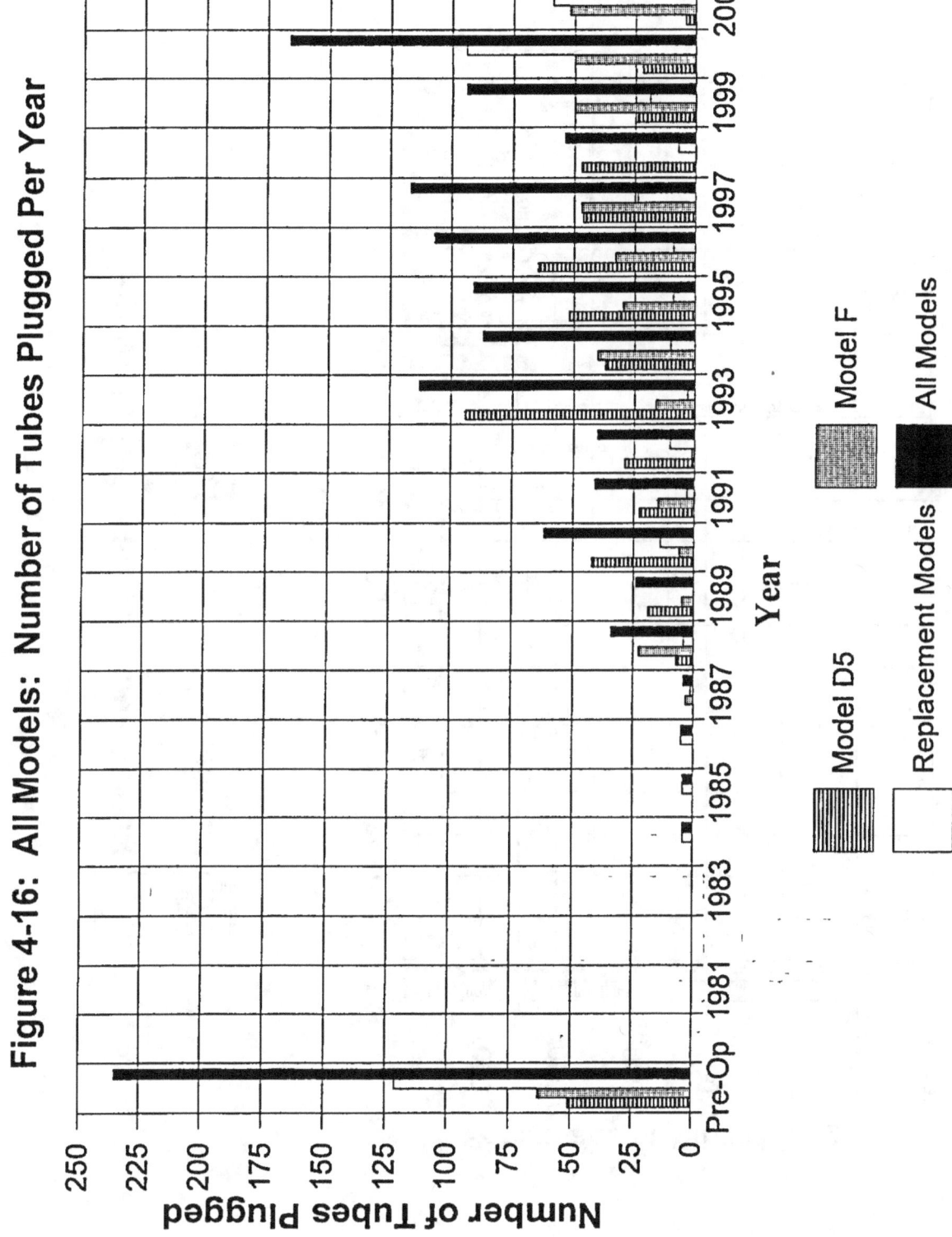

Figure 4-16: All Models: Number of Tubes Plugged Per Year

Number of Tubes Plugged

Year

Model D5
Model F
Replacement Models
All Models

-211-

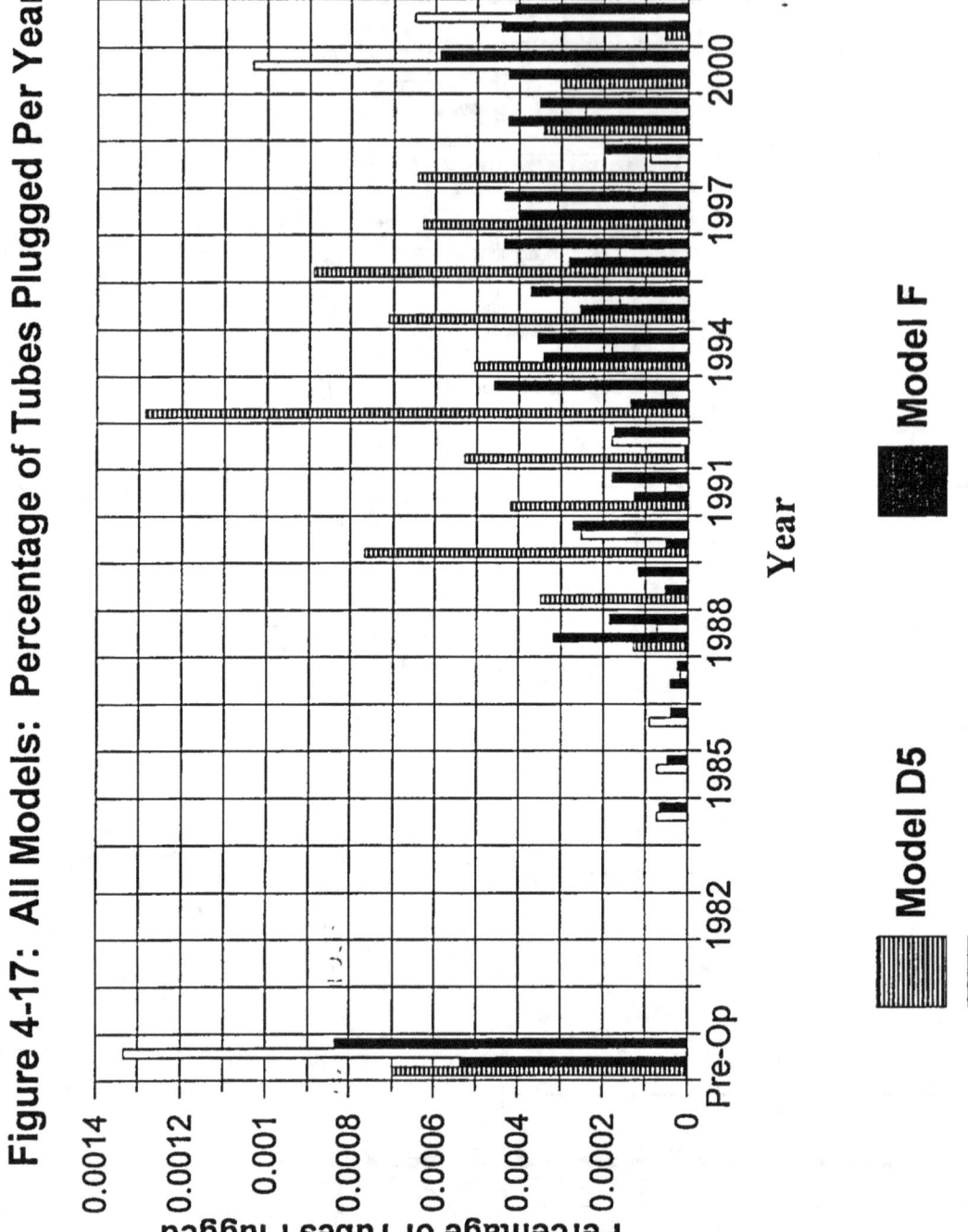

Figure 4-17: All Models: Percentage of Tubes Plugged Per Year

Model D5   Model F
Replacement Models   All Models

-212-

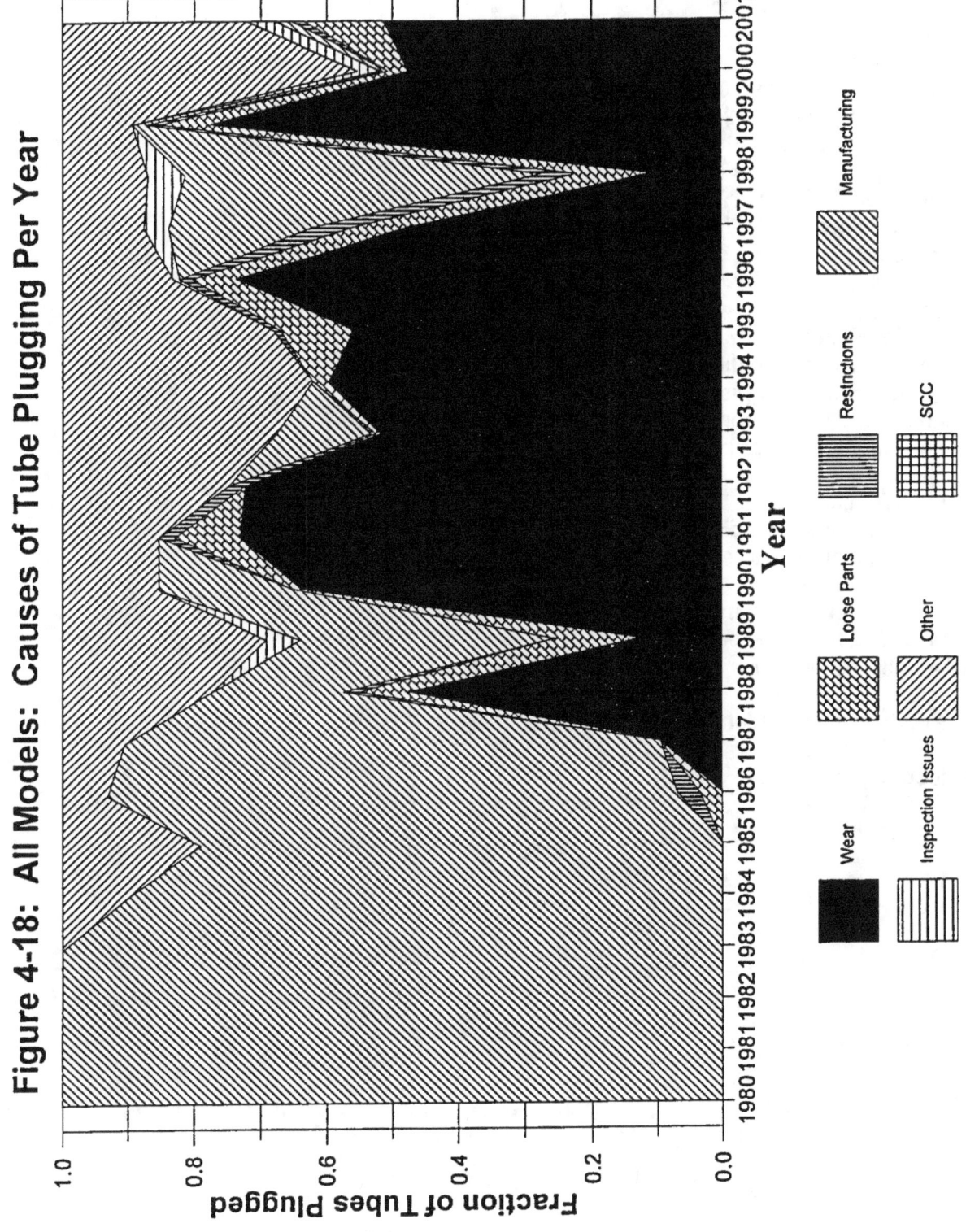

Figure 4-18: All Models: Causes of Tube Plugging Per Year

Legend: Wear, Inspection Issues, Loose Parts, Other, Restrictions, SCC, Manufacturing

APPENDIX A: ACRONYMS

ADI	absolute drift indication
ADS	absolute drift signal
AVB	anti-vibration bar
AVT	all volatile treatment
BPH	hot-leg flow distribution baffle (baffle plate hot)
CLP	confirmed loose part
EFPM	Effective Full Power Month
EFPY	Effective Full Power Year
FBH	hot-leg flow distribution baffle (flow baffle hot)
FS	freespan
gpd	gallons per day
gpm	gallons per minute
ID	inside diameter
MAI	multiple axial indication
MBM	manufacturing burnishing mark
NDF	no degradation found
NQI	non-quantifiable indication
NRC	Nuclear Regulatory Commission
OD	outside diameter
ODI	outside diameter indication
ODSCC	outside diameter stress corrosion cracking
PLP	possible loose part
psi	pounds per square inch
PWR	pressurized-water reactor
PWSCC	primary water stress corrosion cracking
RFO	refueling outage
SAI	single axial indication
SG	steam generator
TSP	tube support plate
TT	thermally treated
UT	ultrasonic testing

APPENDIX B: BIBLIOGRAPHY

General

Regulatory Guide 1.121, "Bases for Plugging Degraded PWR Steam Generator Tubes"

Generic Letter 91-04 "Changes in Technical Specification Surveillance Intervals to Accommodate a 24-Month Fuel Cycle," April 2, 1991

NUREG-0966, "Safety Evaluation Report Related to the D2/D3 Steam Generator Design Modification"

NUREG-1014, "Safety Evaluation Report Related to the D4/D5/E Steam Generator Design Modification"

Generic Letter 95-03, "Circumferential Cracking of Steam Generator Tubes"

Bulletin 89-01, "Failure of Westinghouse Steam Generator Tube Mechanical Plugs"

U.S. Nuclear Regulatory Commission Information Notice 2001-016, "Recent Foreign and Domestic Experience with Degradation of Steam Generator Tubes and Internals," October 31, 2001.

U.S. Nuclear Regulatory Commission, "Steam Generator Tube Failures," NUREG/CR-6365, April 1996.

U.S. Nuclear Regulatory Commission, "Circumferential Cracking of Steam Generator Tubes," NUREG-1604, April 1997.

U.S. Nuclear Regulatory Commission Information Notice 2002-21, "Axial Outside-Diameter Cracking Affecting Thermally Treated Alloy 600 Steam Generator Tubing" June 25, 2002.

Braidwood 2

Letter from S.C. Hunsader, Commonwealth Edison, to the NRC, dated May 7, 1990, "Braidwood Station Unit 2, First Fuel Outage, Steam Generator Inservice Inspection Results, NRC Docket No. 50-457." NUDOCS Accession No.

Letter from A.R. Checca, Commonwealth Edison, to the NRC, dated April 22, 1991, "CECo Braidwood Unit 2 First Outage, Steam Generator Inservice Inspection Results, NRC Docket No. 50-457." NUDOCS Accession No.

Letter from T.W. Simpkin, Commonwealth Edison, to the NRC, dated November 19, 1991, "Braidwood Station Unit 2, Second Refueling Outage, Steam Generator Inservice Inspection Results, NRC Docket No. 50-457." NUDOCS Accession No. 9112020194

Letter from T.W. Simpkin, Commonwealth Edison, to the NRC, dated August 25, 1992, "Braidwood Station Unit 2, Second Refuel Outage Steam Generator Inservice Inspection Results, NRC Docket No. 50-457." NUDOCS Accession No.

Letter from K.L. Kofron, Commonwealth Edison, to the NRC, dated April 12, 1994, "Braidwood Station Unit 2, Steam Generator Tube Inservice Inspection Report, Docket No. STN 50-457." NUDOCS Accession No. 9404180410

Letter from K.L. Kofron, Commonwealth Edison, to the NRC, dated October 27, 1994, "Braidwood Station Unit 2, Cycle 4 Refuel Outage, Steam Generator Tube Inservice Inspection Report, Docket No. STN 50-457." NUDOCS Accession No.

Letter from T.J. Tulon, Commonwealth Edison, to the NRC, dated October 24, 1995, "ComEd Braidwood Station Unit 2 Fourth Refuel Outage, Steam Generator Inservice Inspection Report, Docket No. STN 50-457." NUDOCS Accession No. 9510270004

Letter from T.J. Tulon, Commonwealth Edison, to the NRC, dated April 23, 1996, "Braidwood Station Unit 2, Fifth Refuel Outage, Steam Generator Inservice Inspection Report, NRC Docket No. STN 50-457." NUDOCS Accession No. 9605070344

Letter from T.J. Tulon, Commonwealth Edison, to the NRC, dated January 15, 1997, "ComEd Braidwood Station Unit 2 Fifth Refuel Outage, Steam Generator Inservice Inspection Report, Docket No. STN 50-457." NUDOCS Accession No. 9701280276

Letter from T.J. Tulon, Commonwealth Edison, to the NRC, dated October 23, 1997, "Braidwood Unit 2, Sixth Refuel Outage, Steam Generator Inservice Inspection Report, NRC Docket No. STN 50-457." NUDOCS Accession No. 9710290024

Letter from T.J. Tulon, Commonwealth Edison, to the NRC, dated October 23, 1997, "ComEd Braidwood Station Unit 2 Sixth Refuel Outage, Steam Generator Inservice Inspection Report, Docket No. STN 50-457." NUDOCS Accession No. 9710300202

Letter from T.J. Tulon, Commonwealth Edison, to the NRC, dated May 13, 1999, "Steam Generator Tube Inspection Report from Braidwood Station Unit 2 Refueling Outage Inspections." NUDOCS Accession No. 9905190243

Letter from T.J. Tulon, Commonwealth Edison, to the NRC, dated April 13, 2000, "Commonwealth Edison (ComEd) Braidwood Unit 2 Cycle 7 Steam Generator Eddy Current Examination 12 Month Summary Report." ADAMS Accession No. ML003704386

Letter from T.J. Tulon, Commonwealth Edison, to the NRC, dated November 9, 2000, "Eighth Refuel Outage Steam Generator Tube Inspection Report." ADAMS Accession No. ML003769511

Letter from G.K. Schwartz, Exelon Generating Company, LLC, to the NRC, dated January 26, 2001, "Braidwood Station, Unit 2 Inservice Inspection Summary Report." ADAMS Accession No. ML010360111

Letter from J.D. von Suskil, Exelon Generating Company, LLC, to the NRC, dated October 18, 2001, "Braidwood Station, Unit 2 Eighth Refueling Outage Steam Generator Tube Inspection Report." ADAMS Accession No. ML020150065

Byron 2

Letter from R. Pleniewicz, Commonwealth Edison, to the NRC, dated February 9, 1989, "Steam Generator Tube Plugging From Byron Unit 2, Cycle 1 Refueling Outage (B2RO1)." NUDOCS Accession No.

Letter from R. Pleniewicz, Commonwealth Edison, to the NRC, dated April 3, 1989, "Commonwealth Edison Byron Unit 2 Eddy Current Inspection." NUDOCS Accession No.

Letter from M.H. Richter, Commonwealth Edison, to the NRC, dated June 16, 1989, "Byron Station Units 1 and 2, Braidwood Station Units 1 and 2, Zion Station Units 1 and 2, Response to NRC Bulletin 89-01, Failure of Westinghouse Steam Generator Tube Mechanical Plugs, NRC Docket Nos. 50-454/455, 50-456/457, and 50-295/304." NUDOCS Accession No. 8906210005

Letter from R. Pleniewicz, Commonwealth Edison, to the NRC, dated December 26, 1990, "Commonwealth Edison Byron Unit 2 Steam Generator Eddy Current Examination During the Cycle 2 Refueling Outage." NUDOCS Accession No. 9101240226

Letter from D.J. Chrzanowski, Commonwealth Edison, to the NRC, dated August 9, 1991, "Byron Station Units 1 and 2, Braidwood Station Units 1 and 2, Zion Station Units 1 and 2, Response to NRC Bulletin 89-01, Supplement 2, Failure of Westinghouse Steam Generator Tube Mechanical Plugs, NRC Docket Nos. 50-454/455, 50-456/457, and 50-295/304." NUDOCS Accession No. 9108120228

Letter from D.J. Chrzanowski, Commonwealth Edison, to the NRC, dated October 3, 1991, "Clarification to Response to NRC Bulletin 89-01, Supplement 2, Failure of Westinghouse Steam Generator Tube Mechanical Plugs, Byron Units 1 and 2, Braidwood Units 1 and 2, Zion Units 1 and 2, NRC Docket Nos. 50-454/455, 50-456/457, and 50-295/304." NUDOCS Accession No. 9110100128

Letter from R. Pleniewicz, Commonwealth Edison, to the NRC, dated April 1, 1992, "Steam Generator Tube Plugging From Byron Unit 2, Cycle 3 Refueling Outage." NUDOCS Accession No.

Letter from R. Pleniewicz, Commonwealth Edison, to the NRC, dated June 5, 1992, "Commonwealth Edison Byron Unit 2 Steam Generator Eddy Current Examination During the Cycle 3 Refueling Outage." NUDOCS Accession No.

Letter from D.E. St. Clair, Commonwealth Edison, to the NRC, dated October 4, 1993, "Steam Generator Tube Plugging From Byron Unit 2 Cycle 4 Refueling Outage (September 3-November 2, 1993)." NUDOCS Accession No.

Letter from D.E. St. Clair, Commonwealth Edison, to the NRC, dated January 4, 1994, "Commonwealth Edison Byron Unit 2 Steam Generator Eddy Current Examination During the Cycle 4 Refueling Outage." NUDOCS Accession No.

Letter from T.W. Simpkin, Commonwealth Edison, to the NRC, dated January 31, 1995, "Byron Station Units 1 and 2, Braidwood Station Units 1 and 2, Update on Status of Alloy 600 TT Steam Generator Mechanical Tube Plug Replacement, NRC Docket Nos. 50-454, 50-455, 50-456 and 50-457 ." NUDOCS Accession No. 9502060090

Letter from D.E. St. Clair, Commonwealth Edison, to the NRC, dated March 16, 1995, "Steam Generator Tube Plugging from Byron Unit 2 Cycle 5 Refueling Outage (Beginning February 9, 1995)." NUDOCS Accession No.

Letter from D.E. St. Clair, Commonwealth Edison, to the NRC, dated June 9, 1995, "ComEd Byron Unit 2 Steam Generator Eddy Current Examination During the Cycle 5 Refueling Outage." NUDOCS Accession No.

Letter from J.B. Hosmer, Commonwealth Edison, to the NRC, dated August 2, 1996, "Application for Amendment to Facility Operating Licenses: 'Elimination of Corrosion Testing Requirement for Steam Generator Tube Sleeving'." NUDOCS Accession No. 9608060231

Letter from D.B. Wozniak, Commonwealth Edison, to the NRC, dated September 11, 1996, "Steam Generator (SG) Tube Repairs Resulting from Byron 2 Forced (B2F17) and Refueling (B2RO6) Outages, Byron Nuclear Power Station Unit 2, Facility Operating License NPF-66, NRC Docket No. 50-455." NUDOCS Accession No. 9609170587

Letter from D.B. Wozniak, Commonwealth Edison, to the NRC, dated December 17, 1996, "ComEd Byron Station Unit 2 Steam Generator Eddy Current Examination During B2F17 & B2RO6 - 90 Day Summary Report, Byron Nuclear Power Station, Unit 2, Facility Operating License NPF-66, NRC Docket No. 50-455." NUDOCS Accession No. 9612270082

Letter from K.L. Kofron, Commonwealth Edison, to the NRC, dated September 27, 1996, "Steam Generator Tubes Not Inspected During Outage." NUDOCS Accession No. 9610080408

Letter from K.L. Graesser, Commonwealth Edison, to the NRC, dated May 8, 1998, "Steam Generator Tube Repairs Resulting from Byron Unit 2 Cycle 7 Refueling Outage, Byron Nuclear Power Station Unit 2, Facility Operating License NPF-66, NRC Docket No. 50-455." NUDOCS Accession No. 9805180062

Letter from K.L. Graesser, Commonwealth Edison, to the NRC, dated July 27, 1998, "ComEd Byron Unit 2 Cycle 7 Steam Generator Eddy Current Examination 90 Day Summary Report, Byron Nuclear Power Station, Unit 2, Facility Operating License NPF-66, NRC Docket No. 50-455." NUDOCS Accession No. 9807300182

Letter from R.M. Krich, Commonwealth Edison, to the NRC, dated December 30, 1998, "Byron Station, Units 1 and 2, Facility Operating License Nos. NPF-37 and NPF-66, NRC Docket Nos. STN 50-454 and STN 50-455; Braidwood Station, Units 1 and 2, Facility Operating License Nos. NPF-72 and NPF-77, NRC Docket Nos. STN 50-456 and STN 50-457; Steam Generator Laser Welded Sleeves." NUDOCS Accession No. 9901110021

Letter from W. Levis, Commonwealth Edison, to the NRC, dated November 15, 1999, "Steam Generator Tube Repairs Resulting from Byron Unit 2 Cycle 8 Refueling Outage (B2RO8)." ADAMS Accession No. ML993270004

Letter from W. Levis, Commonwealth Edison, to the NRC, dated February 8, 2000, "Steam Generator Inservice Inspection Summary Report." ADAMS Accession No. ML003684433

Letter from R.M. Krich, Commonwealth Edison, to the NRC, dated July 31, 2000, "Steam Generator Laser Welded Sleeves." ADAMS Accession No. ML003738467

Letter from R.P. Lopriore, Exelon Generation Company, LLC, to the NRC, dated April 23, 2001, "Steam Generator Tube Repairs Performed During the Byron Station Unit 2, Cycle 9 Refueling Outage." ADAMS Accession No. ML011200063

Letter from R.P. Lopriore, Exelon Generation Company, LLC, to the NRC, dated July 12, 2001, "Steam Generator Inservice Inspection Summary Report." ADAMS Accession No. ML011980298

Callaway

Letter from J.D. Blosser, Union Electric, to the NRC dated April 28, 1987, "Docket Number 50-483, Callaway Plant Unit 1, Facility Operating License NPF-30, Special Report 87-03, Number of Tubes Plugging During Second Steam Generator Tube Inservice Inspection." NUDOCS Accession No. 8705040301

Letter from J.D. Blosser, Union Electric, to the NRC dated March 4, 1988, "Docket Number 50-483, Callaway Plant Unit 1, Facility Operating License NPF-30, Special Report 87-04, Results of Second Steam Generator Tube Inservice Inspection." NUDOCS Accession No. 8803150025

Letter from J.D. Blosser, Union Electric, to the NRC dated October 15, 1987, "Docket Number 50-483, Callaway Plant Unit 1, Facility Operating License NPF-30, Special Report 87-11, Number of Tubes Plugged During Third Steam Generator Tube Inservice Inspection." NUDOCS Accession No. 8710230217

Letter from J.D. Blosser, Union Electric, to the NRC dated August 2, 1988, "Docket Number 50-483, Callaway Plant Unit 1, Facility Operating License NPF-30, Special Report 87-12, Results of Third Steam Generator Tube Inservice Inspection." NUDOCS Accession No. 8808090082

Letter from J.D. Blosser, Union Electric, to the NRC dated May 1, 1989, "Docket Number 50-483, Callaway Plant Unit 1, Facility Operating License NPF-30, Special Report 89-04, Number of Tubes Plugged During Third Steam Generator Tube Inservice Inspection." NUDOCS Accession No. 8905150199

Letter from D.F. Schnell, Union Electric, to the NRC dated June 15, 1989, "Docket Number 50-483, Callaway Plant, Failure of Westinghouse Steam Generator Tube Mechanical Plugs." NUDOCS Accession No. 8906260308

Letter from J.D. Blosser, Union Electric, to the NRC dated March 30, 1990, "Docket Number 50-483, Callaway Plant Unit 1, Facility Operating License NPF-30, Special Report 89-05, Results of the Fourth Steam Generator Tube Inservice Inspection." NUDOCS Accession No. 9004110012

Letter from J.D. Blosser, Union Electric, to the NRC dated November 5, 1990, "Docket Number 50-483, Callaway Plant Unit 1, Facility Operating License NPF-30, Special Report 90-03, Number of Tubes Plugged During Fourth Steam Generator Tube Inservice Inspection." NUDOCS Accession No. 9011090110

Letter from J.D. Blosser, Union Electric, to the NRC dated August 12, 1991, "Docket Number 50-483, Callaway Plant Unit 1, Facility Operating License NPF-30, Special Report 90-04 (SOS 90-3060), Results of the Fifth Steam Generator Tube Inservice Inspection." NUDOCS Accession No. 9108150051

Letter from D.F. Schnell, Union Electric, to the NRC dated July 24, 1991, "Docket Number 50-483, Callaway Plant, Failure of Westinghouse Steam Generator Tube Mechanical Plugs." NUDOCS Accession No. 9107300032

Letter from J.D. Blosser, Union Electric, to the NRC dated May 13, 1992, "Document Number 50-483, Callaway Plant Unit 1, Facility Operating License NPF-30, Special Report 92-02, Number of Tubes Plugged During Sixth Steam Generator Tube Inservice Inspection." NUDOCS Accession No. 9205210002

Letter from D.F. Schnell, Union Electric, to the NRC dated March 11, 1992, "Docket Number 50-483, Callaway Plant, Failure of Westinghouse Steam Generator Tube Mechanical Plugs." NUDOCS Accession No. 9203170366

Letter from D.F. Schnell, Union Electric, to the NRC dated July 2, 1992, "Docket Number 50-483, Callaway Plant, Failure of Westinghouse Steam Generator Tube Mechanical Plugs." NUDOCS Accession No. 9207090165

Letter from W.R. Campbell, Union Electric, to the NRC dated January 29, 1993, "Docket Number 50-483, Callaway Plant Unit 1, Facility Operating License NPF-30, Special Report 92-03 (SOS 92-1293), Results of the Sixth Steam Generator Tube Inservice Inspection." NUDOCS Accession No. 9302120086

Letter from J.D. Blosser, Union Electric, to the NRC dated November 8, 1993, "Document Number 50-483, Callaway Plant Unit 1, Facility Operating License NPF-30, Special Report 93-02, Number of Tubes Plugged During Sixth Steam Generator Tube Inservice Inspection." NUDOCS Accession No. 9311150219

Letter from C.D. Naslund, Union Electric, to the NRC dated February 11, 1994, "Docket Number 50-483, Callaway Refuel 6 Inservice Inspection Summary Report." NUDOCS Accession No. 9403010178

Letter from J.D. Blosser, Union Electric, to the NRC dated September 29, 1994, "Docket Number 50-483, Callaway Plant Unit 1, Facility Operating License NPF-30, Special Report 93-03 (SOS 93-1622), Results of the Sixth Steam Generator Tube Inservice Inspection." NUDOCS Accession No. 9410050108

Letter from J.D. Blosser, Union Electric, to the NRC dated May 11, 1995, "Document Number 50-483, Callaway Plant Unit 1, Facility Operating License NPF-30, Special Report 95-01, Number of Tubes Plugged During the Eighth Steam Generator Tube Inservice Inspection." NUDOCS Accession No. 9505190314

Letter from C.D. Naslund, Union Electric, to the NRC dated August 3, 1995, "Docket Number 50-483, Callaway Refuel 7 Inservice Inspection Summary Report." NUDOCS Accession No. 9508150261

Letter from R.D. Affolter, Union Electric, to the NRC dated April 1, 1996, "Docket Number 50-483, Callaway Plant Unit 1, Facility Operating License NPF-30, Special Report 95-02 (SOS 95-1138), Results of the Eighth Steam Generator Tube In-Service Inspection." NUDOCS Accession No. 9604080153

Letter from D.F. Schnell, Union Electric, to the NRC dated February 1, 1995, "Callaway Plant, Docket Number 50-483, Interim Report on Westinghouse Alloy 600 Steam Generator Mechanical Plugs." NUDOCS Accession No. 9502070285

Letter from D.F. Schnell, Union Electric, to the NRC dated September 26, 1995, "Callaway Plant, Docket Number 50-483, Westinghouse Alloy 600 Steam Generator Mechanical Plugs." NUDOCS Accession No. 9510030346

Letter from D.F. Schnell, Union Electric, to the NRC dated January 12, 1996, "Callaway Plant, Docket Number 50-483, Circumferential Cracking of Steam Generator Tubes." NUDOCS Accession No. 9601170033

Letter from R.D. Affolter, Union Electric, to the NRC dated November 19, 1996, "Docket Number 50-483, Callaway Plant Unit 1, Facility Operating License NPF-30, Special Report 96-003, Number of Tubes Plugged During the Ninth Steam Generator Tube Inservice Inspection." NUDOCS Accession No. 9611260198

Letter from R.D. Affolter, Union Electric, to the NRC dated October 9, 1997, "Docket Number 50-483, Callaway Plant Unit 1, Facility Operating License NPF-30, Special Report 96-02 (SOS 96-1706), Results of the Ninth Steam Generator Tube In-Service Inspection." NUDOCS Accession No. 9710170069

Letter from R.D. Affolter, Union Electric, to the NRC dated May 18, 1998, "Docket Number 50-483, Callaway Plant Unit 1, Facility Operating License NPF-30, Special Report 98-001, Number of Tubes Plugged During the Tenth Steam Generator Tube Inservice Inspection." NUDOCS Accession No. 9805260013

Letter from J.A. McGraw, Union Electric, to the NRC dated July 29, 1998, "Docket Number 50-483, Callaway Plant Unit 1, Union Electric Co., Facility Operating License NPF-30, Interval 2, Period 1 Inservice Inspection Summary Report." NUDOCS Accession No. 9808050141

Letter from R.D. Affolter, Union Electric, to the NRC dated March 25, 1999, "Docket Number 50-483, Callaway Plant Unit 1, Facility Operating License NPF-30, Special Report 98-03, Results of the Tenth Steam Generator Tube In-Service Inspection." NUDOCS Accession No. 9904230071

Letter from R.D. Affolter, Union Electric, to the NRC dated April 28, 1999, "Docket Number 50-483, Callaway Plant Unit 1, Facility Operating License NPF-30, Special Report 98-03, Results of the Tenth Steam Generator Tube In-Service Inspection." NUDOCS Accession No. 9905050080

Letter from R.D. Affolter, Union Electric, to the NRC dated November 5, 1999, "Docket Number 50-483, Callaway Plant Unit 1, Union Electric Co., Facility Operating License NPF-30, Special Report 99-02, Inservice Inspection Results for Steam Generator Tube Inspections - Number of Tubes Plugged or Repaired." ADAMS Accession No. ML993160189

Letter from R.D. Affolter, Union Electric, to the NRC dated June 1, 2000, "Docket Number 50-483, Callaway Plant Unit 1, Union Electric Co., Facility Operating License NPF-30, Special Report 2000-01, Results of the Eleventh Steam Generator Tube In-Service Inspection." ADAMS Accession No. ML003721791

Letter from W.A. Witt, Union Electric, to the NRC dated May 10, 2001, "Docket Number 50-483, Callaway Plant Unit 1, Union Electric Co., Facility Operating License NPF-30, Special Report 2001-01, Inservice Inspection Results for Steam Generator Tube Inspections - Number of Tubes Plugged or Repaired." ADAMS Accession No. ML011350341

Letter from W.A. Witt, Union Electric, to the NRC dated January 29, 2002, "Docket Number 50-483, Callaway Plant Unit 1, Union Electric Co., Facility Operating License NPF-30, Special Report 2001-02, Results of Twelfth Steam Generator Tube In-Service Inspection." ADAMS Accession No. ML020460331

Catawba 2

Letter from H.B. Tucker, Duke Power Company, to the NRC dated February 26, 1988, "Catawba Nuclear Station, Unit 2, Docket No. 50-414, Licensee Event Report 414/88-02, Technical Specification Violation Because of Steam Generator Tube Degradation Due to a Personnel Error and a Management Deficiency." NUDOCS Accession No. 8906290143

Letter from H.B. Tucker, Duke Power Company, to the NRC dated February 29, 1988, "Catawba Nuclear Station, Unit 2, Docket No. 50-414, Steam Generator Tube Inspections." NUDOCS Accession No. 8803080052

Letter from H.B. Tucker, Duke Power Company, to the NRC dated March 11, 1988, "Catawba Nuclear Station, Unit 2, Docket No. 50-414, Licensee Event Report 414/88-04, Foreign Objects on Steam Generator Tubesheet Result in Tube Damage due to a Manufacturing Deficiency." NUDOCS Accession No. 8906290090

Letter from H.B. Tucker, Duke Power Company, to the NRC dated May 6, 1988, "Catawba Nuclear Station, Unit 2, Docket No. 50-414, Inservice Inspection Report, End-of-Cycle 1 Refueling Outage." NUDOCS Accession No. 8805240073

Letter from H.B. Tucker, Duke Power Company, to the NRC dated February 28, 1989, "Catawba Nuclear Station, Unit 2, Docket No. 50-414, End of Cycle 1 Steam Generator Inspection." NUDOCS Accession No. 8903150459

Letter from H.B. Tucker, Duke Power Company, to the NRC dated May 15, 1989, "Catawba Nuclear Station, Unit 2, Docket No. 50-414, End of Cycle 2 Steam Generator Inspection." NUDOCS Accession No. 8905240517

Letter from H.B. Tucker, Duke Power Company, to the NRC dated April 25, 1990, "Catawba Nuclear Station, Unit 2, Docket No. 50-414, Steam Generator Inspection Report." NUDOCS Accession No. 9005040194

Letter from H.B. Tucker, Duke Power Company, to the NRC dated July 26, 1990, "Catawba Nuclear Station, Unit 2, Docket No. 50-414, Inservice Inspection Report, End-of-Cycle 3 Steam Generator Inspection." NUDOCS Accession No. 9007310218

Letter from M.S. Tuckman, Duke Power Company, to the NRC dated August 21, 1991, "Catawba Nuclear Station, Docket No. 50-414, Unit 2 EOC-3 Refueling Outage, Steam Generator Inspection." NUDOCS Accession No. 9108260279

Letter from M.S. Tuckman, Duke Power Company, to the NRC dated December 18, 1991, "Catawba Nuclear Station, Unit 2, Docket No. 50-414, End of Cycle 4 Refueling Outage, 15 Day Steam Generator Tube Inservice Inspection Report." NUDOCS Accession No. 9112270088

Letter from M.S. Tuckman, Duke Power Company, to the NRC dated November 18, 1992, "Catawba Nuclear Station, Unit 2, Docket No. 50-414, Special Report, 12 Month Steam Generator Inspection Report, End of Cycle 4." NUDOCS Accession No. 9211250148

Letter from M.S. Tuckman, Duke Power Company, to the NRC dated March 17, 1993, "Catawba Nuclear Station, Unit 2, Docket No. 50-414, End of Cycle 5 Refueling Outage, 15 Day Steam Generator Tube Inservice Inspection Report." NUDOCS Accession No. 9303220201

Letter from M.S. Tuckman, Duke Power Company, to the NRC dated March 15, 1993[1994], "Catawba Nuclear Station, Unit 2, Docket No. 50-414, Special Report, End of Cycle 5 Refueling Outage, Steam Generator Tube Inspection Report." NUDOCS Accession No. 9403220254

Letter from D.L. Rehn, Duke Power Company, to the NRC dated June 13, 1994, "Catawba Nuclear Station, Unit 2, Docket No. 50-414, Special Report, End of Cycle 6 Refueling Outage, 15 Day Steam Generator Tube Inservice Inspection Report." NUDOCS Accession No. 9406220294

Letter from D.L. Rehn, Duke Power Company, to the NRC dated September 20, 1994, "Catawba Nuclear Station, Unit 2, Docket No. 50-414, Special Report, End of Cycle 6 Refueling Outage, Steam Generator Tube Inspection Report - 12 Month." NUDOCS Accession No. 9409270323

Letter from M.S. Tuckman, Duke Power Company, to the NRC dated January 31, 1995, "McGuire Nuclear Station Units 1 & 2, Docket Nos. 50-369, 370, Catawba Nuclear Station Units 1 & 2, Docket Nos. 50-413, 414, Oconee Nuclear Station Units 1, 2, & 3, Docket Nos. 50-269, 270, 287, Interim Report on Westinghouse Alloy 600 SG Mechanical Plugs Installed at Duke Power Plants." NUDOCS Accession No. 9502070326

Letter from M.S. Tuckman, Duke Power Company, to the NRC dated September 19, 1995, "Catawba Nuclear Station, Units 1 & 2, Docket Nos. 50-413, 414, Response to Request for Additional Information Concerning Generic Letter 95-03." NUDOCS Accession No. 9509250289

Letter from W.R. McCollum, Jr., Duke Power Company, to the NRC dated November 14, 1995, "Catawba Nuclear Station, Unit 2, Docket No. 50-414, Special Report, End of Cycle 7 Refueling Outage, Steam Generator Tube Inspection Report." NUDOCS Accession No. 9511210058

Letter from W.R. McCollum, Jr., Duke Power Company, to the NRC dated April 24, 1997, "Catawba Nuclear Station, Unit 2, Docket No. 50-414, Special Report, End of Cycle 8 Refueling Outage, Steam Generator Tube Inspection Report." NUDOCS Accession No. 9705070030

Letter from G.R. Peterson, Duke Power Company, to the NRC dated October 8, 1998, "Catawba Nuclear Station, Unit 2, Docket No. 50-414, Special Report - Steam Generator Tube Plugging." NUDOCS Accession No. 9810190294

Letter from G.R. Peterson, Duke Energy, to the NRC dated February 9, 1999, "Catawba Nuclear Station, Unit 2, Docket No. 50-414, Special Report - Steam Generator Tube Inspection." NUDOCS Accession No. 9902160167

Letter from G.R. Peterson, Duke Energy, to the NRC dated June 18, 1999, "Catawba Nuclear Stations, Units 2, Docket Nos. 50-414, Steam Generator Tube Inspection Report." NUDOCS Accession No. 9906290060

Letter from G.R. Peterson, Duke Power, to the NRC dated April 13, 2000, "Catawba Nuclear Stations, Unit 2, Docket Nos. 50-414, Steam Generator Tube Inspection Report." ADAMS Accession No. ML003705897

Letter from G.R. Peterson, Duke Power, to the NRC dated June 29, 2000, "Duke Energy Corporation, Catawba Nuclear Station, Unit 2, Docket Nos. 50-414, Inservice Inspection Report, Steam Generator Outage Summary Report for Unit 2 End of Cycle 10 (2EOC10) Refueling Outage." ADAMS Accession No. ML0037313280

Letter from G.R. Peterson, Duke Power, to the NRC dated September 11, 2000, "Duke Energy Corporation, Catawba Nuclear Station, Docket Nos. 50-413, 50-414, Steam Generator Tube Inspection Summary Reports." ADAMS Accession Nos. ML003751571, ML003751594, ML003751637, ML003751640, and ML003751742

Letter from G.R. Peterson, Duke Power, to the NRC dated October 23, 2001, "Catawba Nuclear Station, Unit 2, Docket No. 50-414, Steam Generator Inservice Inspection." ADAMS Accession No. ML020150410

Letter from G.R. Peterson, Duke Power, to the NRC dated October 24, 2001, "Catawba Nuclear Station, Unit 2, Docket No. 50-414, Steam Generator Tube Inspection Report." ADAMS Accession No. ML013410150

Letter from G.R. Peterson, Duke Power, to the NRC dated January 17, 2002, "Duke Energy Corporation, Catawba Nuclear Station, Unit 2, Docket Number 50-414, Inservice Inspection Report and Steam Generator Outage Summary Report for End of Cycle 11 Refueling Outage." ADAMS Accession Nos. ML020420187, ML020420198, ML020420293

Comanche Peak 2

Letter from C.L. Terry, TU Electric, to the NRC dated November 7, 1994, "Comanche Peak Steam Electric Station (CPSES) - Unit 2, Docket No. 50-446, Special Report on the Unit 2, First Refueling Outage, Steam Generator Inservice Inspection Tube Plugging." NUDOCS Accession No.

Letter from C.L. Terry, TU Electric, to the NRC dated February 17, 1995, "Comanche Peak Steam Electric Station (CPSES) - Unit 2, Docket No. 50-446, Submittal of Unit 2 First Refueling Outage Inservice Inspection (ISI) Summary Report (Unit 2: 1986 Edition of ASME Code, Section XI, No Addenda, Interval Start Date - August 3, 1993, First Interval)." NUDOCS Accession No. 9502210330

Letter from C.L. Terry, TU Electric, to the NRC dated March 6, 1995, "Comanche Peak Steam Electric Station (CPSES) - Unit 2, Docket No. 50-446, Special Report on the Unit 2, First Refueling Outage, Steam Generator Inservice Inspection Tube Plugging and Summary Report." NUDOCS Accession No.

Letter from C.L. Terry, TU Electric, to the NRC dated March 25, 1996, "Comanche Peak Steam Electric Station (CPSES) - Unit 2, Docket No. 50-446, Unit 2, Second Refueling Outage, Steam Generator Inservice Inspection Tube Plugging, Special Report No. 2-SR-96-001-00." NUDOCS Accession No.

Letter from M.R. Blevins, TU Electric, to the NRC dated July 23, 1996, "Comanche Peak Steam Electric Station (CPSES) - Unit 2, Docket No. 50-446, Submittal of Unit 2 Second Refueling Outage Inservice Inspection (ISI) Summary Report (Unit 2: 1986 Edition of ASME Code, Section XI, No Addenda, Interval Start Date - August 3, 1993, First Interval)." NUDOCS Accession No. 9607250109

Letter from C.L. Terry, TU Electric, to the NRC dated August 30, 1996, "Comanche Peak Steam Electric Station (CPSES) - Unit 2, Docket No. 50-446, Special Report on the Unit 2, Second Refueling Outage, Steam Generator Inservice Inspection Tube Plugging, Special Report No. 2-SR-96-002-00." NUDOCS Accession No.

Letter from C.L. Terry, TU Electric, to the NRC dated July 10, 1997, "Comanche Peak Steam Electric Station (CPSES), Docket No. 50-445 and 50-446, NRC Inspection Report Nos. 50-445/97-09 and 50-446/97-09, Supplement to Response to Notice of Violation." NUDOCS Accession No. 9707180059

Letter from C.L. Terry, TU Electric, to the NRC dated November 20, 1997, "Comanche Peak Steam Electric Station (CPSES) - Unit 2, Docket No. 50-446, Unit 2, Third Refueling Outage, Steam Generator Inservice Inspection Tube Plugging, Special Report No. 2-SR-97-002-00." NUDOCS Accession No.

Letter from C.L. Terry, TU Electric, to the NRC dated December 23, 1997, "Comanche Peak Steam Electric Station (CPSES) - Unit 2, Docket No. 50-446, Special Report on the Unit 2, Third Refueling Outage, Steam Generator Inservice Inspection Tube Plugging Special Report No. 2-SR-97-003-00." NUDOCS Accession No. 9712310299

Letter from C.L. Terry, TU Electric, to the NRC dated April 15, 1999, "Comanche Peak Steam Electric Station (CPSES) - Unit 2, Docket No. 50-446, Unit 2, Fourth Refueling Outage (2RFO4), Steam Generator Inservice Inspection Tube Plugging, Special Report No. 2-SR-99-001-00." NUDOCS Accession No. 9904210175

Letter from C.L. Terry, TU Electric, to the NRC dated July 16, 1999, "Comanche Peak Steam Electric Station (CPSES) - Unit 2, Docket No. 50-446, Submittal of Unit 2 Fourth Refueling Outage (2RFO4) Inservice Inspection (ISI) Summary Report, 1986 Edition of ASME Code, Section XI, No Addenda, and Containment Inservice Inspection (CISI) Summary Report, 1992 Edition of ASME Section XI 1992 Addenda." NUDOCS Accession No. 9907200177

Letter from C.L. Terry, TXU Electric, to the NRC dated January 28, 2000, "Comanche Peak Steam Electric Station (CPSES) Unit 2, Docket Nos. 50-446, Unit 2 Fourth Refueling Outage, Condition Monitoring Report Special Report 446/00-001-00." ADAMS Accession No. ML003679671

Letter from C.L. Terry, TXU Electric, to the NRC dated October 20, 2000, "Comanche Peak Steam Electric Station (CPSES) - Unit 2, Docket No. 50-446, Unit 2, Fifth Refueling Outage (2RFO5), Steam Generator Inservice Inspection Tube Plugging, Special Report No. 2-SR-00-001-00." ADAMS Accession No.

Letter from C.L. Terry, TXU Electric, to the NRC dated February 2, 2001, "Comanche Peak Steam Electric Station (CPSES)-Unit 2, Docket Nos. 50-446, Submittal of Unit 2 Fifth Refueling Outage (2RFO5) Inservice Inspection (ISI) Summary Report (1986 Edition of ASME Code, Section XI, No Addenda, Unit 2 Interval Dates - August 3, 1993 - August 3, 2003, First Interval)." ADAMS Accession No. ML010370402

Letter from C.L. Terry, TXU Electric, to the NRC dated November 7, 2000, "Comanche Peak Steam Electric Station (CPSES)-Unit 2, Docket No. 50-446, Unit 2 Fifth Refueling Outage, Condition Monitoring Report, Special Report 446/00-002-00." ADAMS Accession No. ML003768963

Indian Point 2

Letter from J.S. Baumstark, Consolidated Edison Company of New York, Inc., to the NRC dated December 11, 2000, "Proposed Technical Specification Amendment - Changes to Primary to Secondary Leakage Limits and Steam Generator Tube Inservice Surveillance Requirements." ADAMS Accession No. ML003779281

Letter from P.D. Milano, NRC to M.R. Kansler, Entergy Nuclear Operations, Inc., dated April 2, 2002, "Indian Point Nuclear Generating Unit No. 2 - Amendment Re: Technical Specification Changes to Secondary Leakage Limits and Steam Generator Tube Inservice Surveillance Requirements (TAC No. MB0770)." ADAMS Accession No. ML020590148

Millstone 3

Letter from S.E. Scace, Northeast Utilities, to the NRC dated December 14, 1987, "Steam Generator Tube Plugging." NUDOCS Accession No. 8712210219

Letter from E.J. Mroczka, Northeast Utilities, to the NRC dated May 3, 1988, "Millstone Nuclear Power Station Unit No. 3, In-Service Inspection Summary Report." NUDOCS Accession No. 8805060165

Letter from S.E. Scace, Northeast Utilities, to the NRC dated June 13, 1989, "Millstone Nuclear Power Station, Unit 3 Steam Generator Tube Plugging." NUDOCS Accession No. 8906200377

Letter from E.J. Mroczka, Northeast Utilities, to the NRC dated June 16, 1989, "Haddam Neck Plant, Millstone Nuclear Power Station, Unit Nos. 2 and 3, NRC Bulletin No. 89-01, Failure of Westinghouse Steam Generator Tube Mechanical Plugs." NUDOCS Accession No. 8906270273

Letter from E.J. Mroczka, Northeast Utilities, to the NRC dated June 29, 1989, "Haddam Neck Plant, Millstone Nuclear Power Station, Unit No. 3, Proposed Revision to Technical

Specifications, Steam Generator Tube Inspection Acceptance Criteria." NUDOCS Accession No. 8907050418

Letter from S.E. Scace, Northeast Utilities, to the NRC dated April 2, 1990, "Millstone Nuclear Power Station, Unit No. 3 Steam Generator Tube Inservice Inspection Report." NUDOCS Accession No. 9004180368

Letter from S.E. Scace, Northeast Utilities, to the NRC dated March 6, 1991, "Millstone Nuclear Power Station, Unit No. 3 Steam Generator Tube Plugging." NUDOCS Accession No. 9103130123

Letter from E.J. Mroczka, Northeast Utilities, to the NRC dated July 30, 1991, "Haddam Neck Plant, Millstone Nuclear Power Station, Unit Nos. 2 and 3, NRC Bulletin No. 89-01, Supplement 2, Failure of Westinghouse Steam Generator Tube Mechanical Plugs." NUDOCS Accession No. 9108060084

Letter from S.E. Scace, Northeast Utilities, to the NRC dated February 18, 1992, "Millstone Nuclear Power Station, Unit No. 3 Steam Generator Tube Inservice Inspection Report." NUDOCS Accession No. 9202260164

Letter from J.F. Opeka, Northeast Utilities, to the NRC dated April 15, 1993, "Millstone Nuclear Power Station, Unit No. 3, Proposed Revision to Technical Specifications, Steam Generator Surveillance Requirements." NUDOCS Accession No. 9304220155

Letter from D.B. Miller Jr., Northeast Nuclear Energy, to the NRC dated August 11, 1994, "Millstone Nuclear Power Station, Unit No. 3, Steam Generator Tube Inservice Inspection Report." NUDOCS Accession No. 9408170294

Letter from J.F. Opeka, Northeast Utilities System, to the NRC dated May 1, 1995, "Millstone Nuclear Power Station, Unit No. 3, Proposed Revision to Technical Specifications, 24-Month Fuel Cycle - Containment Type B and Type C Testing and Steam Generator Tube Inspections and Request for Exemption from 10CFR50, Appendix J." NUDOCS Accession No. 9505050189

Letter from D.B. Miller Jr., Northeast Nuclear Energy, to the NRC dated May 18, 1995, "Millstone Nuclear Power Station Unit No. 3, Steam Generator Tube Plugging." NUDOCS Accession No. 9505250204

Letter from D.B. Miller Jr., Northeast Nuclear Energy, to the NRC dated November 14, 1995, "Millstone Nuclear Power Station, Unit No. 3, Steam Generator Tube Inservice Inspection Report." NUDOCS Accession No. 9511210250

Letter from M.H. Brothers, Northeast Utilities System, to the NRC dated October 16, 1996, "Millstone Nuclear Power Station Unit 3, Steam Generator Tube Plugging." NUDOCS Accession No. 9610180012

Letter from M.H. Brothers, Northeast Nuclear Energy, to the NRC dated September 30, 1997, "Millstone Nuclear Power Station Unit No. 3, Steam Generator Tube Inservice Inspection Report." NUDOCS Accession No. 9710060421

Letter from M.H. Brothers, Northeast Nuclear Energy, to the NRC dated August 6, 1998, "Millstone Nuclear Power Station, Unit No. 3, Proposed Revision to Technical Specification, Steam Generator Tube Inspection Interval (TSCR 3-17-98)." NUDOCS Accession No. 9808120261

Letter from M.L. Bowling Jr., Northeast Nuclear Energy, to the NRC dated September 21, 1998, "Millstone Nuclear Power Station, Unit No. 3, Proposed Revision to Technical Specification, Steam Generator Tube Inspection Interval (TSCR 3-17-98), Request for Additional Information." NUDOCS Accession No. 9809250362

Letter from J.W. Andersen, NRC to M.L. Bowling Jr., Northeast Nuclear Energy, dated September 23, 1998, "Issuance of Amendment - Millstone Nuclear Power Station, Unit No. 3 (TAC No. MA2463)." NUDOCS Accession No. 9809250236

Letter from R.P. Necci, Northeast Nuclear Energy, to the NRC dated March 11, 1999, "Millstone Nuclear Power Station, Unit No. 3, Schedule for Responding to NRC Request for Additional Information Pertaining to Steam Generator Tube Inspection." NUDOCS Accession No. 9903180110

Letter from R.P. Necci, Northeast Nuclear Energy, to the NRC dated June 2, 1999, "Millstone Nuclear Power Station, Unit No. 3, Steam Generator Tube Plugging." NUDOCS Accession No. 9906100051

Letter from R.P. Necci, Northeast Nuclear Energy, to the NRC dated October 5, 1999, "Millstone Nuclear Power Station, Unit No. 3, Withdrawal of 24 Month Steam Generator Tube Inspection Surveillance Extensions." NUDOCS Accession No. 9910130068

Letter from R.P. Necci, Northeast Nuclear Energy, to the NRC dated November 9, 1999, "Millstone Nuclear Power Station, Unit No. 3, Withdrawal of 24 Month Steam Generator Tube Inspection Surveillance Extensions-Reference Revision." ADAMS Accession No. ML993280010

Letter from C.J. Schwarz, Northeast Nuclear Energy, to the NRC dated February 17, 2000, "Millstone Nuclear Power Station Unit No. 3, Special Report - Steam Generator Tube Examination." ADAMS Accession No. ML0036874250

Letter from R.G. Lizotte, Northeast Nuclear Energy, to the NRC dated March 5, 2001, "Millstone Nuclear Power Station, Unit No. 3, Steam Generator Tube Plugging." ADAMS Accession No. ML010720282

Letter from C.J. Schwarz, Dominion Nuclear Connecticut, Inc., to the NRC dated February 15, 2002, "Millstone Nuclear Power Station, Unit No. 3, Special Report - Steam Generator Tube Inservice Inspection." ADAMS Accession No. ML020630236

Point Beach 1

Wisconsin Electric Power Company, "Annual Results & Data Report, 1984." NUDOCS Accession No. 8503140252

Letter from C.W. Fay, Wisconsin Electric Power Company, to the NRC dated March 11, 1985, "Docket Nos. 50-266 and 50-301, Annual Results and Data Report, Point Beach Nuclear Plant, Units 1 and 2." NUDOCS Accession No. 8503250347

Wisconsin Electric Power Company, "Annual Results & Data Report, 1985." NUDOCS Accession No. 8603130049

Wisconsin Electric Power Company, "Annual Results & Data Report, 1986." NUDOCS Accession No. 8703030170

Wisconsin Electric Power Company, "Annual Results & Data Report, 1987." NUDOCS Accession No. 8803040258

Wisconsin Electric Power Company, "Annual Results & Data Report, 1988." NUDOCS Accession No. 8903080484

Letter from C.W. Fay, Wisconsin Electric Power Company, to the NRC dated February 28, 1990, "Docket Nos. 50-266 and 50-301, Annual Results and Data Report 1989, Point Beach Nuclear Plant, Units 1 and 2." NUDOCS Accession No. 9003080460

Letter from C.W. Fay, Wisconsin Electric Power Company, to the NRC dated June 27, 1991, "Dockets 50-266 and 50-301, Addendum to Annual Results and Data Report for 1987, 1988, and 1989, Point Beach Nuclear Plant Units 1 and 2." NUDOCS Accession No. 9107100105

Letter from C.W. Fay, Wisconsin Electric Power Company, to the NRC dated February 27, 1991, "Docket Nos. 5[0]-266 and 50-301, Annual Results and Data Report 1990, Point Beach Nuclear Plant, Units 1 and 2." NUDOCS Accession No. 9103070072

Wisconsin Electric Power Company, "Annual Results & Data Report, 1990." NUDOCS Accession No. 9103060210

Letter from C.W. Fay, Wisconsin Electric Power Company, to the NRC dated May 17, 1991, Docket 50-266, Licensee Event Report 90-002-00, Degradation of Steam Generator Tubes, Point Beach Nuclear Plant, Unit 1." NUDOCS Accession No. 9105280190

Letter from J.J. Zach, Wisconsin Electric Power Company, to the NRC dated February 28, 1992, "Docket Nos. 50-266 and 50-301, Annual Results and Data Report - 1991, Point Beach Nuclear Plant, Units 1 and 2." NUDOCS Accession No. 9203030345

Letter from B. Link, Wisconsin Electric Power Company, to the NRC dated February 25, 1993, "Dockets 50-266 and 50-301, Annual Results and Data Report - 1992, Point Beach Nuclear Plant, Units 1 and 2." NUDOCS Accession No. 9303020493

Letter from B. Link, Wisconsin Electric Power Company, to the NRC dated March 17, 1993, "Dockets 50-266 and 50-301, Annual Results and Data Report - 1992, Point Beach Nuclear Plant, Units 1 and 2." NUDOCS Accession No. 9303230146

Letter from B. Link, Wisconsin Electric Power Company, to the NRC dated February 25, 1994, "Dockets 50-266 and 50-301, Annual Results and Data Report - 1993, Point Beach Nuclear Plant, Units 1 and 2." NUDOCS Accession No. 9403080197

Letter from B. Link, Wisconsin Electric Power Company, to the NRC dated March 30, 1994, "Docket 50-266, Steam Generator Inspection Plan, Point Beach Nuclear Plant, Unit 1." NUDOCS Accession No. 9404060014

Letter from G.M. Krieser, Wisconsin Electric Power Company, to the NRC dated February 23, 1995, "Dockets 50-266 and 50-301, Annual Results and Data Report - 1994, Point Beach Nuclear Plant, Units 1 and 2." NUDOCS Accession No. 9503020244

Letter from G.M. Krieser, Wisconsin Electric Power Company, to the NRC dated February 28, 1996, "Dockets 50-266 and 50-301, Annual Results and Data Report - 1995, Point Beach Nuclear Plant, Units 1 and 2." NUDOCS Accession No. 9603050276

Letter from D.F. Johnson, Wisconsin Electric Power Company, to the NRC dated February 27, 1997, "Dockets 50-266 and 50-301, Annual Results and Data Report - 1996, Point Beach Nuclear Plant, Units 1 and 2." NUDOCS Accession No. 9703050035

Letter from D.F. Johnson, Wisconsin Electric Power Company, to the NRC dated February 27, 1998, "Dockets 50-266 and 50-301, 1997 Annual Results and Data Report, Point Beach Nuclear Plant, Units 1 and 2." NUDOCS Accession No. 9803040445

Letter from V.A. Kaminskas, Wisconsin Electric Power Company, to the NRC dated February 25, 1999, "Dockets 50-266 and 50-301, 1998 Annual Results and Data Report, Point Beach Nuclear Plant, Units 1 and 2." NUDOCS Accession No. 9903100033

Letter from A.J. Cayia, Wisconsin Electric Power Company, to the NRC dated February 28, 2000, "Dockets 50-266 and 50-301, 1999 Annual Results and Data Report, Point Beach Nuclear Plant, Units 1 and 2." ADAMS Accession No. ML003689804

Letter from A.J. Cayia, Nuclear Management Company, LLC, to the NRC dated February 28, 2001, "Dockets 50-266 and 50-301, 2000 Annual Results and Data Report, Point Beach Nuclear Plant, Units 1 and 2." ADAMS Accession No. ML010670316

Letter from T.J. Webb, Nuclear Management Company, LLC, to the NRC dated March 9, 2001, "Dockets 50-266, 50-301, and 72-005, 1999 Annual Results and Data Report Errata, Point Beach Nuclear Plant, Units 1 and 2." ADAMS Accession No. ML010790116

Letter from T.J. Webb, Nuclear Management Company, LLC, to the NRC dated May 2, 2001, "Docket 50-301, Steam Generator Tube Plugging, Point Beach Nuclear Plant, Unit 1." ADAMS Accession No. ML011280137

Letter from T.J. Webb, Nuclear Management Company, LLC, to the NRC dated September 4, 2002, "Docket 50-266, Point Beach Nuclear Plant, Unit 1, Summary of the Spring 2001 Unit 1 (U1R26) Steam Generator Eddy Current Examinations." ADAMS Accession Number not available as of date of preparation.

Robinson 2

Letter from R.E. Morgan, Carolina Power & Light Company, to the NRC dated September 11, 1987, "H.B. Robinson Steam Electric Plant, Unit No. 2; Docket No. 50-261; License No. DPR-23; 90-Day Inservice Inspection Report." NUDOCS Accession No. 8709230338

Letter from R.E. Morgan, Carolina Power & Light Company, to the NRC dated December 16, 1988, "H.B. Robinson Steam Electric Plant, Unit No. 2; Docket No. 50-261; License No. DPR-23; 14-Day Special Report - Plugged Steam Generator Tube." NUDOCS Accession No. 8812200340

Letter from R.E. Morgan, Carolina Power & Light Company, to the NRC dated April 27, 1989, "H.B. Robinson Steam Electric Plant, Unit No. 2; Docket No. 50-261; License No. DPR-23; 90-Day Inservice Inspection Report." NUDOCS Accession No. 8905050159

Letter from R.E. Morgan, Carolina Power & Light Company, to the NRC dated March 10, 1989, "H.B. Robinson Steam Electric Plant, Unit No. 2; Docket No. 50-261; License No. DPR-23; Monthly Operations Report." NUDOCS Accession No. 8903200181

Letter from R.E. Morgan, Carolina Power & Light Company, to the NRC dated May 11, 1989, "H.B. Robinson Steam Electric Plant, Unit No. 2; Docket No. 50-261; License No. DPR-23; Monthly Operations Report." NUDOCS Accession No. 8905180153

Letter from R.E. Morgan, Carolina Power & Light Company, to the NRC dated May 11, 1989, "H.B. Robinson Steam Electric Plant, Unit No. 2; Docket No. 50-261; License No. DPR-23; Monthly Operations Report." NUDOCS Accession No. 8905180158

Letter from D.M. Verrelli, NRC to Lynn W. Eury, Carolina Power & Light Company dated May 18, 1989, "Notice of Violation, NRC Inspection Report No. 50-261/89-08." NUDOCS Accession No. 8906050174

Letter from A.B. Cutter, Carolina Power & Light Company, to the NRC dated June 14, 1989, "H.B. Robinson Steam Electric Plant, Unit No. 2; Docket No. 50-261/License No. DPR-23; Response to NRC Bulletin 89-01, Failure of Westinghouse Steam Generator Tube Mechanical Plugs." NUDOCS Accession No. 8906270150

Letter from A.B. Cutter, Carolina Power & Light Company, to the NRC dated June 26, 1990, "H.B. Robinson Steam Electric Plant, Unit No. 2; Docket No. 50-261/License No. DPR-23; Request for License Amendment, Steam Generator Tube Inspection." NUDOCS Accession No. 9007050031

Letter from J.J. Sheppard, Carolina Power & Light Company, to the NRC dated June 3, 1991, "H.B. Robinson Steam Electric Plant, Unit No. 2; Docket No. 50-261; License No. DPR-23; 90-Day Inservice Inspection Report." NUDOCS Accession No. 9106070289

Letter from G.E. Vaughn, Carolina Power & Light Company, to the NRC dated July 31, 1991, "H.B. Robinson Steam Electric Plant, Unit No. 2; Docket No. 50-261/License No. DPR-23; Response to NRC Bulletin 89-01 Supplement 2, Failure of Westinghouse Steam Generator Tube Mechanical Plugs." NUDOCS Accession No. 9108070023

Letter from R.H. Chambers, Carolina Power & Light Company, to the NRC dated May 11, 1992, "H.B. Robinson Steam Electric Plant, Unit No. 2; Docket No. 50-261; License No. DPR-23; Inservice Inspection: Steam Generator Tube Plug." NUDOCS Accession No. 9205210003

Letter from R.H. Chambers, Carolina Power & Light Company, to the NRC dated September 21, 1992, "H.B. Robinson Steam Electric Plant, Unit No. 2; Docket No. 50-261:; License No. DPR-23; 90-Day Inservice Inspection Report." NUDOCS Accession No. 9209290226

Letter from M.P. Pearson, Carolina Power & Light Company, to the NRC dated October 15, 1993, "H.B. Robinson Steam Electric Plant, Unit No. 2; Docket No. 50-261; License No. DPR-23; Inservice Inspection: Steam Generator Tube Plug." NUDOCS Accession No. 9310210196

Letter from R.M. Krich, Carolina Power & Light Company, to the NRC dated February 11, 1994, "H.B. Robinson Steam Electric Plant, Unit No. 2; Docket No. 50-261; License No. DPR-23; 90-Day Inservice Inspection Report." NUDOCS Accession No. 9402220131

Letter from R.M. Krich, Carolina Power & Light Company, to the NRC dated March 10, 1994, "H.B. Robinson Steam Electric Plant, Unit No. 2; Docket No. 50-261/License No. DPR-23; Monthly Operations Report." NUDOCS Accession No. 9403150515

Letter from R.M. Krich, Carolina Power & Light Company, to the NRC dated April 11, 1994, "H.B. Robinson Steam Electric Plant, Unit No. 2; Docket No. 50-261/License No. DPR-23; Monthly Operations Report." NUDOCS Accession No. 9404190210

Letter from C.A. Julian, NRC to C.S. Hinnant, Carolina Power & Light Company dated April 8, 1994, "NRC Inspection Report No. 50-261/94-10." NUDOCS Accession No. 9404200130

Letter from H. Christensen, NRC to S. Hinnant, Carolina Power & Light Company dated April 15, 1994, "Notice of Violation; NRC Inspection Report No. 50-261/94-08." NUDOCS Accession No. 9405230016

Letter from R.M. Krich, Carolina Power & Light Company, to the NRC dated February 23, 1995, "H.B. Robinson Steam Electric Plant, Unit No. 2; Docket No. 50-261/License No. DPR-23; Response to Request for Information by NRC Made in December 22, 1994, Meeting With Westinghouse Owners Group Regarding Steam Generator Tube Plugs." NUDOCS Accession No. 9503010209

Letter from R.M. Krich, Carolina Power & Light Company, to the NRC dated September 15, 1995, "H.B. Robinson Steam Electric Plant, Unit No. 2; Docket No. 50-261/License No. DPR-23; Submittal of Steam Generator Tube Inservice Inspection Report and 90 Day Inservice Inspection Report." NUDOCS Accession No. 9509220287

Letter from R.M. Krich, Carolina Power & Light Company, to the NRC dated June 27, 1995, "H.B. Robinson Steam Electric Plant, Unit No. 2; Docket No. 50-261/License No. DPR-23; Response to NRC Generic Letter 95-03, 'Circumferential Cracking of Steam Generator Tubes'." NUDOCS Accession No. 9507060083

Letter from R.M. Krich, Carolina Power & Light Company, to the NRC dated July 22, 1996, "H.B. Robinson Steam Electric Plant, Unit No. 2; Docket No. 50-261/License No. DPR-23; Response to Request for Additional Information Regarding Response to Generic Letter 95-03, 'Circumferential Cracking of Steam Generator Tubes'." NUDOCS Accession No. 9507300165

Letter from R.M. Krich, Carolina Power & Light Company, to the NRC dated July 31, 1996, "H.B. Robinson Steam Electric Plant, Unit No. 2; Docket No. 50-261/License No. DPR-23; Response to Request for Additional Information Regarding Response to Generic Letter 95-03, 'Circumferential Cracking of Steam Generator Tubes'." NUDOCS Accession No. 9508080233

Letter from R.M. Krich, Carolina Power & Light Company, to the NRC dated October 11, 1996, "H.B. Robinson Steam Electric Plant, Unit No. 2; Docket No. 50-261/License No. DPR-23; Special Report Regarding Inservice Inspection Steam Generator Tube Plug." NUDOCS Accession No. 9610160372

Letter from H.K. Chernoff, Carolina Power & Light Company, to the NRC dated January 20, 1997, "H.B. Robinson Steam Electric Plant, Unit No. 2; Docket No. 50-261/License No. DPR-23; Submittal of 90 Day Inservice Inspection Report." NUDOCS Accession No. 9701240314

Letter from T.M. Wilkerson, Carolina Power & Light Company, to the NRC dated May 14, 1998, "H.B. Robinson Steam Electric Plant, Unit No. 2; Docket No. 50-261/License No. DPR-23; Monthly Operating Report." NUDOCS Accession No. 9805200189

Letter from T.M. Wilkerson, Carolina Power & Light Company, to the NRC dated July 9, 1998, "H.B. Robinson Steam Electric Plant, Unit No. 2; Docket No. 50-261/License No. DPR-23; Submittal of 90 Day Inservice Inspection Report." NUDOCS Accession No. 9807150082

Letter from R. Subbaratnam, NRC to D.E. Young, Carolina Power & Light Company dated November 18, 1999, "H.B. Robinson Steam Electric Plant, Unit No. 2 (HBRSEP2) - Closeout of Generic Letter 97-06, 'Degradation of Steam Generator Internals' (TAC No. MA0939)." ADAMS Accession No. ML993310066

Letter from R.L. Warden, Carolina Power & Light Company, to the NRC dated November 15, 1999, "H.B. Robinson Steam Electric Plant, Unit No. 2; Docket No. 50-261/License No. DPR-23; Monthly Operating Report." ADAMS Accession No. ML993300069

Letter from R.L. Warden, Carolina Power & Light Company, to the NRC dated January 20, 2000, "H.B. Robinson Steam Electric Plant, Unit No. 2; Docket No. 50-261/License No. DPR-23; Submittal of 90 Day Inservice Inspection Summary Report." ADAMS Accession No. ML003677701

Letter from B.L. Fletcher III, Carolina Power & Light Company, to the NRC dated May 6, 2001, "H.B. Robinson Steam Electric Plant, Unit No. 2; Docket No. 50-261/License No. DPR-23; Steam Generator Tube Plugging During Refueling Outage 20." ADAMS Accession No. ML011300085

Letter from B.L. Fletcher III, Carolina Power & Light Company, to the NRC dated June 12, 2001, "H.B. Robinson Steam Electric Plant, Unit No. 2; Docket No. 50-261/License No. DPR-23; Monthly Operating Report." ADAMS Accession No. ML011690318

Letter from B.L. Fletcher III, Carolina Power & Light Company, to the NRC dated August 10, 2001, "H.B. Robinson Steam Electric Plant, Unit No. 2; Docket No. 50-261/License No. DPR-23; Submittal of 90 Day Inservice Inspection Summary Report." ADAMS Accession No. ML012270378

Letter from B.L. Fletcher III, Carolina Power & Light Company, to the NRC dated July 3, 2002, "H.B. Robinson Steam Electric Plant, Unit No. 2; Docket No. 50-261/License No. DPR-23; Response to NRC Request for Additional Information on the Steam Generator Inservice Inspection Results." ADAMS Accession No. ML021900019

Salem 1

Letter from L.F. Storz, Public Service Electric and Gas Company, to the NRC dated August 12, 1996, "Steam Generator Tube Inspections and Testing; Salem Generating Station Unit No 1; Docket No. 50-272." NUDOCS Accession No. 9608190065

Letter from A.C. Bakken III, Public Service Electric and Gas Company, to the NRC dated December 30, 1997, "LER 272/95-023-01, Salem Generating Station - Unit 1; Facility Operating License No. DPR-70; Docket No. 50-272." NUDOCS Accession No. 9801130415

Letter from D.R. Powell, Public Service Electric and Gas Company, to the NRC dated February 26, 1998, "Technical Specification 6.9.1.5 Annual Reports; Salem and Hope Creek Generating Stations; Docket Nos. 50-272, 50-311 and 50-354." NUDOCS Accession No. 9803060081

Letter from D.R. Powell, Public Service Electric and Gas Company, to the NRC dated March 1, 1999, "Technical Specification 6.9.1.5 Annual Reports; Salem and Hope Creek Generating Stations; Docket Nos. 50-272, 50-311 and 50-354." NUDOCS Accession No. 9903100217

Letter from G. Salamon, Public Service Electric and Gas Company, to the NRC dated October 20, 1999, "Steam Generator Tube Plugging Report; Technical Specification 4.4.6.5.a; Salem Generating Station Unit No. 1; Facility Operating License DPR-70; Docket No. 50-272." ADAMS Accession No. ML993070029

Letter from G. Salamon, Public Service Electric and Gas Company, to the NRC dated February 28, 2000, "Technical Specification 6.9.1.5 Annual Reports; Salem and Hope Creek Generating Stations; Docket Nos. 50-272, 50-311 and 50-354." ADAMS Accession No. ML003691698

Letter from G. Salamon, PSEG Nuclear LLC, to the NRC dated February 27, 2001, "Technical Specification 6.9.1.5 Annual Reports; Salem and Hope Creek Generating Stations; Docket Nos. 50-272, 50-311 and 50-354." ADAMS Accession No. ML010800160

Letter from D.F. Garchow, PSEG Nuclear LLC, to the NRC dated March 28, 2001, "Response to Request for Additional Information in Regards to Request for License Amendment; Increased Licensed Power Level; Salem Generating Station, Unit Nos. 1 and 2; Facility Operating License DPR-70 and DPR-75; Docket Nos. 50-272 and 50-311." ADAMS Accession No. ML011000129

Letter from D.F. Garchow, PSEG Nuclear LLC, to the NRC not dated, "Steam Generator Tube Plugging Report; Technical Specification 4.4.5.5.a; Salem Generating Station Unit No. 1; Facility Operating License DPR-70; Docket No. 50-272." ADAMS Accession No. ML011420106

Letter from G. Salamon, PSEG Nuclear LLC, to the NRC dated February 26, 2002, "Technical Specification 6.9.1.5 Annual Reports; Salem and Hope Creek Generating Stations; Docket Nos. 50-272, 50-311 and 50-354." ADAMS Accession No. ML020710732

Seabrook

Letter from G.S. Thomas, New Hampshire Yankee, to the NRC dated June 15, 1989, "Response to NRC Bulletin 89-01: Failure of Westinghouse Steam Generator Tube Mechanical Plugs." NUDOCS Accession No. 8906230144

Letter from T.C. Feigenbaum, New Hampshire Yankee, to the NRC dated July 30, 1991, "Response to NRC Bulletin 89-01, Supplement 2: Failure of Westinghouse Steam Generator Tube Mechanical Plugs." NUDOCS Accession No. 9108050310

Letter from T.C. Feigenbaum, New Hampshire Yankee, to the NRC dated September 9, 1991, "Steam Generator Tubes Plugged During First Inservice Inspection." NUDOCS Accession No. 9109110217

Letter from T.C. Feigenbaum, North Atlantic Energy Service Corporation, to the NRC dated August 28, 1992, "1991 Steam Generator Inservice Inspection." NUDOCS Accession No. 9209010003

Letter from T.C. Feigenbaum, North Atlantic Energy Service Corporation, to the NRC dated October 9, 1992, "Steam Generator Tube Plugging Report for the Second Inservice Inspection." NUDOCS Accession No. 9210160230

Letter from T.C. Feigenbaum, North Atlantic Energy Service Corporation, to the NRC dated August 25, 1993, "1992 Steam Generator Inservice Inspection." NUDOCS Accession No. 9309020251

Letter from T.C. Feigenbaum, North Atlantic Energy Service Corporation, to the NRC dated June 23, 1994, "Steam Generator Tube Plugging Report for the Third Inservice Inspection." NUDOCS Accession No. 9406270329

Letter from T.C. Feigenbaum, North Atlantic Energy Service Corporation, to the NRC dated April 26, 1995, "1994 Steam Generator Inservice Inspection." NUDOCS Accession No. 9505020200

Letter from T.C. Feigenbaum, North Atlantic Energy Service Corporation, to the NRC dated January 30, 1995, "Response to Request for Additional Information Regarding Steam Generator Tube Mechanical Plugs." NUDOCS Accession No. 9502060335

Letter from T.C. Feigenbaum, North Atlantic Energy Service Corporation, to the NRC dated August 25, 1995, "Action Plan to Respond to Steam Generator Tube Mechanical Plug Removal." NUDOCS Accession No. 9508290157

Letter from T.C. Feigenbaum, North Atlantic Energy Service Corporation, to the NRC dated December 1, 1995, "Steam Generator Tubes Plugged During Fourth Inservice Inspection." NUDOCS Accession No. 9512070142

Letter from W.A. DiProfio, North Atlantic Energy Service Corporation, to the NRC dated November 27, 1996, "Seabrook Station, Steam Generators A and D Inservice Inspection." NUDOCS Accession No. 9612110327

Letter from T.C. Feigenbaum, North Atlantic Energy Service Corporation, to the NRC dated June 18, 1997, "Seabrook Station, Steam Generator Tubes Plugged During Fifth Inservice Inspection." NUDOCS Accession No. 9706250388

Letter from W.A. DiProfio, North Atlantic Energy Service Corporation, to the NRC dated May 15, 1998, "Seabrook Station, Steam Generators Inservice Inspection." NUDOCS Accession No. 9805210123

Letter from T.C. Feigenbaum, North Atlantic Energy Service Corporation, to the NRC dated May 5, 1999, "Seabrook Station, Steam Generator Tubes Plugged During Sixth Inservice Inspection." NUDOCS Accession No. 9905120192

Letter from T.C. Feigenbaum, North Atlantic Energy Service Corporation, to the NRC dated February 25, 2000, "Seabrook Station, Steam Generators Inservice Inspection." ADAMS Accession No. ML003687027

Letter from T.C. Feigenbaum, North Atlantic Energy Service Corporation, to the NRC dated November 17, 2000, "Seabrook Station, Steam Generator Tubes Plugged During Seventh Inservice Inspection." ADAMS Accession No. ML003770486

Letter from T.C. Feigenbaum, North Atlantic Energy Service Corporation, to the NRC dated August 14, 2001, "Seabrook Station, Steam Generators Inservice Inspection." ADAMS Accession No. ML012320140

<u>Surry 1 and 2</u>

Letter from W.L. Stewart, Virginia Electric and Power Company, to the NRC dated January 27, 1984, No Title. NUDOCS Accession No.

Letter from W.L. Stewart, Virginia Electric and Power Company, to the NRC dated December 31, 1984, No Title. NUDOCS Accession No.

Letter from W.L. Stewart, Virginia Electric and Power Company, to the NRC dated March 4, 1986, "Virginia Electric and Power Company; Surry Power Station Units 1 and 2; 1985 Annual Steam Generator Inservice Inspection Report." NUDOCS Accession No.

Letter from W.L. Stewart, Virginia Electric and Power Company, to the NRC dated July 15, 1986, "Virginia Electric and Power Company; Surry Power Station Unit Nos. 1 and 2; Monthly Operating Report." NUDOCS Accession No. 8609120169

Letter from W.L. Stewart, Virginia Electric and Power Company, to the NRC dated August 12, 1987, "Virginia Electric and Power Company; Surry Power Station Units 1 and 2; 1986 Annual Steam Generator Inservice Inspection Report." NUDOCS Accession No. 8708170367

Letter from W.R. Cartwright, Virginia Electric and Power Company, to the NRC dated March 1, 1989, "Virginia Electric and Power Company; Surry Power Station Units 1 and 2; 1988 Annual Steam Generator Inservice Inspection Report." NUDOCS Accession No. 8903090151

Letter from W.L. Stewart, Virginia Electric and Power Company, to the NRC dated May 26, 1989, "Virginia Electric and Power Company; Surry Power Station Units 1 and 2; North Anna Power Station Units 1 and 2; Steam Generator Tube Leak Event Corrective Action and Response to NRC Bulletin No. 89-01." NUDOCS Accession No. 8906020254

Letter from W.L. Stewart, Virginia Electric and Power Company, to the NRC dated March 1, 1990, "Virginia Electric and Power Company; Surry Power Station Units 1 and 2; 1989 Annual Steam Generator Inservice Inspection Report." NUDOCS Accession No. 9003120200

Letter from W.L. Stewart, Virginia Electric and Power Company, to the NRC dated December 27, 1990, "Virginia Electric and Power Company; Surry Power Station Unit 1; Steam Generator Tube Inspection Report." NUDOCS Accession No. 9101080347

Letter from W.L. Stewart, Virginia Electric and Power Company, to the NRC dated February 25, 1991, "Virginia Electric and Power Company; Surry Power Station Units 1 and 2; 1990 Annual Steam Generator Inservice Inspection Report." NUDOCS Accession No. 9103040071

Letter from W.L. Stewart, Virginia Electric and Power Company, to the NRC dated May 21, 1991, "Virginia Electric and Power Company; Surry Power Station Unit 2; Steam Generator Tube Inspection Report." NUDOCS Accession No. 9105300131

Letter from W.L. Stewart, Virginia Electric and Power Company, to the NRC dated August 23, 1991, "Virginia Electric and Power Company; Surry Power Station Units 1 and 2; North Anna

Power Station Units 1 and 2; Response to NRC Bulletin 89-01, Supplement 2." NUDOCS Accession No. 9108290211

Letter from W.L. Stewart, Virginia Electric and Power Company, to the NRC dated February 28, 1992, "Virginia Electric and Power Company; Surry Power Station Units 1 and 2; 1991 Annual Steam Generator Inservice Inspection Report." NUDOCS Accession No. 9203060254

Letter from W.L. Stewart, Virginia Electric and Power Company, to the NRC dated May 8, 1992, "Virginia Electric and Power Company; Surry Power Station Unit 1; Steam Generator Tube Inspection Report." NUDOCS Accession No. 9205190266

Letter from M.L. Bowling, Virginia Electric and Power Company, to the NRC dated February 9, 1993, "Virginia Electric and Power Company; Surry Power Station Units 1 and 2; 1992 Annual Steam Generator Inservice Inspection Report." NUDOCS Accession No. 9302160132

Letter from M.L. Bowling, Virginia Electric and Power Company, to the NRC dated April 19, 1993, "Virginia Electric and Power Company; Surry Power Station Unit 2; Steam Generator Tube Inspection Report." NUDOCS Accession No. 9304220166

Letter from M.L. Bowling, Virginia Electric and Power Company, to the NRC dated February 23, 1994, "Virginia Electric and Power Company; Surry Power Station Units 1 and 2; 1993 Annual Steam Generator Inservice Inspection Report." NUDOCS Accession No. 9403070251

Letter from M.L. Bowling, Virginia Electric and Power Company, to the NRC dated March 15, 1994, "Virginia Electric and Power Company; Surry Power Station Unit 1; Steam Generator Tube Inspection Report." NUDOCS Accession No. 9403220234

Letter from M.L. Bowling, Virginia Electric and Power Company, to the NRC dated February 20, 1995, "Virginia Electric and Power Company; Surry Power Station Units 1 and 2; 1994 Annual Steam Generator Inservice Inspection Report." NUDOCS Accession No. 9502240297

Letter from J.P. O'Hanlon, Virginia Electric and Power Company, to the NRC dated June 8, 1995, "Virginia Electric and Power Company; Surry Power Station Units 1 and 2; Core Uprate - Materials and Chemical Engineering Branch Follow-Up Questions to Previous Request for Additional Information." NUDOCS Accession No. 9506130151

Letter from J.P. O'Hanlon, Virginia Electric and Power Company, to the NRC dated June 27, 1995, "Virginia Electric and Power Company; Surry Power Station Units 1 and 2; North Anna Power Station Units 1 and 2; Response to NRC Generic Letter 95-03; Circumferential Cracking of Steam Generator Tubes." NUDOCS Accession No. 9507030144

Letter from J.P. O'Hanlon, Virginia Electric and Power Company, to the NRC dated October 5, 1995, "Virginia Electric and Power Company; Surry Power Station Units 1 and 2; North Anna Power Station Units 1 and 2; Response to NRC Request for Additional Information Regarding Our Response to Generic Letter 95-03; Circumferential Cracking of Steam Generator Tubes." NUDOCS Accession No. 9510110311

Letter from J.P. O'Hanlon, Virginia Electric and Power Company, to the NRC dated October 12, 1995, "Virginia Electric and Power Company; Surry Power Station Unit 1; Steam Generator Tube Inspection Report." NUDOCS Accession No. 9510240292

Letter from M.L. Bowling, Virginia Electric and Power Company, to the NRC dated March 1, 1996, "Virginia Electric and Power Company; Surry Power Station Units 1 and 2; 1995 Annual Steam Generator Inservice Inspection Report." NUDOCS Accession No. 9603110250

Letter from S.P. Sarver, Virginia Electric and Power Company, to the NRC dated February 10, 1997, "Virginia Electric and Power Company; Surry Power Station Units 1 and 2; Annual Steam Generator Inservice Inspection Summary Report." NUDOCS Accession No. 9702180383

Letter from S.P. Sarver, Virginia Electric and Power Company, to the NRC dated April 8, 1997, "Virginia Electric and Power Company; Surry Power Station Unit 1; Steam Generator Tube Inspection 15 Day Report." NUDOCS Accession No. 9704150140

Letter from R.F. Saunders, Virginia Electric and Power Company, to the NRC dated July 21, 1997, "Virginia Electric and Power Company; Surry Power Station Unit 1; 90 Day Inservice Inspection Summary Report For the 1997 Refueling Outage." NUDOCS Accession No. 9707290048

Letter from J.H. McCarthy, Virginia Electric and Power Company, to the NRC dated February 5, 1998, "Virginia Electric and Power Company; Surry Power Station Units 1 and 2; Annual Steam Generator Inservice Inspection Summary Report." NUDOCS Accession No. 9802180075

Letter from J.H. McCarthy, Virginia Electric and Power Company, to the NRC dated February 12, 1999, "Virginia Electric and Power Company; Surry Power Station Units 1 and 2; Annual Steam Generator Inservice Inspection Summary Report." NUDOCS Accession No. 9902240436

Letter from G.E. Edison, NRC, to Virginia Electric and Power Company dated August 23, 1999, "Closure of Review of Response to Generic Letter 97-05, 'Steam Generator Tube Inspection Techniques' for the Surry Power Station, Units 1 and 2 (TAC Nos. MA0501 and MA0502)." NUDOCS Accession No. 9908300113

Letter from J.H. McCarthy, Virginia Electric and Power Company, to the NRC dated May 17, 1999, "Virginia Electric and Power Company; Surry Power Station Unit 2; Steam Generator Tube Inspection Report." NUDOCS Accession No. 9905210220

Letter from D.A. Christian, Virginia Electric and Power Company, to the NRC dated February 28, 2000, "Virginia Electric and Power Company; Surry Power Station Units 1 and 2; Annual Steam Generator Inservice Inspection Summary Report." ADAMS Accession No. ML003692154

Letter from J.H. McCarthy, Virginia Electric and Power Company, to the NRC dated May 8, 2000, "Virginia Electric and Power Company; Surry Power Station Unit 1; Steam Generator Tube Inspection Report." ADAMS Accession No. ML003715079

Letter from W.F. Renz, Virginia Electric and Power Company, to the NRC dated October 19, 2000, "Virginia Electric and Power Company; Surry Power Station Unit 2; Steam Generator Tube Inspection Report." ADAMS Accession No. ML003762349

Letter from S.P. Sarver, Virginia Electric and Power Company, to the NRC dated February 28, 2001, "Virginia Electric and Power Company; Surry Power Station Units 1 and 2; Annual Steam Generator Inservice Inspection Summary Report." ADAMS Accession No. ML010650310

Letter from S.P. Sarver, Virginia Electric and Power Company, to the NRC dated November 5, 2001, "Virginia Electric and Power Company; Surry Power Station Unit 1; Steam Generator Tube Inspection Report." ADAMS Accession No. ML020090607

Letter from S.P. Sarver, Virginia Electric and Power Company, to the NRC dated February 28, 2002, "Virginia Electric and Power Company (Dominion); Surry Power Station Units 1 and 2; Annual Steam Generator Inservice Inspection Summary Report." ADAMS Accession No. ML020710707

Turkey Point 3

Letter from J.W. Williams, Jr., Florida Power and Light Company, to the NRC dated June 17, 1985, "Turkey Point Unit 3; Docket No. 50-250; Steam Generator Inspection." NUDOCS Accession No.

Letter from J.W. Williams, Jr., Florida Power and Light Company, to the NRC dated October 16, 1985, "Turkey Point Unit 3; Docket No. 50-250; Inservice Inspection Report." NUDOCS Accession No. 8510210046

Letter from J.W. Williams, Jr., Florida Power and Light Company, to the NRC dated September 3, 1985, "Turkey Point Units 3 and 4; Docket Nos. 50-250 and 50-251; 10 CFR 50.59 Report." NUDOCS Accession No.

Letter from C.O. Woody, Florida Power and Light Company, to the NRC dated June 23, 1987, "Turkey Point Unit 3; Docket No. 50-250; Technical Specification 4.2.5.5.a. Report." NUDOCS Accession No. 8706260344

Letter from C.O. Woody, Florida Power and Light Company, to the NRC dated December 15, 1987, "Turkey Point Unit 3; Docket No. 50-250; 1987 Inservice Inspection Summary Report." NUDOCS Accession No. 8712210013

Letter from C.O. Woody, Florida Power and Light Company, to the NRC dated August 31, 1987, "Turkey Point Units 3 and 4; Docket Nos. 50-250 and 50-251; 10 CFR 50.59 Report." NUDOCS Accession No.

Letter from C.O. Woody, Florida Power and Light Company, to the NRC dated June 19, 1989, "Turkey Point Units 3 and 4; Docket Nos. 50-250 and 50-251; NRC Bulletin No. 89-01; Failure of Westinghouse Steam Generator Mechanical Plugs." NUDOCS Accession No. 8906230148

Letter from K.N. Harris, Florida Power and Light Company, to the NRC dated April 6, 1990, "Turkey Point Unit 3; Docket No. 50-250; Technical Specification 4.2.5.5.a." NUDOCS Accession No. 9004170137

Letter from K.N. Harris, Florida Power and Light Company, to the NRC dated September 7, 1990, "Turkey Point Unit 3; Docket No. 50-250; Inservice Inspection Report." NUDOCS Accession No. 9009170013

Letter from K.N. Harris, Florida Power and Light Company, to the NRC dated August 30, 1990, "Turkey Point Units 3 and 4; Docket No. 50-250 and 50-251; 10 CFR 50.59 Report." NUDOCS Accession No.

Letter from T.F. Plunkett, Florida Power and Light Company, to the NRC dated December 30, 1991, "Turkey Point Unit 3; Docket No. 50-250; Inservice Inspection Report." NUDOCS Accession No. 9201070255 and 9201080229

Letter from T.F. Plunkett, Florida Power and Light Company, to the NRC dated October 28, 1992, "Turkey Point Unit 3; Docket No. 50-250; Steam Generator Tube Plugging." NUDOCS Accession No.

Letter from T.F. Plunkett, Florida Power and Light Company, to the NRC dated March 10, 1993, "Turkey Point Unit 3; Docket No. 50-250; Inservice Inspection Report." NUDOCS Accession No. 9303160060

Letter from T.F. Plunkett, Florida Power and Light Company, to the NRC dated November 18, 1993, "Turkey Point Units 3 and 4; Docket No. 50-250 and 50-251; 10 CFR 50.59 Report." NUDOCS Accession No. 9312020007

Letter from T.F. Plunkett, Florida Power and Light Company, to the NRC dated May 2, 1994, "Turkey Point Unit 3; Docket No. 50-250; Steam Generator Tube Plugging." NUDOCS Accession No.

Letter from T.F. Plunkett, Florida Power and Light Company, to the NRC dated August 15, 1994, "Turkey Point Unit 3; Docket No. 50-250; Inservice Inspection Report." NUDOCS Accession No. 9408260153

Letter from W.H. Bohlke, Florida Power and Light Company, to the NRC dated June 22, 1995, "Turkey Point Units 3 and 4; Docket Nos. 50-250 and 50-251; Response to Generic Letter 95-03, Circumferential Cracking of Steam Generator Tubes." NUDOCS Accession No. 9506300133

Letter from T.F. Plunkett, Florida Power and Light Company, to the NRC dated October 11, 1995, "Turkey Point Units 3 and 4; Docket Nos. 50-250 and 50-251; Response to Request for Additional Information - Generic Letter 95-03, Circumferential Cracking of Steam Generator Tubes." NUDOCS Accession No. 9510190030

Letter from T.F. Plunkett, Florida Power and Light Company, to the NRC dated September 29, 1995, "Turkey Point Unit 3; Docket No. 50-250; Steam Generator Tube Plugging." NUDOCS Accession No. 9510060358

Letter from R.J. Hovey, Florida Power and Light Company, to the NRC dated January 3, 1996, "Turkey Point Unit 3; Docket No. 50-250; Inservice Inspection Report." NUDOCS Accession No. 9601110198

Letter from R.J. Hovey, Florida Power and Light Company, to the NRC dated January 17, 1996, "Turkey Point Unit 3; Docket No. 50-250; Steam Generator Tube Plugging Inservice Inspection Report." NUDOCS Accession No. 9601220367

Letter from R.J. Hovey, Florida Power and Light Company, to the NRC dated March 27, 1997, "Turkey Point Unit 3; Docket No. 50-250; Steam Generator Tube Plugging - 15 Day Special Report." NUDOCS Accession No. 9704030004

Letter from R.J. Hovey, Florida Power and Light Company, to the NRC dated July 10, 1997, "Turkey Point Unit 3; Docket No. 50-250; Inservice Inspection Report." NUDOCS Accession No. 9707160093

Letter from R.J. Hovey, Florida Power and Light Company, to the NRC dated March 5, 1998, "Turkey Point Unit 3; Docket No. 50-250; Steam Generator Tube Plugging; Inservice Inspection - 12 Month Special Report." NUDOCS Accession No. 9803170401

Letter from R.J. Hovey, Florida Power and Light Company, to the NRC dated October 14, 1998, "Turkey Point Unit 3; Docket No. 50-250; Steam Generator Tube Plugging 15-Day Report." NUDOCS Accession No. 9810200272

Letter from R.J. Hovey, Florida Power and Light Company, to the NRC dated January 20, 1999, "Turkey Point Unit 3; Docket No. 50-250; Inservice Inspection Report." NUDOCS Accession No. 9902120286

Letter from R.J. Hovey, Florida Power and Light Company, to the NRC dated March 16, 1999, "Turkey Point Unit 3; Docket No. 50-250; Steam Generator Tube Plugging; Inservice Inspection - 12 Month Special Report." NUDOCS Accession No. 9903250292

Letter from R.J. Hovey, Florida Power and Light Company, to the NRC dated March 27, 2000, "Turkey Point Unit 3; Docket No. 50-250; Steam Generator Tube Plugging 15-Day Report." ADAMS Accession No. ML003715540

Letter from R.J. Hovey, Florida Power and Light Company, to the NRC dated April 6, 2000, "Turkey Point Unit 3; Docket No. 50-250; Reportable Event: 2000-001-00; Date of Event: March 11, 2000; Steam Generator Tube Plugging Places Steam Generator 3B in Category C-3." ADAMS Accession No. ML003705889

Letter from R.J. Hovey, Florida Power and Light Company, to the NRC dated June 22, 2000, "Turkey Point Unit 3; Docket No. 50-250; Inservice Inspection Report." ADAMS Accession No. ML003726844

Letter from R.J. Hovey, Florida Power and Light Company, to the NRC dated September 27, 2000, "Turkey Point Unit 3; Docket No. 50-250; Steam Generator Inspection Information." ADAMS Accession No. ML003756946

Letter from R.J. Hovey, Florida Power and Light Company, to the NRC dated March 5, 2001, "Turkey Point Unit 3; Docket No. 50-250; Steam Generator Tube Plugging; Inservice Inspection 12-Month Special Report." ADAMS Accession No. ML021760011

Letter from J.P. McElwain, Florida Power and Light Company, to the NRC dated October 20, 2001, "Turkey Point Unit 3; Docket No. 50-250; Steam Generator Tube Plugging 15-Day Report." ADAMS Accession No.

Letter from J.P. McElwain, Florida Power and Light Company, to the NRC dated January 24, 2002, "Turkey Point Unit 3; Docket No. 50-250; Inservice Inspection Report." ADAMS Accession No. ML020330094

Letter from J.P. McElwain, Florida Power and Light Company, to the NRC dated February 28, 2002, "Turkey Point Unit 3; Docket No. 50-250; Steam Generator Tube Plugging Inservice Inspection 12-Month Special Report - Revision." ADAMS Accession No. ML020720442

Letter from J.P. McElwain, Florida Power and Light Company, to the NRC dated June 25, 2002, "Turkey Point Unit 3; Docket No. 50-250; Inservice Inspection Report - Revision." ADAMS Accession No.

Turkey Point 4

Letter from R.E. Uhrig, Florida Power and Light Company, to the NRC dated August 12, 1983, "Turkey Point Unit 4; Docket No. 50-251; Inservice Inspection Report." NUDOCS Accession No. 8308180180

Letter from J.W. Williams Jr., Florida Power and Light Company, to the NRC dated September 4, 1984, "Turkey Point Unit 4; Docket No. 50-251; Inservice Inspection Report." NUDOCS Accession No. 8409100191

Letter from J.W. Williams Jr., Florida Power and Light Company, to the NRC dated June 18, 1985, "Turkey Point Units 3 and 4; Docket Nos. 50-250 and 50-251; Generic Letter 85-02." NUDOCS Accession No. 8506240503

Letter from C.O. Woody, Florida Power and Light Company, to the NRC dated December 1, 1986, "Turkey Point Unit 4; Docket No. 50-251; Inservice Inspection Report." NUDOCS Accession No. 8612090435

Letter from W.F. Conway, Florida Power and Light Company, to the NRC dated March 18, 1988, "Turkey Point Units 3 and 4; Docket Nos. 50-250 and 50-251; NRC Bulletin 88-02: Rapidly Propagating Fatigue Cracks in Steam Generator Tubes." NUDOCS Accession No. 8803250093

Letter from W.F. Conway, Florida Power and Light Company, to the NRC dated December 7, 1988, "Turkey Point Unit 4; Docket No. 50-251; Technical Specification 4.2.5.5.a." NUDOCS Accession No. 8812140198

Letter from C.O. Woody, Florida Power and Light Company, to the NRC dated September 15, 1989, "Turkey Point Unit 4; Docket No. 50-251; Inservice Inspection Report." NUDOCS Accession No. 8909220142

Letter from W.H. Bohlke, Florida Power and Light Company, to the NRC dated July 30, 1991, "Turkey Point Units 3 and 4; Docket Nos. 50-250 and 50-251; NRC Bulletin 89-01, Supplement 2; Failure of Westinghouse Steam Generator Mechanical Plugs." NUDOCS Accession No. 9108050317

Letter from T.F. Plunkett, Florida Power and Light Company, to the NRC dated January 27, 1992, "Turkey Point Unit 4; Docket No. 50-251; Inservice Inspection Report." NUDOCS Accession No. 9202030140

Letter from T.F. Plunkett, Florida Power and Light Company, to the NRC dated May 4, 1993, "Turkey Point Unit 4; Docket No. 50-251; Steam Generator Tube Plugging." NUDOCS Accession No. 9305140226

Letter from T.F. Plunkett, Florida Power and Light Company, to the NRC dated August 20, 1993, "Turkey Point Unit 4; Docket No. 50-251; Inservice Inspection Report." NUDOCS Accession No. 9308260306

Letter from T.F. Plunkett, Florida Power and Light Company, to the NRC dated October 24, 1994, "Turkey Point Unit 4; Docket No. 50-251; Steam Generator Tube Plugging." NUDOCS Accession No. 9411010123

Letter from T.F. Plunkett, Florida Power and Light Company, to the NRC dated February 9, 1995, "Turkey Point Unit 4; Docket No. 50-251; Inservice Inspection Report." NUDOCS Accession No. 9502210127

Letter from T.F. Plunkett, Florida Power and Light Company, to the NRC dated October 6, 1995, "Turkey Point Unit 4; Docket No. 50-251; Steam Generator Tube Plugging Inservice Inspection Report." NUDOCS Accession No. 9510110118

Letter from T.F. Plunkett, Florida Power and Light Company, to the NRC dated January 31, 1995, "Turkey Point Units 3 and 4; Docket Nos. 50-250 and 50-251; Alloy 600 Steam Generator Mechanical Tube Plugs." NUDOCS Accession No. 9502070106

Letter from R.J. Hovey, Florida Power and Light Company, to the NRC dated January 16, 1996, "Turkey Point Unit 4; Docket No. 50-251; Generic Letter 95-03 - Circumferential Cracking of Steam Generator Tubes." NUDOCS Accession No. 9601220369

Letter from R.J. Hovey, Florida Power and Light Company, to the NRC dated February 27, 1996, "Turkey Point Unit 4; Docket No. 50-251; Generic Letter 95-03 - Circumferential Cracking of Steam Generator Tubes." NUDOCS Accession No. 9603040329

Letter from R.J. Hovey, Florida Power and Light Company, to the NRC dated July 1, 1996, "Turkey Point Unit 4; Docket No. 50-251; Inservice Inspection Report." NUDOCS Accession No. 9607170072

Letter from R.J. Hovey, Florida Power and Light Company, to the NRC dated October 1, 1997, "Turkey Point Unit 4; Docket No. 50-251; Steam Generator Tube Plugging." NUDOCS Accession No. 9710100290

Letter from R.J. Hovey, Florida Power and Light Company, to the NRC dated January 7, 1998, "Turkey Point Unit 4; Docket No. 50-251; Inservice Inspection Report." NUDOCS Accession No. 9801130203

Letter from R.J. Hovey, Florida Power and Light Company, to the NRC dated December 30, 1997, "Turkey Point Unit 4; Docket No. 50-251; Steam Generator Tube Plugging Inservice Inspection Report." NUDOCS Accession No. 9801060277

Letter from R.J. Hovey, Florida Power and Light Company, to the NRC dated June 30, 1999, "Turkey Point Unit 4; Docket No. 50-251; Inservice Inspection Report." NUDOCS Accession No. 9907080066

Letter from R.J. Hovey, Florida Power and Light Company, to the NRC dated October 16, 2000, "Turkey Point Unit 4; Docket No. 50-251; Steam Generator Tube Plugging 15-Day Report." ADAMS Accession No. ML003762437

Letter from R.J. Hovey, Florida Power and Light Company, to the NRC dated January 19, 2001, "Turkey Point Unit 4; Docket No. 50-251; Inservice Inspection Report." ADAMS Accession No. ML010250129

Letter from R.J. Hovey, Florida Power and Light Company, to the NRC dated August 10, 2001, "Turkey Point Unit 4; Docket No. 50-251; Steam Generator Tube Plugging; Inservice Inspection 12-Month Special Report." ADAMS Accession No. ML021760007

Vogtle 1

Letter from J.A. Bailey, Georgia Power Company, to the NRC dated June 13, 1986, "NRC Docket Numbers 50-424 and 50-425, Construction Permit Numbers CPPR-108 and CPPR-109, Vogtle Electric Generating Plant - Units 1 and 2, SER Confirmatory Item 18: Examination of Steam Generator Tubes." NUDOCS Accession No. 8606180002

Letter from W.G. Hairston III, Georgia Power Company, to the NRC dated November 7, 1988, "Plant Vogtle - Unit 1, NRC Docket 50-424, Operating License NPF-68, Technical Specification, Special Report 88-007, Steam Generator Tube Plugged." NUDOCS Accession No. 8811150487

Letter from W.G. Hairston III, Georgia Power Company, to the NRC dated February 22, 1989, "Plant Vogtle - Unit 1, NRC Docket 50-424, Operating License NPF-68, Inservice Inspection Summary Report." NUDOCS Accession No. 8903010197

Letter from W.G. Hairston III, Georgia Power Company, to the NRC dated June 16, 1989, "Plant Vogtle - Units 1, 2, NRC Dockets 50-424, 50-425, Operating Licenses NPF-68, NPF-81, NRC Bulletin 89-01: Failure of Westinghouse Steam Generator Tube Mechanical Plugs." NUDOCS Accession No. 8906200329

Letter from W.G. Hairston III, Georgia Power Company, to the NRC dated March 22, 1990, "Vogtle Electric Generating Plant, Special Report, Number of Steam Generator Tubes Plugged During 1R2." NUDOCS Accession No. 9003280482

Letter from W.G. Hairston III, Georgia Power Company, to the NRC dated July 5, 1990, "Vogtle Electric Generating Plant, Inservice Inspection Summary Report." NUDOCS Accession No. 9007130318

Letter from W.G. Hairston III, Georgia Power Company, to the NRC dated July 31, 1991, "Vogtle Electric Generating Plant, Response to NRC Bulletin 89-01 Supplement 2, Failure of Westinghouse Steam Generator Tube Mechanical Plugs." NUDOCS Accession No. 9108060366

Letter from C.K. McCoy, Georgia Power Company, to the NRC dated February 13, 1992, "Vogtle Electric Generating Plant, Inservice Inspection Summary Report." NUDOCS Accession No. 9202260291

Letter from C.K. McCoy, Georgia Power Company, to the NRC dated November 5, 1992, "Vogtle Electric Generating Plant, Correction to Inservice Inspection Summary Report." NUDOCS Accession No. 9211160103

Letter from C.K. McCoy, Georgia Power Company, to the NRC dated April 22, 1993, "Vogtle Electric Generating Plant, Special Report 1-93-3, Number of Steam Generator Tubes Plugged During 1R4." NUDOCS Accession No. 9304270197

Letter from C.K. McCoy, Georgia Power Company, to the NRC dated May 6, 1993, "Vogtle Electric Generating Plant, Special Report 1-93-3, Number of Steam Generator Tubes Plugged During 1R4." NUDOCS Accession No. 9305130223

Letter from C.K. McCoy, Georgia Power Company, to the NRC dated July 21, 1993, "Vogtle Electric Generating Plant, Inservice Inspection Summary Report." NUDOCS Accession No. 9307270164

Letter from C.K. McCoy, Georgia Power Company, to the NRC dated October 6, 1994, "Vogtle Electric Generating Plant, Technical Specifications Special Report - Unit 1, Number of Steam Generator Tubes Plugged During 1R5." NUDOCS Accession No. 9410120113

Letter from C.K. McCoy, Georgia Power Company, to the NRC dated January 10, 1995, "Vogtle Electric Generating Plant, Inservice Inspection Summary Report." NUDOCS Accession No. 9501230321

Letter from C.K. McCoy, Georgia Power Company, to the NRC dated January 25, 1995, "Vogtle Electric Generating Plant, Steam Generator Mechanical Tube Plugs." NUDOCS Accession No. 9502010150

Letter from C.K. McCoy, Georgia Power Company, to the NRC dated April 1, 1996, "Vogtle Electric Generating Plant, Special Report 1-96-1, Number of Steam Generator Tubes Plugged During 1R6." NUDOCS Accession No. 9604050023

Letter from J.D. Woodard, Georgia Power Company, to the NRC dated July 17, 1996, "Vogtle Electric Generating Plant, Inservice Inspection Summary Report." NUDOCS Accession No. 9607230176

Letter from J.D. Woodard, Georgia Power Company, to the NRC dated June 10, 1996, "Vogtle Electric Generating Plant, Confirmed loose Part 14-Day Report." NUDOCS Accession No. 9606140081

Letter from C.K. McCoy, Southern Nuclear Operating Company, Inc., to the NRC dated October 13, 1997, "Vogtle Electric Generating Plant, Technical Specification Report 1-97-2, Number of Steam Generator Tubes Plugged During 1R7." NUDOCS Accession No. 9710200005

Letter from C.K. McCoy, Southern Nuclear Operating Company, Inc., to the NRC dated November 21, 1997, "Vogtle Electric Generating Plant, Confirmed Loose Part 14-Day Report - Revision 1." NUDOCS Accession No. 9712010215

Letter from C.K. McCoy, Southern Nuclear Operating Company, Inc., to the NRC dated January 16, 1998, "Vogtle Electric Generating Plant, Inservice Inspection Summary Report." NUDOCS Accession No. 9801260450

Letter from J.B. Beasley Jr., Southern Nuclear Operating Company, Inc., to the NRC dated March 29, 1999, "Vogtle Electric Generating Plant, Technical Specification Report 1-99-1, Number of Steam Generator Tubes Plugged During 1R8." NUDOCS Accession No. 9904070055

Letter from J.B. Beasley Jr., Southern Nuclear Operating Company, Inc., to the NRC dated June 21, 1999, "Vogtle Electric Generating Plant, Inservice Inspection Summary Report." NUDOCS Accession No. 9907010009

Letter from J.B. Beasley Jr., Southern Nuclear Operating Company, Inc., to the NRC dated January 12, 2001, "Vogtle Electric Generating Plant, Inservice Inspection Summary Report." ADAMS Accession No. ML010170148

Vogtle 2

Letter from J.A. Bailey, Georgia Power Company, to the NRC dated October 27, 1988, "Plant Vogtle - Unit 2, NRC Docket Number 50-425, Construction Permit Number CPPR-109, SER Confirmatory Item 18: Examination of Steam Generator Tubes." NUDOCS Accession No. 8811030150

Letter from W.G. Hairston III, Georgia Power Company, to the NRC dated January 25, 1991, "Vogtle Electric Generating Plant, Inservice Inspection Summary Report." NUDOCS Accession No. 9102010137

Letter from C.K. McCoy, Georgia Power Company, to the NRC dated August 5, 1992, "Vogtle Electric Generating Plant, Inservice Inspection Summary Report." NUDOCS Accession No. 9208100159

Letter from C.K. McCoy, Georgia Power Company, to the NRC dated October 14, 1993, "Vogtle Electric Generating Plant, Special Report, Steam Generator Tubes Plugged During Third Unit 2 Refueling Outage." NUDOCS Accession No. 9310190094

Letter from C.K. McCoy, Georgia Power Company, to the NRC dated January 11, 1994, "Vogtle Electric Generating Plant, Inservice Inspection Summary Report." NUDOCS Accession No. 9401260247

Letter from C.K. McCoy, Georgia Power Company, to the NRC dated March 24, 1995, "Vogtle Electric Generating Plant, Special Report 2-95-2, Number of Steam Generator Tubes Plugged During 2R4." NUDOCS Accession No. 9504040208

Letter from C.K. McCoy, Georgia Power Company, to the NRC dated June 26, 1995, "Vogtle Electric Generating Plant, Inservice Inspection Summary Report." NUDOCS Accession No. 9507070399

Letter from C.K. McCoy, Georgia Power Company, to the NRC dated October 10, 1996, "Vogtle Electric Generating Plant, Special Report 2-96-3, Number of Steam Generator Tubes Plugged During 2R5." NUDOCS Accession No. 9610170031

Letter from C.K. McCoy, Georgia Power Company, to the NRC dated January 8, 1997, "Vogtle Electric Generating Plant, Inservice Inspection Summary Report." NUDOCS Accession No. 9701170027

Letter from C.K. McCoy, Southern Nuclear Operating Company, Inc., to the NRC dated April 15, 1998, "Vogtle Electric Generating Plant, Special Report 2-98-1, Number of Steam Generator Tubes Plugged During 2R6." NUDOCS Accession No. 9804220100

Letter from J.D. Woodard, Southern Nuclear Operating Company, Inc., to the NRC dated July 13, 1998, "Vogtle Electric Generating Plant, Inservice Inspection Summary Report." NUDOCS Accession No. 9807200156

Letter from J.B. Beasley, Jr., Southern Nuclear Operating Company, Inc., to the NRC dated January 13, 1999, "Vogtle Electric Generating Plant, Correction to Inservice Inspection Summary Report." NUDOCS Accession No. 9901220062

Letter from J.B. Beasley, Jr., Southern Nuclear Operating Company, Inc., to the NRC dated November 1, 1999, "Vogtle Electric Generating Plant, Special Report 2-99-1, Number of Steam Generator Tubes Plugged During 2R7." ADAMS Accession No. ML993140360

Letter from J.B. Beasley, Jr., Southern Nuclear Operating Company, Inc., to the NRC dated January 21, 2000, "Vogtle Electric Generating Plant, Inservice Inspection Summary Report." ADAMS Accession No. ML003679404

Letter from J.B. Beasley, Jr., Southern Nuclear Operating Company, Inc., to the NRC dated May 2, 2001, "Vogtle Electric Generating Plant, Technical Specification Report 2-2001-1, Number of Steam Generator Tubes Plugged During 2R8." ADAMS Accession No. ML011310386

Letter from J.D. Woodard, Southern Nuclear Operating Company, Inc., to the NRC dated July 23, 2001, "Vogtle Electric Generating Plant, Inservice Inspection Summary Report." ADAMS Accession No. ML012070394

Wolf Creek

Letter from B.J. Youngblood, NRC, to Kansas Gas and Electric Company and Union Electric Company dated December 20, 1983, "Comments on Steam Generator Tube Plugging Margin Analysis." NUDOCS Accession No. 8312280150

Letter from B.D. Withers, Wolf Creek Nuclear Operating Corporation, to the NRC dated October 27, 1987, "Docket No. 50-482: Special Report 86-09." NUDOCS Accession No. 8711190087

Letter from J.A. Bailey, Wolf Creek Nuclear Operating Corporation, to the NRC dated November 14, 1989, "Docket No. 50-482: Special Report 88-005." NUDOCS Accession No. 8911220024

Letter from J.A. Bailey, Wolf Creek Nuclear Operating Corporation, to the NRC dated April 19, 1990, "Docket No. 50-482: Special Report 90-001 - Steam Generator Tube Plugging Report." NUDOCS Accession No. 9004250110

Letter from J.A. Bailey, Wolf Creek Nuclear Operating Corporation, to the NRC dated April 3, 1991, "Docket No. 50-482: Special Report 90-003." NUDOCS Accession No. 9104110107

Letter from J.A. Bailey, Wolf Creek Nuclear Operating Corporation, to the NRC dated May 29, 1992, "Docket No. 50-482: Special Report 91-007." NUDOCS Accession No. 9206020253

Letter from O.L. Maynard, Wolf Creek Nuclear Operating Corporation, to the NRC dated April 7, 1993, "Docket No. 50-482: Special Report 93-002 - Steam Generator Tube Plugging Report." NUDOCS Accession No. 9304130322

Letter from O.L. Maynard, Wolf Creek Nuclear Operating Corporation, to the NRC dated December 10, 1993, "Docket No. 50-482: Special Report 93-003." NUDOCS Accession No. 9312220195

Letter from O.L. Maynard, Wolf Creek Nuclear Operating Corporation, to the NRC dated October 21, 1994, "Docket No. 50-482: Special Report 94-003 - Steam Generator Tube Plugging Report." NUDOCS Accession No. 9410270268

Letter from O.L. Maynard, Wolf Creek Nuclear Operating Corporation, to the NRC dated March 30, 1995, "Docket No. 50-482: Special Report 94-004." NUDOCS Accession No. 9504040153

NRC Inspection Report 50-482/94-11. NUDOCS Accession No. 9412230099

Letter from O.L. Maynard, Wolf Creek Nuclear Operating Corporation, to the NRC dated March 13, 1996, "Docket No. 50-482: Special Report 96-001 - Steam Generator Tube Plugging Report." NUDOCS Accession No. 9603200179

Letter from C.C Warren, Wolf Creek Nuclear Operating Corporation, to the NRC dated January 14, 1997, "Docket No. 50-482: Special Report 97-001 - Steam Generator Tube Inspection Results." NUDOCS Accession No. 9701220349

Letter from C.C Warren, Wolf Creek Nuclear Operating Corporation, to the NRC dated November 18, 1997, "Docket No. 50-482: Special Report 97-002 - Steam Generator Tube Plugging Report." NUDOCS Accession No. 9711250038

Letter from R.A. Muench, Wolf Creek Nuclear Operating Corporation, to the NRC dated March 16, 1998, "Docket No. 50-482: Response to NRC Generic Letter 97-05." NUDOCS Accession No. 9803230460

Letter from R.A. Muench, Wolf Creek Nuclear Operating Corporation, to the NRC dated October 20, 1998, "Docket No. 50-482: Special Report 98-002: Eighth Steam Generator Tube Inspection Results." NUDOCS Accession No. 9810270006

Letter from R.A. Muench, Wolf Creek Nuclear Operating Corporation, to the NRC dated May 7, 1999, "Docket No. 50-482: Special Report 99-001 - Steam Generator Tube Plugging Report." NUDOCS Accession No. 9905130185

Letter from R.A. Muench, Wolf Creek Nuclear Operating Corporation, to the NRC dated February 15, 2000, "Docket No. 50-482: Special Report 99-002 - Ninth Steam Generator Tube Inservice Inspection Results." ADAMS Accession No. ML003685730

Letter from R.A. Muench, Wolf Creek Nuclear Operating Corporation, to the NRC dated November 1, 2000, "Docket No. 50-482: Special Report 00-002 - Steam Generator Tube Plugging Report." ADAMS Accession No. ML003767139

Letter from R.A. Muench, Wolf Creek Nuclear Operating Corporation, to the NRC dated October 10, 2001, "Docket No. 50-482: Steam Generator Tube Inspection Report." ADAMS Accession No. ML012890479

NRC FORM 335 (2-89) NRCM 1102, 3201, 3202	U.S. NUCLEAR REGULATORY COMMISSION **BIBLIOGRAPHIC DATA SHEET** *(See instructions on the reverse)*	1 REPORT NUMBER (Assigned by NRC, Add Vol., Supp., Rev., and Addendum Numbers, if any.) NUREG-1771

2 TITLE AND SUBTITLE

U.S. Operating Experience With Thermally Treated Alloy 600 Steam Generator Tubes

3	DATE REPORT PUBLISHED	
	MONTH	YEAR
	April	2003

4 FIN OR GRANT NUMBER

N/A

5 AUTHOR(S)

Kenneth J. Karwoski

6 TYPE OF REPORT

Technical

7 PERIOD COVERED *(Inclusive Dates)*

1/1980 through 12/2001

8 PERFORMING ORGANIZATION - NAME AND ADDRESS *(If NRC, provide Division, Office or Region, U.S. Nuclear Regulatory Commission, and mailing address; if contractor provide name and mailing address.)*

Division of Engineeering
Office of Nuclear Reactor Regulation
U.S. Nuclear Regulatory Commission
Washington DC 20555-0001

9 SPONSORING ORGANIZATION - NAME AND ADDRESS *(If NRC, type "Same as above"; if contractor, provide NRC Division, Office or Region, U.S. Nuclear Regulatory Commission, and mailing address.)*

Same as above

10 SUPPLEMENTARY NOTES

11 ABSTRACT *(200 words or less)*

Steam generators placed in service in the 1960s and 1970s had tubes primarily fabricated from mill-annealed Alloy 600. Over time, this material proved to be susceptible to stress corrosion cracking in the highly pure primary and secondary water chemistry environments of pressurized-water reactors. The corrosion ultimately led to the replacement of steam generators at numerous facilities, the first U.S. replacement occurring in 1980. Many of the steam generators placed into service in the 1980s used tubes fabricated from thermally treated Alloy 600. This tube material was thought to be less susceptible to corrosion. Because of the safety significance of steam generator tube integrity, this paper evaluates the operating experience of thermally treated Alloy 600 by looking at the extent to which it is used and results from steam generator tube examinations

12 KEY WORDS/DESCRIPTORS *(List words or phrases that will assist researchers in locating the report.)*

PWR
steam generator (SG)
steam generator tube
Alloy 600, Inconel 600
thermally treated
eddy current testing
nondestructive evaluation

13 AVAILABILITY STATEMENT
unlimited

14 SECURITY CLASSIFICATION
(This Page)
unclassified
(This Report)
unclassified

15 NUMBER OF PAGES
260

16 PRICE

NRC FORM 335 (2-89)

This form was electronically produced by Elite Federal Forms, Inc.

Federal Recycling Program